THE JUNGLE IS NEUTRAL

F. Spencer Chapman D.S.O.

The Lyons Press

Guilford, Connecticut

An imprint of The Globe Pequot Press

Published by Times Books International
An imprint of Times Media Private Limited
A member of Times International Publishing
Times Centre, 1 New Industrial Road
Singapore 536196

Times Subang
Lot 46, Subang Hi-Tech Industrial Park
Batu Tiga, 40000 Shah Alam
Selangor Darul Ehsan, Malaysia

Published in North America by The Lyons Press.

The Lyons Press is an imprint of The Globe Pequot Press

10 9 8 7 6 5 4 3 2 1

Printed in Malaysia

ISBN 1-59228-107-9

The Library of Congress Cataloging-in-Publication data is
available on file.

CONTENTS

FOREWORD

This is a story of endurance and survival beyond the normal human capacity for survival. The title of Colonel Spencer Chapman's work implies that if human beings have the fortitude to bear the malevolence and hazards of the jungle and the resource to use what benefits it produces, it has no particular objection to their living in it. But the neutrality of the Malayan jungle, as Colonel Spencer Chapman warns us, is armed. He himself was on one occasion dangerously ill for two months on end, including a period of unconsciousness for seventeen days; he suffered at various times from black-water fever, pneumonia, and tick-typhus, as alternatives or additions to almost chronic malaria; it took him once twelve days' hard marching to cover ten miles through the jungle; and he was marching barefooted six days without food on another occasion. Armed neutrality indeed! One can hardly help sympathising with the six British soldiers who in such conditions died, 'not of any specific disease but because they lacked the right mental attitude.'

When one discovers that, besides this 'neutral' jungle and declared enemies like the Japanese, Colonel Spencer Chapman had to combat doubtful ones like many of the local inhabitants, including such professed disturbers of the peace as Chinese bandits, the fact of his survival becomes still more surprising. He was twice wounded, once by a steel nut from a home-made cartridge; was captured both by Japanese troops and by Chinese bandits and escaped from both; and after nearly three and a half years 'out of circulation' emerged into civilisation again so little the worse for wear in body or spirit as to return to the same jungle within a few months. 'The spirit truly is willing but the flesh is weak' is a poor text; if the spirit can endure, the flesh will usually find the capacity to do so.

The story of Colonel Chapman's adventures is typical of the British way of war, and therefore begins with a complete lack of preparation. He was posted in August 1941 to a school of guerilla warfare in Singapore, which had as one of its main objects the organisation of parties to stay behind in parts which the Japanese

5

might overrun. Since, however, the Malayan Command had no belief in the ability of the Japanese to invade Malaya, let alone overrun it, nothing was allowed to be organised till a considerable portion of Malaya had already been overrun. But when the inevitable tragedy had occurred and the return match had to be staged, British capacity both for improvisation and detailed organisation asserted itself as usual – 'still as Saxon slow in starting, still as weirdly wont to win.' The uncoordinated efforts – because communication was impossible – of Colonel Chapman and a number of similar adventurers, the majority of whom eventually fell victims to their foes or to the jungle, caused the Japanese much trouble and loss. Colonel Chapman found the Jap, in spite of his boasted efficiency in jungle fighting, easy money for ambushes and sabotage, so long as explosives and ammunition lasted. Meanwhile, unknown to them, a great effort was gradually being built up overseas. In the end touch was established, and a powerful weapon was forged inside Malaya for the discomfiture of the enemy when the time for invasion came. The Japanese surrender made the return match in Malaya a walkover; had it been played the result would have been an innings defeat for the Japanese, in which the guerilla forces organised within the Peninsula would have played a large part.

We have been inclined to believe that our armed forces are excessively professional and regular. This war has shown, as others have done before it, that the British make the best fighters in the world for irregular and independent enterprises. Our submarines, commandos and airborne forces, to whom a special memorial was rightly unveiled in Westminster Abbey recently, have proved that where daring, initiative, and ingenuity are required in unusual conditions unrivalled commanders and men can be found both from professional and unprofessional fighting men of the British race. The spirit which found its most renowned expression in the Elizabethan adventurers lived before them and still lives. It will surprise other foes in other wars, if wars are still to be.

Inevitably Colonel Chapman's adventures and achievements recall those of a famous character of the last war, T. E. Lawrence, who also endured greatly and survived by the high quality of his spirit. As Dogberry said, comparisons are odorous, but if anyone wishes to fortify himself by reading of feats of endurance and of the triumph of the spirit over the body, let him supplement this tale of Colonel Chapman's endurance from some chapters of the *Seven Pillars*, such as the camel rides in Chapters 31 and 32, or 81.

Colonel Chapman can claim no such political and material successes as were Lawrence's as the fruit of his toil and endurance. Though his tale is well and simply told with many a keen and humorous turn of phrase, and though his pen has recaptured some sharply focused snapshots of the natural life of the jungle, he has not T.E.'s literary genius; nor his introspection. He does not reveal the innermost thoughts that came to him in the many hours he lay alone waiting for his fevers to pass over. Colonel Chapman has never received the publicity and fame that were his predecessor's lot; but for sheer courage and endurance, physical and mental, the two men stand together as examples of what toughness the body will find, if the spirit within it is tough; and as very worthy representatives of our national capacity for individual enterprise, which it is hoped that even the modern craze for regulating our lives in every detail will never stifle.

Field-Marshal Earl Wavell
June 1948

CHAPTER ONE

War Comes to Malaya

To foster resistance movements in the Far East brings one up against many problems not encountered in Europe. The native populations are a hotch-potch of various racial, religious, and political elements, and among them include the colonies of three major European Powers. What patriotic or ideological driving force could such countries have to help them to resist an invader? Again, no European can live for a day in an Asiatic country without being recognised as a white man. Therefore, unless a safe area among a friendly people can be found, a European must be perpetually in hiding, with obvious bad effects on his health and morale; and if he operates at night or in disguise the strain will be even greater. There is also the problem of language: few Englishmen can speak Siamese, Chinese, Karen, or even Malay, like a native.

Then there are almost insuperable geographical difficulties. A country like Burma or Sumatra has, in its mountainous or swampy jungles, an infinite number of hiding-places where guerillas can go to ground; but life is very precarious and unhealthy in such places even for a native, much more so for a white man. Food is hard to get; distances are vast, and communications difficult. It may take a month's hard travelling, even for a fit party, to cover a distance of a hundred miles on the map. So vast are the distances that there may be no possibility of supplying the guerillas with arms and other equipment, or of the interchange of agents: Malaya, for example, until the arrival of the new Liberator bomber in 1944, was out of range of any available plane flying from any base in India or Ceylon except the old Catalina seaplane, which is far too slow and vulnerable for modern warfare. And the west coast of Malaya is so shelving as to be almost inaccessible to submarines.

In 1941 the High Command in Malaya were not in the least interested in guerilla warfare in any of its forms. At that time the war in Europe had set no example of a successful resistance movement, and there were too many at Far Eastern Headquarters who still thought in terms of the last war. The idea of stay-behind parties consisting of Europeans and Asiatics seemed an extravagant and impracticable notion; the defence of Malaya was considered to be a purely military undertaking and to be already well under control 'through the proper channels.'

Early in 1941 a small organisation had been sent out to Singapore to deal with certain aspects of irregular warfare. No. 101 Special Training School was the instructional and operational arm of this organisation and was commanded by Lieut.-Col. J. M. L. Gavin, R.E. His school at Singapore had only been going for six weeks when I arrived by air from Sydney early in September 1941, as his second-in-command. Later I was to take over from Gavin, leaving him free to go on tour and concentrate on the planning side. The War Establishment of the school consisted of ten officers and about fifty other ranks; of these, the specialists came out with Gavin and the rest had been recruited locally. The object of the school was to train all types of personnel – military and civilian, European and native – in irregular warfare, and to supply special intelligence and carry out certain operations at the orders of G.H.Q., Far East, with whom Lieut.-Col. A. Warren, R.M., was the liaison officer. By December 8 plans were well under way for directing irregular warfare in China and for stay-behind parties in Hong Kong, French Indo-China, Burma, and South Thailand.

It was only three months before Pearl Harbour and the air-raid on Singapore that I arrived in Malaya. In Australia the impression I had gathered was that the outbreak of war with Japan was only a matter of months, but that Australia at least was in no way ready to defend herself. In Malaya my impression was just the opposite. From the Press and from conversation with people who should have known, one gathered that Japan was economically incapable of declaring war, but that, if she did, the British and American Pacific fleets would prevent her reaching Malaya, and in any case the defence of the Peninsula, especially of Singapore, was impregnable.

Entering Singapore produced a comfortable feeling of security. Uniforms of all kinds were to be seen everywhere. Aeroplanes droned incessantly overhead, and at night the sky was streaked with the pale beams of searchlights. There was the great Naval Base, which had cost £60,000,000 and taken nearly twenty years to build. By day and night one heard firing practice from the fifteen-inch guns which defended the island. The 'whisky-swilling planter' is a myth: the planters were all in the Volunteers, whose eight battalions had not been mobilised, as their officers were considered to be more valuable where they were – on the estates and mines.

But this appearance of strength was an illusion. There were virtually no ships. An 'expert' had said that tanks could not be used in Malaya, so there were no tanks and very few anti-tank guns. There were not enough planes and what there were were out of date, not enough anti-aircraft guns, above all not enough men. The necessary arms and men were simply not available. The attack on Malaya came only eighteen months after the disaster of Dunkirk, and in those months the home army had had to be re-equipped, the Battle of Britain had been fought and won, large numbers of men and a vast amount of stores had been sent to the Middle East, and great quantities of arms had also been supplied to Russia.

It was assumed that there would be plenty of time for reinforcements of men and materials to arrive, and it was known that a string of airfields had been prepared from the Middle East to Malaya. It was anticipated that if the Japs did declare war, they would not be allowed to secure control of the sea routes leading to southeast Asia. Their nearest base was at Hainan, 1,500 miles away, and they would surely be prevented from securing land bases from which Malaya could be attacked.

The possibility of an overland invasion of Malaya down the length of the peninsula was always seriously considered. But here again the Japs would have to launch their attacks across the Gulf of Siam, and this could surely be prevented or at any rate so interfered with as to delay their advance until our reinforcements arrived. The Japs had marched into southern Indo-China in the summer of 1941, thus bringing their advanced base a thousand miles nearer Malaya, but it was assumed that the Siamese would be willing and able to withstand the increasing Japanese pressure. Indeed, the British Ambassador at Bangkok had done all he could to prevent the organisation with which I was connected from operating in Siam, on the ground that any such preparations were unnecessary and would merely upset the people. The possibility of having to fight in the 'impenetrable' jungle – as seen on either side of the motor roads by Staff Officers – seems hardly to have been taken seriously. No specialised jungle technique or equipment had been evolved, and of all the troops stationed in Malaya only the 2nd Battalion of Argylls had had any serious training in jungle warfare. Nor had the natives of the country been in any way prepared to expect or resist invasion. There was no united front.

In August 1941 a detailed plan for the organisation of stay-behind parties throughout Malaya was put up to Sir Shenton Thomas, the Governor and C.-in-C. Malaya for approval. Each party was to be in charge of a military officer specially trained in irregular warfare and would include one or more police officers, planters, or other Europeans who knew the languages of the country and, whenever possible, had a detailed knowledge of the particular locality where they would operate. The parties were also to include Chinese, Malays, and Indians, carefully selected for their reliability and knowledge of the country. The role of the parties would be to supply intelligence and, in the event of being overrun by the enemy, to operate against his lines of communication. They would also organise sabotage and anti-Japanese propaganda and act as nuclei for raiding parties sent in from unoccupied areas.

After various official delays the matter was discussed on a high level and, early in October, was turned down without any alternative suggestions being made. We were told that the scheme would be too great a drain on European manpower, and that in any case white men would not be able to move freely in occupied territory. Objection was taken to the employment of Asiatics on the ground that a scheme which admitted the possibility of enemy penetration would have a disastrous psychological effect on the Oriental mind. Nor might any Chinese be armed, since many of them belonged to an illegal organisation, the Malayan Communist Party – this in spite of the fact that the Chinese had already been fighting the Japs for four years and had made a magnificent name for themselves in exactly the type of warfare we envisaged. I am sure there were excellent reasons for all these decisions, but to us it seemed that nobody at a high level was the least interested in stay-behind parties in Malaya.

On December 8, 1941, when the Japs landed at Kota Bharu and bombed Singapore, we were at last allowed to proceed with the scheme that had been put up some four months earlier. By this time it was far too late for the plan to be effective and we had to improvise at the last moment what we had hoped to organise beforehand in a careful and orderly manner.

Not long after the outbreak of war in the Far East, the Malayan Communist Party had put up a proposal to the Government that the Chinese should be allowed to form a military force to fight the Japs, and that it should be armed by the British. The C.-in-C. at first refused to allow this, but as the war situation rapidly deteriorated he eventually gave permission for the organisation to train and use a certain number of Chinese selected and supplied by the Malayan Communist Party. Where necessary, sanction for their release from jail for this purpose was also given.

Liaison with the M.C.P. was effected through two Chinese-speaking police officers of the Special Branch, both of whom were authorities on Chinese secret societies in Malaya. On December 18 a meeting was convened between one of those police officers, two Chinese (one of whom was the Secretary-General of the M.C.P.), and myself, representing the organisation. This conference took place in a small upstairs room in a back street of Singapore. To complete the air of conspiracy, both Chinese wore dark glasses.

It was agreed that the M.C.P. would provide as many young Chinese as we could accept at 101 Special Training School (S.T.S.) and that after training they could be used against the Japanese in any way we thought fit. It was arranged that the School transport would pick up the fifteen Chinese students for the first week's course at a certain corner in Singapore on December 20, and that as soon as we could increase our instructional staff and accommodation this number should be doubled or, if possible, trebled. It was too late to make up mixed parties of British and Chinese, as in our original scheme, and these men were to be trained and armed as stay-behind parties, and established in the jungle ahead of the advancing Japanese. I made a point of staying at 101 S.T.S. long enough to welcome and give the opening lecture to the first course on December 21. I was much impressed by the enthusiasm of these young Chinese, who were probably the best material we had ever had at the School.

On December 19 Colonel Warren instructed me to hand over command of the School and to prepare to proceed to Kuala Lumpur on December 22. It appeared that Warren and I had been attached as General Staff Officers to 3rd Corps Headquarters 'expressly to organise and lead reconnaissance and operational parties behind the enemy lines.' At that time I had a large scarlet Ford V-8 coupé, and while Warren, Sergeant Sartin (a demolition instructor from the School), and I sat in front, we piled the dicky high with tommy-guns, cases of P.E. (plastic high explosive), grenades, and an assortment of demolition and incendiary devices. It was an ideal way of going to the war, and I felt so like a Crusader that when we passed a wayside Chinese temple I almost suggested that we should go in and have our tommy-guns blessed.

The Corps Commander was extremely keen for us to organise raiding parties behind the enemy lines. Apart from the material value of such raids, some definite information was required to counteract the growing myth of the invincibility of the Jap as a jungle fighter. Accordingly, we were given every possible assistance.

By this time the war situation had steadily deteriorated. The Japs had sent a force across from Kota Bharu to Grik, and this threatened to reach Kuala Kangsar and cut the communications of the 11th Division in Kedah. Although a Company of the Argylls and the Malayan Independent Company fought a most gallant delaying action down the Grik road, the 11th Division had had to fall back, and were now defending a line along the Perak river. The Division was re-organised and re-equipped. Now, a river, with thick jungle coming right up to its banks, is an impossible line to hold, and the 11th Division was about to withdraw to the open tin-mining country round Kampar where its artillery, which was superior to that of the Japanese, would have more scope. The Japs were expected to cross the Perak river before Christmas.

Such was the military situation in Malaya when Warren, Sartin, and I arrived at Kuala Lumpur – in the middle of an air-raid – on December 22, 1941.

CHAPTER TWO

Reconnaissance Behind the Japanese Lines

(See Map No. 5)

There had been considerable discussion of a plan for a series of hit-and-run raids behind the enemy lines. Finally it was decided that these raids were to be made in light motor craft based on a coastal steamer. The first operation was to be a night landing at the mouth of the Trong river, on the coast of Perak, whence a party could move inland and attack any suitable targets, particularly along the Jap lines of communication from Taiping to the pontoon bridge over the Perak river at Tanjong Blanja.

The more I thought about it, the more convinced I became, not only that the raid would be very much more effective if it were based on a target reconnaissance, but that such a journey would have a much wider value. Very little was then known about Japanese equipment and transport, or their general method of advance, and any information on the subject would be valuable. Thus I hit upon the idea of going through the Jap lines from the front and crossing the strip of enemy-held country between the Perak river and the coast to meet the raiding party on arrival at the Trong river. Accordingly Christmas Eve found Sergeant Sartin and myself driving the scarlet V-8 Ford up the road to report to advance headquarters a hundred miles away at Tapah. We set off armed with a note from headquarters to Major Anderson, the Corps Intelligence Officer, asking him to supply me with a Malay-speaking Volunteer who knew that part of Perak.

The consensus of opinion at advance headquarters was that I was absolutely crazy and ought to be forcibly detained. It needed all my powers of persuasion to be allowed to proceed at all. Fortunately the commander of a Volunteer Gunner Battery stationed up the road at Kampar was on a visit to the mess, and he agreed to take me back with him and to try to find a suitable interpreter to

15

accompany me. Major Anderson also gave me a signed letter to the officers commanding the various front-line units that I should have to pass through on my way to the Perak river.

The latest information was that the small town of Parit below the demolished pontoon bridge at Blanja had been bombed all day by the Japs, and that they were expected to cross the river during the night or first thing in the morning. Our troops had been withdrawn from Parit, but it might just be possible for us to cross the river under cover of darkness, though I was warned that all boats had been taken downriver or destroyed. Major Anderson gave me a questionnaire that he had prepared with a view to finding out something about the Japanese numbers, transport, armament, equipment, and morale, and to what extent the local people were helping them.

When we reached Kampar, twelve miles north of Tapah, we found the Battery celebrating Christmas Eve, but the C.O. soon found us a volunteer in the person of Battery Sergeant-Major Ian Patterson, an inspector in the Mines Department, who spoke Malay fluently, though he did not know the actual area in which we were going to operate. The C.O. also lent me a sergeant who would accompany us to Parit and drive my V-8 back to Tapah.

The road to Parit took us through Gopeng, Batu Gajah, and Siputeh, a distance of about thirty-five miles. We seemed to be the only traffic going forward and had the greatest difficulty in getting through the pickets across the road, as everybody seemed to think we were Fifth Columnists. Christmas Eve seemed to be a very dangerous time to be taking risks with the nerves of a retreating army, though it was a good time for collecting volunteers. Patterson later told me that at any normal time he would never for a moment have considered accompanying such a crazy enterprise! As we approached Parit, soon after midnight, we found several very large craters in the road and had to complete the journey on foot, having taken what we needed from the car and sent it back. Parit itself, consisting of a single street of stone shop-houses running down to the river, was a derelict and smoking ruin, though the wrecked shops were still full of merchandise.

Our plan was to find a boat and cross the river before it was light, then to cut northwest to the Blanja-Bruas road and to make our way westward parallel to it in the rubber and jungle. Once it was dark we hoped to be able to follow the road up to Trong, taking cover in the roadside whenever we met a Jap convoy. The whole distance from Parit to the rendezvous at the mouth of the Trong river was only about forty miles by road, and we had two days and two nights in which to do it. We were essentially a reconnaissance party, but had to be sufficiently well armed to fight our way out of any tight corners in which we might find ourselves. We had to take enough food to enable us to keep going for a week and to find our way back through the Jap lines. We each took a tommy-gun and three spare mags, a .45 automatic pistol, and several grenades; and though we took no blankets, groundsheets, or spare clothes, we were heavily overloaded, especially since we took only two rucksacks so that the man in front could be unencumbered. Sartin also insisted on taking some P.E. (plastic high explosives) and various gadgets that he wanted to try out if he had a chance.

For a boat, we only succeeded in finding a cumbersome twenty-foot motor ferryboat with a glass cabin, which had been badly holed and was lying half submerged at the edge of the river. To cross without a boat was out of the question, as the Perak river after the recent torrential rains was a swirling brown flood about five hundred yards wide. Patterson and Sartin, being engineers, set to work to repair the engine, while I plugged the bullet-holes with scraps of cloth and bailed her out with a four-gallon kerosene tin.

The engine, alas! was waterlogged, but was so near to starting that it was already full daylight by the time we had realised we should have to do without it and paddle ourselves across with floorboards – there being no oars. This operation proved to be extraordinarily difficult, and though we all paddled on the port side we could make little headway and seemed to be rushing seaward at a crazy speed while the boat gradually filled with water through its many leaks. There were several enemy aircraft about, and out in the middle of the river in broad daylight we felt horribly vulnerable; but they all seemed fully occupied a mile or two further north, where bombing and machine-gunning had started soon after dawn.

At last, after drifting a good mile downstream, we managed to make a landing on a low shore covered with coarse grass and bushes. As we were afraid a plane might become interested in us at any moment, and since we had no intention of returning this way, we pushed off the now waterlogged boat and were only too glad to see her swirl away downstream, gradually turning round and round. It was then that we discovered that we were on an island and that another hundred yards of rushing water separated us from the further bank. Fortunately just then an aged Malay boat-man appeared, standing up and poling a most precarious dugout canoe. Patterson hailed him in Malay, and he at once agreed to ferry us across. There was only an inch of freeboard with the old man alone in the boat, and though we went over one at a time, lying flat and hardly daring to breathe, it was only just possible to get across without capsizing.

The Malay told us that no Japs had visited his *kampong* (native village) yet; but there was a bicycle path along the river bank, and we were pretty certain that they would soon appear. Indeed, all the time I was precariously balancing the dugout I had been keep-ing an eye on the bank, expecting to be shot at. Sure enough, no sooner had we all crossed over and were crouching in the jungle talking to a group of terrified Malays, then a patrol of a dozen Jap cyclists passed rapidly down the path within fifty yards of us. We overcame with difficulty the temptation to shoot them up.

The Malays did everything they possibly could to help us, but were so completely and pathetically bewildered that we were afraid they would be equally helpful to the Japs. These were the first Malays I had ever met – alas! I could not speak to them – and on seeing these poor creatures so helpless and demoralised with fear, I could not help feeling ashamed that we, who had taken over their country and deliberately stamped out their inherent fighting spirit, could now do so little to help them. The headman of the *kampong* took us into his house and gave us rice and delicious curried fish, followed by coffee and jack-fruit.

When we had finished our meal we put on our rucksacks, which we very soon realised were far too heavy for travelling over rough ground in the heat of the day, and followed a guide the headman had provided. We soon left the Malay *kampong*, with its vegetable gardens and patches of rubber trees, and found ourselves in the jungle.

It was the first time I had been in real jungle. The thing that astonished me most was the absolute straightness, the perfect symmetry of the tree-trunks, like the pillars of a dark and limitless cathedral. The ground itself was covered with a thick carpet of dead leaves and seedling trees. There was practically no earth visible and certainly no grass or flowers. Up to a height of ten feet or so a dense undergrowth of young trees and palms of all kinds hid the roots of the giants, but out of this wavy green sea of undergrowth a myriad tree-trunks rose straight upwards with no apparent decrease in thickness – that was the most extraordinary thing – for a hundred or a hundred and fifty feet before they burgeoned into a solid canopy of green which almost entirely shut out the sky. The tree-trunks, though similar in that they were all straining straight upwards towards the light, were of every colour and texture of bark – smooth and black like Purbeck marble, red and scaly as our own Scots pine, pale grey or ghostly green like the nightmare jungles in *Snow White and the Seven Dwarfs*, or beautifully marbled and dappled like a moth's wing.

Next to the remarkable symmetry of the tree-trunks, the most astonishing thing was the amount of parasitic growth. Many of the boles of the trees were almost hidden by a network of creepers, occasionally breaking out into huge leaves but usually bare and often as thick as a man's thigh. In other places the vines and creepers hung straight down from the branches to the ground, where they had taken root again and looped themselves from tree to tree like the crazy rigging of a thousand wrecked ships. Up in the tree-tops where the great trunks suddenly burst into branches were huge hanging gardens of mosses and ferns, whose rotting foliage seemed to provide its own soil so that the whole mass might be six or eight feet in diameter and was festooned in its own little world of lianas and creepers.

Tactically the jungle gave me a great feeling of assurance, for had a patrol of Japs suddenly appeared, in one dive I could have been completely hidden in the dense undergrowth and it would have been easy enough to elude pursuit. In this jungle the average visibility for two men standing up was at the most only twenty-five yards, though it varied from place to place. This gave us a great sense of confidence, though it was soon lost when we had to leave the jungle and cross a large area of absolutely open paddy-fields, where we should have been an easy target for a Jap machine-gunner.

From further east there was now a tremendous racket as our twenty-five-pounders opened up on the Japs, who were presumably preparing to cross the Perak river. There was also the stutter of machine-guns and intermittent rifle fire, and Japanese reconnaissance planes were flying low up and down the road to the north. The noise of all this was too much for our guide, and he refused to come any further. He also refused to accept any payment for his services.

Our way soon left the paddy-fields, much to my relief, and after crossing a narrow strip of jungle we quickly reached the open trees of a rubber estate. It was very noticeable that these small patches of jungle, where plenty of light could enter from the sides, were very much thicker than the big jungle where the almost impenetrable ceiling of greenery shut out the sunlight and fresh air. In these isolated patches, rattans and other thorns flourished, and the palms, ferns, bracken, and seedling trees rose in such a mad scramble towards the open space above and all round them that, away from the path, progress was impossible unless one hacked a way through with a *parang* (Malay jungle-knife).

We spent some time trying to work our way westward, but the palm-oil and rubber plantations soon stopped and there seemed to be no track through the jungle. By the middle of the day the atmosphere was exactly that of the Orchid House at Kew, except that not only did the heat seem to rise up and strike us from the ground but a burning sun shone mercilessly everywhere but in the thick jungle. Our clothes were soaked with sweat which, in that already saturated air, could not evaporate, and we were tortured with thirst. It was as if every dram of energy was being sucked away, and all we wanted to do was to lie down and sleep – which, as a matter of fact, we did whenever we stopped to rest. At last we were forced to give up the idea of travelling through the jungle and decided to wait for nightfall and then try to follow the road.

Four o'clock in the afternoon found us lying at the edge of the rubber in a very good position overlooking the road and the factory buildings of a rubber estate which the Japs seemed to be using as a halting-post. Here there was no question of falling asleep, since we lay only a hundred yards from the road and could see the enemy, hundreds and hundreds of them, pouring eastwards towards the Perak river. The majority were on bicycles in parties of forty or fifty, riding three or four abreast and talking and laughing just as if they were going to a football match. Indeed, some of them were actually wearing football jerseys. They seemed to have no standard uniform or equipment, and were travelling as light as they possibly could. Some wore green, others grey, khaki, or even dirty white. The majority had trousers hanging loose or enclosed in high boots or puttees. Some had tight breeches, and others shorts and rubber boots or gym shoes.

Their hats showed the greatest variety: a few tin hats, topees of all shapes, wide-brimmed planters' hats or ordinary felt hats, high-peaked jockey hats, little caps with eyeshades or even a piece of cloth tied round the head and hanging down behind. Their equipment and armament were equally varied and were slung over themselves and their bicycles with no apparent method. We noticed with delight that their weapons – tommy-guns and rifles – were usually tied on to the frames of the bicycles, so that they would have taken some time to go into action had they been suddenly attacked. Every now and then a convoy of staff cars and lorries would go past heavily camouflaged with palm fronds. There was little need for this, as the Jap planes seemed unopposed and flew very low up and down the road.

The general impression was one of extraordinary determination. They had been ordered to go to the bridgehead, and in their thousands they were going, though their equipment was second-rate and motley and much of it had obviously been commandeered in Malaya. This was certainly true of their means of transport, for we saw several parties of soldiers on foot who were systematically searching the roadside *kampongs*, estate buildings, and factories for bicycles, and most of the cars and lorries bore local number-plates. Their cooking gear was also of the lightest, and they were living off the country by collecting rice, fowls, and vegetables from the roadside villages.

After a time it came on to rain and we had to put away our notebooks, but even the cloudburst rain of Malaya did not stop the

Japs. They all produced efficient mackintosh capes with hoods – apparently the only standard equipment that they carried – which covered themselves and the paraphernalia on their bicycles. Although there were several buildings beside the road, we saw none of the men stop to take shelter.

As the waves of cyclists and motor transport continued without interruption, we realised we should not be able to cross the road until dark. It was Christmas Day and, standing there in the rain, we ate a miserable Christmas dinner of bully beef, wet biscuits, and wet chocolate, washed down with a minute flask of Australian brandy.

This rain was terrific. Within half a minute we were soaked to the skin, and having been unbearably hot all day were now equally disconsolate with cold. The rain came down so hard that it actually hurt our bare heads and hands, and we had to take shelter under a grove of coconut palms. The huge drops splashed up from the ground in a pale knee-deep mist. The roar of the rain on the leathery leaves above our heads was so loud that we had to shout to make each other hear, and the small stream between us and the road rose visibly, as we watched it, to become a turbid flood.

Since the stream was rising higher every minute, and the torrential rain had hurried on the twilight, we made a move rather earlier than we should have done, and this very nearly proved our undoing. The stream came above our waists and was so swift that we had to swim across, though we managed to keep our rucksacks dry. Some elephant grass gave us cover to the edge of the road, and there we lay concealed in the ditch, watching the Jap cyclists pass within a few yards of us, whistling and singing as they pedalled sturdily along with their heads down. We had intended to wait until it was really dark, but we grew colder and colder. As there were occasional gaps in the procession I decided it would be a fair risk to dash across, although there was a sharp corner to the west of us and we could not see far up the road. Just as I left the cover of the ditch a large party of cyclists came rapidly round the bend and I was nearly run over. I had left my tommy-gun and rucksack, but was afraid that they would recognise me as a European. All I could do was to put up my arm to hide my face and wave to them. Much to my surprise, they waved back. It was getting dark and raining, and I suppose they did not expect to see any Englishmen there, but it still amazes me that they did not recognise me as a white man.

Once it was really dark we returned to the road and started to walk along it, but this proved quite impossible because the volume of traffic seemed to increase rather than diminish and several times we almost trod on parties of Japs resting or mending their bicycles by the roadside. After an hour's attempt, in which we ran great risk of detection and were only able to make a few hundred yards, we gave it up and decided to wait until dawn. We collected a pile of twigs to insulate us from the soaking ground, and lying close up against each other for warmth tried to sleep. But the mosquitoes attacked us in force and it was so cold that we passed a miserable night.

At dawn, as soon as we had eaten some chocolate and biscuits and drunk some river water – which we sterilised in our water-bottles – we set off through the rubber on a compass course parallel to the road. There were a good many Tamils and Malays wandering about the estates and we had to be very careful not to be seen. Fortunately there were patches of excellent cover and even small areas of jungle, so we moved fairly fast. There was no sign of the Japs, though once when we passed the back of some estate buildings we heard orders being shouted, and whenever we saw the road the eastward procession did not seem to have decreased in volume.

Soon we met the road coming south from Kuala Kangsar and crossed it a mile or so north of its junction with the Blanja-Bruas road. There was much less traffic on this road, which was more vulnerable to artillery fire from our positions on the other side of the Perak river. Having watched the road for an hour and made a careful count of all that passed in that time, we tried to work our way southwest to cut across to the Bruas road. Almost at once we ran into difficulties. There had once been cleared land here, but it had gone back to secondary jungle – what is known on the maps by the Malay name of *belukar*. This is quite the most terrible going it is possible to imagine. We had only brought a small *parang* with us, and found this jungle virtually impenetrable. In one hour of grilling and exhausting work, we made only about a hundred yards.

We recrossed the road and tried again further down, but were always stopped by swampy thickets of thorn or bracken, through which it was quite impossible to force a way. At last, completely exhausted and driven to distraction by the bites of a peculiarly vicious type of red ant, we had to admit defeat.

It was now apparent that we could not hope to reach the R.V. (rendezvous) at the mouth of the Trong river and meet the raiding party in time; however, as all our information concerned the Perak river area, it would be far more valuable to Corps headquarters than to an isolated raiding party. I found I had the answer to almost every question in Major Anderson's questionnaire. It was obvious that we must try to find our way back across the Perak river. The trouble was that by now the Japs would have crossed the river and it would be very difficult to know exactly where the front line was. On the other hand, as the Japs were moving south as well as east, we might be able to slip down the Perak river at night until we were right through to safety. It seemed unlikely that the Japs could already have reached Teluk Anson, fifty river miles south of Parit.

Having made this decision, we spent the rest of the afternoon lying up in some paddy-fields only thirty yards from the road, in the shade of a little thatched shelter on stilts. From here, with our field-glasses, we had a wonderful view of the road and could not only make exact notes of the Japanese numbers and equipment, but could get some idea of their morale and character. On the far side of the road and less than a hundred yards distant were some estate buildings, which the Jap officers seemed to be using as a halting-place. Several of the staff cars flew pennants, and we could easily identify these as well as the badges of rank worn by the officers themselves.

These were the first enemy Japs I had been able to examine at close quarters, and I was astonished by their extraordinary resemblance to current caricatures of them – little evil blustering spectacled popinjays with huge ears, projecting front teeth, and toothbrush moustaches, wearing high-peaked jockey caps and untidy uniforms. Some officers who arrived in staff cars had several Chinese and Malays with them, and these were being bullied and beaten up by an interpreter. Once a squat and pompous Japanese major thoroughly boxed the ears of an unfortunate Malay, and then threatened him with his sword. I wished I could understand their uncouth language. At this stage there was no question of the Chinese or Malays collaborating, but both were obviously frightened to death, and it was clear that the Japs were completely ruthless and would have had no compunction in cutting off their heads.

As soon as it was dark we crawled through the grass to the road, and were lying in the ditch ready to dash across when a small dog from the estate buildings picked up our scent. Coming close to us, the brute barked and growled with such persistence that two Japs came out to see what was the matter – possibly thinking there was a tiger. We had already noticed that the Japs, who are very much afraid of the dark, always carried huge torches with them, and we were terrified of being discovered. We lay flat in the bottom of the ditch with our tommy-guns ready, while the Japs flashed the light all round us and passed on down the road. It was a frightening moment – and those Japs will never know how near they were to being shot.

During the night we retraced our steps on a compass course through the rubber, recrossed the Bruas-Blanja road at the exact point where I had waved to the Jap cycle patrol, and lay up for the last few hours of darkness just where our path entered the thick jungle. As soon as it was light enough to travel we found our way back to the Malay *kampong* south of Parit where the headman had entertained us, but alas! the houses were now deserted, though we found a dugout canoe hidden in the undergrowth. While we were searching for paddles we saw a movement in some hibiscus bushes, and discovered that we were being observed by a young Malay. He signalled us to join him under cover and said that Jap bicycle patrols passed regularly up and down the path beside the river. He said that the Japanese had crossed the river at Blanja two days before and that our forces had been driven back to Batu Gajah. He could give us no news of what was happening further south, except that many boatloads of Japs had gone downriver that morning.

We decided to make for Teluk Anson in the boat we had found. The river was even higher than it had been when we had crossed only two days before, and as long as we did not capsize we should certainly get along fast enough. The Malay promised to return at dusk with a paddle and gave us a very welcome bunch of bananas before he returned to the jungle.

As soon as it was dark the Japs no longer used the path and we began to prepare for our journey. We were just carrying the dugout down to the waterside when a party of very frightened Malays appeared, including our friend of the morning, who signalled to us to follow him. He took us some distance downstream, where he showed us a tiny craft which, being flat-bottomed and very beamy, was exactly the boat for the job. I gave him a ten-dollar note – though the boat probably did not belong to him – and he disappeared into the rain and darkness.

Our boat was less than ten feet long and pointed at each end, but we found that, with the two rucksacks packed in the stern, we could just fit in one behind the other if we stretched out our legs on either side of the man in front. There should have been a moon, but fortunately the sky was completely overcast, since it was raining as if it had never rained before. We pushed out into the river and were soon swirled away in the formidable current.

Almost at once we found that the boat was leaking very badly indeed, though we could not tell how much of the water we were sitting in was lapping over the sides and how much was due to the torrential rain. Fortunately Patterson had a large felt hat and this made an excellent bailer, but so much water came in that one of us had to bail as hard as he could all the time. The man in the bow kept his tommy-gun ready and peered into the darkness to try to see where we were going, while the man in the stern tried to keep the boat straight with the paddle. There was no need to add to our speed.

All night long we were swept along by the flooded river. We tried to keep in midstream, since we were just as likely to be shot at by the British as by the Japs, and from either bank, but most of the time we had little idea whether we were in the middle of the stream or near the side. It was most exhilarating to be whirled along at this speed, but also frightening to be so completely at the mercy of the river – and we were terrified of crocodiles. The noise of the rushing flood and the tropical rain beating on the water was terrific, and in some places the river seemed to be breaking and lines of white water rushed at us out of the night. We found that the man at the stern could not hear the orders of the lookout and could not even see his signals, so we gave the paddle to the man in the bow. This allowed two of us to bail – an advantage, because one man could only just keep pace with the leak.

The river was very shallow in parts, and often the boat would scrape over sandbanks or strike submerged branches. Once we ran right up on to an island which we had not seen till the moment of impact, and we clambered out and stretched our numbed legs for a few minutes. We took this opportunity to pull the boat out of water and examine her bottom. The cause of her excessive leakage was not far to seek – she had a large bung-hole, but no bung! A stick and a piece off my shirt soon put this right, and after that the bailing could easily be done by one man. Thereafter the one whose turn it was to sit in the stern could go to sleep, for by this time we were all worn out with our efforts to keep the boat afloat.

Once, when I was steering, I suddenly saw what appeared to be a boat rowed by several pairs of oars approaching at terrific speed out of the darkness. I could see the irregular shape of its occupants and the white water as the oars splashed, and as it rushed past only a few yards to port there was a loud roaring noise. For a second I thought it was an apparition, for no human could possibly row at that speed against such a current. Then I realised that what I had seen was a stationary waterlogged tree. It was our own boat that was moving at such speed, and the current rushing against the branches of the tree had produced the white water and the noise.

In the early hours of the morning the rain stopped. As we did not know where we were, we landed and slept until it was light enough to find a habitation where we could get some news. At dawn we found a Malay *kampong* standing well back from the left bank, and the men were already astir. The first Malays we hailed turned and ran, but soon we held up a man on a bicycle, and after he had recovered from the shock of thinking we were Japs we got some sense out of him. We were at Kampong Pasir Panjang. During the night we had covered some forty river miles and Teluk Anson was only ten miles distant in a straight line. The Malay had seen no Japanese soldiers and certainly Teluk Anson was still in our hands.

We continued our voyage, keeping close to the bank in case any Jap aircraft turned up. After some time we were hailed in English from the bank, and pulled in to talk to a very well-dressed Malay whose dark glasses hid a sinister squint. He told us that he was a member of the royal house of Brunei and that it was most unsafe for us to continue by boat, because there was little cover further down and the Japs were very busy bombing any craft they saw. As he implemented his advice by offering to lend us three bicycles and a guide in exchange for our boat, we accepted his offer – dismissing the suspicion that he merely coveted our re-doubtable craft.

We then joined a large party of Malays and Chinese who were bicycling to Teluk Anson. Soon the path stopped and we had to ferry across the river, keeping an anxious eye on the sky. On the far side the jungle was flooded for considerable stretches and we had to cycle or push our machines through two feet of mud and water. After some time the track stopped altogether, and we sent our bicycles back. We were given a lift on a Chinese sampan which, together with innumerable other craft, was going downriver to Teluk Anson for rice. After a shave in the local barber's shop, and a hot meal, we continued our way by thumbing a lift in another Chinese sampan. Before dark we reached Teluk Anson.

General Paris, who had recently taken over the 11th Indian Division, was in Teluk Anson at that time, and I had a long inter-view with him and gave him a summary of the information we had collected. As he seemed very pleased with what we had done, I made bold to ask him for five hundred men, or even one hundred, to train for one week and then to take behind the Jap lines to operate in small parties. He put a hand on my shoulder and said, 'My dear boy, if I had them, you should have them today; but at the moment I can't spare you even ten men – no, not one!' And that was that.

At Kuala Lumpur I submitted a detailed report, the reconnais-sance had justified itself, and I had learned a great deal about the Japs and the country. I was more than ever convinced of the great opportunities for trained guerillas.

CHAPTER THREE

Stay-behind Parties

On December 30, 1941, I spent the evening with Frank Vanrenan and Bill Harvey, the two planters who had acted as guides to the Trong raiding party mentioned in the last chapter. As a result of this venture behind the Jap lines, they shared my belief in the enormous possibilities of raiding or stay-behind parties, and were not only tremendously keen to join such a project themselves but knew several other planters whom they were quite certain would be equally enthusiastic. I sat up the rest of the night working out the details. Next day I put up a scheme through Colonel Warren to the Corps Commander, the substance of which was that a chain of small self-contained European parties should be installed in the jungle at strategic points along a line running from Kuala Kubu to Kuala Lipis. Between these towns the entire land lines of communication between the Japanese forces (then in south Perak) and the rest of Malaya would be constricted in a bottleneck only fifty miles wide.

Each party was to consist of five to ten British officers, including at least one demolition expert from 101 S.T.S., and several Malay or Tamil speakers – if possible, men who knew the area in which they would operate. There were no Chinese-speaking Europeans available at that time, though there were some English-speaking Chinese who had been trained as wireless operators at 101 S.T.S.

Communication was a serious problem. At this time there was practically no suitable light-weight wireless equipment in the Far East, and such equipment as had been obtained for the School was already in use elsewhere. In fact the only available set capable of working from the field to Singapore, much less to India, was a cumbersome, antiquated apparatus which, with its petrol generator, fuel, and batteries, needed six men to carry it. The other parties would have to take ordinary receiving sets, and the only way I could communicate with them would be by sending a message to our station in Singapore, whence it would be relayed to them in the guise of after-news announcements.

Stores were to be brought up to Kuala Lumpur from 101 S.T.S., or procured locally. A master list was compiled and each leader could add to it as he thought fit. Each party was to have demolition, ammunition, and food supplies for three months on full scale. In addition, they were to take in seeds and gardening and forestry tools, so that with the vegetables grown, augmented by fishing and hunting, they would be able to exist for at least a year even without help from the Chinese. A general reserve dump to be hidden near Tras would serve as a general R.V. for all parties in case of emergency. I hoped that once the area was completely overrun by the enemy it would be fairly easy to use the roads at night. Every man was to take a bicycle and suitable clothes, stain, etc., to be able to disguise himself as a Malay, Chinese, or Indian. In the event of the fall of Singapore (an eventuality which one only mentioned in a whisper), preparations were to be made for a getaway by sea to Sumatra or India, in which case the various parties would be told by wireless to assemble at Tras. Vanrenan and Harvey had already made friends with a Malay at Trong who had a large and sea-worthy boat, and they had given him a substantial present and told him that later on they might need his boat.

There were any number of volunteers for the stay-behind parties, but they had to be selected with the utmost care. I felt that six was the ideal number. They could then operate in three pairs or as two parties of three. A larger number would be stronger in attack and defence and would be able to carry more explosives, but at night – and they would only operate at night – a team of three is, in my opinion, ideal, as it can move very fast and with practice can almost think and operate as one man. Experience had shown me that to be successful an enterprise of this nature must be run more on the lines of a polar or climbing expedition than a military exercise. In the former the discipline is just as strong but much more light-hearted, though a basis of military training and knowledge is essential. It seemed to me that planters who had been in the Volunteers were exactly what I wanted, especially as they all seemed to have a well-developed sense of humour – a virtue indispensable in a small party, whether one is climbing a mountain or fighting in the jungle.

My own party had to be rather larger than the other, since we would have to deal with the main railway line and with the most important trunk road in Malaya. We also had the only wireless transmitter and were responsible for the reserve supply dump at Tras. At this stage my party included Frank Vanrenan, second-in-command, two planter friends of his – Boris Hembry and Richard Graham – Bill Harvey, and, of course, John Sartin, who was now given a commission. As wireless operator there was Ah Lam, a Mandarin-speaking Chinese trained at the School. I planned to get all our stores and men in position by January 10.

(See Map No. 1)
On January 1 Harvey, Sartin, and I set off in my old Ford for Kuala Kubu and the Gap road. Our object was to choose a site for the central dump at Tras. On the way we were bombed several times and kept on having to drive the car off the road into the rubber. After Kuala Kubu the road winds up through magnificent virgin jungle in a series of formidable S-bends till the summit of the Gap is reached, where the boundary between Selangor and Pahang runs, at 2,793 feet. From here a road goes off to the north and climbs another 1,500 feet to Fraser's Hill, one of the two larger hill stations in Malaya. Up at this height tree-ferns were abundant and the jungle growth seemed even more luxuriant than down below.

On the very top of the pass, just sixty miles from both Kuala Lumpur and Kuala Lipis, is a well-built two-storied stone rest-house and a smaller bungalow belonging to the chief Game Warden of Malaya, E. O. Shebbeare, whom I had known in India when we were both concerned with climbing in the Himalaya. Although he was well over fifty at this time, he was full of energy and enthusiasm, and with his knowledge of the jungle I thought he would be a most valuable addition to my party. As I had hoped, he agreed at once to join us, together with a Forest Officer named Shepherd who was working with him at that time on a pathfinding job for the Military. It was agreed that they should join us as soon as they were free of their present commitments.

We then drove down the east side of the Gap past Walsh's Corner, from which there is an incomparable view over the blue jungle-clad hills of Pahang, which stretch as far as the eye can see. On Shebbeare's advice we went through Tranum – where we joined the road that skirts the eastern side of the Main Range – and Tras,

31

then turned left up a tiny side road to Sungei Sempan, where is the power station for Raub Australian Goldmine. This was an ideal place for our dump. The roadhead was five miles up a narrow but motorable lane, and from the power station a pipeline ran steeply uphill into jungle which stretched unbroken to the summit of the Main Range and down the other side to the west coast road and railway. There was a tiny path up to Fraser's Hill and another one following the pipeline to Raub.

We called at the only bungalow and introduced ourselves to Mr. Alves, a little grey-haired Eurasian Tamil who was the electrician in charge of the power station. He was extraordinarily helpful and at once agreed to lend us his Sikh foreman and fifteen Malay coolies to carry our stores up the pipeline into the jungle. This place seemed so perfect for a hideout that I decided there and then to make a self-contained operational camp here, so that if things got too hot for us on the other side, we could simply walk or bicycle over the Gap road and start work again in an entirely new area.

On our return to Kuala Lumpur we were machine-gunned twice by Jap aircraft and were very nearly hit. We stopped at Kuala Kubu and smeared wet mud all over the clean red paint of the V-8, having discovered that she was far too attractive a target for Jap pilots. On January 2 Vanrenan and I went up the west coast road to find a site for our main camp. Kuala Kubu itself did not seem very suitable, nor did Kerling, as we could not find a suitable roadhead far enough into the jungle. It was not till we reached Tanjong Malim that we found an excellent position at the jungle edge four miles north of the town. It was at the head of the side road to a tin mine which had been derelict for some years. All the plank bridges on this side road had been removed to stop the Japs using it, but when we had replaced them, we found it just passable. The country here was old tin-mining ground – known as tin-tailings – and resembled a landscape in the moon. For some distance on either side of the track the jungle had been cut down, the powerful hydraulic drills of the tin-miners had removed all the soil and subsoil, and the rains and rivers had eroded the unprotected laterite rock into crumbling red and ochre cliffs and pillars of fantastic shape, surmounted by a tangled growth of bracken, Straits rhododendron, elephant grass, and ground orchids.

Two miles up this lane we came to the Sungei Salak (barking river) and found several Chinese houses where the people were growing bananas, tobacco, and vegetables on the fertile slope above the valley. There were only Chinese here, which augured well for the security of our camp. We immediately made friends with two *towkays* (merchants) who promised to help us in every way. Leu Kim had fled to the jungle after the bombing of Tanjong Malim, where he owned rubber estates and engaged in business. He was a small, shrewd, humorous man of middle age whom we liked at once. Lee Fee, the other *towkay*, normally lived in this valley and, as far as we could gather, made a living by illicit tin-mining. Unlike Leu Kim he was a countryman and was one of the strongest and best-built men I have ever seen. Each had twenty or thirty coolies, and they promised to help us to carry our stores from the roadhead into the jungle. As a token of good faith we presented them with the two bicycles we had brought with us to reconnoitre beyond the roadhead.

From the abandoned mine a bicycle path led across more tin-tailings to the foot of a steep pipeline which ran several miles into the jungle to the headwaters of the Sungei Bernam. We determined to site the camp in the jungle, a short distance up, and to one side of, the pipeline. An advantage was that from the head of the pipeline it was only ten miles in an easterly direction to the head of a footpath which the map showed running in from our dump at the head of the Sungei Sempan pipeline. As the crow flies, the camps would be only about fifteen miles apart, though to go from one to the other would involve climbing 4,000 feet to cross the Main Range. We determined to open up a jungle track connecting the two camps, so that we could go from one to the other without using the road. In our innocent enthusiasm we even planned to have a private hill station halfway across where we could open up a vegetable garden and retire for sanctuary if we got tired of blowing up the Japs, or if things got too hot for us at our operational camps.

That night I drove to Kuala Lumpur, leaving Vanrenan to find a suitable site for our hideout and to make everything ready for the rest of the party and the stores, which I promised to send up from Kuala Lumpur as soon as possible. I myself arranged to return to Tanjong Malim on January 8 with Harvey and Sartin and, if possible, Shebbeare, Shepherd, and Joli. Thus the party would consist of ten – Vanrenan, Harvey, Graham, Hembry, Sartin, Shebbeare, Shepherd, Ah Lim, Joli, and myself. I was very pleased with this party. The two Chinese were young and cheerful and experts in their own jobs, Sartin was a regular Sapper, and though I should always be chary of taking a regular soldier on a job like this, he had become sufficiently irregular after instructing for five months at 101 S.T.S., while Vanrenan, Harvey, Graham, and Hembry were rubber-planters with commissions in the Volunteers, and absolutely ideal men for such work. They had spent all their working lives in Malaya and spoke Malay and Tamil fluently. Shebbeare was rather old, but he was one of the toughest men I have ever met and had the enthusiasm of a schoolboy. Both he and Shepherd knew the jungle well.

January 3 and 4 were spent rushing round Kuala Lumpur trying to get the stores together, which could not have been done without Gavin's help. As a regular soldier, he carried much more weight than I, and above all he knew exactly whom to approach in each department. The next problem was transport. There were plenty of trucks but no drivers, and in the end we had to take volunteer drivers to bring the trucks back. Thus it was that no less than three of them were overturned. It was quite unsafe to drive by day, since the Japanese had complete control of the air and used to fly up and down the roads bombing and machine-gunning any vehicles they saw.

On January 6 I went down with my first attack of fever. I had a terrible pain behind the eyes, ached in all my joints, felt alternately boiling hot and freezing cold, and ran a high temperature. I staggered to Kuala Lumpur hospital for a blood test and was told I was suffering from 'benign tertiary' – a virulent, but not the most serious, variety of malaria. Next day I was worse.

That afternoon, January 7, there was a rumour in Kuala Lumpur that the Japs had broken the line at Slim and our troops were falling back to Tanjong Malim. I sent a message up by motorcycle to tell Vanrenan I should meet him at Escot Estate Bungalow if the bridge were blown; but the dispatch rider returned with my note to say that the bridge at Tanjong Malim had already been destroyed and he could not get across. It was impossible for me to join

Vanrenan's party or even to communicate with it. The only thing I could do was to join Harvey and Sartin at Sungei Sempan and, as soon as I was better, to walk with them over the Main Range to Vanrenan's camp. The question was: would Vanrenan stay?

On the following day I was no better, but determined to go to Sungei Sempan whatever happened. Gavin agreed to drive me up in my redoubtable V-8, which had by now been covered with earth several times, but had escaped more serious injury. Before we left Kuala Lumpur I met Shebbeare, almost distraught with fury because he could no longer reach his bungalow at the Gap where all his possessions, including his books and diaries, still were. I explained to him exactly where my camp at Sungei Sempan was and he promised to join me by jungle paths as soon as he had wound up his present commitments – but I was to see nothing more of him or Shepherd or Joli.

At Sungei Sempan it was difficult to realise that there was a war. After a few days we heard that Jap convoys were pouring past Tras, four or five miles to the southeast, but none of them turned aside to enter our side road. There were two wooden bridges between us and the main road which we had intended to blow up, but to do so now would only draw attention to our presence.

Alves' family consisted of his elderly Malay wife, a son, and two daughters, all of whom spoke excellent English. Their comfortable home was an ideal place to recuperate. While I lay in the front room of his bungalow, Harvey and Sartin, with the help of the Sikh foreman and fifteen Malay coolies, worked all day carrying our stores up the steep hill to the top of the pipeline and then along a level track beside the pipe to a little *atap* (thatched) hut near the reservoir. From here we intended to carry them half a mile up the Sungei Sempan and then by a small steep tributary to a perfect camp site they had found in a grove of bamboos. For the second stage of this move we intended, for greater security, to use the services of four Chinese vegetable gardeners who had settled nearby. As there was still no sign of any Japanese in our valley, Harvey and Sartin used to return each night to Alves' bungalow, and we planned that as soon as I was well enough to travel we should all move up to our jungle camp.

At dawn on January 13, the day on which I was to go outside for the first time, we were woken by what sounded like a miniature battle at the head of the pipeline. We grabbed our tommy-guns and rushed up to the *atap* shelter where all our stores were hidden, to find that it had been raided. Several boxes of grenades and explosives were missing, a few firearms, our precious case of books, most of our tobacco and whisky, and $2,000 in small notes – almost our entire supply of money – which had been hidden in a hole in the floor. It appeared that after fortifying themselves with a whole bottle of whisky, the robbers had tried out the grenades, as well as the firearms, for the outside of the plank walls of the hut – which contained 1,500 lb. of high explosive – was pitted with bomb fragments and bullets. It was easy to see that the thieves had crossed the dam at the foot of the reservoir and followed the steep path down the left bank of the river. We raced after them, ready to shoot anybody to regain our possessions, but they had too much of a start. However, they had discarded most of the loot as they ran, and we recovered everything except a few firearms, most of the grenades, a case of whisky, and all our money apart from a few hundred dollars I had in my pocket. We learned later that this was the work of a well-known Chinese robber gang; some weeks afterwards, much to our delight, as a result of their throwing our grenades about the town of Raub, the heads of two of the leaders were removed by the Japs and displayed on poles at the entrance to the town. The exact position of our dump must have been divulged by the Malays or the Chinese working for us, and of course each nationality blamed the other or the Sikh foreman.

After this we moved into the jungle and installed ourselves in a tent, while we carried up the rest of the stores and hid them in two more tents which we camouflaged with the greatest care. For this work we had to use the four Chinese, as I was still not strong enough to carry heavy loads and it would have taken the other two several weeks to do the job alone. It was not until January 17 that the stores were adequately hidden, and I was fit enough to set off to join Vanrenan at Tanjong Malim.

We almost persuaded Alves to take us round by car at night, at least as far as Kuala Kubu, but at the last minute his courage failed him. The Japs had still not entered our side road, but we heard they were using the Gap road and had turned Fraser's Hill into a hospital or convalescent home. There was supposed to be a track straight up to Fraser's Hill from Sungei Sempan, a distance of only four miles in a straight line, but it appeared to be completely overgrown and neither Alves nor we could find it. This was disappointing, for neither Shebbeare, Shepherd, nor Joli had joined us at Sungei Sempan, and before leaving this camp I was anxious to visit the Gap to see if I could find any trace of them. The news that we heard on Alves' wireless and later on our own set was most disquieting, and it seemed that the Japs had already reached Johore. We were therefore anxious to join the other party at Tanjong Malim and start operations as soon as we possibly could.

The distance from camp to camp in a straight line was only fifteen miles. The pipeline on the west side took two miles off this, and a footpath marked on our maps along the Sungei Sempan reduced this by another three, leaving a distance of only ten miles. Surely, I thought, however hard the going might be and even if we did have to cross the Main Range, we could make at least two miles in the day, and that gave us five days – call it a week, to be on the safe side. Harvey agreed with me, saying that there were paths everywhere in the jungle and we could shoot any number of pig and deer with our tommy-guns, as well as find all sorts of edible fungi, leaves, nuts, roots, berries, and fruit. Also there were friendly aborigines called Sakai living all over the Main Range, and they could supply us with fish, meat, and vegetables. Alas! how little I knew in those days about the Malayan jungle!

Although we cut our loads down to the absolute minimum, we carried at least 25 lb. each. This included two tommy-guns with eight full magazines, six grenades, a pistol each, a week's food, one change of clothes, groundsheets (but no blankets), medical gear, a pair of field-glasses, maps, compass, *parangs*, matches, etc. Unfortunately there had been no concentrated rations available at that time in Malaya, so we took tins of meat and vegetables for the first part of the journey – when we expected the going to be easier – and oatmeal, sugar, and biscuit for the last few days. These, as well as the matches, were packed in tins and sealed with adhesive tape. Each of us dressed as he thought best. Harvey wore a shirt, shorts, and a pair of gym shoes. This, he said, was what he always wore in the jungle, his theory being that he could see the leeches crawling up his bare legs and pull them off before they got a hold. Though I did not know much about the jungle, I had had plenty of experience of leeches in Sikkim on the way to the Himalaya, so I wore some soft leather boots with a heavy rubber sole and sewn-in tongue with the tops laced tightly over my khaki drill trousers. Sartin wore army boots and puttees.

After a magnificent farewell party with the Alves family, we left our camp at dawn on January 18, having set lethal booby traps all round our tents, and warned our Chinese and Malays that we had done so. It was a nightmare journey – perhaps the most unpleasant journey I have ever done. I had not realised that in the Malayan jungle a mile on the map may mean four or five miles on the ground and that without a track it may take several hours to cover a single mile. Nor did I realise that though a footpath may be marked on the map, it will be completely grown over in a year unless it is kept open by regular use and cutting – and our maps, excellent though they were, were more than ten years out of date. The footpath shown on our map as running several miles up the right bank of the Sungei Sempan took us for a mile up the left bank and then stopped at a deserted Chinese hut. By then it was raining hard and we were soon soaked to the skin. We started to follow a rudimentary track upstream, but presently had to use our *parangs*, as we intended to cut a wide path which we hoped to use regularly between the two camps. Had we not been cutting this track, we could have gone much faster.

In the absence of any path the valley of the river provided the worst possible going. The watercourse itself was too deep and rough to follow, and the sides were so steep and so covered with bamboo, thorns, *atap* (this word is also used for the type of palm used for thatching), and thickets of every kind that our progress was lamentably slow. As soon as the ground was wet we found it almost impossible to keep a footing on the steep traverses, and our hands were torn with clutching at twigs to prevent falling. The tommy-gun in the jungle is a source of considerable grief and bad language. It is far too heavy and is covered with knobs, swivels, handles, catches, guards and other protuberances which, however you carry it, scrape and bruise your hip bone, dig you in the ribs, and still more infuriatingly, catch on every twig and creeper in the jungle.

The first night found us still beside the Sungei Sempan. We camped on a sandbank several feet above the waterline, as it was the only more or less level place we could find. When we undressed to bathe in the river, we found many bloated leeches stuck to various parts of our bodies. I had been bitten round the waist and neck, since the foul creatures, being unable to get at my legs, had worked their way up my clothes until they could find an opening. I had pulled off scores during the day and did not know any had crawled through until I felt the blood running down my chest. Harvey was very badly bitten about the ankles and hands. He had been using a stick and the leeches had crawled up it to reach their favourite of all places – the weblike flesh between the bases of the fingers. Sartin had also been bitten all over the legs, as they had crawled through the eyeholes of his boots and through the folds of his puttees. As we removed the surfeited leeches, Harvey regaled us with charming stories of people who had died from leeches – or the swelling resulting from their bites – blocking the more intimate orifices of the body. The theory is that leeches should not be pulled off, as their teeth stay in and fester. They should be removed by touching them with salt, tobacco, a solution of areca nut, or a cigarette end. My experience is that the wounds bleed just as much and are just as likely to become infected, however they are removed.

The rain continued, and with some difficulty we managed to make a fire. Harvey had said that bamboo, however wet, will always burn. This is true only when you have once kindled a fire, and I had yet to learn that one must always take a piece of rubber or resin to start the fire. Since our packs were so heavy, we ate up as much of the tinned rations as we could. We then cut a pile of branches to sleep on and made a lean-to-shelter out of our three groundsheets. The rain was coming down harder than ever and we went to bed soaking wet and very miserable. During the night it rained very heavily indeed and the river rose so rapidly that, finding ourselves on an island, we had to strike camp and cross a roaring torrent to the bank, where we sat shivering disconsolately until daylight.

Next day was pugatory. We wasted half a box of matches before we could persuade the sodden bamboo to light; then it started

39

to rain again and we gave up the attempt to dry our clothes. We now climbed out of the river valley and set a course due west, making for a col halfway between Gunong Liang (6,341 feet) and Gunong Semangko, which, at 3,985 feet, is the lowest point in that section of the Main Range watershed.

All the third day it poured with rain, and night found us on the top of a ridge about 3,000 feet high. We had not intended to camp so high up, but in the afternoon, to our great delight, we had come across the remains of what had once been a fairly wide path running straight up a ridge to the northwest, and we had made very good time. That evening, by a strange anomaly, we suffered tortures from thirst as we could find no water and for once it had stopped raining. This is the only time I can ever remember being really short of water in the jungle. During the night it began to rain again and we collected the water in a groundsheet. That night, although we huddled close together, we suffered so much from the cold that it was almost impossible to sleep. We determined that on the following night we would keep a huge fire burning until dawn.

Next day we followed our ridge up and up until we came to the summit, which appeared to be above the tree-line, though in fact surveyors had probably cut down the vegetation to get a view and the tall trees had never re-established themselves. The last hundred feet were covered with rhododendron scrub, some of which was in flower, and coarse shrubs and moss which were so thick that we clambered over the top of them without touching the ground at all. From here there was one of the most wonderful views I have ever seen. For the first time I realised the terrifying vastness of the Malayan jungle.

In every direction there were tree-clad hills, peak after peak and ridge after ridge, purple at first, then violet and blue, fading at last into the paler blue of the distance. There was no clearing of any sort to be seen, and the only sign of human beings was the conspicuous cluster of red bungalows on the top of Fraser's Hill about six miles to the south. By working out back bearings from Fraser's Hill and another peak that I could recognise, I discovered that we were on the summit of Bukit Kubang Babi (or the hill of the wild boar's wallow), 3,990 feet above sea level. The track had taken us rather further north than I had intended, and I had to work out a new course along a prominent ridge to the southwest.

The satisfaction of being able to fix our position gave us new life, but our optimism was soon shattered. Once again it rained heavily all the afternoon, and when we stopped to camp we found that the continual soaking had removed the adhesive tape from the tin containing our matches, which had completely disintegrated. The same thing had happened to our sugar, and most of it had disappeared in solution through an ill-fitting lid, while what was left of our biscuit and oatmeal was a sodden pulp. Had we known that the journey was still to take us another week we should certainly have turned back. That night we finished the last of the tinned food and for the rest of the journey had only raw oatmeal – of which, fortunately, we had brought a fairly large bag – mixed with water each morning and each evening. For the last two days we had water alone.

Where we went after leaving our rhododendron-covered hill I have no idea, though I tried to keep steadily a little south of west. The going grew worse and worse. Sometimes we clambered up hills so steep that we had to hold on to the vegetation with both hands to pull ourselves up, and on the descents had to lower ourselves from branch to branch. We seemed to meet every kind of thicket – bamboo, rattan, *atap*, scrub, and thorn. The worst going of all consisted of whole valleys full of huge granite boulders half covered with a treacherous layer of moss and roots, so that a false step was liable to land us in the stream below. Our packs seemed to get heavier and heavier, and the tommy-guns nearly drove us demented. Though it was usually dry in the mornings, it rained steadily almost every afternoon and most of the night, so that we were never dry and the wet clothes rubbed away the skin in the most tender parts of our bodies, so that it was agony to start off again in the morning. Though my boots were as good at the end of the crossing as at the beginning and I did not get a single blister on my feet, the others' footwear rotted away and by the end of the journey had almost completely disintegrated.

We soon developed a regular drill. The man who was in front did not carry a tommy-gun, but cut a path so that he could just

41

pass through. The second man widened the track and marked the route more clearly by bending saplings down or blazing tree-trunks, and the third man merely followed and checked the course with a compass. For, unless he were carefully watched, the leading man might turn through half a circle in a few minutes without being in the least aware of it, as we could not see the sun and there were no landmarks save the interminable tree-trunks on which to march. Every half-hour we changed places. Our hands, unused to the continuous hard work of using the *parang* and softened by being always wet, blistered terribly. Our clothes as well as our hands and faces were soon lacerated by thorns. Two of us had deep wounds resulting from our lack of skill with the *parang*. We were so bitterly cold at night that we were only too glad to set off the moment it was light enough to travel, at about six o'clock, and by three in the afternoon we usually stopped, not only because we were too exhausted to continue, but so that we could rest before it became too cold to sleep.

As soon as we stopped, we de-leeched ourselves, washed away the clotted blood, and then made a leaf shelter for the night. We quickly became adept at this. We used to make a low framework with a sloping roof and lash it firmly in place with vines, then, collecting the largest leaves we could find, we thatched them into the framework of the roofs. We then made a huge pile of branches and leaves as a mattress, put on all our clothes, and covered ourselves with our groundsheets. How we wished that we had brought both sweaters and blankets! When I had made out the list of stores, I had not even thought of including sweaters, as I had always been under the impression that Malaya was a hot country.

While the light was still good, I used to work out the course by dead reckoning from the compass direction we had endeavoured to keep and the approximate distance we had covered. I tried to fit the particular ridges and valleys we had crossed during the day with the endless maze of ridges and valleys shown on the map – but always without success. I tried to preserve my optimism, but in reality I had absolutely no idea where we were.

Before we went to sleep, we used to take it in turn to read aloud from the only book we had brought – C. E. Montague's *The Right Place*, my particular *vade mecum* – and this was the only happy hour of the day. Beneath the groundsheets we generated a comforting warmth and the book took us away from our present miseries to a faraway world of its own. As darkness closed in, the jungle chorus, which had been hushed during the day, came to life, and was so deafening that we had to raise our voices to be heard against it. Every imaginable species of grasshopper, cicada, and tree-frog tuned its individual contribution – musical, unmusical, rhythmic, or strident – to the cacophonous medley. One made a noise like an alarm clock and fully as loud, others like bicycle bells, cymbals, hunting horns, road drills, fishing reels, the infuriating clicker with which a lecturer asks for his next lantern slide, the brakes of a cart going downhill, or the maddening hum of a bee imprisoned beneath a glass. In each camping place the chorus would vary in nature and intensity, depending upon how high up we were and on our nearness to water. The only bird that disturbed our slumbers was the hornbill, whose loud discordant voice resembles that of a heron. In the daytime we would occasionally hear the extraordinary loud rhythmic beat of their wing pinions and, if there happened to be a break in the tree-tops, we would see the huge black ungainly form, and on its head the fantastic white bony structure from which it gets its name.

One of our chief troubles at night was from insects. In the daytime they did not trouble us much, for there are not nearly so many mosquitoes in the great jungle as in the rubber, or near cultivation in the plains; but at night they bit us severely. Worse even than the bite is the shrill humming that seems to be just beside your ear. However much you slap your face, the noise soon breaks out again. Far worse than the mosquitoes were the midges, whose wings made no noise, but whose bite was really a bite and itched like a nettle-sting. These were particularly bad in the early morning and often woke us up long before dawn. As a result of the bites we received in the night, our faces would be so enlarged and distorted that in the morning we were almost unrecognisable. Often our cheeks were so swollen that the eyes were closed and we could not see until we had bathed them in the cool water of a stream.

The going grew worse instead of better, and one of the ridges we crossed was so high and steep that it took us a whole day to climb it. On the top we found stunted scrub and mosses, but unlike the rhododendron summit there was no view here and we still had no idea where we were. We even wondered if the compass were wrong – always the last resort of unskilled travellers – and whether we were wandering north or south along the axis of the Main Range.

By this time – it must have been the ninth or tenth day – our strength was beginning to give out and we had only a small amount of oatmeal left. Both Harvey and I were very worried about Sartin. He rarely spoke and was behaving strangely. We did not think he would be able to carry on much longer. Harvey himself, normally large and rather heavily built, had lost so much weight that he looked quite slight and thin, and had taken in six holes on his belt. Sartin said pathetically he was not used to this sort of thing – implying that Harvey and I were in the habit of making similar little trips! I was still feeling the after-effects of malaria and was not going really well, but the stimulus and responsibility of leadership gave me additional strength and I think I seemed less exhausted than I was. Harvey, as jungle expert, said that he thought we ought to go back at once before it was too late. Realising that none of us would ever willingly make this journey again, we had for some days given up cutting a wide track; but he still thought we could follow our trail back. I was determined to go on. I still had faith in my navigation and knew we must be very near the western edge of the mountains.

It would be so disheartening to have to retrace our steps that I dreaded such an attempt far more than the unknown dangers ahead. Also Frank Vanrenan and his party were waiting for us. If we were to return now, it would be months before we could reach Tanjong Malim either by trying this journey again with better equipment or by walking or cycling round by road. Sartin, on being asked his opinion, said that either course would be equally bloody, but in any case he did not think he could go on much longer – and that was truer than he realised. 'There is nothing either good or bad, but thinking makes it so' – and Sartin was a regular soldier, though rather an exceptional one. Harvey and I were quite certain we could carry on for another week though we should cover less and less ground each day as our strength ebbed. So we went on.

That night we finished our oatmeal. To lighten our loads I suggested that we should dump one of the tommy-guns and possibly return for it later. Sartin's whole training rebelled instantly at such an idea and, rather ashamed of myself, I apologised for the suggestion. The next day, January 28, and the eleventh day of our journey, on the top of a high ridge we found signs of men having once been there. The trees had been blazed, though some years before. We found an empty beer bottle, and there were unmistakable vestiges of a track running down a long spur to the southwest. We followed it for some time, stopping and casting to left and right whenever we were in doubt, until at last it became a definite path. By this time it was dark and we had to camp.

It was quite extraordinary what a good influence this ray of hope had on our spirits and strength. Instead of progressing in gloomy and resigned silence, we now talked and whistled, and went at twice the speed. Next morning we were ready to start the very moment it was light enough to find the path, and going downhill steeply we soon reached a wide stream where there were the remains of a dam at the head of a pipeline. This was the Bernam river. We had come down the long spur between this stream and its tributary, the Sungei Lempong. The odds against striking a line running parallel to our course after such a journey are so great that it must be considered a miracle of good fortune rather than good navigation. Had we been a mile or two further north or south, where the mountains continue much further westward, we should probably not have had the strength to get through.

Beside the pipeline there was an excellent track with naked footmarks along it of recent date. The pipeline ran steadily westward, traversing in and out of the hill and crossing ravines on crazy scaffolding. As soon as we came out of the jungle into an open patch of ground where the trees had been felled, we took off our clothes and basked in the warm sunshine. It was astonishing to see how much weight we had lost in a mere twelve days. Our bones stuck out everywhere. Our skin, except where it was mottled with the purple spots of hundreds of leech-bites, was a sickly yellow. Our clothes were in ragged tatters, and our hands, knees, and faces were covered with a network of cuts and thorn scratches. As we lay in the sun we watched the antics of a gibbon – *wah-wah* as the Malays call them – swinging himself from branch to branch

45

with his long arms, and I realised that this was the only animal, or even sign of an animal, that we had seen on the whole journey.

Halfway down the pipeline we met a party of men, the foremost of whom wore khaki uniform and carried a double-barrelled shot-gun. For a horrid moment I thought they were Japanese. Then I was sure they were Gurkhas, for the leader had pronounced Mongolian features and far paler skin than the average Malay, and wore a wide-brimmed felt hat. They turned out, however, to be Malays, whose job it was to look after the pipeline. They were very friendly indeed and took us back to their *kampong*, which lay a short distance to the south.

Malay *kampongs*, with their thatched houses on stilts, their fruit trees, coconut palms, hibiscus flowers, and vivid green paddy-fields, are always attractive. But after this nightmare journey we seemed to be in very heaven as we lay on the soft grass in the sun, eating bananas and pineapple, and watching brightly coloured bee-eaters and bulbuls hawking for flies overhead. Soon we had a magnificent curry with chicken, eggs, fish, and several vegetables. We were disappointed to find how little we could eat, as our stomachs seemed to have shrunk to nothing. The Malays could give us no news of the rest of our party, but they said that a great many British soldiers, many of them in the last stages of exhaustion, had passed southwards on the edge of the jungle, but that they had not dared to go outside the jungle for some time as they were terrified both of the Japs and of the Chinese. We were filled with excitement at the near prospect of joining Vanrenan's party, so, after a Malay cheroot and several cups of warm sweet coffee, we returned to the pipeline. To reach it we had to climb a steep hill. Much to our surprise we found that the strength seemed to have deserted our legs, and we had to stop and rest every minute.

We descended the steep hill and followed the footpath along the edge of the open tin-tailing ground to Leu Kim's *kongsi*-house (literally company-house) a mile down the valley. The old man was out, but his womenfolk gave us coffee and sweet cakes while they sent a boy to look for him. We must have looked the most awful desperadoes with our swollen features, emaciated bodies, twelve days' beard, and scarred hands and faces. At first the Chinese were so terrified that they started to hurry the children into the jungle which came right up to the back of the house. When they discovered we were Englishmen and that one of us spoke Malay, their curiosity overcame their fear; but in answer to our questions about Vanrenan, they maintained an impassive countenance. We began to fear the worst.

At last Leu Kim returned with his eldest son, Abang (Malay for elder brother), who spoke quite good English. Although I had spent an hour or two with Leu Kim only a month before, he was unable to recognise me and I had to relate various circumstances of our conversation to convince him of my identity. He was then most astonished to find that I had indeed come back.

His story was very incoherent, and it was some time before we could make any sense of it. It appeared that as soon as the stores had arrived on January 5, Vanrenan, Hembry, Graham, and Ah Lam, assisted by a large gang of coolies provided by Leu Kim and Lee Fee, had started to move them into the edge of the jungle. Their plan was to get the cases out of sight of the road and bicycle path as soon as possible, and later to carry them up to the hideout further into the jungle. On the following afternoon, when half the stores had been moved, a Chinese rushed up the side road shouting, 'The Japs are coming! The Japs are coming! They have already reached Tanjong Malim and are at this moment coming up here.' This rumour proved to be entirely untrue, but such was the prevalent state of panic and uncertainty that the coolies disappeared within a few seconds, and Vanrenan's party, hastily collecting their tommy-guns and a few essentials, hid in the jungle. When it came on to rain they went up the pipeline and spent the night in the *atap* hut there.

Next morning at dawn they returned to the stores to find that every single packing-case had disappeared – not only those outside but the ones that had already been hidden in the jungle. There was no sign of the Japanese nor of the coolies. Vanrenan then sought out Leu Kim, who was in tears, and who told him that, as some of the cases had been broken open, the coolies knew that they contained food and tobacco. During the night, he said, Lee Fee's coolies had returned and, unknown to Leu Kim, had carried off all the stores into the jungle. Leu Kim and Vanrenan started to search, but not a single case was left. Even the radio equipment and bicycles, which had been put under cover in a deserted *atap* hut, had completely disappeared. On going over to Lee Fee's *kongsi*-house, they found that it was empty and tracks showed that its occupants had all taken to the jungle.

Vanrenan, finding himself without stores and apparently deserted by his leader, had no option but to set off through the jungle to try to join up with the retreating British forces. About January 10, Leu Kim thought, Vanrenan and his party had said goodbye to him and set off up the pipeline. Four years later I discovered what happened to them. They succeeded in reaching Singapore. Hembry went down with fever, but Vanrenan and Graham made their way via Sumatra and across the Malacca Straits to Port Selangor in search of my party. Unfortunately they were caught by the Japs. They managed to escape, but were recaptured and beheaded at Kuala Lumpur.

CHAPTER FOUR

The Mad Fortnight

(USE MAP NO. 1)

Our failure to join up with the rest of the party was a bitter disappointment, and our own position seemed both hopeless and desperate. With no explosives and only our eight magazines of tommy-gun ammunition it was impossible to go into action. Without the transmitter and wireless operator we could not even get in touch with our headquarters, much less supply any intelligence. All we could do was to try to escape from Malaya and make our way by boat to Sumatra, which would be difficult enough with no food and only a few hundred dollars. The one ray of hope was that Leu Kim had told us that Lee Fee's coolies, unable to carry away all the loot at one time, had dumped some of it just inside the jungle. After Vanrenan had gone, Leu Kim had collected together a few of his more reliable men and during the night they had recovered these stores and hidden them in a cave. But he warned us there was no food there.

We had hoped to spend the night in the warm *kongsi*-house, but Leu Kim said he was afraid this would not be possible, as some of his wives had already objected strongly to our presence, saying that if the Japs were to find out that they had sheltered Europeans, all the inhabitants of the *kongsi*-house would have their heads cut off. However, he agreed to hide us for that night in the jungle and to bring us some food, but said that next day we must return whence we came. Once away from his wives – of whom he had no less than seven – Leu Kim became an entirely different man. He told us that some time before, he had prepared a number of hiding-places further up the valley, in case of air-raids, and that he and Abang would look after us there and bring us food every morning and evening until we had recovered our strength and had time to make a plan to get away.

He then took us to the most perfect hideout imaginable. We followed the footpath back towards the pipeline, with steep untouched jungle on one side, and on the other level tin-tailings covered with a thick growth of bracken and purple-flowered Straits rhododendron. We turned aside over dry stony sand that left no footprint, then, entering a grove of bamboos, followed a tiny track uphill. Here we entered a deep trench as wide as a man which, after about thirty feet, ended in a chamber of ten feet square and the same height, hollowed out of a steep bank of red clay. The back, where a bamboo sleeping-bench had been made, was roofed with *atap*, while the front was open to the sky to let in light. A belt of tangled bamboo, fifty feet high and therefore tall enough to hide the smoke of a dry wood fire, surrounded the cave; and beyond this was a desolate waste of scrub-covered laterite rock broken into cliffs and ravines.

Leu Kim left us here and returned some time later with a grass mat to cover the sleeping-bench, three scarlet blankets, and an earthenware pot of fragrant boiled rice – dry and tacky as only Orientals can prepare it – with fried salt fish, a china dish of brinjols (or egg-fruit, the French *aubergine*) flavoured with soyabean sauce and ginger, and a bottle of sweet strong coffee. While we were eating this delectable meal, he explained that though the Japs had not yet entered this side valley, his people lived in continual fear, because the Malays and many of the Chinese were helping the Japs and one never knew who might be an informer – indeed, he could not even trust all his own coolies. He told us that the Japs had repaired the road bridge at Tanjong Malim and that every day and night convoys of men and equipment poured southwards on their way to the front line, now in Johore. The railway was also being used both by day and night, and no British aircraft was ever seen.

That night, before we fell into a dreamless sleep that lasted until Leu Kim returned late next morning, we determined that if only there were some explosive in Leu Kim's cache of stores, we would start operations as soon as our strength had returned. There might yet be time to justify our stay-behind party – for in those days we still believed in the impregnability of Singapore. Next day, led by Leu Kim, we waded up a reddish stream to a large crack in the waste of laterite where he had stowed the stores, covered them with a tarpaulin, and skilfully camouflaged the cache with bracken.

Apparently the looters had been primarily interested in food and tobacco and had put aside the heavier boxes to remove later, for here we found much of the explosive, grenades, and ammunition, as well as a case of books, another of medical supplies, a roll of maps, and bundles of clothing and gym shoes. The only food was a half-empty case of tinned sardines – for which Leu Kim was most apologetic. It was clear to us that the old man had done a little looting on his own – but who could blame him?

We were still unable to use the explosive without fuses and detonators, and the various delays and other devices necessary for our purposes. But Leu Kim now told us he knew where Lee Fee had buried some of the boxes for which he had no immediate use, so that night we took a *changkol* (the large hoe which replaces the spade in Malaya) and dug up the cache. Here we found most of the missing devices and fuse – but still no detonators, so we decided to go at once to Lee Fee's house in the jungle and make a surprise search. Leu Kim promised to take us along the path to Lee Fee's hut, but having shown us where it was, he must not appear or his life would be in peril.

Accordingly, the middle of the night found us outside a huge *kongsi*-house half a mile into the jungle, calling loudly for Lee Fee. The culprit soon appeared, shaking with fear at the sight of our tommy-guns, at the head of about fifty men, women, and children. He protested that it was Leu Kim's coolies and not his that had looted our stores and that he knew nothing whatsoever about it. Indeed, he had heard that Leu Kim had already given us back some of our stores, and that proved Leu Kim's guilt and his own innocence. We searched the house and several surrounding huts, but found nothing except some cigarettes which were of the same rather obscure make that the Army had supplied to us, but Lee Fee quickly said these had been given to him by Leu Kim. We were quite certain from his demeanour that he was guilty, but we could prove nothing. Harvey then called all the people together and made an impassioned speech in Malay and made them promise to help us against the iniquitous Japanese and not to betray us to the common enemy. As a result of this speech they gave us six fowls, about thirty eggs, and a case of our own raisins – which, apparently, the Chinese did not like. All we now needed was detonators, and Sartin assured us that he could take these off the primers supplied with the grenades.

Next day, when Leu Kim brought our breakfast of curried chicken and cucumber soup, we took him into our confidence. We intended to attack the road and railway that the Japanese were using. If we could paralyse their lines of communication, even for a few days, it might have a very considerable effect on the progress of the battle then being fought in Johore. Though the effect of the efforts of three men might seem to him to be of little avail, yet we might, especially if the other stay-behind parties had also gone into action, be able to hold up the Japs so that the reinforcements that were known to be on their way to Malaya would have time to arrive. We could not do anything without Leu Kim's assistance. Would he help us by allowing us to remain in his hideout and by bringing us food? As Harvey poured out his fluent and persuasive Malay, a gleam came into the old man's eye and I could see at once that we had won the issue. The Chinese are born conspirators and Leu Kim was no exception: also he was a good Chinese. He made a long and eloquent speech – not that I could understand a word of it without translation – explaining how his people in China had already been at war with the dastardly Japanese for four long years; and now he would help us in any way that lay in his power as long as no harm came to his family.

It took us several days to recover from the effects of our journey. We had all lost much weight and were so weak and giddy that if we stood up suddenly the blood rushed to our heads and we fell down in a momentary faint. One morning when I was up early I was overcome by one of these fits of giddiness and fell into the fire. The others pulled me away, but not before one arm was slightly burned. It is noteworthy that at this time, probably because we were new to the jungle, none of our cuts or even leech-bites became infected – an immunity we were to lose in a few months' time. We shaved off our beards, lay in the sun, bathed in the stream, put on new clothes and gym shoes, slept the clock round every night, and ate vastly of the delicious meals that Leu Kim himself cooked. After three days we were ready to start work.

While we were resting, I drew a three-inch-to-the-mile map enlargement of the area in which we should operate, so that I could gradually add more detail such as footpaths and short cuts as we discovered them. One of the first things to be done was to find a way from our hideout to the road without using the lane, as there were several Chinese houses right beside it – we had heard that one of the men had a Japanese wife – and it was essential that nobody besides Leu Kim's and Lee Fee's people should know of the presence of Europeans in the valley. One afternoon, therefore, leaving Sartin to sort out his demolition gear, Harvey and I, who were always glad of an excuse to leave the hideout when Sartin was sawing the detonators off the grenade fuses, set off to find a way round behind Tanjong Malim to reach the road and railway further south through Escot Estate.

Behind our hideout the pipeline crossed an open patch of broken laterite and, plunging into very heavy jungle again, ran for another mile to the southwest. The pipe, being three feet thick, made an excellent causeway and, as we were walking silently along it in our gym shoes, we saw an enormous tiger bound over the pipe some distance ahead and disappear into the jungle again without making a sound of any sort. It was the first wild tiger I had ever seen, and it gave me an impression of infinite grace and strength. The muddy ground on either side of the pipe was broken up where pig had been rooting, and the tiger was probably hunting them. We had no fear, as it is only diseased and toothless tigers that become man-eaters and this one seemed to be in his prime. Here, on the edge of cultivation, we saw in half an hour more signs of game than we had noticed in twelve days in the real jungle. From the end of the pipe we followed a little stream which led us through the rubber to the Bernam river. On the other side of it was Escot Estate, through which, as I already knew, four miles of easy walking along footpaths and estate roads would lead us to an iron railway bridge that was to be our first target.

Slinking furtively through the rubber and the edge of the jungle, and having to take cover whenever we saw a Tamil, Malay, or Chinese even in the distance, Harvey and I realised that it would be necessary, even at night, to go out in disguise so that we should not instantly be recognised as Europeans. As soon as we returned from our reconnaissance we tackled this problem. We were all too tall to pass as Malays or Chinese, so we determined to disguise ourselves as Indians and to dress like Tamils. All we needed was a white shirt, a *dhoti* or *sarong* round our middles, and a dirty white cloth tied round our heads and left hanging down behind. Tamils are notoriously timid folk, and in these disturbed days, when no wise or law-abiding man ventured out after dark, it would not excite undue comment if we seemed rather reluctant to meet other people. The matter of complexion caused us some difficulty. After various experiments we found that a strong solution of lamp-black, iodine, potassium permanganate, and coffee blackened us thoroughly and was sufficiently permanent for our purpose.

On the night of February 1 we went into action and for the next fortnight operated almost every night. Although, as I write, it is four and a half years ago, every detail of that mad fortnight remains in my mind with far more clarity than many events that have happened since. Our routine was to leave the hideout at about 5 p.m., with our faces and hands darkened and wearing battle-dress carefully camouflaged with patches of mud. Each of us carried a tommy-gun, a pistol, and two grenades, as well as army packs filled with explosive and the various requisites for making up charges.

In order to protect the people in the valley, as well as for the security of our hideout, we made it a definite rule at first never to operate within five miles of our base, except in Tanjong Malim itself, which was just under four miles away. Normally we tried to return to the edge of the jungle well before dawn and then to find our way back to the hideout with a torch, which Leu Kim had given us. To follow a jungle path, even on a moonlit night, it was necessary to use a light of some sort, so we put a green leaf inside the glass, not only to make the torch less bright, but to accustom our eyes to a dim light. Outside the jungle we made a point of never using a torch at all, and it was remarkable how quickly our eyes became used to the dark. When our only battery ran out, we discovered that a few fireflies or luminous centipedes in the reflector of a torch gave quite enough light to read a map, lay a charge, or even follow a path. We all gave up smoking, as our lives depended on our senses working at full efficiency, and the use of tobacco certainly affects one's sense of smell.

As I was responsible for the navigation, and because my eyesight seemed to be much better than that of the others, I always went in front, followed by Sartin and then Harvey, whose cheerful bulk gave me great confidence as rearguard. We invariably walked in single file within touching distance if it were dark and further apart out in the open or in moonlight.

We evolved a special system of signals, so that it was rarely necessary to talk. We made a clicking noise between the upper teeth and side of the tongue – the sound used to encourage a horse. This is an excellent signal, as it can be made very softly and on a still night will carry a great distance. It is a sound that does not unduly attract attention, as it might well be a bird, an insect, or a rubber nut falling. A single click meant *Stop* or *Danger*, and two clicks indicated *Go on* or *O.K.* The only other signal we needed – for such signals must be as few as possible and absolutely unmistakable – was a rallying cry, which I alone made, to call the party together again if one of us were lost or if we had scattered in a sudden emergency. The signal used was the hunting cry of the British Tawny Owl. This piercing cry carries for a great distance even in thick woodland, cannot be confused with any other cry heard in the Malayan jungle, yet to the uninitiated – and we included the Japs in this class – it passes without notice in the variety of weird nocturnal voices.

Before setting out we practised walking and running past each other to make sure that no bit of metal caught the light and nothing such as a half-empty box of matches could betray us by its rattle. We even wrapped our tommy-guns in adhesive tape to stop them shining in the moonlight. With a little practice we learned to walk heel first on hard ground and toe first on soft ground, so that we passed absolutely silently, and with our camouflaged clothes and darkened faces were virtually invisible. To walk in this way requires much practice and, as it calls into use muscles not normally used, is extraordinarily exhausting at first. It was certainly very effective, for time and time again we passed within a few yards of natives, and unless they happened to be looking straight at us they would be unaware of our presence. Often, seeing us moving silently in the darkness superstitious Malays and more particularly Tamils would frighten us in turn by uttering a scream and rushing away.

If we were operating far from our base or ran into trouble, we did not take risks in order to hurry home, but returned in broad daylight in our disguise as Tamils. As soon as we saw the dawn approaching we would make for the jungle, go in some distance (later always walking up the course of a stream because the Japs brought two Alsatian police dogs to Tanjong Malim to track us), eat some food, and sleep for a few hours. If the water in the streams looked unhealthy, we could always be sure of finding uninfected water in the cups attached to the rubber trees to catch the latex – though it was often thick with the wriggling larvae of mosquitoes. Sometimes, if we were far enough away from a path, we would even light a fire as in the jungle smoke disperses long before it reaches the tree-tops. Then we would take our tommy-guns to pieces and pack them, our battle-dress, army packs, and anything else suspicious, into innocent-looking gunny-bags that we had brought for the purpose, make up our faces, arms, and legs, and put on our Tamil clothes. We always kept a pistol and a grenade tucked into the tops of our *sarongs* in case of emergency.

Here Harvey came into his own, as he was a born buffoon and not only spoke Tamil fluently but had all the right gestures of arm and head, and really looked like a Tamil – indeed, he even smelled like a Tamil, for the *kampong* dogs, which at once saw through Sartin's and my disguise, never barked at him. Often we came upon people too suddenly to turn aside, and Harvey usually made a point of talking to them. I do not know what the genuine Tamils thought about it, but I am convinced that the Chinese and Malays, and certainly the Japs, were taken in by our disguise. Quite often we saw in the distance patrols of Japanese cyclists, presumably looking for us, and once we had to stop and speak to them. I was terrified, but Harvey rose to the occasion admirably and whined to them in abject Tamil.

In spite of the equality of all races in their much-vaunted brotherhood of New East Asia, if you met a Japanese – whether you were a Chinese, Malay, or Tamil – you had to cover your face with both hands and bow down low before him. If you were afraid that you were rather tall for a Tamil, that your features were rather European, and that some of the stain had run off your face with the sweat, you were only too glad to cover your face with your hands and bow down before anybody. I consoled myself with noticing that the Japs did not have their weapons ready, and as I bowed low I pressed my elbow reassuringly against the butt of my .38, which I could have drawn at the least sign of danger.

We would walk home through the rubber and jungle, avoiding as far as possible the *kampongs* and roads. When we reached our hideout, we would bathe in the stream which ran only fifty yards away, eat the enormous meal that Leu Kim always left for us, tell the old man all about our last raid if he were there, then sleep solidly until it was time to get ready to go out again.

As we were far too small a party and far too tired to be able to maintain a sentry during the day, we had to rely on booby traps which only Leu Kim and Abang knew how to pass in safety. Also we prepared a getaway through the back of the hideout into a ravine which led across the tin-tailings towards the pipeline. Our only scare was when some passing Malays, probably the men who guarded the pipeline, saw us bathing in the stream; but nothing happened and probably they had the sense to hold their tongues. During our fortnight's operations – except on this occasion – we were never once, as far as I know, recognised as Europeans, though we must have been seen by hundreds of Japs, Indians, Malays, and Chinese.

Our first raid was carried out immediately to the south of Tanjong Malim. We crossed the Bernam river into Escot Estate as soon as it was really dark, then followed the wide estate road past the coolie lines to the railway and underneath it to the road. As this area was only three hours' walk from our camp, we had at least six hours in which to operate. Our objective was the bridge a mile south of the railway station, but when we reached it we found that it was a much more formidable target than I had remembered.

It was of the heavier type of those used on the Malayan railways, in which the bridge is suspended from semicircular girders. It was far too solid to demolish with the small amount of explosive that the three of us were able to carry – always our limiting factor – so we buried a charge of about 30 lb. of P.E. (plastic high-explosive) in the middle of the line against the abutment of the north side of the bridge. This charge was connected to a pressure switch placed beneath the rail, so that it would be set off by the weight of the engine. We hoped that the next train to pass would thus be derailed and, with any luck, would fall against one side of the bridge and overturn the whole structure, so that both train and bridge would crash into the river and road below.

Having hidden every sign of our handiwork, we walked up the line to our next objective – a heavy masonry bridge by which the road crosses the railway. This again was quite beyond our means, so we contented ourselves with walking back up the line, setting a number of five-pound charges, each of which was to be detonated by a simple delayed-action device called a time pencil. In this type of device, the operator, when all is ready, squeezes a copper tube and thus breaks a phial of acid which gradually eats through a fine wire. When this wire is dissolved, a spring is liberated which forces a striker against a percussion cap, thus igniting an instantaneous fuse. The length of the delay (denoted by coloured bands on the outside of the pencil) is regulated by the thickness of the wire and varies from half an hour to twenty-four hours.

The advantage of both pressure switch – which is set off by the weight of the locomotive, though the charge may be some distance ahead – and time pencil is that the operator has time to get well clear of the scene before things start to happen; but the time pencil is not so effective as the pressure switch, which will not only demolish the line but will derail, and possibly wreck and overturn, the train that sets it off. A fog signal placed on top of the line is as effective as a pressure switch, but as it is clearly visible it should only be used if it is quite certain that the train will arrive before daylight. Time pencils, however, were very useful to detonate small charges set up and down the line on either side of a derailing charge – as long as none of them went off before the arrival of the train. The point of this is that once a train has been derailed, the line keeps blowing up on either side of the wreckage for another twenty-four hours so that breakdown gangs are distinctly discouraged, if not actually prevented, from reaching the scene of the original demolition. It will be seen that demolishing a railway line gives plenty of scope for ingenuity. It has been said that the dynamiter's dream is to cause the head-on collision of two trains, both full of troops, in the middle of a tunnel. Though we never achieved this, we did our best to keep the Japs from getting stale.

By now we had used up our night's ration of explosive – 100 lb. was the most the three of us could carry in addition to our weapons and other gear – but before we started for home I swarmed up the telegraph posts in several places and cut the lines with pliers. There were about thirty wires, and I dared not cut all of them in any one span lest the resulting tension on only one side of the post should pull it down – and me with it. As we were on our way through the rubber, we heard to our unspeakable delight a train leaving Tanjong Malim station half a mile away and starting very laboriously down the line. Our excitement was so great that we could scarcely breathe.

The train came on down the line so slowly that it seemed hardly to be moving. We gripped each others' hands to control our agitation. The train drew nearer and nearer, yard by yard, clanking and chugging and wheezing. Surely it must have reached the charge! Had something gone wrong? Suddenly there was a most blinding flash followed by a crash that shattered the night and reverberated across the valley. Fragments of metal whizzed into the air and fell with a loud thud some seconds afterwards, hundreds of yards from the scene of demolition. The train clanked to a standstill and there was a loud noise of escaping steam and shouting.

We longed to go and look at it, but there was now a brilliant moon and we thought it wiser to get home and ask Leu Kim next day to find out how much damage we had done. On our way home we heard two more explosions and the Chinese reported several others next day. We discovered to our disappointment that the train had merely left the line after being derailed and had neither turned over nor done much harm to the bridge, but the locomotive was completely wrecked.

As we heard that the Japs had sent armed patrols round the *kampongs* to the south of Tanjong Malim and had arrested several Chinese, we decided on the following night to go in the other direction. Our first attempt to reach this target area was abortive. A night later we tried to cut straight across to the railway, our objective being a group of iron bridges just south of Kampong Behrang and about seven miles up the line from the scene of our last raid. It took us more than three hours to cover the two miles of Behrang Estate between the end of the Sungei Salak lane and the railway.

The ground was a maze of small hillocks, streams, isolated strips of jungle, and patches of seedling rubber. Soon after we had started walking north up the railway line, we saw what we thought was a Japanese patrol approaching us. The moon was behind us, and seeing them some distance away, we hid in the long grass beside the line. Some wore wide-brimmed hats, and they walked very noisily and seemed exhausted. As they passed there was a peculiar odour of sour sweat and tobacco which was strangely familiar. It was not till some time after that we realised they were probably British soldiers. But I decided not to go after them. We might be wrong, and in any case they would only be an embarrassment to us (and to Leu Kim), and we could have done little to help them.

We started putting charges on the line. Sartin used to supervise this work, while I helped him and Harvey kept guard. We had found an ideal place for a derailment, where there was a curve above an embankment, and had just finished laying the charge when Sartin suddenly gasped and said, 'Christmas! You're lucky men!' It seems that we certainly were! Ten pounds of gun-cotton had been carefully placed beneath the outer rail and connected by detonating fuse to the pressure switch, which then had to be packed up carefully with stones so that it just touched the lower surface of the rail. While doing this, Sartin had pushed it up too hard and the spring had gone off – but, by the grace of God, the cap was a dud and had failed to detonate the charge.

Dawn was not far distant, so we decided to put all the rest of our explosive, about 25 lb. of P.E., on a small girder bridge just south of Kampong Behrang station, and to detonate it with a pressure switch. A job like this used to take us about half an hour, as separate charges had to be placed against every rail and girder, each one connected by detonating or instantaneous fuse so that as the pressure of the train fired the switch, all the charges would detonate simultaneously. Then each lump of P.E. had to be carefully lashed or jammed in position so that it would not be shaken off by the vibration of the approaching train. As far as possible we prepared the charges before we left camp, but there was always a good deal of work to be done at the last moment, usually against time and in darkness.

On this occasion we had almost finished the job when I thought I heard a train far away to the north. The others listened, but as they could hear nothing I came to the conclusion I was mistaken. Soon afterwards, however, we heard a definite whistle. There was no doubt that a train was approaching fast. We had intended to detonate the charges with a pressure switch placed at some distance from the charges so that the bridge would be demolished in front of the train and – with any luck – it would be unable to get across the gap and be thrown down the embankment in a glorious tangle. But now, hearing the train so near, we simply put a fog signal on top of the line and hastily connected it with the main fuse leading from the charges.

Suddenly the train whistled again as it came through the station less than a mile distant. In a minute it would be upon us. We hastily finished off the job and, collecting our bits and pieces, pushed them into our packs. It took us some time to find the precious pliers, and then Sartin remembered he had put his box of detonators in a safe place on the bridge. By now the train was in sight, just up the line. With one accord we started to race down the footpath beside the track, having no desire to be run over as well as blown up. Over our shoulders we could see the dark mass of the train bearing down on to the bridge with sparks spouting from its funnel. On one side of the line there was a hill covered with thick jungle, so we turned and dashed down the banking, only to find ourselves up to our waists in a foul swamp. At this moment there was a blinding white flash, which gave me a glimpse of the other two, open-mouthed and holding their tommy-guns up out of the water.

Almost at the same moment came a shattering explosion, which nearly burst our eardrums and shook even the soft mud in which we were stuck, followed by a frightful grinding and rending of metal. A shower of missiles roared and whistled above us to crash into the jungle or splash into the wide swamp on the other side of the line. To our horror the train did not stop, but dragged itself slowly on over the bridge, clanking hideously. We were momentarily floodlit as the cab, bristling with Japs, passed less than ten yards in front of us and came to a standstill a little further on. Above the loud hiss of escaping steam we heard some altercation.

Then two chattering Tamil drivers with an escort of Jap soldiers armed with tommy-guns and flashing their torches walked back between us and the goods-wagons to examine the wrecked bridge. We covered them with our tommy-guns as they passed, but they did not see us, and after a few minutes they returned accompanied by three more Japs, presumably from the brake-van at the back of the train. As the locomotive was quite useless, they abandoned it and set off down the line towards Tanjong Malim.

As soon as they were out of sight, we extricated ourselves from the bog and went to have a look at the engine. We dared not approach too near, as water and steam were gushing out on to the line and we expected it to blow up at any moment. Harvey insisted on lobbing a grenade into the open door of the furnace, and we took cover as it exploded. We found that both the twelve-inch steel girders of the bridge and one rail were cut through, but the charge on the other rail had apparently been displaced by the vibration of the train. Both brick abutments had crumbled, and the rails, especially the severed one, sagged right down, yet the train had been able to drag itself over the gap and remain on the rails on the other side.

By this time it was already beginning to get light, and as we were afraid some Japs might appear from Behrang station, we made our way through the rubber, being careful to avoid being seen by the Chinese and Malays who were already abroad, having been woken up by the explosion. At last we reached a patch of thick jungle, and here we knew we were safe.

After a few more expeditions against the railway we came to the conclusion that we needed a change. A single line, the nearest point of which was three and a half miles away from our base, did not give us much scope without returning too often to the same spot, unless we could somehow procure bicycles. Since we were now beginning to meet Jap patrols on the line it became obvious that the railway was no longer a healthy place for us. Also we were not quite certain how effective our demolitions had been, since we dared not return to the scene of our operations. True, we used to hear our charges exploding at all hours of the day and night, and Leu Kim used to bring up encouraging reports of trains wrecked and lying on their side, but we were afraid that several of the charges had not gone off – presumably owing to dud caps – and that even when they had detonated, the damage was not as great as it should have been.

Where we had been able to examine the results, our demolitions had not been entirely successful, and Sartin even began to wonder if the explosive had deteriorated from damp in the jungle. Another cause of mistrust of the efficiency of our methods was the extraordinary speed with which the Jap breakdown gangs managed to get the line in running order again; and I came to the conclusion – though Sartin would never agree to this – that a train, at any rate a Malayan train, can jump a six-foot gap in one rail. To make quite certain of the job at least ten feet should be cut, preferably of both rails. Yet another worry was that on the railway we were getting through our explosive at the rate of a hundred pounds a day. Leu Kim had averted a crisis by securing a tin of 500 detonators, a roll of safety fuse, and several hundred pounds of blasting gelignite from a tin-mining friend, but even so we were finishing the explosive too fast and not making use of any of our large supply of tommy-gun ammunition or grenades. My conclusion was that we should turn our attention to the main road.

On our visits to the railway line south of Tanjong Malim, which for several miles is only separated from the main road by a narrow strip of rubber, we had had plenty of opportunity of observing the road traffic at night, and while returning by daylight from more distant raids on the line north of the town, we had spent many hours making careful traffic counts. In the daytime practically all motor transport, including a few armoured vehicles, innumerable lorries and staff cars, and a good many motorcycles, moved southwards, and there seemed to be little attempt to drive in convoys. There were also large patrols of cycle troops going south and a few civilian cyclists and pedestrians moving in either direction. At night civilians seemed to avoid the road entirely and we saw no cyclists, but large convoys of trucks and staff cars moved southwards at any hour of the night, driving very fast with headlights full on and with no proper interval between vehicles. In other words, they were just asking to be ambushed.

One night, when returning home from the railway, we noticed

a pile of glowing embers at the roadside, and on investigating we found that six 20-cwt. trucks were parked almost touching each other in the grass beside the road. There were no sidelights burning and no signs of the drivers or any sentries, though we dared not go too close in case they were being really clever and watching from a distance. Unfortunately we had no explosive left, but Sartin remembered that we had hidden about 20 lb. of P.E., which we had left over one night, in the roots of a rubber tree less than a mile away. While Harvey stayed to watch the trucks, Sartin and I collected the explosive as fast as we could. When we returned – after giving and receiving the double click of recognition – Harvey said that judging from the snoring he had heard coming from the trucks, they were full of troops, though it might have come from the sentries or the drivers. While Harvey, with his tommy-gun ready, continued to keep watch, Sartin and I crawled underneath the lorries and jammed 2 lb. of P.E. on each one just between the crankcase and the clutch. As we worked our way along the line of trucks, we connected the charges together with detonating fuse – a job which took over an hour to complete. As we wanted to see what would happen, we set off the charge with a copper-tube igniter and four feet of safety fuse, thus giving us two whole minutes to crawl away and hurry to a safe distance down the road. When the charges exploded, we were most disappointed that not one of the trucks caught fire – though neither they nor their drivers were much further use to the Japanese war effort. After this we usually took with us a few clams – small magnetic bombs which adhere to metal and can be set off with a time pencil – to use against vehicles parked by the roadside. Once we were able to attach three of these while the drivers were sitting round a fire a short distance away.

Our first road ambush was quite fortuitous, as it resulted from our desire to try out a new bomb we had invented. We had several hundred pounds of gelignite which had suffered so much from the climate that all the nitroglycerine was running out of it. The textbooks say that such gelignite is very dangerous and should be thrown away, but in our circumstances we were very reluctant to waste good explosive. As the stuff was very sticky, Sartin had stored it inside a section of bamboo – and this had given me an idea. We had often discussed the possibility of setting mines in the roadway, but had given up the idea as we had no apparatus for boring holes through the metal of the road. We had, indeed, suggested scooping out a hole in the soft side of the embankment to set a crater charge beneath the middle of the road, but, though this would crater the road and cause a certain amount of annoyance, it would use up a great deal of explosive, it would not damage any vehicles, and the Japs would soon fill up the crater again. But it struck me that a bomb on the surface, concealed in a section of bamboo – which, on a Malayan road, would not attract attention – would be very effective and would be easy to prepare.

The bomb would be detonated by a pull-switch, a device similar in principle to a pressure switch. This switch is buried in the explosive or connected to it by instantaneous fuse. Then, at the required moment, the operator from a safe distance pulls a length of piano wire (which is quite invisible at night), and detonates the charge. A great advantage of detonating a mine by this means is that it gives much more control. Not only can you choose the exact moment for detonating the charge, but, if an unsuitable target appears, you can let it pass harmlessly over the danger spot and wait for better game. If it is unwise to wait, a trip wire can be laid across the road so that whatever runs into it is automatically blown up.

Our first trial of the bomb was carried out early one morning on the way back from an expedition to Kalumpang railway station, three miles south of Tanjong Malim. Along this section of the line we had left about fifty separate charges to be detonated with time pencils. Each one consisted of two-pound slabs of gun-cotton placed just beneath the junction of two rails so that both of them would be damaged and would have to be replaced. We had discovered that the Jap repair gangs were very quick at filling up large craters and replacing damaged bridges, but we thought a fusillade of small explosions at odd intervals of time up and down a mile or two of line might keep them away and render the railway unusable for at least twenty-four hours.

We had already prepared a bomb consisting of a section of bamboo about eighteen inches long, filled with 5 lb. of gelignite and a pull-switch. On the way down the line earlier in the night we had crossed over from the railway to the road and found an excellent place for our ambush just by the fiftieth milestone (from Kuala Lumpur). Indeed, our bomb, which was oozing nitroglycerine, seemed to be in such a dangerous state that we hated carrying it further than was necessary and we hid it behind the milestone and collected it again on our way back.

The rubber came up to the edge of the road and ended in a low bank which gave sufficient cover from the explosion, while a little path back to the railway provided an excellent getaway. We scattered several other bits of bamboo on the road, so that if any driver was suspicious he could satisfy himself that they were quite innocent. We then put the bomb in the middle of the road, anchored it to the milestone, and took up our position behind the bank.

Success in an operation of this sort depends very largely on careful planning, and before we had left our hideout each of us knew exactly what he had to do. Sartin was to have the honour of pulling the line if I hit him on the back, which I would do if I decided that the target was worthy – but not too worthy – of our attention. In this ambush, as we were such a small party and not in a very good defensive position, I decided that I would only stop a single Jap car or a very small convoy. Sartin was to pull the line just as the nose of the first car passed over the bomb, then we would all take cover and hope for the best. The moment after the explosion, Harvey and I, from behind the bank, would each throw two grenades. As soon as these had gone off, we would each empty a tommy-gun magazine into any target that we could see, then race like hell to the railway line, on the far side of which we would rendezvous to make sure all was well, cross the Sungei Inki by a footbridge that we had placed there some time before, and go home straight across Escot Estate.

Unfortunately this ambush, like many more important battles in history, did not go exactly as planned, because we had gone into it far too light-heartedly at the end of a heavy night's work. It was a brilliant moonlit night and we lay behind the bank in a state of intense excitement. There was a sharp explosion to the south – this was one of the shorter delays we had put on the line. Then we heard a train coming down from the north and we wondered if it would be able to get over the gap cut by the explosion that had just occurred; but the train stopped at Tanjong Malim – probably a night-watchman had heard the explosion and they were holding up all traffic until they had examined the line. Suddenly we saw headlights approaching down the road.

The great moment had come. I counted the lights of six cars, but I could not tell what sort of vehicles they were. As this might be our last chance that night, I hit Sartin on the shoulder and we all pressed our bodies down into the soft soil. Harvey and I pulled the pins out of our grenades. As far as we could make out on reconstructing the scene later, the bomb must have exploded beneath the petrol tank and ignited that too, for not only was there the usual flash and explosion, which almost threw us upright, but the flash was followed by a steady and brilliant blaze which lit up the whole scene like a stage setting. As I threw my grenades, I caught a glimpse of another large closed truck crashing into the burning wreckage and the third one turning broadside on with a scream of brakes. After the explosion there was a harsh stutter as Harvey emptied his tommy-gun in one burst up the road. I did the same and then found myself racing down the path, floodlit by the funeral pyre of the Jap lorries.

It was not until we had reached the railway line that the Japs opened fire, at first sporadically and then at an increasing tempo. Apparently they were not expecting trouble and none of them had his weapons ready. As we dashed across the line, we saw in the clear moonlight a party of men with lanterns a hundred yards up the track. They opened fire too and started shouting though for all they could see we might easily be Japs escaping from the blazing convoy. This must have been a patrol sent down the line from Tanjong Malim on hearing the earlier explosion down to the south. As we plunged through the rubber and then raced along a footpath to gain the estate road, on which we could run even faster, the night was hideous with the noise of rifle, machine-gun, and even mortar fire. Our whole action had taken only half a minute, yet the Japs kept up their firing practice – for they could not possibly have seen anything to shoot at – for over an hour. It was really most frightening, though none of the bullets or bombs came very near us. Having safely passed the estate coolie lines, we lay down to rest and recover our breath, congratulating ourselves on a very successful, though very terrifying, ambush.

67

This experience taught us a great deal, and as the Japs would probably be prepared in future, we determined from now on only to carry out an ambush in cuttings, so that we should have adequate protection from enemy fire and the bursting of our own grenades as well as the possible explosion of the vehicles. We remembered having noticed several suitable places where there were small cuttings on the west side of the lonely four miles of road between the end of the Sungei Salak lane and the turning off to Behrang station. There was rubber on the upper side of this road and virgin jungle on the other. Although this section of the road was rather nearer to our hideout than we had intended to operate, it was the only suitable stretch within reach of our camp. But as most of our operations hitherto had been to the south of Tanjong Malim, the Japs would, we hoped, conclude that we were based on that side of the town and leave the northern side in peace.

We now improved our ambush technique. In order to cover a greater number of vehicles, the three of us took up positions about thirty yards apart, depending on the nature of the cutting. As our supply of grenades was limited and they were rather heavy to carry so far, we made our own bombs by putting a stick of gelignite, with detonator and fuse attached, inside a tin or a section of bamboo, then filling it up with several pounds of road metal. The fuse was lit by pressing a small igniter in a copper tube, thus obviating the use of matches. One great advantage of making our own bombs was that we could vary the length of the fuses, so that the explosions would continue for some time after we had left the scene and would discourage the Japs from answering our fire till we were well back in the rubber or jungle. We continued to stop the leading vehicle with a bomb operated with a pull-switch, then emptied our tommy-guns in a few short bursts, threw several grenades, changed the magazines of the guns while waiting for the bombs to explode, fired another magazine, then threw as many home-made bombs as we had had time to make, and ran back along prearranged routes to an R.V. at my signal. All through the action, we shouted and yodelled at the tops of our voices not only to encourage ourselves, but to make the enemy think we were a considerable force.

Sometimes the vehicles contained stores only and then there was little opposition, but more than once we attacked convoys of troops, and this always started a scrap which lasted until we were far out of range. After we had carried out three full-scale ambushes along this section of road, in a different place each time, and one more to the south, the Japs defeated us by the simple expedient of not using the road at all at night.

Our second ambush on the road to the south was very nearly disastrous. As the country there was fairly level, there were no real cuttings, and Sartin's first grenade bounced back off the canvas cover of a lorry and exploded within a few feet of where he lay behind a low bank, stunning him and covering him with earth. When we retired, he failed to appear at my usual rallying cry and we had already given him up for dead when he joined us, having had to wait until the Japs ceased fire before crawling back. He reported that on this occasion the Japs were firing into the rubber on both sides of the road. He also saw at least thirty casualties.

After we had been operating for about a fortnight we came to the conclusion that we should have to move. Now that we had been forced to operate so near home that our battles were plainly audible from Leu Kim's *kongsi*-house, the old man was getting more and more embarrassed by our presence. He said that his wives gave him no peace and insisted that we should go, and that he was afraid some of the coolies would soon betray us. Wholesale massacres had been carried out in several *kampongs* south of Tanjong Malim, and Jap patrols had already come halfway up the Sungei Salak side road, and Leu Kim was afraid that somebody had given some information against him. He could not sleep at night for fear of what would happen to him and his people if the Japs found out anything further.

By now we were completely and absolutely exhausted and our muscles and nerves could stand no more. On each raid, carrying loads of 40 or 50 lb., we had covered an average of ten or twelve miles and been away from our base for as many hours. Already we were very short of explosive and fuse, and had run out of some vital demolition devices and would have to visit our dump at Sungei Sempan to obtain any more. The Japs seemed to have stopped using the road and railway at night altogether, so there was not much we could do here until we had given the area a good rest and allowed the Japs to regain confidence. We decided to leave the area on the night of February 15, the very day that Singapore fell.

One of our greatest difficulties was to obtain accurate information and to find out the results of our work. Leu Kim told us the Japs had now posted sentries on all bridges and were patrolling the road and railway all night. He also informed us that about 2,000 men had been held at Tanjong Malim and Kuala Kubu especially to hunt us down. It was impossible to estimate the amount of damage we had done.

As far as we could judge from what we saw ourselves and from what Leu Kim and other Chinese told us, and from what I learned after the war was over, we actually derailed seven or eight trains, severely damaged at least fifteen bridges, cut the railway line in about sixty places, damaged or destroyed some forty motor vehicles, and killed or wounded somewhere between five and fifteen hundred Japs. Altogether we had used a thousand pounds of explosive and over a hundred grenades or home-made bombs. The results of this fortnight's work more than justified our original appreciation of the possibilities of Asiatic stay-behind parties led by Europeans.

If only we had been vouchsafed a small measure of support by Malaya Command and had been allowed to start preparations even a few weeks earlier, there would have been a large number of British officers, backed by hundreds of trained Chinese, Malays, and Indians, operating under ideal circumstances; and it is reasonable to argue from the achievements described in this chapter that had such a force been in operation from the very time the enemy set foot in Malaya, the advance of the Japanese would have been delayed sufficiently to allow the 18th Division – which landed at Singapore just in time to be interned – and the 9th Australian Division – which only reached Java on its way to Malaya – to go into action. What effect this would have had on the campaign it is impossible – and perhaps fruitless – to assess.

CHAPTER FIVE

A Chapter of Perilous Journeys

(Use Map No. 1)

When Harvey, Sartin, and I had first reached Sungei Salak, I had asked Leu Kim if there were any Chinese guerillas in the neighbourhood and, if so, whether it would be possible for him to put us in touch with them. Accordingly, about January 8, two very smartly dressed youths arrived on bicycles and were brought up to our hideout. They told us that in Perak the guerillas had not yet been organised into jungle camps, but were very strong further north at Slim, where they had collected a great number of weapons abandoned by our forces after the Slim river debacle.

It was agreed that as we all had the same ultimate object – to drive the Japs out of Malaya – we could help each other in many ways. In the first place, we should like their help in transporting stores and explosives from our depot at Sungei Sempan to this side of the mountains. If the worst happened and Singapore fell, it might be necessary for some of us to get out by sea to India. If they helped us to reach the coast we could repay them by handing over whatever remained of our weapons and stores. The Chinese said they could make no definite plans for cooperation without consulting their leader, but they would certainly help us to move our stores. They arranged that twelve Chinese cyclists would be at our hideout not later than 3 p.m. on February 15. We expected to take three nights to walk the sixty miles to Sungei Sempan, but as they wanted to visit Kuala Lumpur *en route* we should all reach Sungei Sempan about the same time.

We waited until dusk on February 15, but as there was still no sign of the Chinese, I decided we ought to leave. It was not fair to Leu Kim to delay our departure for another day, and if we waited any longer we should pass the Japanese Garrison at Kuala Kubu too near dawn to be safe. Our journey was an eventful one, for we had to pass through ten miles of the country that we ourselves had stirred up. We each carried a tommy-gun and a pack of about 20 lb., in addition to 30 lb. of P.E. with which we intended to bid a suitable adieu to the area. As we crossed the railway line from Escot Estate to meet the road near the 50th Mile, we placed a charge of 15 lb. of explosive a foot below a sleeper in the centre of the track and connected it to a pressure-switch beneath each rail. We were crossing the road bridge over the railway half a mile further on, when to our great delight we heard a train approaching from the south.

As the train passed beneath us, I overcame with difficulty the temptation to try to drop a grenade down the funnel – a thing I always wanted to do – and presently there was the usual blinding flash and reverberating explosion, followed by the whizzing of pieces of metal through the air and the dull thuds as they crashed into the rubber. From the parapet of the bridge we had a magnificent grandstand view of the demolition, but were disappointed to see that the train was merely derailed, and not overturned – but it was only a goods train, and probably empty at that.

Half an hour later we saw headlights approaching from the south and went to ground in some rubber beside the road. Seven open lorries rushed past at a furious speed, filled with Japs in tin hats with their weapons ready. Presumably Tanjong Malim, thinking that they had not enough troops to deal with us, had rung through to the garrison at Kuala Kubu for reinforcements.

Passing through Kerling was hazardous, as we had to walk down a street between two rows of shops and houses. But there was no moon and the town was absolutely still and dark, though we were rather afraid of some lightning which had been flickering intermittently over the mountains to the east. The only sign of life was a glowing point of light on the other side of the street where somebody was standing still smoking a cigarette. As we tiptoed stealthily along the pavement we could hear the heavy breathing and snoring of sleepers in the open verandas above the street.

Some time after this we were suddenly aware of the lights of motorcars behind us and, thinking that it might be the Jap patrol returning to Kuala Kubu, we dashed into some seedling rubber on the right of the road – only to be inextricably entangled in a barbed-wire fence. I just had time to say, 'For God's sake, keep still: don't move a muscle!' when we were floodlit by the headlights of the trucks. We were caught in the strangest attitudes, spread-eagled several feet above the ground impaled on the wire. Indeed, a prong entered my forehead and made a scar which I carry to this day. We must have been unusually conspicuous with our tommy-guns and square army packs, though our faces were darkened and our clothes camouflaged – yet the trucks never stopped.

We had saved our last 15 lb. of P.E. to attack a magnificent target that the Chinese guerillas had told us about. This was a temporary wooden bridge which carried the railway line over a road cutting. It had been built by the Japs to replace a stone bridge destroyed by our retreating army. Leu Kim and the guerillas had told us that many of the bridges were now guarded at night, so we were approaching very circumspectly, feeling uncomfortably trapped in the deep cutting, when a sudden flash of lightning revealed two sentries at the side of the road leaning against the wooden piles of the bridge. Fortunately they had not seen us. We had to be content with placing the charge, with our longest delay, in a culvert beneath the road a mile further on.

As if we had not had enough frights for one night, we were to have another terrifying experience before we reached Kuala Kubu. We came to a stretch of the road where there were several steep cuttings. After our earlier experience we fully realised the danger of getting caught in these by the headlights of a car, and arranged that if any appeared we should lie flat in the gutter. Since our packs would be very conspicuous on our backs, we carried them in our hands, having previously camouflaged them with a few sprays of greenery, so that if a car appeared we could put the packs on the ground and lie down behind them. It was fortunate that we had taken these precautions, for just when we were in the middle of the longest cutting, of which we could hardly see the end, the glow of headlights appeared behind us and a large convoy went south. We carried out our plan and it worked perfectly, but it was very frightening to lie in the road while lorry after lorry rumbled past within a few feet of us, lighting up the whole cutting like a stage.

After twelve miles along the road we reached the turning to Kuala Kubu. From a considerable distance we smelled the pungent fragrance of Japanese tobacco, then saw the glow of a cigarette and realised there must be a sentry on duty as we had expected. There was a small triangle of grass at the crossroads, and the Japs had put up a sentry box facing the main road. We tiptoed past, keeping well in to the left of the road, and as the sentry was inside the box we were soon out of sight.

Kuala Kubu we reached at four o'clock in the morning. Here all the bungalows on the left of the road were lit up, and through the windows we could see uniformed figures striding about. There was a good deal of shouting and singing – probably in celebration of the fall of Singapore, though we did not hear about it until two days later – and we had some trouble with drunken soldiers staggering about the road. But we managed to get through without being seen.

A short distance beyond the town, near the 45th Mile, we found a woodcutter's track leading steeply uphill into the jungle on the right of the road. Here, beside a stream, we found a very pleasant place to spread out our groundsheets and go to sleep. In lieu of a sentry, we fixed up a booby trap consisting of a creeper as a trip-wire attached to a pull-switch and a short length of instantaneous fuse.

We slept all next day without being disturbed, and as soon as it was dark set off for the Gap, a distance of over seventeen miles, involving a climb of 2,500 feet. After we had passed the villages of Peretak and Sangka Dua, we had the road to ourselves, save for occasional Tamil bullock-carts. Once we tried to steal a lift on one of these, and had managed to climb on without the driver being aware of it. Suddenly, however, he caught sight of his three passengers and, with a piercing scream, ran wildly up the road. I had always imagined that any fool could drive a pair of bullocks, but this is certainly not so. The united efforts of all three of us had no effect whatsoever and we could not make the stubborn animals move an inch.

As we climbed the long winding hill, we grew more and more tired and our packs seemed filled with lead. Whenever we stopped to rest, we could not keep awake, and when we passed a road-worker's *atap* shed beside the road we went inside and slept for a few hours. Because of this delay, it was almost dawn when we reached the Gap. Here there were a few small bungalows perched in the jungle above the road, as well as Shebbeare's house, and the two large two-storied stone rest-houses. As the whole place seemed deserted, we entered all the buildings and had a good look round. Shebbeare's bungalow had been looted and looked very squalid, but I found several copies of the *Himalayan Journal* and one of his Everest diaries, which I rescued, as I thought he might want it some day.

We had intended to sleep in the jungle, but as dawn broke, the cold mountain mist turned into rain and we decided to stay in the rest-house, which would be the last place the Japs would expect to find us. Here only the smaller furniture had been looted, and in the best bedroom there were some excellent spring bedsteads. As the windows directly overlooked the road, there was no chance of our being surprised, but to make things quite safe we barricaded the door and prepared a getaway over a wardrobe to a trap-door in the roof. It was beyond our dreams of luxury to lie on real beds again, and we slept soundly most of the day. A good many Japanese cars and lorries passed immediately below our window – so close that we could easily have dropped grenades into them – but none stopped. In the afternoon we searched the garden, which was safe from observation, being built up above the road, and here we found some kidney beans and English potatoes, which we cooked in the rest-house kitchen. As we were on the move, we felt it was safe to go and talk to a Chinese who lived down the road; and he sold us a couple of fowls, which we cooked and ate also. The Chinese said that the Japs had broadcast that Singapore had fallen two days before, but we refused to believe it.

At nightfall we set off again, but it seemed very laborious and stupid to have to walk over twenty miles downhill to Sungei Sempan, so we determined to visit Tamil coolie lines a few miles down the road and buy some bicycles. Shortly before dawn we reached Sungei Sempan without meeting a soul on the road. We concluded that bicycling was the ideal way of getting from place to place and wished that we had realised this earlier. Our first shock was to find that the power-station, which had been derelict before, was now running and ablaze with light. The second was to see a large Japanese flag nailed on to the wall of Alves' house, which shook us so much that we hid our bicycles in the jungle and went straight up the pipeline to our hideout, instead of calling in for breakfast with Alves as we had intended.

Next morning, having watched the bungalow long enough to make sure that there were no Japs in possession, we paid a call on Alves, only to find that he had entirely changed. He still wanted to help us, but the Japs had already visited him and frightened him to such an extent that he had completely lost his morale. He said the valley was now full of Chinese and Malay informers, and Jap officials might arrive on a visit of inspection at any moment. His Malay coolies had all fled and were shortly to be replaced by Tamils. As Alves' wireless was still working, we heard that Singapore had indeed capitulated on February 15, and we listened to a Japanese broadcast in English from Singapore itself.

We were relieved to find that our camp had not been touched, and were so delighted to get back that we were very nearly blown up by our own booby traps – Sartin remembered them just in time. After a meal of porridge with milk and sugar, which we had been looking forward to more than anything else, we rolled ourselves up in our blankets, deciding not to think about the future until we had had a really good sleep.

Next day, after discussing the matter in all its aspects – none of which was particularly cheerful – we decided that since the whole of Malaya had fallen, it was obviously no good continuing to stick pins into the Japs. Not only would this bring down their wrath on our heads, but it would mean that anybody who helped us would have to risk torture and death. Our first object must now be to get out of the country and, in the light of our experience, start training a select force to return with us when the time should be ripe to carry out the same work on a much larger scale. Our second object would be to hand over all our spare stores and weapons to the Chinese guerillas and, if time allowed, teach them how to use them. We should then go back to Tanjong Malim and get in touch with the guerillas. Harvey would go over to Trong and see if the boat that he and Vanrenan had already earmarked was still available. Then, making use of the northeast monsoon, which normally blows until the middle of April, the whole party would set sail for India, possibly accompanied by a few Chinese who were willing and suitable to be trained as officers. But before we started putting this plan into action we must have a full week's rest.

Our week's rest here was one of the most pleasant holidays I have ever had. Certainly I have seldom needed one more. The first thing to be done was to make the camp secure. The way to our hideout already led half a mile up the course of the river, along two fallen trees, up a side stream, and finally through a bamboo thicket – which retains no footprints. We fixed up trip-wires with jangling tins and lengths of instantaneous fuse which would make a loud bang but would do no harm to anybody. All noisy operations such as chopping wood and listening to our wireless were restricted to the hours of darkness, and we soon accustomed ourselves to speaking softly at all times.

To make our camp more comfortable, we levelled a platform outside the tent and built a table and three armchairs out of packing-cases. We made a roof with bamboo split in half and placed alternate ways up to make a rain-proof covering. In the small patch of garden at the top of the pipeline we had found beds of roses and a camellia bush in flower, and we always kept a large bamboo vase of these on our table. In the same garden we also found plenty of tapioca growing – a plant whose tuberous roots were to be my staple diet for the next three years.

One day, about February 22, we were catching fish by dropping small charges of gelignite into the pools. All three of us were splashing about stark naked in the river recovering the half-dazed fish, when we suddenly became aware of two bearded faces in the jungle on the bank. Thinking we were surrounded by Japs, we dashed for our pistols, but before we had time to take any action, the intruders introduced themselves as Pat Garden and Clark Haywood from the camp at Sungei Gow.[1]

All was well there, they said, though some of their stores had been stolen before they could move them into the jungle. They had been so busy laying dumps, cutting paths, and making other preparations that they had not had time to start operations before they heard the melancholy news of the fall of Singapore. They had then gone on quarter rations and were proposing to hibernate in the jungle until the British returned to Malaya.

---

[1] The Sungei Gow camp had been established a few miles northwest of Karak by a stay-behind party which had left Kuala Lumpur on January 4, 1942.

Garden had cut his hand very deeply with his *parang* and could not travel for a few days. In any case they both needed a rest, as they had walked over thirty miles along the road, quite apart from a stretch of jungle going at each end of the journey. Both the newcomers readily fell in with my plan, especially Haywood, who had formerly been in the R.N.V.R. and was a keen yachtsman. They thought that if I myself put the project to the rest of their party, they would all wish to throw in their lot with us. They readily agreed to return by bicycle to Sungei Gow, and about February 26 the three of us set off, leaving Harvey and Sartin to start burying the stores we should have to leave behind.

Now that we had decided to avoid further operations against the Japs, we gave up disguising ourselves as low-caste Indians and wore uniform, including badges of rank, and carried identity cards. The idea was that if we were caught we should pretend to be officers accidentally left behind and now trying to get out of the country. In this way we hoped to be treated as prisoners of war and not shot out of hand as spies. We invented and memorised a careful cover story, and Harvey, pretending to be a Jap, cross-questioned each of us in a most realistic way to find out any weak points in our stories.

We got through to Sungei Gow in a single night with no difficulty. It was most exhilarating free-wheeling in the darkness down the steep pass between Tranum and Bentong, where the road falls 500 feet in a few miles. Bicycling through half a mile of the streets of Bentong was quite exciting, but we passed through at two o'clock in the morning, when the town was deserted, though the hospital, police station, and rest-house were all brilliantly lit up. There was a sentry post at Kampong Ketari, where the Genting Sempak road from Kuala Lumpur comes in, but no one interfered as we free-wheeled silently past. There were a number of other cyclists on the road, mostly Chinese – we hoped. Many of them were dressed very smartly and carried suitcases on their carriers. At this time the Japs had imposed a curfew, forbidding the use of roads at night, so that when two parties of cyclists met, each looked straight ahead and pretended not to see the other.

Three miles short of Karak we turned to the right off the main road and followed a timber track for three miles steeply uphill to reach their camp, 2,000 feet above sea level, by the headwaters of the Sungei Gow. Garden's party had made friends with a Chinese timber *towkay* (merchant) and they had taken on one of his woodmen who lived with his wife a few miles down the valley. He had looked after the party and built the attractive *atap* hut in which they lived. It had a sleeping-bench of *atap* stalks and above it a loft of the same material, on which two of the five slept. The climate up here was the most pleasant, and at night we needed two or three blankets.

Garden and Haywood I had known at Kuala Lumpur, but the other three I now met for the first time. Chrystal and Robinson were rubber-planters from north Perak; both were married, had fought in the last war, and were the wrong side of forty-five. Chrystal also suffered from duodenal ulcers. It was, therefore, all the more courageous of them to have volunteered for work of this nature. Frank Quayle, the remaining member of the party, was a New Zealander who, after spending much of his life at sea as an engineer, had worked for the last few years on a tin mine in Siam, where he had been recruited to carry out a 'scorched-earth' job. From there he had gone to 101 S.T.S. and had become an instructor in demolitions.

I explained my plan to these three, and they at once volunteered to join our party. An immediate advantage of this decision was that they need no longer stay on quarter rations. Indeed, we could eat as much as we wanted, for most of the supplies were to be left with the *towkay* on condition that he would look after any of us who might come back. Before we returned to Sungei Sempan five more bicycles were needed, as the party going to the coast would now be eight. The *towkay* agreed to buy them for us, but he took so long about it that it was not until the beginning of March that we were able to return to Tras.

This journey was most unpleasant, as our bicycles were extremely rickety, and they were heavily loaded with stores that we needed for the journey to the coast. In addition, we had to wheel two extra machines. This was simple as long as we could ride, but extremely difficult on the five-hundred-foot climb between Bentong and Tranum.

On this journey we were often scattered over five or six miles of road, which proved to me that it was quite impossible without a great deal of practice for even six cyclists to keep in touch on a dark night. A small compact party can cycle silently and swiftly past a danger spot and will be out of harm's way before any action can be taken – unless there is a barrier – but if the bicycles straggle over a distance, those in front stir up trouble which is visited on the ones behind. A case in point was the fearful rumbling noise produced as we passed one after another over the planks of the improvised bridges put up by the Japs. The bicycles constantly broke down, and some miles before Tranum we were delayed by two punctures. Garden and Haywood volunteered to retire into the jungle to mend them and to join us the following night, so the rest of us pushed on to reach our camp very shortly before dawn.

We now busied ourselves in making preparations for the bicycle trip to the coast and the subsequent voyage to India. For the two journeys I allowed six weeks' rations on full scale, though these would last for very much longer with the additional food we expected to get from the guerillas while staying in their camps, and the bulk stores of rice and salt fish we hoped to pick up at Trong. The day's ration per man weighed 2 lb., including tins and packing, and was made up of biscuit, butter, bully, sardines or herring, raisins, and sugar. With arms and ammunition, spare clothes, groundsheets, medical and cooking gear, maps, books, and tobacco, our loads came to about 100 lb. per man This was slung on either side of the back wheel in two army packs, while each of us carried a 'getaway' emergency haversack of essentials loosely tied to the handlebars. All eight bicycles were in appalling condition, and before they were fit for the journey, Haywood and Quayle, the two engineers, had to spend three days patching them up in a shed behind Alves' house.

Before we left camp we concealed our remaining stores, in all about 2 tons, so that they would be there in reserve in case we had to return or if we wanted to hand them over to the guerillas. We buried them most carefully in the holes torn by uprooted trees, wrapping the wooden cases in tarpaulins and standing them on bamboo platforms which were carefully drained. In one we put arms, ammunition, and explosives, in another, cases of food, and in a third, clothes, books, and odds and ends. I left our wireless set in Alves' care and showed him where the dump was, saying that if neither we nor the Chinese guerillas appeared to claim them within six months, he could consider them his own. The old man was in a state of extreme depression these days and, though he obviously longed to help us more, he had to think first of his wife and children. Before we left Sungei Sempan the original three of us went to say goodbye to him, and both he and his wife wept to see us go.

As a patrol of eight cyclists would be too unwieldy, especially on the hairpin bends of the Gap road, I divided the party into two, with one engineer in each to keep the bicycles in running order. Haywood and I left with the 'old men' – Chrystal and Robinson – on March 8, leaving Harvey, Garden, Quayle, and Sartin to finish sealing up the stores and to follow two nights later.

The journey that followed was altogether disastrous. We hoped that the district would have calmed down in the three weeks that had elapsed since we had last used the road, but by now the Japs had had time to tighten their grip on the country, and the newly formed Chinese guerilla patrol at Kerling had stirred the Japs up afresh. The first stage of the journey, which we hoped to complete in two nights' travel, was to our old hideout at Sungei Salak. This involved only sixty miles of road work, but in the fifteen miles from Tranum to the Gap we had to push our heavily laden bicycles up more than 2,000 feet of ascent.

As there was no moon until after midnight, it was impossible to ride along the five miles of narrow, torturous, stony Sungei Sempan lane. Because we had not yet become used to wheeling such back-heavy bicycles, we had many crashes. We also ran into a party of Malays, who flashed a torch in our faces and then fled into the rubber. Then, on the mile and a half of road between Tras and Tranum, some headlights appeared, and in taking cover on the right of the road – there was a bank on the left – two of the bicycles went down a thirty-foot slope into the river and had to be unloaded before we could get them back on the road. By the time we had pushed our loads up a few miles of the Gap Hill we were already exhausted, and as the 'old men' had fallen behind, Haywood and I sat on the side of the road to wait for them.

As it was a pitch-dark night, I spread a towel in the middle of the road, as arranged, in case they could not see us. Unfortunately Haywood and I fell asleep and the others went through without seeing the towel. We wasted some time waiting and going back down the road before we realised what had happened and then hurried after them, but dawn was already breaking, and we had to search rapidly for a place near water where we could hide the bicycles and ourselves. This took some time, and we were nearly seen by some Tamil coolies going to work. Next night we waited at the emergency R.V. – the wooden seat at Walsh's Corner – and soon heard somebody whistling 'The Lambeth Walk,' which was our signature tune. We joined forces once more, having discovered that the two pairs had camped within a hundred yards of each other without knowing it.

That night we passed the rest-house at the Gap and knew that the worst part of the journey was over. Nobody else seemed to be on the road at night and, except for the terribly exhausting work of pushing our loads up the hill, all had gone well. It was a great disappointment to find that it was too dark to be able to free-wheel safely downhill, as there were innumerable S-bends and most of the way there was a deep embankment on the right of the road. We only reached the 50th Mile (eleven miles short of Kuala Kubu) before dawn broke, and once again we were almost seen by Tamil coolies and some Chinese cyclists before we could find a suitable place to lie up for the day.

Next night we were able to ride, and I was waiting for the others, still astride my bicycle with one foot on the ground, when my back wheel suddenly subsided with the weight of the heavy load. As I was the only one who knew the road and our destination, I changed bicycles, and left Chrystal and Robinson in the jungle to await the next party. Haywood and I then pushed on, having promised to send a Chinese back with a spare wheel from Tanjong Malim. A mile or two further on, the front forks of my new machine broke and I fell heavily on to my shoulder in the road. Haywood with remarkable skill managed to repair the damage, but as it was obviously impossible for the bicycle to continue with such a load, I dumped my two packs under a small bridge by our old camp at the 45th Mile, planning that the Chinese who brought the spare wheel to the other two would be able to collect my load on his return journey. After this the machine went quite well, though somewhat noisily.

When we reached the top of the little hill in Kuala Kubu at half-past three in the morning, we saw that there was a dazzling arc-light fixed high above the centre of the road and tilted so as to shine straight up the slope towards us. We watched for some time with my field-glasses, but could see no sign of any movement, though there might have been a sentry immediately beyond the light where there was absolute darkness. There was a road further south, which bypassed the town, but we were already half a mile past the turning and I knew from previous experience that this road was barricaded. We discussed the matter and eventually agreed that as the road ran downhill from us to the light, we should get up speed and dash past it before the sentry – if there were one – could do anything to stop us. The only danger was that there might be a barrier in the dense shadow beyond the light.

As we flashed past, I had a glimpse of several men sitting, apparently asleep, on the running-board of a truck drawn up on the left of the road, and as we passed beneath the light there was a clatter of arms and a loud startled voice shouted, '*Hudu*' – whatever that may mean. There was no barricade, and we were safely past and rushing through the black night, only hoping that the road ran straight on.

We were afraid that there might be a telephone line to the sentry box which we knew to be at the corner two miles ahead, and hurried on to pass it before the sentry that we had just woken up had time to telephone. The road ran downhill all the way, and somehow we were on to the crossroads much sooner than we expected. Instead of being able to dismount and wheel our bicycles quietly past in the edge of the road, as we had intended, we were still pedalling furiously and our decrepit machines were groaning and creaking This was enough to warn the sentry. He flashed a light on to us, then shot three times as we sped down the road, all the time, for some strange reason, shouting at the top of his voice. Haywood's chain broke at this moment, but we were going so fast that we free-wheeled almost as far as the turning down to Kuala Kubu railway station. We went down this road and, following an inspiration of Haywood's, cut a length from one of the telephone wires and wound it in and out so as to short-circuit all the others. Our idea was to prevent Kuala Kubu from warning Tanjong Malim.

If cars came after us in pursuit, we could easily get off the road and hide, but if an ambush were to be prepared in front of us, it would be the end. It was essential that we should push on to Tanjong Malim, or by the next night the whole district would be roused and there would be a reception committee at every corner.

We safely passed through the streets of Kerling, which I had been afraid might prove a deathtrap, and in less than ten miles would be safely past Tanjong Malim. At this stage my front forks finally and irreparably collapsed and we had to dump the machine in the rubber. While we were doing this, two trucks full of troops passed from Kuala Kubu and we realised it would now be unsafe to try to get through that night.

We decided to camp as soon as we could get out of the rubber, which rarely affords a large enough area of good cover to be really safe from encirclement. Haywood rode the remaining bicycle and I ran alongside carrying my tommy-gun. In this way we reached the level area of overgrown tin-tailings a mile short of Kalumpang and, fearing that the men who had already passed us in the trucks might be waiting for us, we lay up for the day, not daring to light a fire and taking it in turns to keep watch.

Since we had only a few miles to go, I decided to leave as late as possible the next night. We had stopped riding the bicycle and only used it as a beast of burden. There was nobody astir in the mile-long village of Kalumpang, but the night was alive with alarming sounds. Once, as we tiptoed past in the soft dust at the edge of the road, there was a loud cough just beside us. Another time somebody ahead lit a cigarette and we lay in the rubber and watched a party of six men pass by. They carried arms, but we could make out nothing more. Twice in the darkness, as we passed the end of a side road, we heard a metallic clatter as if a sentry were leaping to his feet, but nothing further happened. It was out of the question to pass through Tanjong Malim, but I was in my own country here and knew every little track. We hid the bicycle and, dividing its heavy load, followed our old route through Escot Estate to reach the hideout at Sungei Salak just before dawn.

The next week was one of the most depressing times I have ever known. Our first shock was to find that Leu Kim's *kongsi*-house had been burned down and there was no sign of the old man or any of his coolies. At last we met a Chinese whom we knew, who told us that Lee Fee had informed against Leu Kim. But the Japs, beyond insisting that the latter's whole family should return to the town, had taken no action against him. The whole area was full of informers, and the Japs had been making every effort to round up anybody who could give any information about the recent operations against the road and railway. Almost every day they or their agents visited the valley. The Japanese were in the habit of collecting all the people of a suspected *kampong* into one *kongsi*-house. They would then give them lectures and afterwards, in their capricious way, either tommy-gun or bayonet them, or let them go free. Once further north, they had driven over a hundred Chinese including old men, women, and children, into an *atap* shed and had then burned them to death.

Our only consolation was that this Chinese told us the guerillas were now much stronger and better organised. He was in touch with them, and only a few days before they had asked him if he knew where we had hidden our surplus stores, which they were very anxious to acquire. I then wrote a letter to the leader of the Perak guerillas, explaining that I had formerly commanded 101 S.T.S. where their original parties had been trained. I asked that one of their English-speaking leaders should come at once to confer with me, as I needed their assistance urgently and at the same time thought I should be able to help them.

Our Chinese friend then took us to a hut in the jungle where he and about twenty others were living, and after a good meal led us to a small hideout some distance further into the jungle. It was absolutely typical of the Chinese that, though we were entirely responsible for bringing this trouble upon them, not one of them showed the least resentment and they continued to help us in every possible way.

Harvey and I had arranged a 'letter-box' underneath a log table in a deserted *atap* hut in the jungle which we had formerly used as a halting-place on our way to and from the road. Each night I visited this place, but my letter to Harvey had not been collected and there was still no news. We were terribly afraid that his party had run into trouble, and I blamed myself for not having stopped to warn them. We waited miserably in our hut, being brought meals by the Chinese, until at last, after three days, two guerillas appeared.

These men told me that they had come from the camp of the Anti-Japanese Forces at Slim, which was their Perak headquarters and that in a few days their leader would arrive to confer with me. Meanwhile, they had been instructed to help us in any way they could. I immediately sent them by bicycle with a letter to Chrystal and Robinson, telling them that they should stay where they were and that as soon as possible I would send a party of guerillas to take them to the camp at Slim, where they would find us. The two Chinese also agreed to find out anything they could about the fate of Harvey's party. I then spent some time trying to teach them how to whistle 'The Lambeth Walk,' so that they should more readily find Chrystal and Robinson. Next day the messengers returned with a letter from Chrystal saying that they were well, though they had been seen by some Malays; that Quayle had joined them, as his bicycle had broken down, but that they had had no news of Harvey, Garden, and Sartin after they had gone by on their way towards Kuala Kubu. The two guerillas also reported that three Europeans and some Chinese had been seen in the back of a Japanese lorry being taken back to Kuala Kubu.

The same night the three alleged leaders of the Perak guerillas reached our camp. These were Lee Far, a very intelligent English-speaking Chinese, Chen Ping (alias Wong Ping, or C.T.P.), a young and attractive Hokkien who was later to become Britain's most trusted guerilla representative, and Itu, then and until the end of the war, the military head of the Perak guerillas. We held a most cordial four-hour conference squatting in the clearing in front of the Chinese hut. Twice we were interrupted by lights seen approaching, but it was only some belated Chinese.

It appeared that the guerillas at Ulu Slim had been in camp for several weeks. They had collected a considerable supply of weapons, ammunition, and explosive left by the retreating British forces, but they had little idea how to use them. It was therefore agreed that Haywood and I should at once return to Ulu Slim with them; that they should send next day to bring Chrystal's party and stores to Ulu Slim, and, because it was now too late for us to take advantage of that year's northeast monsoon, we should stay at their headquarters and concentrate on training the guerillas. As soon as we had done this we should hand over to them all the stores we had left in Malaya and they would try to help us to sail across to Sumatra, where they would put us in touch with the Chinese Communists, who would help us to get a boat to sail to Australia or India, depending upon the time of the year. They also promised to deliver a letter from me to the Secretary-General of the M.C.P. inviting him to come up to the Slim camp to confer with me.

Next night, accompanied only by Lee Far, we set off for Ulu Slim, and for the next five days we travelled due north on the edge of the jungle. From our camp to theirs the distance was only twenty miles in a straight line, though we must have walked four or five times that distance. Lee Far, who travelled in the jungle in a spotless white shirt, lavender-coloured trousers, thin leather shoes, and a white topee, did not know the way, but at each stage he collected one or more local men who acted as guides and carried his spare clothes.

The route led us due north, contouring round the steep extremities of no less than ten parallel spurs running westwards from the Main Range, and across the valleys of the intermediate rivers. On the spurs we usually climbed to a height of a thousand feet, and through windows in the steep jungle wall caught occasional exciting glimpses of the Slim road bordered by rubber estates, at first only two miles further west. The track led us continually in and out of the mountain to cross steep little torrents, and by the end of the journey we were sick to death of walking on the same traverse. Ten rivers had also to be crossed, and as they were still in the mountainous part of their courses, they were foaming torrents ten yards wide, rushing headlong between boulders and slabs of granite. We had to choose our crossing place very carefully and help each other from rock to rock, for in places a slip might have been fatal, especially when the current was even swifter than usual after a rainstorm in the hills.

For the first part of the journey we followed the boundary of the Behrang Forest Reserve, where a wide track had been cut some years before and kept more or less open ever since. All the way up the edge of the hills we continually crossed the deep tracks where water buffaloes had been used to drag out the heavy tree-trunks.

We usually camped in a deserted woodcutter's hut beside one of these, so that in the evening one of the Chinese could go outside to buy rice and vegetables, and sometimes a chicken or some eggs. Twice we spent the night in deserted Sakai villages far into the jungle, where all the houses were made of bamboo and built high up off the ground. Much to my disappointment we did not meet any of the aborigines themselves, as at this time of the year they were up in the hills clearing the jungle to grow tapioca and maize.

At last we emerged from the jungle at the head of a beautiful valley where the river was bordered with meadows of green grass kept short by the water buffaloes, and with trim Chinese vegetable gardens. We did not show ourselves until it was dark, and then walked through some rubber smallholdings to cross the Slim river a mile south of Kampong Ulu Slim. The river here was waist deep and about fifty yards wide, but it was quite easy to wade across. We followed up the river past the village and along more green meadows to a huge derelict tin dredge which looked like a cross between the Ark and a traction engine. After fording the river, we spent the rest of the night in a Chinese house beside the Sungei Beresih. At dawn next morning we followed a timber path for an hour until we reached the headquarters camp of the Perak guerillas or, as they called themselves at this time, No. 5 Independent Anti-Japanese Regiment.

CHAPTER SIX

We Join the Chinese Guerillas

(Use Map No. 1)

When Haywood and I reached the Ulu Slim camp, we found that Chen Ping and Itu had already returned and had prepared a tremendous welcome. They met us at the guard post and conducted us to the roughly levelled parade-ground, which was about the size of a tennis-court. Here was a motley guard of honour consisting of about twenty Chinese, including two girls, armed with service rifles and shotguns. We were saluted with Communist clenched-fist salute, and then followed several speeches of welcome which Lee Far translated and to which we had to reply through the same medium. Few of the men were more than twenty-five years of age; indeed the majority were under twenty, and there was one boy who could not have been more than twelve. They wore no uniform, and while some were dressed like coolies in faded blue trousers, others wore clean white shirts, well-creased grey trousers, and smart felt hats. I discovered later that those who went out to the *kampongs* for food or on other work dressed as smartly as possible, since at that time ragged Chinese were always suspected of being guerilas. The girls wore the severe but attractive black Chinese blouse and trousers, had their hair bobbed, and used no make-up.

After inspecting the men and weapons we went across to the camp quarters, which were built beneath the overhanging sides of an enormous single boulder. Only an *atap* lean-to roof had been added to these natural caverns to provide a kitchen, a lecture-room which would accommodate the sixty or so occupants of the camp, and sleeping-benches for about half this number. The rest of the men lived in an *atap* house fifty yards up the hill above the boulder and parade-ground. This hut consisted simply of a high-peaked roof, of which the *ataps* were still green, and a sleeping-bench of flattened bamboo running round three sides of it about

89

two feet above the ground. From the boulder a small path ran down a steep bank to a fair-sized stream which provided water for the camp. The latrines were built out over the stream some yards further down – a most insanitary system, as there were several houses a few miles below. On the other side of the stream an extraordinarily steep bamboo-clad hillside ran up to the summit of Bukit Kilap (2,150 feet).

The armament of the patrol was a Bren machine-gun, three tommy-guns, twenty rifles, five shotguns, and five pistols, most of them in a shocking state of repair. Some had actually spent several weeks at the bottom of the Slim river. At Itu's request we immediately set about teaching the men how to use these weapons, and in the evenings gave them lectures on demolition, jungle craft, and minor tactics. At this time they knew absolutely nothing – not even how to use the sights of a rifle or to fire a tommy-gun; but it would have been impossible to find men keener to learn. We also started physical-training classes in the early morning and half an hour of games in the evenings.

On April 3, after we had been about a fortnight in this camp, Chrystal, Robinson, and Quayle arrived after a fifteen days' journey from beyond Kuala Kubu. As all three of them were indifferent travellers, they were absolutely worn out. Their story was as follows: For three nights after Haywood and I had left them they had hung about the edge of the road whistling 'The Lambeth Walk' whenever they heard a sound resembling a bicycle passing in the night. At last the other party arrived, using torches (contrary to my orders), and spread over two miles of road. They had started a day late because a Jap patrol had visited Sungei Sempan – probably as a result of my party being seen by a Malay. They took two nights to reach the Gap and had slept in the rest-house. On the way down the hill they had lost another day, as Sartin had ridden over a twenty-foot embankment and had badly shaken himself as well as his bicycle. Quayle's bicycle had also broken down, and when he was greeted by the strains of 'The Lambeth Walk' he was wheeling his machine, having entirely lost touch with the others. He was, therefore, only too glad to stay behind with them.

Three and a half years later, when Garden and Sartin were liberated from a Japanese prisoner-of-war camp, I learned what had befallen them. On reaching Kuala Kubu they had seen the same brilliant light above the road that had halted Haywood and me, and after some discussion they decided to wheel their bicycles past it. Just as they were level with the light a number of Japanese soldiers suddenly closed in on them, and as each waited for the others to start shooting, they put up no resistance and were easily taken prisoner. This lack of initiative was very unlike Harvey, who was in charge of the party, and I can only put it down to extreme exhaustion resulting from the physical strain of pushing their heavily laden bicycles over the Gap. The Japs confiscated their diaries and other papers but, with characteristic stupidity, immediately returned them, so that anything incriminating was destroyed before they were cross-questioned. Next day they were taken by car to Kuala Lumpur, where they were confined in Pudu jail. Later Harvey, together with Vanrenan and Graham, managed to escape but they were caught and were finally executed.

On the night after the arrival of Chrystal's party I was suddenly woken up by a strange and exuberant Chinese who shook me by the hand, pulled down my blanket and examined a large scar I have on the back of my right knee, then shook my hand still more warmly. At first I thought he was mad – and then I remembered that when I had given the welcoming address to the first class of Chinese students we had at 101 S.T.S. I had shown them this scar and said that if any of them were to meet me later on in the jungle they would be able to recognise me. The man was Tan Chen King, the leader and interpreter of the first course of students at the school.

He told me that my letter had been received at guerilla headquarters and that he had been sent up here to get in touch with me. Before the war Tan Chen King had been a workman at the Ford factory at Singapore and a keen M.C.P. member. He was about twenty-two years of age, extremely well built and athletic, and was a man of much greater intelligence and wider vision than the average guerilla official I was to come to know only too well in the years that followed. At that time he was directly in touch with, if not an actual member of, guerilla headquarters. He told me that the Secretary General and other high officials of the M.C.P. had narrowly escaped from Singapore by boat and had set up their headquarters in Johore.

He said that the Secretary General already knew that I was still in Malaya and wanted to meet me, having expressed great satisfaction at the efforts of S.T.S. in training and supplying his men, and that guerilla headquarters would soon be moving to the Kuala Lumpur area, where he, Tan Chen King, would arrange a conference. We agreed that I should be attached to, or at least be permanently in touch with, general headquarters to advise on policy, to help with their intelligence and propaganda departments, and to set up a school for training their leaders. It appeared that Tan Chen King and Ah Piow (who had been second-in-command at the first course at 101 S.T.S.) were the leaders of the Selangor group of guerillas whose headquarters were near Batu Caves, and it was decided that I should go there as soon as possible.

Tan Chen King told me that the guerillas in Selangor and Negri Sembilan had been extremely active and had attacked Japanese police stations and even convoys on the road, and as a result they had had to move their camps very often. They were very short of arms and wanted me to let them have any weapons and supplies that I could spare. He also told me that two Chinese-speaking British officers, whom I recognised from his description as Captains Broome and Davis, who had worked with the Singapore organisation, had reached the Selangor coast from Sumatra at about the time of the fall of Singapore. They had taken a minor guerilla official back with them to Sumatra, arranging that he should return to Malaya and bring a representative from headquarters to meet them at Labohan Bilek on the Sumatra coast in a week's time. Tan Chen King himself had sailed across the Malacca Straits in a junk to keep this R.V., but had found the Japanese in possession and no European there. He had been most disappointed, as he had hoped to make arrangements for arms and supplies to be dropped to the guerillas by parachute. Now he had met me again, he said, he hoped that it might still be possible to put this plan into operation.

The same day – for we had talked from midnight until well after daylight – Tan Chen King returned to Selangor by bicycle. Haywood and I were to follow him by jungle paths as soon as possible, while Chrystal, Robinson, and Quayle stayed at Slim to continue the school for the Perak guerillas. I gave Chrystal complete freedom of action, and I told him that as soon as I had arranged for a boat to take us out of the country I should let him know, and we would then try to arrange an R.V. on the coast, so that Haywood and I could pick his party up on our way across the Straits. The only money that we had in the whole party was $200, and this we divided up before the two of us went south. Before I left this camp I gave Chrystal the two closely written volumes of my diary for the last three months, and he agreed that if he had to leave this camp he would bury them in a waterproof gun-cotton tin at the foot of a certain tree beside the hut where we had lived. This he did when the camp was attacked by the Japs some months later, but some Sakai, with their unerring eye for seeing where the ground had been disturbed, dug them up and gave them to some Malays who handed them over to the Japs.

Perfect liaison with guerilla headquarters seemed assured, and in high hopes Haywood and I left Ulu Slim camp on April 6. Ten Chinese accompanied us as far as Tanjong Malim to carry back the remainder of the stores which we had hidden there and which I had promised to hand over to the Slim patrol. We made a fairly rapid journey south, picking up at each camp fresh guides, who often enlisted local Chinese when they lost their way. This happened very frequently, as Europeans could not be taken through the rubber or even along the edge of the jungle in daylight, so that we had to travel at night or, if by day, use jungle paths with which they were not familiar.

We passed through Kampong Ulu Slim before dawn, and three days of strenuous jungle going brought us to Tanjong Malim. The jungle between here and Kuala Kubu is very precipitous, and we had to go outside and travel at night through Chinese *kampongs* and rubber, sometimes following the roads for short distances. This stage of the journey should have taken only two or three nights, but our guides continually lost us, having no idea of the direction once they were in new country and obstinately refusing to listen to me, though I knew every little track in this area and in any case could have kept them right by compass or the stars. Instead of skirting the coolie lines of Escot Estate they became involved in some bamboo cattle-pens and, losing their heads, started crashing down the poles. As a result we were chased by a large party of Sikhs and Tamils, who presumably thought we were cattle-thieves.

This upset our guides so much that nothing went right, and we spent the rest of the night plunging through flooded rubber land, occasionally being shouted at or pursued by angry Chinese and Malays. It had been raining heavily and all the streams were in flood, so that we had the greatest difficulty in crossing them. Once, where a bridge had been washed away, one of the guides, who unfortunately was carrying our spare clothes and food, waded in to see if he could cross and was incontinently swept out of sight into the night. He was recovered some time later, none the worse for his bath but without our precious bag. By this time dawn was breaking, and as we could no longer reach the Chinese house for which they were making, we had to lie up in a patch of swampy undergrowth, where we were bitterly cold – having lost our dry clothes – and were devoured by a swarm of large and voracious mosquitoes.

Next night we had to take to the jungle to get past Kalumpang, and near the tin dredge we ran into a party of Malay police who chased us. Fortunately they were only armed with sticks and we soon outran them, though it took nearly an hour to collect the party together again. Here we picked up two new guides. Much to our surprise they had a car ready for us and took us a mile or two up a side road into the jungle. We were now in the country of the Kerling guerillas, but they were on the run at this time and we could not use their camps or outside contacts. We had to pass two more miserable days lying up in mosquito-ridden *atap* huts or deserted coolie lines, while our guests went outside to buy food. The one consolation of an otherwise detestable journey was that we had wonderful meals, as at this time almost anything could still be bought in the shops – tinned milk, meat, butter, cheese, sugar, and even white bread and cake.

At last we slipped round Kuala Kubu at midnight and crossed the wide Selangor river by a wooden bridge, passing by the old flooded town beside miles of open water and sandy tin-tailings. Here we took to the rubber again, and eventually followed up the Sungei Kinjai to the Kuala Kubu camp, which we reached soon after daylight about April 20. Here there were some forty men and the usual three or four girls, in charge of Ah Leow – another member of the first party trained at 101 S.T.S. They were all living in a single *atap* hut almost overhanging a stream in a narrow gorge completely shut in by the jungle – a most depressing camp. Apparently they had had to move from a more open site where they had already made a clearing and parade-ground, as Jap aircraft had flown very low over it and they were certain it had been detected. In this camp they were very short of arms, having only one tommy-gun and eleven rifles.

While we were here I insisted on returning by night to Kuala Kubu, where we had been told that Harvey, Garden, and Sartin were still confined. I spent the day lying up in a small patch of jungle overlooking the town and watching with my glasses for any signs of the prisoners. Though I had a most interesting day and watched the Japs drilling and having mortar practice, I saw no sign of any Europeans.

From the Kuala Kubu camp three long, hard days of jungle travel took us right round Rasa and Batang Kali and brought us into the Sungei Liam valley a few miles south of Ulu Yam Bharu. In the long, straight valley all the Chinese *kampong* houses displayed Jap flags, but it was a very good guerilla area, and we travelled openly by day, being welcomed and given wonderful meals by everybody we met. Another day took us over the watershed by the old road trace and down into the Sungei Batu valley. We were told by our Chinese guides that the Japanese had been led this way by the Malays in their advance towards Kuala Lumpur.

When we reached the edge of Sungei Tua Malay Reservation, our guides left us in the edge of the jungle and went in search of the Batu Caves guerillas. After three hours they returned disappointed, saying that the patrol had moved camp and we must return to Ulu Yam. This, however, we refused to do, and sent the guides out again. This time they were successful, and returned about midnight with a party of bicyclists and two extra machines for us. Before setting off we were told to shoot any Malays we should see on the way, but as we had to cycle right through a Malay Reservation, Haywood and I decided it was the close season – which was just as well, for most of the houses were still lit up and we passed several Malays on the road.

After our laborious days of wading through swamps, toiling up and down jungle ridges, and lurking in mosquito-ridden rubber estates, it was a marvellous sensation to be speeding through the night on bicycles, but all too soon we had to leave the road and take to the rubber once more. At last we reached the camp, about two miles northeast of Batu Caves and only a few hundred yards from the edge of the rubber. The airline distance from Ulu Slim camp was just under fifty miles. The journey had taken us exactly a fortnight, although we were both extremely fit and carrying light loads. We had actually travelled for seven and a half nights, often for ten or even twelve hours at a stretch.

The Batu Caves camp consisted of a low *atap* hut about sixty feet long with a sleeping-bench along each side, a cookhouse by the stream, and the headquarters hut about fifty yards from the rest of the camp. There was also the usual parade-ground. Although the jungle had been cleared around the camp, it was so deep in a valley that it would only have been visible from aircraft exactly overhead. The chief danger was that the rubber came within half a mile of the camp on one side, and though a sentry was posted here, the camp was in a singularly vulnerable position.

There were about seventy Chinese, including five girls, in camp. Tan Chen King spent much of his time here, but as he was a member of the Selangor Group headquarters, if not of the general headquarters, he took no part in the actual running of the camp. This patrol was fairly well armed, having two machine-guns, four tommy-guns, seventeen rifles, six pistols, and a considerable amount of explosive and demolition devices which had originally been supplied to the Chinese stay-behind parties by 101 S.T.S. In all, there were four men who had been at the School at Singapore, but so far they had not done much about training the others.

There were also six Europeans, all of whom were suffering from beri-beri and were in a very poor state of physical and mental health. The best was Sergeant Regan, whom I had met before. He was a tin-mining engineer from Siam, trained at 101 S.T.S. as a wireless operator. He had already been with this patrol for several months. There was also a British mortar sergeant whose limbs were terribly swollen with beri-beri. He died two days after we arrived. The other four were privates – two very young Argylls and two gunners. The two former were suffering from V.D. as well as beri-

beri. I knew that beri-beri is caused simply by vitamin-B deficiency, and I managed to procure some groundnuts and rice bran, which soon reduced the swelling, though it needed more than vitamin B to cure their mental attitude, which was slowly but surely killing them.

My experience is that the length of life of the British private soldier accidentally left behind in the Malayan jungle was only a few months, while the average N.C.O., being more intelligent, might last a year or even longer. To them the jungle seemed predominantly hostile, being full of man-eating tigers, deadly fevers, venomous snakes and scorpions, natives with poisoned darts, and a host of half-imagined nameless terrors. They were unable to adapt themselves to a new way of life and a diet of rice and vegetables. In this green hell they expected to be dead within a few weeks – and as a rule they were. The other school of thought, that the jungle teems with wild animals, fowls, and fish which are simply there for the taking, and that luscious tropical fruits – paw-paw, yams, breadfruit and all that – drop from the trees, is equally misleading.

The truth is that the jungle is neutral. It provides any amount of fresh water, and unlimited cover for friend as well as foe – an armed neutrality, if you like, but neutrality nevertheless. It is the attitude of mind that determines whether you go under or survive. 'There is nothing either good or bad, but thinking makes it so.' The jungle itself is neutral.

This camp at Batu Caves was most unhealthy, and both Haywood and I felt ill there. Haywood even developed the first symptom of beri-beri, which is a puffiness round the knees, ankles, and wrists, so that when the flesh is pressed with a fingertip the dint remains. The diet was no worse than usual – wet rice in the morning, dry rice in the evening, and a small amount of vegetables or fish. But the sanitary conditions were revolting, and to this the poor standard of health could be attributed. The latrine, which was only thirty yards from the camp – and upwind at that – consisted of two poles over a pit full of a stinking mass of seething maggots, and was so nauseous that most of the men used the stream immediately below the camp – a stream that was in any case far too small for this purpose. All the refuse from the cookhouse was thrown into open pits just across the stream, and these were overflowing and black with flies.

One of the gunners was suffering from persecution mania and had already tried several times to escape from the camp. He also thought that the others were trying to do him out of his share of tobacco and food and were even plotting to kill him. Tan Chen King, who was very much concerned for the safety of the camp, asked me to shoot him. This I refused to do, though (with Regan's agreement) I gave him permission to do so if, after I had gone, he further endangered the lives of the others. Regan was in good spirits in spite of his swollen legs, but it was obvious that the other four had given up hope and could not last long, although the guerillas did everything they possibly could to help them.

One afternoon, after we had been in this camp for a few days, a rifle shot suddenly rang out from the sentry post at the edge of the rubber. While we were hastily packing up everything, ready to scatter into the jungle, Tan Chen King ran up to the guard post and returned to say that two Malays had been seen prowling about in the rubber obviously looking for the camp. The sentry had shot at them, but missed, and the Malays had run away. It was probable that the camp would be attacked next day, so we set about making preparations for leaving it. It struck me that this was a heaven-sent opportunity to study the Jap methods of attack. So, leaving Haywood to look after the sick men on the march, I spent the rest of the evening preparing a hideout overlooking the camp. Tan Chen King very reluctantly agreed to let one Chinese remain with me to take me on to the new camp site on the following night.

As soon as it was dark we made ourselves as comfortable as we could in the hideout and took it in turns to keep guard. At earliest dawn, about 5.45 a.m., without a sound to warn us of what was coming, two or possibly more mortars opened up from the rubber and plastered the whole area with bombs. After the first few bombs I found myself alone. It was the first time my friend had been under fire, and certainly some of the explosions were alarmingly close to us. Apparently the Japs had nobody spotting, for the later shots were no more accurate than the earlier ones, but they systematically raked the whole area of the camp, and every hut was hit without actually being destroyed. After this there was silence for some time and then machine-gun fire broke out from the hill above the camp and continued for about ten minutes. Of course, there was no target other than the empty huts, and even if the camp had been occupied at the time of the attack, we should all have disappeared into the jungle after the first mortar bomb, and only the heavy baggage would have been lost. After this about a hundred Japanese soldiers and as many Malays and Indians charged down the hill with loud shouts and fixed bayonets. They then stood in a huddle on the parade-ground, gazing round them like a party of tourists, and I only wished I had a machine-gun with me. After shouting and talking excitedly for some time, they set fire to all the huts and retired hurriedly.

I later learned that at about four o'clock that morning the Japs had surrounded the Chinese *kampong* which lay a mile from the camp and had sent the 160 inhabitants – men, women, and children – away in the lorries which had brought the troops. When they had reached a deserted area of tin-tailing ground on the way to Kuala Lumpur, they had made the men dig a trench and had then stood everybody in a row beside it and had tommy-gunned them to death. When the Japs had departed, my Chinese returned and, after waiting for nightfall in his father's house at the edge of the jungle, we made our way westwards across the Sungei Tua side road down which we had bicycled a week before. A few hours' walk through vegetable gardens and rubber estates brought us to a large number of long, low *atap* huts, built by the British as emergency shelters in case Kuala Lumpur should be heavily bombed. The others had spent the day here and gone on as soon as it was dark, leaving a small party to wait for us and show us the way.

We crossed a high ridge and, following a jungle track northwards for a few hours, caught up with the main body. They could be heard from a considerable distance, as the cook insisted on carrying his largest rice-pot with a loose ladle inside, which made a noise like the beating of tom-toms in the night. The march was not going well, as the guides had lost the way and half the party had gone ahead and were out of touch. The Europeans were in a very bad way and one of the gunners had a temperature of 104 degrees and had to be carried. Worst of all, the party had been seen by some Malays when crossing the Sungei Tua road the night before, and were afraid that they were being shadowed. At last we reached a small Chinese *kampong* by the Sungei Udang at the head of a woodcutter's path and were given a huge empty *atap* shed as a resting-place.

As soon as it was light an advance party of about twenty men went ahead to choose a site and start building the camp. I was included in this party, as my height would be useful in making the framework of the huts. Haywood was anxious to stay with the gunner, as he still hoped to save his life. We found a very good camp site in some old tin-mining ground beside the Sungei Kanching about two miles northeast of the 12th Milestone on the Batu Caves-Rawang road. We needed a remote part of the jungle, well away from any paths which might be used by prying Malays, yet not too far from the *kampongs* which would supply us with food. A good defensive position was needed for the guard post, if possible on the only way in to the camp. Water must be at hand, and *atap* suitable for thatching should be found nearby.

This camp took the usual form: a small piece of ground capable of being levelled for a parade-ground; two long huts nearby for the men; a smaller headquarters house a little back from the others, and a cookhouse beside the stream. Five- or six-inch poles of green timber were cut for the framework, and when possible we used standing trees, especially to support the main beam of the roof. Most of the Chinese were expert axemen, and while they were felling and trimming the poles the rest of us went out and collected rattan to bind the joints.

The rattan is a creeper which may be hundreds of feet in length. It coils along the ground and then climbs to the summit of the tallest trees to burst into a palm-like clump of ferny leaves. I have seen rattans more than two inches thick, but the ideal size for this work is one-third to half an inch in diameter. As soon as one of suitable size was found, two or three of us would haul it in, pulling it out of the ground or down from the trees. The jointed green cane of the rattan is protected by a thorny shell, but this easily strips off, and the pliable stem is coiled up like a rope and brought home. Now comes the skilled part of the job. Each rattan must be split with a sharp knife into two, or for finer lashings, strips and then the inner pith cut away and discarded. This is particularly difficult, as the cane has no grain, and unless the cut is kept absolutely true, the knife slips to one side or the other and the rattan is ruined.

While we were building the framework of the huts, the rest of the men and the girls came up and started plaiting *atap* for the roofs. There were great dumps of *atap* palms along the top of a ridge above the camp with drooping fronds twenty or thirty feet long. The fronds were pulled down with a crook and the top eight feet of the pithy stalk cut off, stacked in special racks to prevent the leaves being damaged, and then carried back to the camp in bundles. With all able-bodied men and women on the job, it took us two days to make the camp ready for occupation and another day to complete it. Tan Chen King explained that they were not going to build a lecture-room here, as it was not a very good place for a camp. It was too near the main road, and also the Rawang patrol lived only four miles to the west-northwest and this was really their area. As soon as new food lines could be prepared, they intended to move to the jungle near Kajang to the southeast of Kuala Lumpur.

Before we had all moved into the new camp, the sick gunner died, and we buried him – as we had buried the mortar sergeant – in a grave at the edge of the jungle. I could not procure a Prayer Book in order to read the Burial Service, so we had to be content with saying the Lord's Prayer and Fidele's Dirge from *Cymbeline*, after which the guerillas sang 'The Red Flag.'

Altogether Haywood and I spent about a fortnight with this patrol, and at the leader's request we ran a concentrated course of lectures for the section commanders. As most of them had absolutely no military knowledge, it was very difficult to compress the course into such a short time. I also worked far into the night preparing a number of simple manuals on each of the weapons, and on demolitions and elementary tactics. Tan Chen King intended to translate these in Mandarin, have them duplicated, and then issue them to all the camps in Selangor. Every day I asked Tan Chen King when the Secretary General was coming and when it would be possible to confer with him and other leaders with a view to my being attached to headquarters. I was told it was very difficult for a man of such importance to travel about the country, and it seemed that it might be several weeks before he would reach Selangor.

101

One of the chief drawbacks to life in the Chinese camps was that we could get absolutely no news of the progress of the war. We had heard no authentic news since the fall of Singapore, though there were stories that the Japs had overrun Burma and landed on Ceylon. When I suggested that we should go over to Sungei Sempan and collect the wireless set which I had left with Alves, or to Sungei Gow for the set that Garden's party had left with the timber *towkay* there, Tan Chen King and Ah Piow were delighted with the idea, especially when I told them that they could have the few weapons and considerable supplies of ammunition and explosive that we had cached at each of these places. On the way we intended to visit the dumps that Haywood's party had hidden at the 20th Mile on the Genting Sempak road and at Chagar Mine, and to hand most of that over to them too. Haywood and I were getting very tired of a diet of rice, salt fish, and leaves, and we thought that the sugar, biscuits, and tinned foods that were there would be most welcome and might save the lives of the surviving Europeans, who were still in a very poor state of health. Tan Chen King told me that the Pahang guerillas had just established themselves near Bentong, but as there had been little fighting on that side of the Main Range, they were very short of weapons. They had recently suffered a very severe setback in that their leader had been killed by the Japs. The new leader, one Ah Loy, had come over to visit Selangor head-quarters and was staying in a *kampong* near Batu Caves – he was not allowed in the camp on security grounds. Tan Chen King suggested that Ah Loy should accompany us and, while Ah Piow's men should have the supplies at the 20th Mile, which was only about fifteen miles from Batu Caves, we should let the Pahang group have what we did not want of the three dumps on their side of the Main Range, as it would be very difficult to bring these stores right back over the Genting Sempak. This seemed an excellent plan. We should get away from this rather depressing camp and fill in the time until the Secretary General should arrive. Also our surplus weapons and supplies hidden in various dumps in Pahang and Selangor would be made use of, and we should collect our wireless receiver and be able to find out what was happening in the rest of the world.

CHAPTER SEVEN

Skirmish on the King's Highway

(Use Map No. 1)

The road distance from Batu Caves to the Sungei Gow camp was about fifty miles. After our recent experiences Haywood and I were of the opinion that walking in Japanese-occupied Malaya was a much more healthy pastime than bicycling. But Tan Chen King assured us that, whereas the Kuala Kubu road where our companions had been caught was a main road, here we should only be using minor roads which he and Ah Loy could guarantee had not been used by the Japs at night since the occupation. If we kept at the back of the party, we should not even run the risk of being recognised as Europeans. Accordingly we agreed to go on bicycles. Again recalling our bitter experience, we insisted that the machines should be in really good condition and that a set of tools should be procured for Haywood to take in case of trouble.

We left the Batu Caves camp about May 1, 1942, and after a few hours' walking reached the hut where Ah Loy and the bicycles were waiting for us. Here we had a wonderful meal of fresh dry rice, chicken, pork, and curried brinjols, followed by bananas, pineapple, and coffee. Ah Loy was a genial, rather coarse Cantonese who put great energy into everything he did – especially eating. He spoke a little English and, unlike most of the guerilla leaders, was very informative. During the meal we learned that he was the younger son of a rich pawnbroker at Bentong who, though he kept eleven wives, had refused to educate Ah Loy, who therefore ran away from home and joined the famous 8th Route Army guerilla school at Shensi in North China and became a Communist. Ah Loy was very good company and extremely courageous, but he was too impetuous and quarrelsome to be a good leader.

The journey started very badly, for, in order to avoid using the road round the south of Batu Caves, we had to cycle for several miles through rubber estates along tiny muddy paths which shot suddenly downhill to cross irrigation ditches or spanned them perilously on narrow plank bridges. Haywood and I had not been on bicycles for some months and were not accustomed to this sort of steeplechase going. Consequently we had several bad crashes and both of us were soaked by falling into rivers. At last we reached the road to the southeast of Batu Caves and found infinite pleasure in rushing silently through deserted Malay *kampongs* with tall coconut palms overhanging the road. After a few miles we started to climb rapidly, and, trying to keep pace with the others who were used to cycling, we realised how much we had lost condition living on poor food in the unhealthy Batu Caves camps. The long grind up the Genting Sempak, in which we climbed a thousand feet in the last seven miles of the night's ride, was most exhausting. It was all we could do to keep the others in sight, as they insisted on riding the whole way up the hill.

At last, shortly before dawn, we reached the 20th Mile, but although there was a brilliant moon Haywood could not find the steep narrow track which led through the thick roadside jungle to the derelict charcoal-burner's oven in which the stores had been hidden four months before. Accordingly we spent the rest of the night drinking *samsu* (spirit distilled from rice) in a coffee-house half a mile up the road, which was kept by two very old Chinese who behaved as if it were in no way out of the ordinary to entertain Englishmen at such a time.

Next morning, as soon as it was light, we went down to the dump, but even so only narrowly avoided being seen by some Tamil coolies and Chinese cyclists who were already on the road. We found the charcoal-burner's oven without difficulty. It was flooded with water and it appeared that bears had broken into it, for the four-gallon tins of rice, sugar, and oil had all been smashed and everything was topsy-turvy. However, the explosive, ammunition, grenades, and smaller tins of food were intact, and these were taken back to the camp in broad daylight by a party of ten of Ah Piow's men, who arrived for this purpose at dawn on bicycles with large suitcases on the carriers.

We lay up for the whole of that day in an old clearing high above the road, from which we had a wonderful view of a series of

S-bends above us where the road toiled through magnificent jungle to reach the summit of the Genting Sempak three miles further on. There was little traffic on the road, and I spent my time sleeping in the sun or making notes on the innumerable varieties of birds, most of which were new to me.

As I knew there was a sentry at Kampong Ketari, where the Karak road turns off, I insisted we should not start until midnight so as to pass him at about 2 a.m. We spent the early part of the night very pleasantly, eating rice and curried fish with the two old Chinese in the coffee-shop. From them we heard something of conditions in Malaya now. I listened to frightful accounts of the innumerable cold-blooded massacres of Chinese perpetrated by the Japs, especially in areas where the guerillas were known to be active, and I was astonished – though it was so universal that I ceased to wonder at it later – that these old men showed absolutely no reluctance to help us, although it would have been certain death for them had they been caught. The Chinese throughout Malaya, especially in the country districts, were filled with a most bitter hatred of the Japanese and yet felt themselves completely impotent to do anything about it – except to support the guerillas, which they were prepared to do to the limit.

This night's journey was a lamentable example of the fundamental incompetence of the Chinese guerillas – even the leaders of the Selangor and Pahang Groups – when it came to getting a job done. Before we set off they absolutely refused to make any sort of plan, Ah Loy saying that it was unnecessary and that he would just shoot up anybody who should dare to try to stop us. It was a brilliant moonlit night and there were a good many Chinese cyclists on the road and, even at this hour of the night, some Tamil bullock-carts toiling slowly up the pass. Tan Chen King, Ah Loy, and another Chinese who accompanied us, again insisted on riding up the hill.

Haywood and I were soon completely exhausted as well as soaked through with sweat in our efforts to keep up, for we felt it was most dangerous to be spread over several miles of road. Fortunately it was only three miles – in which we climbed over 500 feet – to the summit of the pass at 2,080 feet. Then we knew there were twenty miles of free-wheeling to the crossroads at Kampong

Ketari, with a further ten miles downhill to Sungei Gow, a few miles short of Karak.

On the way up we had had some trouble owing to the chains of our bicycles breaking from the undue strain, but Ah Loy, who had the usual Chinese genius for improvisation, managed to mend these with wire. The descent was magnificent. In the brilliant tropical moonlight we could go as fast as by daylight, and it was glorious to see the huge jungle trees rush past us and to feel the cool fecund night air on our faces. Then Tan Chen King's tyre burst and it was discovered that Ah Loy, who had the only puncture-mending outfit, had gone on ahead. It took over an hour for the third Chinese to overtake him and bring him back.

At about the 75th Mile, soon after we had rattled at long intervals over a plank bridge, I had halted for a moment with one foot on the ground to wait for the other Chinese, whose bicycle had been giving trouble and who had been out of sight for some time. Suddenly three cyclists overtook me and, as one of them came right alongside, I saw he was a Malay policeman and had a double-barrelled shotgun across his handlebars. Recognising me as an Englishman, he gave a loud grunt and attempted to seize my handlebars. I had my .38 revolver thrust into my belt, but at that time I did not feel I was at war with Malays, and the idea of shooting him never even entered my head. Instead of that, I gave his arm a terrific blow with the side of my hand and, handing off another Malay who had stopped in front of me, I shouted, 'Go like hell!' to Haywood and pedalled furiously down the road. The Malay shot four times. His third shot succeeded in bursting my back tyre and hitting the muscle of my left calf, so that the leg was completely useless. By this time we were well ahead, and though my flat tyre made an appalling noise, I held on to Haywood and we soon caught up Tan Chen King and Ah Loy, who had hurried back on hearing the shooting.

The moment we reached the dark shadow of some rubber trees on the left of the road, I stopped the party and we clambered a short distance up a steep bank and waited. Soon two of the Malays rode up and we opened fire with our pistols. The Chinese shot before I gave the order, but we dropped the leading Malay ten yards in front of us. He was a very brave man, for as he lay he fired two barrels at us and then crawled away into a dense patch of jungle bananas on the other side of the road.[1] The other two Malays had by now disappeared, and we were afraid that they were holding the other Chinese. Haywood and I thought we ought to try to rescue him – especially as he had all the tinned food we had brought from the dump at the 20th Mile – but Tan Chen King said he must look after himself. He returned to Batu Caves two days later, but without his bicycle or load.

It was already about 3 a.m. and we were afraid that the whole neighbourhood would have been aroused by the shooting and that the other Malays would ring up the Japs at Bentong, who would then be waiting for us at Kampong Ketari, only six miles ahead. Thus the first thing we did was to cut the telegraph wires. If it had not been for the wound in my leg, we should have returned to the 78th Mile and walked seven miles due east along the Forest Reserve boundary which led right to our destination – Haywood's old camp at Sungei Gow. But my calf was bleeding profusely and was already extremely painful. The bone seemed to be untouched, but the injury to the muscle made the ankle numb and useless. As it was too dark to dig out the shot, we tied on a first-field-dressing and hoped for the best. We then hid my ruined bicycle carefully, in case its owner should be traced, and taking the Malay's bicycle from the road, I sat on it and was towed along by Ah Loy, who was as strong as a mule. Finding there was no sentry at Kampong Ketari, we passed it without any trouble and had the surprisingly good fortune to reach the Sungei Gow turning before dawn without meeting a single person on the road – or so we thought.

As soon as it was light enough we washed the blood from my leg and discovered that the wound consisted of a single large hole. Tan Chen King then made a probe and a pair of forceps out of bamboo and started excavating the wound. Fortunately I fainted and was thus spared the pain. When I came to, I found that they had extracted a half-inch motorcar nut – apparently the Malay had made up his own cartridges – and I was extremely grateful that none of his shots at close range had found their mark. Haywood

---

[1] In 1945 the Malay District Officer of Bentong told me that this policeman had been admitted to Bentong Hospital with wounds in his arms and legs. I am glad to say that he recovered.

told me that Ah Wan had chewed up some leaves from a certain tree and, filling his mouth with stream water and holding a piece of bamboo between his lips, had thoroughly syringed the wound. His somewhat primitive surgery – aided by the iodine from my medical set – was certainly very effective, for though I could not move the ankle without great pain for some days, the wound never showed any sign of infection and the swelling gradually subsided.

We now had only two miles to go to reach the house of the Chinese called John who had formerly helped Haywood and his party. We found that a series of clearings had been opened up since we were last here, and instead of following a pleasant jungle track we had to crawl under and over a maze of newly cut bamboo, treacherously slippery with the early morning dew. I can remember few more unpleasant three hours in my whole life.

At last, at midday on May 2, we reached John's house, and I collapsed with high fever and pneumonia. I have only a hazy recollection of what happened in the next few weeks. For the first few days I could eat nothing, had great difficulty in breathing and, as if that were not enough, was visited with an attack of dysentery. The first time I went out I was left alone at the emergency latrine over the edge of the path. I fainted and rolled right down the hill to the stream. After a few days John told us the Japs were combing the jungle edge for us, so I was carried on a stretcher right up the hill to the camp where Haywood and his party had formerly lived. We found that the timber *towkay* had already got rid of most of the stores that we had left here – as he had been given permission to do – but we succeeded in recovering the wireless set, though at first we could get no batteries. Unfortunately a Chinese informer had already told the Japs that the *towkay* had formerly helped our party, and he was closely watched and dared not help us, although he sent his man John up to us from time to time.

After a few days in the upper camp Haywood collapsed, and for two months we were both very seriously ill, running extremely high temperatures and being daily shaken by violent rigors. Fortunately our crises occurred at different times, so that we were able to look after each other to a certain extent. Luckily there were some sulphathiazole (M. & B.) tablets in my medical set, and it was probably due to them that I did not die of pneumonia. At that time, indeed throughout the years in the jungle, I kept a very full diary and wrote it up each evening. On May 5 I felt so ill that I thought I was going to die, so I started to write my will, but soon had to dictate it to Haywood. Then one day I suddenly thought to myself, 'My goodness, I haven't written my diary today or yesterday!' Haywood handed it to me and told me the date was now May 23. I had been unconscious of time for seventeen days! Haywood told me that I had lain completely comatose for the greater part of them – so much so that he had often had to examine me carefully to make sure I was still alive. Apparently I had been an ideal patient. When I shivered he covered me with blankets, and when I panted and groaned with the heat of the fever he took them off again. I swallowed whatever medicine or food he gave me and asked for our improvised bedpan whenever necessary.

As soon as I was more or less convalescent, Haywood became exceedingly ill, but *he* was certainly not a good patient. In the middle of the morning he would complain of almost unendurable cold and I would fill our empty bottles with hot water and cover him with every spare blanket we had. All the colour would drain from his face and his lips would fade to a bluish-grey. Then he would start shivering and for an hour would be shaken by the most frightful rigors so that his teeth rattled, the whole sleeping-bench shook, and his breath came in horrible gasps and sobs. He would fall into a feverish sleep, from which he always awoke in a state of delirium.

While I was looking after Haywood I gradually recovered my strength and interest in life. I found that the small clearing round the hut was a wonderful place for birds, and as I still had my small Zeiss field-glasses with me, I spent much of the time identifying new species and making voluminous notes on their appearance and habits. Since I now had the most wonderful opportunity to study the natural history of the jungle, it worried me very much that I did not know anything whatsoever about the flora and fauna of Malaya, and for all I could tell, the vivid blue flycatcher or scarlet minivet I was observing might be the commonest species in the country or entirely new to science. I had to invent my own names for them and to give them numbers, and there were so many varieties in this jungle clearing that after a month's study I had reached Number 107. I also started making a collection of pressed flowers for Kew Herbarium. I had always made a point of doing this in any country I ever visited for any length of time, and I saw no reason why the presence of the Japs should prevent me now. But wild flowers are very rare in the real jungle and I only collected about twelve species, being very disappointed to find only one kind of tree orchid.

At last, in the middle of June, Haywood turned the corner and no longer suffered from rigors and fits of delirium, but he was terribly weak and like me had lost a great deal of weight. In this respect I had suffered more. My normal weight is 170 pounds, and when we reached Sungei Gow I was already at least 15 pounds lighter owing to the poor food and bad conditions in the Batu Caves camps, but after this double illness I was reduced to 100 or 110 pounds and would not have believed it possible to lose so much flesh and yet remain alive.

Tan Chen King and Ah Loy had had to return to their respective camps, but they came over to see us once or twice. When they had first had to leave us, they had put us in touch with the two young Chinese *towkays* of Karak. These men undoubtedly saved our lives. Ah Kow, the younger of the two, was extremely well educated and spoke perfect English, and more or less appointed himself our guardian. He left one of his coolies with us, and through him supplied us with fruit, eggs, fowls, oatmeal, flour, and tinned milk and other foods. At great personal risk – for the Japs were still searching the jungle for us – he came up to our camp almost every week. He would not accept a dollar in return, only taking summaries of the news which we were able to get on our wireless, though it was very difficult even for him to supply us with batteries that were any good.

He proved a most valuable source of reliable intelligence. The Japs allowed him to go to Kuala Lumpur and elsewhere by car, and he took the trouble to make special journeys to find out what I wanted to know, for at that time we were still hoping to get out of the country, and we knew that in India any information about conditions in Japanese-occupied Malaya would be invaluable. From Ah Kow's information I completed a very full report of the location and conditions in the prisoner-of-war and civilian-internee camps, of Jap atrocities, dispositions of garrison troops, naval and air bases, and the general conditions of the people. He told us that the more wealthy Chinese, though some had been pro-Japanese at first, were now willing to support and subsidise the guerillas, though they did not necessarily agree with their politics.

Though Haywood was no longer delirious, he showed no real signs of recovery, and I was afraid that he would die if we stayed here much longer. I was suffering from a terrible dry cough which kept me awake night after night, and from intermittent dysentery. However, with the excellent food provided by Ah Kow I was gradually putting on weight, and I used to walk up and down the path from our hut to the stream to get my muscles back. Haywood was still in bed and could not walk at all without help. I was most anxious to return to Batu Caves before the Secretary General went away again, as it seemed to me of paramount importance to get in touch with guerilla headquarters. The first scheme we considered was that Ah Kow should send us round by road hidden in one of the banana lorries that he was in the habit of sending to Kuala Lumpur, but as we discovered that the Japs were searching every vehicle, we had to give that up. Meanwhile, all we could do was to put the camp in a state of siege by lashing a tommy-gun to the framework of the hut so that it pointed straight down the track and could be fired by either of us by pulling a cord which hung down over the sleeping-bench.

One day Ah Kow brought three other Chinese to see us. One was Lah Leo, the political leader of the new guerilla camp at Menchis, of which Ah Loy was the military leader; the others were Ah Ching, one of his helpers from Kampong Menchis who accompanied him as interpreter, and Chu Mei, a very friendly and well-dressed rubber contractor who produced marvellous testimonials from former British employers.

Ah Kow dare not stay a moment longer than necessary away from his house at Karak, and having introduced the newcomers, left Ah Ching to interpret. It appeared that the Pahang guerillas were most concerned for our safety, and they suggested we should join their camp at Menchis, twenty-five miles south of Karak. They had a Chinese doctor there and could supply us with plenty of

111

good food, and as soon as we were fit again they would help us to return to Selangor or wherever else we wanted to go. In return we should give them the balance of our weapons and military stores and set up a training centre for the Pahang guerillas.

We readily agreed to this suggestion. Haywood and I kept only a pistol and a grenade each, and all the rest of the gear – 2 tommy-guns, 10 rifles, 100 grenades, 3,000 rounds of ammunition, and about 1,500 lb. of explosive, and all the demolition devices – we handed over to the Pahang Group. Lah Leo would transport these and the precious wireless set by bicycle to his camp. He wanted us to ride too, but as Haywood could hardly walk, much less bicycle, they agreed to carry him by stretcher to the road and then to continue the journey by car. This rather surprised us, as motoring seemed an even more uninsurable occupation than bicycling. But they assured us that it was absolutely safe, since the Karak-Menchis road had never once been used by the Japs at night since the beginning of the occupation.

(Use Map No. 2)
We left the Gow camp on July 9. It took two days for relays of Chinese to carry Haywood down through the jungle and along the edge of the rubber round Karak to Sabai Estate factory. At this slow speed I found I could walk quite easily, and once away from the depressing Gow camp I seemed to recover very quickly, though I was still suffering from dysentery. The Chinese towkay at Sabai Estate looked after us very well and agreed to lend us his 8-h.p. Morris saloon, which his brother would drive. The Japs had removed the wiring and headlight bulbs of all motorcars, but the guerillas produced some others and we soon had the car running.

We left the estate factory on the night of July 11 at 9 p.m. This seemed to me dangerously early, but the guerillas were full of confidence, and Ah Loy, who was in charge of the party, was in a hurry to get on. The *towkay's* brother and two other Chinese squashed into the front seat, while Haywood and I and a third man sat behind. Ah Loy and another guerilla, armed with our two tommy-guns, stood on the running-board and hung on to the roof. All our personal gear was lashed on to the back, while the other weapons and stores were carried by a large party of cyclists who set off an hour ahead of us. Haywood and I were each armed with a pistol and grenade, and I had my diaries and intelligence summaries rolled up in the pouches of my web equipment. I also carried my field-glasses and first-aid set.

The estate road from the factory to the main road was overgrown with four feet of vegetation, and we carried planks to improvise bridges. With seven of us besides the driver we were able to manhandle the car very effectively. At last we reached the main road, which was in perfect condition, and it was most thrilling and satisfactory for us after all our recent vicissitudes to be rushing through the night in a tunnel of brilliant light which revealed the tall elephant grass by the roadside and patches of rubber alternating with jungle.

Suddenly, between the 90th and 91st Mile, we saw the headlights of an approaching car. Ah Loy leaned over and shouted excitedly, 'Japun! Japun!' I said to myself, 'This is the end!' and to Haywood, 'Give me your grenade. Get out the moment we stop and lie in the ditch. I'll try to create a diversion. Then get away as fast as you can.' And while I held a grenade in each hand he pulled out the pins. It then struck me that it would be far more sensible to drive off the road – there was rubber on the right and newly cleared land on the left – and to abandon the car as soon as we were no longer floodlit by the Jap headlights. I was shouting to Ah Loy to do this when the driver swerved violently to the left to avoid hitting the Jap lorry, and both vehicles pulled up within a few yards of each other.

The Japanese lorry was bristling with troops, who shouted triumphantly and began to jump out on to the road. As Haywood and the six Chinese poured out of the car and made for the rough ground on the left, I hid behind the Morris and lobbed both grenades into the crowded lorry, then crawled underneath the car for cover. By this time half the Japs were out of the lorry and lining the left-hand side of the road, so that I had to run into the rubber on the other side, thus having to cross the path of their headlights. I now created far more of a diversion than I had intended and not only received the full attention of the Japs but was in the line of fire of my companions, who were shooting from the clearing on the left. Before I could take cover by lying down behind a rubber tree, a bullet passed through my left arm and another severed the cartilage where my left ear joins my head and grazed my cheekbone. Oddly enough, I was far more conscious of the latter wound, though it turned out to be a very slight one and thinking that I had been shot right through the head and must soon lose consciousness, I hastily scratched a hole in the ground and buried my diaries.

By now the noise of battle was terrific. The Japs had at least one mortar in action, and the stutter of machine-guns and tommy-guns was almost continuous. Finding that I was still quite intact, though my left arm was useless, I stupidly abandoned my safe position behind the tree and tried to work my way round through the rubber, fearing that if I did not rejoin Haywood before he reached the jungle, we should have the greatest difficulty in finding each other again. I ran parallel to the road, which I wanted to cross over once I was out of the glare of the headlights and join the others, as I did not think I could get far without help. I had only gone a short distance when a mortar bomb burst beside me and I was thrown violently against a rubber tree. Again I was surprised to find myself still alive and apparently unhurt, though there was a terrible buzzing in my head. I raced across the road and as far as I could through the clearing beyond. Here the trees had only recently been felled, and in the normal way of clearing the jungle, the undergrowth had been burnt off and in many places was still smouldering. Just in front of me a tommy-gun opened fire. Hoping this was Ah Loy, I made my way towards it, crawling over the fallen tree-trunks and shouting, 'Ah Loy, Ah Loy! Don't shoot! Don't shoot!'

Ah Loy had had the end of one thumb shot off, but was otherwise unscathed. I gave my rallying cry for Haywood, but there was no answer. Ah Loy said he thought he had seen him fall soon after leaving the car. There was no sign of any of the other Chinese, and we assumed they were either casualties or had got away into the jungle. It was certainly no use looking for them. Those who were still alive would eventually make their way to the Menchis camp, and Ah Loy assured me that all the Chinese in this area were reliable and would help them.

The Japs were still firing furiously, so we crouched in the deep bed of a stream for a quarter of an hour. The first thing I did was to be violently sick, and then for the rest of the night I suffered from acute attacks of dysentery. The whole of my left side was caked with blood from the wounds in the side of my head and my arm. At that time I thought it was broken, so Ah Loy and I put a first-field-dressing on it and tucked the hand into the braces of my webbing belt to keep it out of the way. The Japanese were raking the ground systematically from end to end with mortar and machine-gun fire, and there was no answer from the guerillas. Ah Loy, at least, had run out of ammunition. We decided to follow down the stream, whose bed gave us a certain amount of cover, and strike the road again to the south of the action. Once more I gave the rallying cry, but as there was still no answer we set off down the road. Conversation with Ah Loy was always difficult, as he could only speak a little English, though he spoke fluent Malay, while my Malay was as bad as his English

He said that we must get beyond Menchis, a distance of fourteen miles, before dawn, as the Japs would start combing the jungle edge as soon as it was light, but that I could probably rest for a few days at a house at the edge of the rubber before going on to the camp. Ah Loy asked me if I could do it. The alternative was to go to the first Chinese house we could find and ask them to hide us in the jungle until the hue and cry was over. There was considerable risk in this, since Ah Loy came from Bentong fifteen miles north of here and did not know who could really be trusted among the *kampong* Chinese in this district.

I have a theory, which I have never yet disproved, that on level ground or downhill one can always go on as long as consciousness lasts. There never comes a time when one literally cannot go another step. Of course, as in any other form of overdraft, one has to pay up afterwards, but as long as a man is reasonably fit the capabilities of the human body are almost unlimited – as I knew from my acquaintance with polar exploration. The trouble was that the last two days' walk was my first exercise for two months, and I had lost a considerable amount of blood from my wounds and was also suffering from severe dysentery pains. Nevertheless, I was certain I could do it as long as we kept to the level road. Meanwhile, the Japs were still pouring lead into the jungle. They kept it up continuously for about three hours and must have wasted thousands of rounds of ammunition.

Just before the village at the 93rd Mile we were suddenly halted by a bamboo barrier across the road. Torches were flashed on us and we were confronted by men in dark blue uniform armed with shotguns. I thought they were Japs, and, being a few yards behind, I dived for cover and was about to open fire with my revolver when Ah Loy shouted to me not to. They were Chinese police in Japanese employ – as I soon saw by their rising-sun armbands – and after a loud altercation with Ah Loy they made us return by the way we had come. As soon as we were out of hearing, Ah Loy explained that the guerillas had an amicable arrangement with these men, but that their officer, who really was pro-Japanese, was within earshot, hence their apparent ferocity.

Ah Loy now attempted to make a detour round the police post. We left the road and entered an area of vegetable gardens and isolated *atap* houses. Unfortunately Ah Loy had no sense of direction and we spent at least an hour wandering in circles through tapioca plantations, paddy swamps, and thorny thickets, with all the dogs in Asia barking at us. At last, when we had passed the same house and been barked at by the same dog three times, I insisted on taking charge. I had recognised the red star Antares through a gap in the clouds. Knowing that it must be in the southeast at that hour of the night, we marched upon it and soon came out at the concrete road bridge over the Sungei Padak.

On the road I could keep up a good pace, in spite of frequent halts caused by my dysentery, and we walked past Kampong Menchis Police Station just before dawn and reached a *kongsi-*house a mile into the rubber at the jungle edge. Here, after washing off as much blood as I could, I was given a Chinese coolie's suit consisting of a jacket buttoning up to the neck and a pair of baggy trousers. I did not disturb the dressing on my arm, which was completely numb and therefore not painful, though very much swollen. After a large meal, I was given a bed in a little loft beneath the *atap* roof and fell asleep, hoping that it would not be necessary to travel for several days.

About an hour later I woke up to find Ah Loy shaking my shoulder. Apparently a lorry-load of Japs had already reached Menchis and were carrying out a house-to-house search of the village. We had to leave for the camp at once. This should have

116

been a three hours' march – about three miles on the map – through rather hilly but not mountainous jungle. But my legs, which had worked mechanically on the road, now simply refused to function when it came to climbing the slightest rise, and it took us nine hours to reach the camp. Ah Loy, though full of energy and courage, was in many ways singularly obtuse, and his somewhat unsympathetic efforts to hurry me along were most unsuccessful. When he walked slowly, I followed him a yard behind, step by step, and with my mind miles away (I had many serious problems to keep it fully occupied) I could keep going; but the moment he started to hurry and thus left me behind, I fell right back and went at only half the speed I had maintained when subconsciously drawn along, as it were, behind him – an interesting sidelight on the psychology of travel.

We were the first of the ambushed party to reach the camp, and for the next week stragglers returned. It seemed that Haywood had been shot through the chest and had fallen only ten yards from the car. The Chinese who later buried him were certain that he must have died at once. The driver of the car – the *towkay's* brother – was also killed and two other Chinese were wounded. At some time in the night – I could never discover exactly when or where – the party of twelve cyclists carrying the wireless set and the more valuable weapons and stores ran into this or another party of Japs and had to abandon their loads and bicycles, though they got away with their rifles.

After the war, when I was at Bentong, I discovered that there were forty-two Japanese soldiers on this one lorry. It was with great satisfaction that I heard that my grenades had accounted for eight of them and wounded many more.

CHAPTER EIGHT

The Menchis Guerillas

(USE MAP NO. 2)

I was still alive, but I had lost my congenial companion Haywood. Also those of my party who had not been taken prisoner were more than a month's journey away to the north. Gone, too, were all the comforts of life that, largely through the generosity of Ah Kow, we had collected at Sungei Gow – blankets, clothes, books, food, and medicines. I had lost my private diaries for the period since leaving the camp at Ulu Slim, as well as my collections of bird notes, butterflies, and plants, which had been in the rucksack on the back of the car.

When I reached the guerilla camp at Menchis, I had only my .38 revolver, field-glasses, wristwatch, and the clothes I stood up in. Haywood had been carrying our last few dollars, so I had no money. The guerillas had been so confident that we could not possibly meet any Japs on the road at night that we had made no plans for such a contingency and I had even left my compass and maps in the rucksack. I joined the Menchis patrol on July 13, 1942, and I stayed with them for more than a year. For the first eleven months, except for one week when I visited a camp in Johore, I saw no white men.

No. 6 Independent Anti-Japanese Regiment was one of the last to be formed, and whereas the other five then in existence had all been built up round the nucleus of men and weapons put in by 101 S.T.S., this group had grown up on its own. Like all the others, it was vaguely in touch with guerilla general headquarters. Its men were recruited from Raub, Bentong, Mentakab, and Menchis, a predominantly Chinese area on the east side of the Main Range containing no real towns but having immense tracts of mountainous jungle intersected by a network of rivers.

Their first patrol was formed in March 1942, when about fifty of them went into camp near Bentong in the buildings of a tin mine high up in the hills. Here, through treachery, they were suddenly attacked by the Japanese. They fled into the jungle, and now in command of Lah Leo, moved about thirty miles to a new camp near the summit of an isolated mountain seven miles west-south-west of Mentakab. Here they were attacked again in May 1942. Once more they fled into the jungle, where some of them wandered for as much as a week. As the numbers in this camp had by now risen to a hundred, they formed two patrols, one moving a further twenty miles southeast to the vicinity of Triang, and the other going the same distance southwest of the jungle west of Menchis, where I joined them.

This camp was not in Pahang at all, being just over the border in the state of Negri Sembilan on the upper waters of the Sungei Sertang. It was only three miles west-southwest of Kampong Menchis, but the distance on the ground must have been about seven miles and took a fit man three hours to walk. The patrol had moved to Mentakab because Lah Leo, the leader, had been a shop-keeper there before the war. As he had also been a member of the Malayan Communist Party, he had many friends round about who were willing to arrange the food lines to the camp. Lah Leo was a little quiet-spoken Cantonese with a whimsical expression and great charm of manner, but when roused he became very excited and eloquent. During the fighting he had been engaged in moving a load of abandoned arms into the jungle for the use of the guerillas, when some Malays had appeared and tried to prevent him. In the ensuing struggle he had half an ear cut off with a *parang*. I liked Lah Leo very much indeed, and he invariably treated me with absolute fairness and honesty.

The move to Menchis was due to the support of Ah Ching, a small shopkeeper there who was a business friend of Lah Leo – though by no means a Communist. Ah Ching became my greatest friend among the guerillas. He was about twenty-five years of age and had the build and movements of an athlete. His greatest ambition was to represent Pahang in badminton so that he could have in his house a large picture of himself standing beside the silver challenge cup. He was a tremendously keen hunter. Before the war he had often taken Englishmen out after pig and deer, and consequently he understood our ways and could speak a certain amount of English. In contrast to the bombastic fearlessness usually expressed by the Chinese in the camps, he admitted that he hated the idea of being shot at, and above all of being caught and tortured. Ah Ching had considerable initiative. During the period between the retreat of the British forces from Menchis and the arrival of the Japanese, he had convened a meeting in his own house of the leaders of the Chinese and Malay communities, and they had made a joint plan to prevent looting and lawlessness, so that in Menchis, unlike many of the country villages, there had been no inter-racial conflict or anarchy.

As I had expected, having overdrawn on my reserves so heavily, I was very ill for my first few weeks in the camp. In the first place, having walked for a long distance when completely out of training, my leg muscles seized up with such acute stiffness that for several days I was unable to walk a single step and had to be supported by two men. One of the girls was a skilful masseuse, and after a week I could get about without pain. My dysentery was also so much worse that I was passing blood and had to have a special 'armchair' latrine built for me, as I sometimes used to faint with the pain.

The doctor and the wonderful food that Ah Ching had promised turned out to be a myth. Apparently for their first month in this camp a Chinese doctor from Menchis used to visit them from time to time, and as the Japs had not discovered where the patrol had moved after leaving Mentakab, their food lines were undisturbed and they could get whatever they liked to eat. Ah Ching, from his shop in Menchis, had organised the collection of food, but on security grounds had never visited the camp himself. In those days the men could have dry rice twice a day, plenty of vegetable in the morning, fish or meat in the evening, and chicken, eggs, and even fresh milk for the sick. But Menchis was now full of informers, and Ah Ching and his food collectors had had to come and take sanctuary in the camp. There was no longer a doctor, there was only a meagre supply of Chinese medicines, and the food was very poor indeed. In the morning we had watery rice and boiled tapioca with sweet-potato leaves as the vegetable, and in the evening dry rice with a limited amount of pumpkin, brinjol, beans, or some other vegetable. It was almost impossible to obtain meat or fish.

At this time many of the Chinese who had joined the guerillas in a fit of enthusiasm were becoming disillusioned. They hated the rigorous camp discipline which even prevented them from visiting their *kampongs*, and found the food inferior to what they were used to in their own homes. In the early days there seemed every hope of keeping the Japanese out of Malaya, but now it looked as if they had come to stay. Consequently there were many desertions, either back to the *kampongs* or even to become informers to the Japanese. Chu Mei was a typical example. At first he had kept in with the guerillas and even won their confidence. Then, when he had some information worth selling, he went over to the enemy and as a result secured a good job for himself. It was interesting that he did not, as far as I could find out, inform against Ah Kow, though he knew enough to get him beheaded had he wanted to do so.

The facility with which the Chinese, otherwise so single-minded in their hatred of the Japanese, could turn informer was a perpetual source of astonishment to me. In the year that I spent with this patrol, no less than six of its members were tried for treachery and summarily shot, and several others who had fled from the camp and turned informer were hunted down and dispatched outside. Those who have a better understanding of the Oriental mind tell me that among the uneducated Chinese, personal pique can reach such limits that a man will be quite prepared to kill himself – let alone sell himself – if he thinks that it will cause sufficient harm to his rival.

As soon as I had settled down in this camp and recovered my health, I set about trying to get in touch with general headquarters, but in this I was completely unsuccessful, and when I left Pahang more than a year later I was still no nearer achieving this object. The reasons were partly geographical and partly political. The Pahang group of guerillas, living on the eastern side of the Main Range and having organised themselves some time after the other groups, were very much cut off from their neighbours. When it actually came to getting a job done, the guerillas proved themselves extraordinarily dilatory and incompetent, a weakness most of all exemplified in the gross inefficiency of their communications. In the year that I spent with this patrol we were in touch – so

121

far as I know – only three times with the Selangor group and through them with general headquarters, three or four times with the Negri Sembilan group to the southwest, twice with Perak, and once with the isolated guerillas in east Pahang. I did not receive a single letter from Regan or Tan Chen King at Selangor and, though I wrote several, I do not believe that they were delivered.

At the same time I flatter myself that the Pahang guerillas did not want me to leave them, and it is quite possible that they deliberately prevented any communication between me and general headquarters. They were so parochially minded that they were quite prepared to keep me as an instructor for their recruits and junior leaders. On the other hand, it is possible that general headquarters themselves preferred me to remain in Pahang. Tan Chen King, when I met him at the Slim camp in March 1942, was certainly not of this opinion, but he, alas! was killed in a skirmish with the Japs a few months after I joined the Pahang guerillas. There was another consideration too. When I went into the jungle in January 1942, I understood that I was to be the liaison officer to the Chinese guerillas in the event of it being possible for the stay-behind parties to cooperate with them. But owing to the disorganisation caused by the speed of the British retreat, nobody had actually informed M.C.P. headquarters of this. Tan Chen King, as I have said, remembered meeting me at 101 S.T.S. and had been prepared to accept me as an ambassador. But so security-minded were the majority of the guerilla officials that it is quite possible they refused to accept me without more definite credentials.

The control of guerilla general headquarters, in spite of its geographical vagueness, was absolute and all-embracing, being limited only by the difficulties of communication. Policy, discipline, routine, ethics, and above all political ideology were entirely regulated from above – and as the penalty for disobedience was death, opposition in word or spirit was practically unknown. Within these limits, group and patrol leaders had complete power within their commands but none outside, nor would they ever dare to take the initiative. Even a patrol leader could not visit another camp in his group without permission from group headquarters, and there was no communication between groups except with the express permission of general headquarters. Every detail had to be referred above and the answer, if it came at all, would take several months to receive.

The ordinary man in the camps knew nothing of general headquarters except that it existed, but all knew the name of the Secretary General, who was credited with innumerable attributes, being able to pilot an aeroplane, drive a tank, speak many languages, and hoodwink the Japanese in any way he desired. The group leaders themselves merely knew that general headquarters was somewhere in Selangor. They did not know the names or number of its members.

Group headquarters usually consisted of four permanent officers: the political leader, whose power was absolute and who was usually a full M.C.P. member; the military commander, not necessarily a Party member and definitely junior to his political colleague; the quartermaster in charge of supply and finance; and a teacher-cum-propaganda-worker who was invariably a Party member and probably the second most important officer of the four. Attached to group headquarters were usually one or more outside workers whose status depended on their own personality or their standing in the M.C.P. Their task, perhaps the most important of all, was to cultivate the minds of the outside people so that they would support the camps, to allocate the areas of influence and the food lines between the various patrols, and to supervise the systematic discovery and eradication of traitors and informers. These men, who were usually the best educated and most intelligent of the guerillas – and often most charming and delightful people – spent only a small proportion of their time in the camps and the rest in the *kampongs* or on tour.

Patrol headquarters was a replica of group headquarters, but there was in addition a military second-in-command who supervised the guard and training. Its members were allowed very little initiative and would often go to any length to avoid responsibility. The schoolmaster was usually helped by one of the girls, who in general tended to be better educated and much more intelligent than the men. His job was to teach Mandarin, singing, and general knowledge – with a strong 'left' bias – to organise concerts, and produce a camp magazine.

The political leader of the Pahang group was a Hokkien called

Ah Chong. I did not get to know him until I had lived with the Menchis guerillas for some months, as he was then living with the Triang patrol. Ah Chong had a lean and hungry look, a very large nose, wore glasses, and had been educated far beyond his intelligence – all characteristics, in my experience, of a fanatic. He was a keen M.C.P. member. Before the war his job had been to visit the mines and foment strikes; and his character had not changed since then. Ah Chong always regarded me with suspicion, and I honestly believe he thought I had been deliberately left behind by the British Government to spy upon the activities of the M.C.P. Quite often – so Ah Ching told me – when I was away hunting he used to go through my papers in search of evidence. Although I always found myself more in sympathy with the men in the camps than with their political leaders, Ah Chong was one of the few I really disliked, largely because he was incapable of telling the truth.

Of the members of the patrol headquarters, Lah Leo and Ah Loy have already been mentioned. Ah Ching became quartermaster, but as he was not a keen Communist he was only attached to headquarters and did not attend any of their important meetings. The schoolmaster member was called Whu Bing. He already spoke a little English, and was so intelligent that he soon learned to speak fluently. I saw a great deal of him. As he had a good brain and was extremely musical, his work was to teach Mandarin and singing and to edit the fortnightly camp magazine, which he transcribed in beautiful Chinese characters and which I illustrated with watercolour drawings.

The Menchis patrol was divided into sections of ten to twelve men, each commanded by a junior leader. These men were given so little initiative that their power was negligible, and they were thus the weakest link in the guerilla set-up. There were never enough natural leaders to go round, and no attempt was made to encourage or train this quality. The normal complement of the patrol was about a hundred men and half a dozen girls, but numbers would rarely be up to full strength. Parties might be away for weeks or even months on end collecting arms, growing vegetables, or pursuing spies and informers, while as much as a quarter of the men might go out each day to carry back food or patrol the approaches to the camp.

The rank and file were absolutely magnificent. I can hardly find words to express my admiration for their courage, fortitude, and consistent cheerfulness in adversity. In the Menchis patrol they were mostly Hakkas. The majority of them were rubber-tappers – as were three of the girls – and there were a few tin-mining coolies, vegetable gardeners, squatters, and woodcutters, as well as the odd barber, coffee-shop attendant, and house 'boy.' The best jungle men had been *jeluton*-tappers (*jeluton* being a kind of wild rubber tree from which chewing gum is manufactured) or illicit tinworkers known as *dulangers* (the *dulang* being a wooden bowl in which the earth is swilled away from the heavier particles of tin).

In each patrol there were usually five or six girl guerillas. These were of two distinct types – the better-educated ones who taught Mandarin and singing, and the tougher ones who helped in the kitchen and did at least their full share of the heaviest and dirtiest chores. All of them also acted as nurses and seamstresses. The girls were very keen to fight the Japanese. But only in a few camps, where there were enough weapons to go round, could they go on guard and attend all parades with the men. In none of the camps I visited were there any girls on the headquarters staff, but some of them, who had been connected with the M.C.P. before the war, acted as secretaries and helped with the teaching and propaganda work.

Often they showed incredible bravery, and when we were on the run or moving to a new camp, they carried just as heavy loads as the men and certainly showed no less fortitude. I have the greatest admiration for these girls. They exerted a very good influence in the camps, and though they could be as pitiless and cruel as the men in dealing with a captured Jap or traitor, they had a certain humanising effect on the rougher coolies who predominated in the camps. The girls expected to be, and were, treated exactly like the men. In all my time in the jungle camps I heard of no single instance of sex complications interrupting the harmony of our personal relationships.

The average age in this camp was about twenty-three, and the headquarters staff would lower rather than raise this average. In most camps there were one or two boys, often in their early teens and sometimes no taller than the service rifle with which they tried to drill. They were usually homeless orphans whose parents had been killed by the Japs. Like the girls, they were a humanising influence in the camps, but they were terribly spoiled by the rest of us, who were starved of the companionship of children. They acted as messengers, and their treble voices were a useful addition to the camp choir.

The girls always lived in the headquarters hut, as did any visitors and a certain number of privileged people, chief among whom were the guides. Of these there were two or three in each patrol. Their duty was to carry letters and messages and to act as guides for headquarters officials and others travelling from camp to camp. For reasons of security one man was usually kept on the same run, as it was a general and excellent principle that the less a man knew the less he could divulge if caught and tortured. As a rule they were the fittest men in the camp. Not only did they obtain extra food outside, but in some camps they were given a special issue of coffee and sugar.

The daily routine was much the same in all guerilla camps throughout Malaya. Sundays were free – although Christianity, together with all other religions, was officially disbelieved in, and there were other free days usually corresponding with Soviet or Chinese holidays. Here is the programme of a typical working day in the Menchis camp when training was in progress:

4 a.m.

The cooks got up to prepare food for those leaving camp at dawn – the guard relief, food-carrying parties, and perhaps a headquarters official with a runner setting off on a long journey. The cooks were usually men who were too stupid to learn Mandarin and therefore to join in the life of the camp, or for some reason incapable of fighting – either too old or infirm.

5.30 a.m. (in some camps 5.45 a.m.)

A whistle blew. We all got up at once, and as we slept fully dressed with our weapons, spare clothes, and other gear ready packed in canvas or rattan bags beside us, we were on parade, fully armed and equipped, within five minutes of the whistle blowing. It was still only half light and fairly chilly, but nobody showed any signs of bad temper while section commanders called the roll and saw that all their men were present. Some of us had a quick wash before P.T.; others preferred to wait until it was fully light.

5.45 a.m. to 6.15 a.m.

P.T. on the parade-ground taken by Ah Loy or his assistant who used to be a professional teacher of Chinese shadow-boxing, and sometimes by myself. Everybody in the camp, except the runners and a few of the headquarters men who had been working far into the night, turned out. The exercises were much too strenuous and prolonged, considering our low diet. Sometimes, instead of P.T., and usually after it, we marched and ran interminably round and round the diminutive parade-ground. The guerillas had a most curious habit, at a given order, of counting in unison up to five or ten at the top of their voices in time with their paces as they ran round. This may have taught new recruits to run in step but was most dangerous, as in the still jungle dawn the noise of their shouting could be heard from a great distance.

6.15 a.m. to 6.30 a.m.

It was now daylight in the clearing round the camp but still fairly dark in the jungle. We went down to the stream at the bottom of the camp and washed our faces and cleaned our teeth. All the Chinese had miniature face towels (nearly all with 'Good morning' printed in red across one end in English and Chinese). They washed with these, then wrung them out and used them for drying. Toothbrushes were bought through friends in the *kampongs*, but most of us knew how to make our own out of pig-bristles.

The Chinese have another early morning ceremony – that of scraping the tongue, especially at the back, with a thin pliable strip of metal which is usually kept attached to the toothbrush. Judging by the amount of whitish sediment that is got rid of in this way, it should be a very healthy habit. We then dressed for the day, those that were lucky enough to have them taking off the long trousers and long sleeved shirts worn since the evening before to ward off mosquitoes and keep us warm at night. In order to preserve the proprieties in a mixed camp, each man wore a small pair of cotton underpants with a sliding cord round the top. Clothed in these, he could change or even bathe in public, only removing them in the privacy of an *atap* bathing-hut. The Chinese as a race are extremely modest in such matters.

In later years, uniform of khaki shorts, shirts, and military caps ornamented with one or three red stars was worn by everybody, but in the early days we wore what we could get – long or short trousers, shirts or Chinese coats, of any colour, the original material often patched with rubber latex – though there were some Chinese, usually outside workers, who always contrived to be immaculately turned out with spotless white shirts, creased trousers, scented hair, and the latest style in felt hats.

The girls, as is the way of Chinese girls, always looked attractive. Their straight black hair was cut in a short bob and their slim figures showed to advantage in wide black trousers and long-sleeved, high-necked smocks of gay colour and pattern. Jewellery and cosmetics were not used; but the girls were often to be seen plucking each other's eyebrows, and removing superfluous hair by a most painful-looking process in which one girl stretched a string figure-of-eight between her hands like a 'cat's cradle', then ran it up and down the other girl's face so that the hairs were caught between the two taut strings and pulled bodily out.

Shoes were always a problem, and most of the Chinese solved it by doing what they had done all their lives – going barefooted. About the camps they often wore home-made wooden clogs held on by rubber toe-strap and known as *terumpa*, from the curious musical noise made by the heels dragging on a hard road, for each clog of a pair invariably gives out a different note.

6.30 a.m.

Formal parade. All in the camp, except the sick, the cooks, and the men whose duty it was to sweep the huts and paths, fell in in two lines in front of the flagstaff at one end of the parade-ground. The flag was run up the mast and we saluted – the Chinese with fist clenched in Communist style, I alone with my fingers extended.

To begin with, we had a large Soviet flag with the hammer and sickle sewn on in white, but later these emblems gave way to three yellow stars representing the Chinese, Malay, and Indian elements in the republic – the Sakai and British, presumably, not being sufficiently important to count. Then we would sing 'The Red Flag,' Whu Bing conducting, having given us the first line – *'Pyow yang di hong-chi'* – so that at least we started at the same pitch. When sung with speed and vigour as a marching tune, this is an excellent song; but the Chinese were too apt to drag it out as a hymn. After 'The Red Flag' Lah Leo or Ah Chong gave a 'pep' talk which might last for as much as half an hour. Sometimes several of the leaders spoke in turn, on politics, camp discipline, Soviet war successes, etc.

7 a.m. to 8.30 a.m.

Military training, arms drill, grenade throwing, or just marching. The Chinese, though I have unlimited respect for their fighting spirit, are surely the most unmilitary nation in the world. I had never imagined it was possible for men to drill so badly. Having been brought up to appreciate smart drill, it always made me most uncomfortable to watch them. The leaders simply did not see faults, much less try to correct them.

The men in the camps had an extraordinary obsession for hard facts and irrelevant detail. They were not particularly interested in learning the rules of aiming or the correct use of cover and camouflage. But they wanted to know the exact distance at which a service rifle would kill, the precise muzzle-velocity of a tommy-gun, how many rounds per minute a Lewis gun fired, and the number of turns of rifling in the barrels of each kind of weapon – and they had little faith in an instructor who could not give the answers. Every man kept a small notebook, in which he would enter every kind of abstruse and useless detail. Yet they had no idea how to peep through, rather than over, cover, and they invariably tied their tin mugs to the outside of their packs so that every twig in the jungle drummed against them.

They were fascinated by machinery. As soon as we obtained any new kind of weapon they would strip it down with great skill and quite often put it together again so that it worked. At the same

129

time they entirely neglected safety precautions. I saw over a dozen accidents in this camp alone, some of which resulted in men being maimed for life. Grenades were an ever-present source of danger, and had it not been for the fact that most of the caps were dud, there would have been even more accidents. They used, however, to replace these with the percussion caps from Japanese rifle ammunition. Their normal way of carrying a primed grenade was to suspend it by the ring attached to the split pin, and every few days they would take them to pieces for cleaning – a process which I always watched with fascinated horror.

One of the greatest disabilities from which the guerillas suffered was that, except for the Japanese, they were quite the worst shots imaginable. Whereas an Englishman, from successive practice with a water-pistol, air-gun, and often a sporting gun, has from earliest youth been accustomed to closing one eye and aiming, many of the Chinese appeared to be handling a weapon for the first time, and about one man in three was constitutionally incapable of closing his left eye only. Others who could close only the right eye, used to shoot from the right shoulder and aim with the left eye – a considerable contortion – and as the service rifle was in any case too long in the stock and too heavy for them, it is not surprising that they could not hit the target.

8.30 a.m. to 9 a.m.

A short break for cleaning arms, etc.

9 a.m.

Breakfast. On the welcome sound of the whistle, each man would collect his tin mug and spoon, fall in on the parade-ground, and march down the steep muddy path to the cookhouse by the stream. We filled our mugs with watery rice from the four-gallon kerosene tin in which it had been boiled, and squatted in circles of six or seven round a huge bowl of boiled tapioca, cut into chunks, and a smaller bowl of vegetable – usually sweet-potato or other leaves. When sweet potato took the place of tapioca, it was boiled up with the rice. We would then wait for the whistle and fall to, each man taking tapioca and morsels of vegetable from the central bowls with his chopsticks. Only fifteen minutes were allowed for the meal, and there must be no talking. This meant that all meals had to be gobbled.

After the whistle went at the end of the quarter of an hour, each man had a drink of hot water – tea or coffee only appeared on very special occasions – washed his mug and spoon in the stream, and returned to his hut to gossip, smoke, read, or do whatever he wished. Meanwhile the girls ministered to the sick, and there would be a long queue of patients waiting to have their horribly ulcerated legs bathed in hot water to which a few drops of disinfectant had been added. Forceps and cotton wool were in fair supply, but one bottle of Lysol had to last the whole camp for several months.

9.30 a.m. to 10 a.m.

Discussion of the day's programme. The outline was allotted by patrol headquarters, but each section discussed how it was to be carried out. If a man criticised a leader's decision in private, he was liable to be severely punished; but in public he could say whatever he liked, and any disagreement with a superior could be taken to higher authority. The control of section commanders was thus very much undermined, and the men tended to go into committee about every decision instead of getting on with the job. This was particularly noticeable on a journey when the leader of the party was uncertain of the way: then they went into a huddle and discussed the matter in loud voices and at great length.

10 a.m. to 11 a.m.

Mandarin lesson in graded classes. The beginners started by tracing characters with a stick on the dust of the parade-ground. They were often old woodcutters or squatters who had never been taught to write, and as this class was often taken by a boy or girl fourteen or fifteen years of age, it was an amusing spectacle. More advanced classes read aloud from broadsheets printed in the camp or supplied by central headquarters – usually extracts from books on Russia. One of the first things I did was to set about learning Mandarin, and I was given special instructions by one of the girls. I am tolerably good at picking up a language if I set myself to it, but I

131

was astonished to find how little progress I seemed to make until one day Ah Ching explained what was really happening. Apparently Ah Chong did not want me to learn Mandarin. He had no desire for a British officer to be able to understand the various conferences that went on at headquarters, and it appeared that I was being taught a different Chinese dialect each week!

11 a.m. to 1 p.m.

Manual work: building huts, cutting down trees or splitting logs for firewood, bringing in supplies from hideouts, etc. In the early days the only available rice was from the large stocks which had been distributed by the British to prevent it falling into the hands of the Japs, and which contained a large amount of lime to preserve it; it also contained a phenomenal number of small black weevils. Every morning, therefore, half of us used to spend an hour winnowing this rice on flat plates and picking out the weevils and lime. The Chinese, when they were eating rice, never worried very much about the weevils – after all, they were largely made of rice even though they were crisp and black. At first I used to pick out every one I saw. Later I pushed them under so that I did not actually see them on my chop sticks, and finally I completely ignored them.

1 p.m. to 2 p.m.

General knowledge lecture: geography and history of Russia, Malaya, or China, citizenship and community life in the camps, etc. These lectures were given by one of the officers. There was one special lecture on Love which was always very well attended. Here they were told that love is quite a good thing – after all, you have to keep up the supply of little guerillas and Communists – but it must be excluded in the camps, as it interferes with the work of fighting the Japs. And they certainly lived up to the theory. Ah Chong, for instance, had been engaged since before the war to one of the girls in the camp – and a most attractive girl she was; but, though I lived in the same hut with them, I saw nothing in their demeanour to indicate a deep attachment.

The guerillas were remarkably unself-conscious and lacking in humour, and their behaviour in these matters of the heart is perhaps the best example of the high seriousness with which they took themselves. If, as sometimes happened, a married couple joined the guerillas, they would be put into different camps lest they should put ideas into the heads of the rest of us. If a man and a girl in the camp fell in love, the whole patrol would meet to discuss the matter, and they would seriously consider whether, in the interest of the work, it was good that they should marry. No other course was ever considered. The Chinese as a race are anything but undersexed, yet, as I have already said, the moral tone of the camps was extraordinarily high in every respect. Quarrels were practically unknown and if they occurred were immediately brought before a higher authority for arbitration. And in all the years I lived in the camps I did not come across a single instance of stealing, though such things as tobacco, books, pencils, eating utensils, and even blankets were considered as common property.

No one in the patrol was allowed to spend money on himself or to possess luxuries denied to the others. Ah Loy made himself very unpopular in this respect, as he used to get special rice from his brother's shop in Bentong on the plea that the limed rice made his joints swell, but he was made to share out the rice. Ah Ching, as quartermaster, used to buy whatever toothbrushes, cloth, shoes, sewing material, tobacco, etc., he could, and it was shared out equally among the men. The officers did, in fact, have a little extra food, especially the occasional cup of coffee and sugar, since they frequently worked till the small hours of the morning either in conference or composing lectures. When I had finished my first course of instruction I received – much to my surprise – a ten-dollar note so that I could buy myself a small present, and this note, like the widow's cruse, lasted me the whole year, for though I could now ask Ah Ching to buy me such things as cheroots, coffee, sugar, and a new toothbrush or piece of soap, I was never once allowed to pay for them.

2 p.m. to 3 p.m.

Lecture on public speaking and propaganda organisation. Everybody in the camp was taught to get up and make a speech on any subject. Nearly all the leaders were most able speakers, and though I could not understand what they said, I could see them emphasising each point, working up to a climax, and using all the devices of a trained orator.

One day in the headquarters hut Lah Leo was having a most impassioned argument with the junior singing instructor. As Lah Leo was making magnificent gestures with his outstretched hands, thumping on the bamboo table, and using in turn every possible modulation of his voice, I thought at least the younger man was being accused of some unspeakable crime, especially as he was almost in tears. However, I later discovered that the question was whether it was right or wrong for the girls to make underpants out of a large flag of the Chinese Republic which we happened to have in the camp. Lah Leo maintained that as they owed suzerainty to the Malayan and not the Chinese Republic, it was eminently justified, especially as there was no other cloth available, but his opponent considered it a flagrant insult to the Generalissimo.

3 p.m. to 4 p.m.

Personal work: washing and mending clothes, writing up lecture notes, special tuition, etc.

4 p.m. to 4.30 p.m.

Bath. The Chinese in the camps were certainly the cleanest people I have ever lived with – far cleaner than British soldiers. None would think of not cleaning his teeth at least once a day and, though the water in the mountain streams was bitterly cold, they would soap and wash themselves daily from head to foot behind the little *atap* screens made for this purpose. They did not find a deep pool and immerse themselves as an Englishman would have done, or even make a spout or shower with a pipe of bamboo. The Chinese way was to scoop up water in a mug or dipper and pour it over one's head. Each man had his towel-cum-washcloth and a piece of soap, and in the early days toothpaste was available – the commonest brand having the attractive name of 'Girl in the Moon.'

4.30 p.m.

Supper. This was the more important meal of the day. We had dry rice, usually mixed with sweet potato or tapioca, and latterly rationed to about a pint per man – a very great privation this, as a working Chinese can eat three pints at a sitting, and undiluted rice at that. The vegetable in the evening was rather more appetising than in the morning, and was often garnished with some dried or salt fish. The cooking in this camp was even plainer than was necessary, on the mistaken policy that guerillas must live hard and get used to a minimum diet. I am sure that as a result of malnutrition, the general efficiency of the men was only about 75 per cent.

5 p.m. to 6 p.m.

Singing lesson. The guerillas used singing very much as a vehicle for propaganda and for keeping up morale. These songs were, in general, unbelievably dreary and humourless, like the old Moody and Sankey hymns, and except by a few expert performers they were droned out with little rhythm and no expression. The tonic sol-fa scale was taught, and every man had to learn to read music using a numerical notation and to keep a small notebook into which he laboriously copied the words and music of the traditional songs. Whu Bing, who had a lovely tenor voice, trained a choir consisting of the twenty best musicians in the camp, men and women, which used to sing old Chinese folk music and part songs. These were a joy to listen to.

6 p.m.

Parade of all hands to take down the Colours and sing 'The Red Flag.'

6.15 p.m. to 7.15 p.m.

Silent hour, in which men wrote up their notes or read some improving book. The camp library contained a remarkable and varied selection of works and, just as in their medicine the ideal seemed to be one small pill or powder which was the elixir for all ills, so there were always a few encyclopaedic works which seemed to embrace all knowledge as their subject. I could not read the Chinese characters, but in these books there was an English translation of any quotation and there were English names under many small portraits, so that I could usually get some idea of what the book was about. I recall one page on which there were pictures of Joseph Chamberlain, Catherine the Great, Nietzsche, and Longfellow, and the only quotation was from Karl Marx – something about dialectical materialism!

7.15 p.m. to 9 p.m.

A general debate, usually in the men's hut, on such diverse subjects as: Is smoking a good thing? How did Malaya fall? Should Japanese prisoners be put to death or converted to Communism and liberated? Also very personal discussions and confessions on Oxford Group lines. In these debates everybody was encouraged to get up and express his opinions, and they certainly did so without any self-consciousness or reserve.

Some of the camps voluntarily decided to give up smoking, but I must admit that many of the Chinese were extremely heavy smokers, some of them even waking up several times in the night to roll and smoke a rank cigarette. Usually I smoked a pipe made out of gnarled bamboo root. This was one of the sweetest pipes I have ever possessed, but alas! the Japs got it eventually. When the Chinese smoked a pipe, which they did very occasionally, they would fill up the bowl with a cement made – oddly enough – of Ovaltine, leaving a cavity no thicker than a pencil. Some of the older men also smoked hubble-bubble pipes, in which the smoke is sucked through water contained in a bottle of bamboo.

9 p.m.

A whistle blew for lights out, and there was no more talking, except in the headquarters hut, where work usually continued until midnight.

From this account of the daily programme it will be seen that the spirit in the camps was one of great cheerfulness and enthusiasm, though of rather an adolescent nature. Although they took their politics, fighting the Japs, and especially themselves very seriously, they were always laughing, and when they played games, they made as much noise as a girls' school. But the greatest recreation was the camp concert. These were usually held to celebrate some Soviet or Chinese festival, and they were preceded by a day given up to speech-making followed by a feast for which the local *kampongs* provided a pig, a few ducks or fowls, and some coffee and sweet cakes. The cooks and a few extra assistants would spend all the afternoon preparing the meal, which would consist of un-limited dry rice, one dish of morsels of fat pork, perhaps with sweet-sour sauce, another of curried chicken, and a huge bowl of soup made from chicken giblets and flavoured with groundnuts and ginger. On these occasions the Spartan tradition of cooking was relaxed.

The audience sat on huge logs round three sides of the parade-ground, whose remaining end was curtained off with blankets hung over rattan lines to form a stage. Lighting was given by several lamps consisting of a floating wick in a glass container of coconut oil, though in some camps we had a pressure lamp which only appeared on these occasions. The concert started, inevitably, with a long speech from Ah Chong or Lah Leo explaining the occasion for our concert. The whole show would last between three and four hours. Whu Bing had arranged and rehearsed several plays and made a certain number of people promise to do a turn of some sort, but half the programme was usually extempore. The concert would begin, quietly, with a few of the everyday anti-Japanese or political songs. Then a Hokkien or Hailam was per-suaded to sing one of the folk songs of his own country, which was greeted with uproarious derision by the predominantly Hakka audience.

This might be followed by a demonstration of Chinese shadow-boxing – perhaps by Ah Ching, who was a great expert. The per-former leaped about the stage and halted in studied attitudes simi-lar to those of Balinese and Cambodian dancers, then struck at imaginary opponents and jumped away again with astonishing agility. In another variety of this art the exponent was armed with a stout pole and appeared to defend himself against a number of assailants at the same time. At this stage there might be calls for 'Chepmin-*tongtse*' (Comrade Chapman) and I would have to sing one of the camp songs in Chinese (half a dozen of which I had memorised though I had no idea what the words meant), an Eskimo song I had learned in Greenland or a yodelling solo. I also introduced wrestling, and in this being taller than all but two of the Chinese I always just contrived to hold my own.

Now there would be a short play in three acts. These were almost always variations of the same theme, and I soon got to know them by heart. In the first act a Chinese family discussed the war; the son of the house asked his father for permission to join the guerillas, but this was refused. In the next scene, the Japs – hideous and ridiculous little men with small black moustaches and huge spectacles – entered the house led by an informer. They ravished the daughter, tied up or killed the parents and, finding a bottle of *samsu*, became incapably drunk. In the final scene, the son of the house, who had run for aid into the jungle, reappeared with a band of guerillas who overpowered the Japs and rescued any compatriots who were still alive. After two hours of this there was a short halt for sweet coffee and cakes made of grated coconut, palm sugar, and spices. Then the concert continued in the same strain for another hour, to conclude at last with more speeches, and the 'Internationale' shouted by everybody into the still, starlit jungle night, and so to bed.

Although I was very happy in my personal contacts with the guerillas, had enough food to keep me alive, got plenty of excitement in exploring the jungle in search of game, and had enough work to keep me busy, I suffered all the time from a sense of frustration and impotence. In the first place, as I had proved, the Jap was a sitting target for a trained and enthusiastic guerilla fighter, yet it was now obviously the wisest policy not only to leave him alone myself but to preach evasion tactics to the Chinese. It was also very embarrassing for me to live with people who had lost every shred of faith in the British, considered that they had been badly let down by us, and did not hesitate to say so. They questioned not only our military competence but our very integrity and courage. I was fortunate in that I was known to have had no part in the much-maligned pre-war Government of Malaya and was thus exonerated from blame.

Once I had thrown in my lot with the guerillas, I was virtually their prisoner and lost all freedom of movement. In the first place they considered themselves personally responsible for my safety, and as I knew the position of more of their camps than did any single one of them, they dared not risk my being caught and tortured by the Japanese. I had collected a vast amount of information about the Japanese occupation and knew that it would be of enormous value if only I could get it out of the country, but owing to the language difficulty I felt I could only do this through guerilla headquarters or by getting in touch with other Europeans who knew the country and languages. But the Chinese put every obstacle in the way of my leaving the camp. I could easily have gone and lived in a *kampong* or with the Sakai, or even returned to live alone in the jungle at Sungei Sempan, where at least I had an English-speaking friend, plenty of food, and a wireless set to boot. But none of these things was what I had been put into the jungle to do. I felt I could have helped them so much – and yet for petty political reasons I was never allowed to do so. It seemed to me that a few of the leaders at least in the early months, were more concerned with the establishment of the Republic of Malaya than with fighting the Jap.

Then, if I were to make plans to escape from Malaya, where should I go? My only source of information about the progress of the war was the Japanese newspapers printed in English. From these I gathered that Burma had fallen within a month of Singapore; the Dutch East Indies had gone; the Philippines had gone; Australia had gone; the whole of Bengal had been evacuated; the British fleet had been sunk off Ceylon; the Germans had broken through the Caucasus and were preparing to shake hands with the Japanese in India; Britain had been so badly blitzed that the Government had gone to Canada; all China had gone. Where then could I go? The guerilla news-sheets, on the other hand, were equally fantastic in the opposite direction. The Japanese papers, though I knew they were pure propaganda, had such a depressing psychological effect that after a time I refused to look at them.

Another source of frustration was scientific rather than military. On every other expedition I had made I had collected birds and insects for the British Museum, plants or seeds for the herbarium at

Kew, or specimens for the Cambridge Anthropological Museum. Here in Malaya, though I had the most wonderful opportunities for such work, I had so little previous experience of the tropics that I did not know what was rare and what was commonplace. And as far as the aborigines were concerned, my lack of information was an even greater handicap, for I could have kept myself fully occupied and contented studying them and thereby making a valuable contribution to knowledge.

Apart from not being able to get on with the job or even to employ my time usefully, my greatest privation – ignoring the lack of reading material – was the absence of sunlight and colour. Because I am unmusical, perhaps, I am particularly susceptible to colour. In the Pahang jungle we seldom saw the sky. In the daytime only small islands of sunlight filtered through the leafy canopy overhead, and at night it was rare to be able to see enough stars to identify more than one or two constellations. In the camps we dared not cut down any of the larger trees or even remove the bamboos and saplings over the huts themselves, for fear of being observed by enemy aircraft which daily passed above us. The monotony of the colouring in the jungle was most depressing, for there were no Sakai clearings near the Pahang camps, and only where the jungle on one side of a valley had been cut down can one look across and appreciate the wonderful variety of colours that goes to make up its gay and variegated roof. Only in the invisible tree-tops, far above our heads, were the brilliant flowering creepers and orchids, the gay butterflies and rainbow-hued birds that I had always associated with the tropical jungle.

Much as I admired and liked the Chinese, they could be most exasperating to live with, especially if one were sick and undernourished. As I have said, the evasion and equivocation of some of the leaders drove me to distraction, and I never knew whether they were telling the truth or not. Even friends like Whu Bing and Ah Ching were precluded by the Chinese sense of politeness from giving me any information which they thought I should not like. Again, life in one of their huts was sheer bedlam. There was no such thing as privacy, and the Chinese – fortunate people – seemed to have no sensibility whatsoever. In the headquarters hut I might be sitting at my desk making a life-sized portrait of Maxim Gorky or Karl Marx from a vignette the size of a postage stamp in one of their books, watched by a group of the men who would be volubly admiring my drawing and making helpful suggestions. Lah Leo would be having an impassioned argument with several others. Whu Bing would be learning a new song, several more might be practising other songs, a mechanic filing furiously and nonchalantly at a live round of ammunition to extract the cap for some purpose, and several others sitting in the medley absorbed in some tattered tome and monotonously reading the characters aloud to themselves, completely oblivious of their surroundings.

Even if one of the men were lying seriously sick with malaria, his compatriots would practise bugling in the hut, smoke cheroots, and stamp across the springy bamboo sleeping-benches. The fever-stricken victim would show no malice, and in justice it must be admitted that the offenders would expect to be treated exactly the same if they were ill. Another Chinese custom which infuriated me at first was their way of roaring with laughter if anybody hurt himself. Even the victim, who had perhaps accidentally shot himself in the foot, slashed his knee with a *parang*, or been stung by a hornet, would join in the general merriment.

What the Chinese really thought of me I do not know. Certainly I was a source of considerable interest. Many of them had never before seen an Englishman at such close quarters, or so intimately, and when I first joined the Menchis patrol, they used to stand and gaze at me as if I were some new kind of animal. The Chinese have a tremendous respect for academic learning, and the fact that I was a graduate of Cambridge University impressed them much more than my being a major in the British Army or the fact that I had specialised in the very type of fighting they would have to do. But, though they may not have appreciated my military qualifications, I enjoyed a great reputation as a marksman, and perhaps my greatest practical contribution to the camp was the amount of fresh meat in the form of deer, pig, and above all monkeys, that I contributed to the larder. I believe it was a great source of surprise and disappointment to the gueril
as that, though I identified myself with them as a comrade in arms, I made no attempt to accept their party views or aspirations and resolutely refused to discuss politics.

CHAPTER NINE

The Bandit Camp in Johore

(SEE MAP NO. 2)

Towards the end of 1942 the Japanese, having subdued the *kampong* Chinese by systematic torture and massacre, were concentrating their efforts against the guerillas in the jungle. Fortunately the traitor Chu Mei had never been allowed to visit the Menchis camp, but he must have known its approximate location, and ever since the disastrous night when Haywood had been killed, the Japs had spared no effort in trying to run us to ground. By September strong patrols of Japanese accompanied by Indians and Malays frequently entered the jungle from the road to the east of us and approached dangerously near our camp. It now became almost impossible for anybody to go outside to collect food, and had it not been for the supplies of rice we had saved from better days and for the tapioca grown by the Sakai, we should have had to move even earlier than we did.

About September 20 the whole patrol migrated to a new area on the other side of the Menchis-Karak road in the foothills, four miles due east of the 96th Mile. We all carried very heavy loads, and the journey, though only six miles in a straight line, took us three days, as we had to make a detour to the north to avoid the vicinity of Menchis. It was all jungle going except for the crossing of the road, so we could travel by daylight.

It rained practically all the time on this journey, and under Ah Loy's incompetent leadership, we invariably went on until it was too late to find a good camp site or even build a lean-to shelter. On the first evening, as a result of half the party taking the wrong turning, we were benighted on the summit of a high ridge far from water and not only suffered from the bitter cold but from hunger and thirst as well. The second night we spent in a deserted Sakai village and, though we were grateful for the shelter, their huts

142

were infested by such a plague of small cockroaches that sleep was almost impossible. We dashed across the road at dusk and then, because some of the party were missing, spent two miserable hours crouching in pouring rain in the rubber being gradually devoured by a swarm of mosquitoes. After this, presumably through another hitch in the plans, we had to make our way in darkness across a strip of newly felled jungle which had been burned off so recently that incandescent tree-trunks stood up in the night like the pillars of flame that guided the Israelites when they too were wandering in the wilderness.

We had the greatest difficulty in crossing the flooded Pertang river, where one of the girls was washed away and very nearly drowned, but at last we reached our new camp about 1,000 feet above sea level at the headwaters of the Sungei Menchis. This camp site was most unsatisfactory, as it seemed to be in the path of violent gales known in Malaya as *Sumatras*. On the very day we reached it, one of these storms occurred. It was a terrifying experience. First we heard a loud roaring noise in the distance which gradually increased in volume until it sounded like a squadron of fighter aircraft zooming just overhead – indeed, I thought it was an air-raid, especially as the Chinese started shouting excitedly and all rushed outside. In the narrow path of the *Sumatra* huge trees were blown to the ground and rotten branches came crashing down right and left. One tree fell right across the headquarters hut, and a sick man, whom we had all forgotten, was decapitated.

This camp was unfortunate for me also. One day I was out hunting alone, as was my habit. I had followed a timber track down to the larger path beside the Sungei Pertang and was walking very cautiously along it when somebody fired at me with a shotgun. A pellet lacerated the end of my right thumb, three were embedded in the stock of my shotgun, and several more entered my right buttock and thigh. I never saw or heard anything of my assailant, but I imagine he was a Malay out for the reward that the Japs had offered for my body dead or alive. The moment I felt the pain and heard the explosion I instinctively turned and ran before he had time to fire the second barrel or reload, and I am ashamed to say I dropped my gun and left it – though I collected it again next day. The wounds gave me great pain for some hours, but fortunately the pellets had only lodged in muscle and must have been fired at considerable range, for they were fairly easily extracted by Ah Loy and Ah Ching with a pocket knife. I lost considerable 'face' for leaving my gun behind and for being so stupid as to follow a track so near the outside.

After we had been in this camp a few weeks, three Chinese informers were brought in. Two, after being burned with brands and beaten almost to death with rattans, were finished off with a bayonet in the grave that had already been prepared for them; but the third, whose guilt was less manifest or because they still hoped to get more information out of him, was kept with his hands tied behind him for further 'trial' on the following day. Somehow he managed to escape during the night, and as he knew our camp and all about us, we had to move at once.

We now migrated to a much more pleasant part of the jungle some six miles further northwest at the end of a low spur. To reach the new camp, we travelled continuously for a day and a night – the nocturnal part of the journey being necessary to traverse Peng Ann and Kampong Padah rubber estates. Here there were several vast *atap* huts housing at least a thousand Chinese coolies. These men had been prepared for our arrival by our outside propaganda workers, and though a few of the weaker brethren had to be eliminated from time to time to prevent their informing, they kept us well supplied with food. A party of about twenty recruits joined the patrol from among these coolies, but none of those who did not sign on as full-time guerilla was ever allowed to visit the camp.

Because of the excellent arrangements that had been made by our outside workers, the food was very good in this camp. The hunting also was much better here, and when I was not training the new recruits, I used to explore the jungle in search of pig, *kijang* (barking deer), or monkeys. In the swamps of the Ayer Palong there were a great many mud turtles, which are about the size of half a football. The moment you saw a slight cloudiness in the mud, as if something had just moved there, you had to make a scoop with your hand and with any luck you would find a turtle. These make most delicious soup, and the meat is very tender and tasty too. We also ate snakes – whose meat is excellent, being similar in taste and texture to a mixture of chicken and lobster.

Another delicacy was the meat of the monitor lizard – a reptile six or seven feet in length. Its eggs also were very tasty.

It was near this camp that I had my only adventure with a bear. I was hunting in a valley I had not hitherto visited, about two hours' walk from the camp. As I was after monkey, I carried my old single-barrelled shotgun. This weapon had been made in Connecticut many, many years ago, and a peculiarity of it was that each time the gun was 'broken' to put in a new cartridge, it came completely apart, so that I was left with the barrel and fore-end in one hand and the stock in the other. Since the cartridges had swollen in the damp jungle conditions, the only way to extract the empty cases was to ram them out with a stick. At that time I had only four cartridges: a lethal ball – consisting of a single large round lead shot; an S.G. – large buckshot – which had already misfired once; and two No. 4, which were all right for monkeys but not much good for anything bigger. I was walking down a steep track, when I disturbed a large greyish animal which ran off with a rolling gait quite unlike the precipitous dash of a pig. A glance at the footprints – just like those of a man's bare feet, but with all the toes of the same size – confirmed that it was indeed a bear. I went through the complicated movements of changing the No. 4 shot for the lethal ball and hurried after the tracks, which were very easy to follow.

Suddenly I heard a hideous roaring from further down the valley. It came from more than one animal, and sounded to me exactly like the noise in the lion-house at the Zoo just before feeding-time. I went cautiously towards this din, and all at once I saw an old bear coming silently towards me with his wicked black head and round ears swinging from side to side. He had been digging in the red clay, and this had stained the white on his muzzle. I went down on one knee and waited until he was only ten yards from me, and as his throat was out of sight, aimed straight between the eyes. I actually saw a white streak appear in the dark fur of his forehead, but the round ball must have glanced off without penetrating the skull, for the bear, far from stopping, came straight at me with a roar of fury. I dashed away up the hill and, as I paused to take out the empty case and put in the doubtful S.G. cartridge, I heard him milling around in the undergrowth and growling ominously. When I returned he had disappeared, though a sparse trail of blood led into a dark thicket where two trees had fallen across a small ravine. After a moment's hesitation I decided I had not spent a year in the jungle to be killed by a bear – a Jap would have been a different matter – and I ran back to the camp for a rifle. By the time I returned, accompanied by Ah Ching and several others, a downpour of rain had obliterated all tracks, but we entered the thicket. Above the tremendous roar of the falling rain I heard a thud, as of a sack falling on to soft ground, and hurrying to where I thought the noise came from, I found fresh blood on the leaves – but we saw no more of the animal, though I returned again next day.

This camp, being a little more than three miles from the Karak-Menchis road, was never very secure, and after three very happy months here we migrated again. We moved in the first week of November 1942, going twelve miles in a northeasterly direction to the very camp site from which the patrol had been driven out by the Japs six months before. The journey took us right across the low-lying swampy jungle of Kemasul Forest Reserve, and most of the way we were able to follow an excellent track. It crossed the winding Pertang river no less than eight times, but as the course of the stream was fairly level – it drops only a hundred feet in ten miles – there was little danger of anybody being drowned. We were very much afraid of crocodiles, which were reported to have taken a Sakai only a month before. Although we travelled from dawn to dusk each day the journey took us three days. It was a route regularly used by the guerillas on their way between the Menchis and Triang camps and consequently there were *atap* shelters we could use and even little huts built right up in the trees to be out of the way of elephants.

The new camp, in which the patrol were to live undisturbed for about a year, was the best natural site of all those I visited in the country. I could well understand why they had returned, although it was known to the Japs and Malays. The huts were built just over the summit of an isolated saddleback hill which rises 821 feet out of untracked swampy jungle. Though only three miles southwest of the corner of Semantan Estate, it was five very long miles from Mentakab, the nearest town, and four miles from the above-mentioned track and from the Karak-Mentakab road.

The guard post was sited on the brow of a steep five-hundred-foot slope, and the huts nestled in a little basin ten minutes' walk and two to three hundred feet lower down on the north side of this horseshoe ridge. The mouth of this little valley was entirely shut in by almost impenetrable rattan and thorn jungle, with more creepers to the square yard than I had believed possible. Although we soon cut a path through to the huge area of swampy jungle that surrounds the headwaters of the Belengu river, it would have been virtually impossible for anyone but a Sakai to have found the camp from that direction.

One great joy in this camp was that we frequently had as much fresh fish as we could eat. When we arrived here the rivers were fairly low and we poisoned several miles of water with *tuba* root (or derris). Several man-loads of *tuba*, which appeared to be the fine roots of a vine, were brought up from the *kampongs*, and all available men spent several hours on the flat rocks beside the river pounding these with wooden cudgels. This produced enough milky fluid to fill several four-gallon kerosene tins. The solution of *tuba* root was then emptied into the river and allowed to flow downstream. Almost immediately small fry were seen to be in difficulties, and soon quite large fish floated belly-upwards to the surface. Very often, especially in deep pools, the fish were only slightly stunned and we had to dive in and grapple them with our hands. At one time, after an unusually long drought, the rivers were so low that we were able to capture enormous quantities of fish by the simple expedient of emptying out the water. This method of fishing was employed in the deep peaty rivers which wound their way through low-lying ground and, owing to the drought, had already ceased to flow. The Chinese would build a series of earthen dams across the river and then work downstream, emptying a section at a time.

I became extremely fit and could travel and carry loads as well as any of the Chinese. Though I was never allowed to visit the *kampongs* where our food was grown, I used to meet the carrying-parties and help to bring back the bags of rice, sweet potatoes, and vegetables up the steep hill to the camp. My existence was so secure in this sheltered valley that I suffered from boredom, and to add some spice to life and at the same time practise myself in the difficult art of jungle navigation, I used to go out and deliberately get lost so that I was forced to use all my resource and energy to find the way home again. Sometimes I failed to get back before dark, and on several occasions had to spend a night out.

This was most valuable experience. At first, as light faded in the jungle and I was far from home and completely lost I would be overcome by panic. I seemed to be an intruder in a hostile and predatory world. The unaccountable snapping of a twig and the stealthy rustling of leaves would prey upon my nerves until I was so certain I was being followed by a tiger that a cold sweat would break out all over my body and the small hairs on the back of my neck would creep with fear, and I found myself going faster and faster until I was running. Then I would have to take myself firmly in hand and convince myself by steady reasoning that there was nothing there but imagined terrors. After a time my confidence grew and, armed with a *parang*, a box of matches, and a piece of rubber to start a fire going, and a rifle, I would be perfectly happy in the knowledge that if I was benighted I could build a fire, make a small shelter of *atap* or wild banana leaves, and with the unlimited fresh water that the jungle provides, could last for a week if necessary until I found my way back to the camp.

At this time it was very difficult to get rubber shoes of any kind, as the Japs did not allow them to reach the shops, so I had to accustom myself to going barefooted in the jungle, a process which took about three months. On paths I could travel fast in absolute silence, but with no rubber sole to take up the concussion, one had to be very careful not to make a thudding noise on hard beaten earth. Off the track one was forced to go carefully, and when hunting this was a great advantage. At first I was afraid of putting my foot on a snake, centipede, or scorpion, but most of the Chinese and all the Sakai went barefooted in the jungle, and I had never heard of them treading on anything worse than thorns, and by a fortunate providence the soles of one's feet never seemed to become infected. The only time I ever seriously injured my feet was against sharp stones or stumps in deep mud.

It was even more difficult to get English books near Mentakab than it had been elsewhere, and the lack of reading matter was always my greatest privation. But I was kept very busy in this camp, as I ran a six weeks' course of training for section commanders and also helped the leaders with their propaganda. At Lah Leo's request I drew from various photographs and sketches a series of life-sized portraits of Stalin, Lenin, Marx, Engels, and other famous Communists, also Mao Tse Tung and Chu Teh, the 8th Route Army Leaders, and Churchill and Roosevelt. These drawings were used to ornament the camp lecture-room, which was large enough to seat the full hundred members of the patrol. They were a great success, and I had to make several more sets for the neighbouring camps at Triang and in Negri Sembilan. The outside propaganda workers also asked me to make a number of posters for use among the Chinese, Malays, and Tamils, and I produced a whole series of coloured posters, each four feet by three, showing the iniquities of the Japanese regime. Whu Bing continued to produce his fortnightly camp magazine, an intricate work of art about four feet square, which was hung on the notice-board in the lecture-room. I used to help to illustrate this with coloured drawings.

When I had first joined the Menchis patrol I asked if I could be allowed to publish a paper in English to be read by the better-educated members of each race in Malaya. This request had to be approved by general headquarters, and it was not until we were installed in the Mentakab camp four months later that permission came through and I started to publish *Truth (Old Order): A News-Letter for all English-speaking Malayans*. The first number, which I wrote in longhand and cyclostyled in blue and red ink, came out in November 1942. Although we only printed a hundred copies of *Truth* owing to scarcity of paper, it had a very wide circulation, since each copy was handed on after being read – a proceeding which was accelerated by the knowledge that to be found in possession of it would have meant certain death. The leader in my second number was followed (by request) by an article on India, but this smacked too much of Imperialism and was suppressed. It was typical of the Chinese or Communist way of doing things that instead of telling me that the article was unsuitable or asking me to rewrite it, they printed the full number of copies and told me that they had been distributed, and it was only by accident that I later discovered the whole issue had been burned. And that was the end of *Truth*.

The hunting in this camp was even better than it had been at the last one. Almost every morning I used to go out alone as soon as it was light enough to follow a track – about 6 a.m., though it would not be possible to see the sights of a rifle in the jungle for another hour. In the thick jungle where there are no tapioca clearings or rubber estates to provide them with food, the pig – judging by their tracks, which I must have followed for hundreds of miles – almost invariably feed singly. When they are in herds, they can be fairly easily located and approached by a skilful hunter, as the noise they make when feeding is considerable, but a lone pig will lift his snout to listen and sniff the air intently every few minutes, and he is almost certain to hear the approach of a man long before he is within range. After following a track with the utmost caution for several hours, all one hears is a sharp bark and a sudden precipitous rush. After his first fright the pig usually stops and there is a loud blowing noise as he clears his nostrils the better to catch the scent of his adversary. Once he is alarmed, it is impossible to get a second chance, even if you wait for half an hour to let the pig recover from his fright.

Elephant were very plentiful in this area. At night they would sometimes come so close to the camp that we all had to turn out and light fires and beat empty tins to frighten them away. The noise they made was terrifying – not only their tremendous trumpeting, which started on a shrill note like a horse whinnying and went in one long roar right down the scale to a deep reverberating growl which seemed to set the whole jungle vibrating, but the mighty crashing sound as they dragged huge creepers bodily off the trees and pulled down fifty-foot bamboos as if they were asparagus stalks. Where elephant have been feeding, the whole jungle is devastated as if it had been swept by a tornado. Where they have bathed, the trees and foliage are plastered with mud to a height of ten or fifteen feet. If we had to follow in their wake, we ourselves were soon completely covered with grey mud and clay.

I must confess to a great respect for elephant, not only because they seemed to be so much at home in the jungle that I felt it would be impossible to elude them if they wanted to catch me, but also because of their uncanny way of becoming invisible in the jungle and disappearing without a sound. The larger and more intelligent an animal is, the more I dislike shooting it, and I hated the idea of killing an elephant, whose intelligence is in many ways superhuman; besides, at this time only about one in three of our rifle cartridges went off and the cordite had surely deteriorated from the damp. Hence it would have been a most uninsurable occupation to have gone elephant-shooting with my old service rifle. I was therefore particularly glad when the Chinese told me that elephant meat was inedible (though I knew they were mistaken) and there was thus no need for me to shoot them. But somehow the animal – or the danger of his presence – fascinated me.

One day I was returning alone from tracking a *rusa* (a large deer), when I heard a strange loud intermittent hissing noise which, for some reason, filled me with fear. I crept up a stream towards it and, suddenly turning a corner, was astonished to see only fifty yards away an elephant standing in the water spraying her 'child' with water from her trunk. This was the first time I had ever seen a wild elephant, though I had often heard them, and I was impressed more than ever by the fantastic shape of the animal, with its enormous head and ears, its sinuous writhing trunk, and its ridiculous little tail.

On another occasion, when I was out after pig, I heard an elephant trumpeting quite near me and turned aside to see if I could get a view of him. This part of the jungle was very thick indeed and the visibility was only about ten yards, so I had to approach very close before I could see anything. These elephant – for there was a whole herd of them – were making the most extraordinary variety of noises: one seemed to be hammering against a tree-trunk with his tusks, another was pulling at creepers which came away or broke with a loud rending noise, while a third was making a tremendous thudding sound, presumably by hitting the ground with his trunk. Elephant, as one would expect from any animal that puts away many hundredweights of vegetable matter per day, seem to suffer from violent indigestion, and their flatulence, belching, and abdominal rumblings must be heard to be believed.

Before I could get a view of one of these elephant they seemed to pick up my scent, for after a single loud bellow which set every leaf – and certainly myself – trembling, the whole herd began to move, and the moment I saw the undergrowth and creepers sway-ing I turned and ran for my life. In this part of the jungle there seemed to be only small trees, which the elephant could have trodden down without noticing them, or huge trunks which were impossible to climb; but at last I found a tree festooned with creepers and managed to run up it like a monkey. I hung there with my rifle slung over one shoulder as the herd crashed past below me, and I just caught a glimpse of a huge grey back on either side of my tree. At the time I was convinced that the elephant were hunting me, but later I discovered that I had approached from the direction of the track by which they had entered the thicket and, having caught my scent, they were probably only running back by the way they had come.

Perhaps the most dangerous of all the animals in the jungle is the *seladang*, the wild ox or bison of Malaya. This huge animal will sometimes attack at sight, and its cunning and persistence when wounded are proverbial. Though I often saw them, I only had one shot at a *seladang* in all my years in the jungle, and that was in the huge swamp to the south of the Mentakab camp. That day I was out after porcupine and therefore carried my old single-barrelled shotgun. I was walking very quietly along a hunting track I had cut, when I suddenly saw a huge brown animal standing well above the bushes on which it was browsing. I noticed which way it was moving and worked round so as to intercept it. Then, having loaded an S.G. cartridge (buckshot), I went down on one knee to wait. A peculiarity of this gun was that the safety-catch had to be pushed forward and then eased back slightly, otherwise it would jam.

Suddenly the *seladang*, who must have caught my scent, hur-ried past me at a fast walk, only eight or ten yards in front of me. There was a strong sweet smell of cattle, and I caught a glimpse of a huge rough-coated bull with his head and massive grey horns held high and stretched straight out as if sniffing the air. So large was he that as I aimed just behind his shoulder, I seemed to be pointing the gun uphill. I pulled the trigger, but in my excitement I had automatically pushed the safety-catch forward again. It jammed, and there was only a sharp click. The *seladang* crashed through the undergrowth like a tank, and for some seconds afterwards I heard the noise of his bursting through the jungle, getting fainter and fainter in the distance. For nights afterwards I used to dream about this bitter disappointment.

As the weeks went by I grew tired of teaching this one patrol. Since it no longer seemed possible to get in touch with general headquarters or even to re-establish contact with the Selangor Group, I turned my thoughts to those Europeans whom I knew to be still in the jungle, with a view to joining up with them and planning some way of getting out of the country. Alone, and with such poor command of Chinese and Malay, I felt it was impossible to escape. I thought that if only I could find some kindred spirit, who could speak one or more of the local languages, we might reach the coast and set sail for India with the northeast monsoon in the following year.

The Chinese told me it was quite impossible for me to reach Perak at that time, though in October I had received a letter from Chrystal. It had been heavily censored, but I gathered that he, Robinson, and Quayle were all right, though the two latter had been very ill. He told me they had moved to a new place where they had met an Englishman called Pat Noone, and that he (Chrystal) and Noone had left the guerillas. Noone, whose name I knew though I had never met him, was a noted expert on the Sakai. The guerillas had often told me that he was with one of their patrols in the north, and I had more than once sent a letter to him in an attempt to arrange a meeting.

I had also had several letters through the Triang patrol from two Englishmen who signed themselves Cotterill and Tyson. Ah Loy told me they were living with some Chinese bandits (a term used by the guerillas for any Chinese of a rival political party) near Segamat in north Johore – much too far away for me to pay them a visit. There were also persistent rumours of large numbers of Australian soldiers still living near Titi in Negri Sembilan, and of a party in Johore who had a wireless transmitter and were so independent that they refused to let any Chinese into their camp.

Soon after we had reached the Mentakab camp I was asked to go over to Triang to train the two guerilla patrols there. I welcomed this plan, as I hoped it might be possible to go on from there to Negri Sembilan and Johore. The Triang camp proved to be six miles south of the small town of Triang on the Sungei

Mengkuang. The airline distance from camp to camp was twenty-five miles, but the route we had to follow was well over fifty. However, I was then extremely fit, and with Ah Ching and the strongest of the runners as companions, I did the journey in two days, starting as soon as it was light and finishing long after sunset.

We left Mentakab camp at 5.45 a.m., but in spite of the early hour the whole camp paraded to see us off and to listen to the inevitable speeches from Lah Leo and Ah Loy. The whole day was spent in the low, rolling, swampy jungle of the Kemasul Forest Reserve, usually following its boundary path, which provided excellent walking, though it had not been cleared since the occupation and we were continually having to make small detours to avoid fallen trees. We met the Triang river just as darkness fell. We now had to be particularly careful, as the Japs, who knew the guerillas were using this route, used to come up the river from Triang by motorboat and stop and search every Chinese they met. The river here was a hundred yards wide and very deep and swift, but the runner knew where a sampan was hidden. Having waited till it was almost dark, we set off downstream, keeping well out in the middle of the river to avoid underwater snags. Suddenly we heard a commotion on the further shore, and I could make out a line of crouching men. At the same moment I heard the rattle of bolts, and thinking it was a Jap ambush, I automatically jumped into the water, but kept a hand on the gunwale of the boat as the bullets screamed overhead. The men turned out to be a party of Triang guerillas, who were waiting to catch an informer. Whether they were aiming at us or merely trying to stop us I do not know, but they did not even hit the boat. All Ah Ching had to say was that the Triang river was full of crocodiles and I really ought to be more careful!

We slept in a Chinese *kampong* that night and set off again before dawn next morning, accompanied by the six Triang guerillas who had so frightened us the night before. For some reason we returned across the river and followed a series of tracks along the northern bank and then crossed it again in the rubber at the edge of Triang Estate. For the rest of the day we travelled southwards, parallel to the railway, either in the rubber or at the edge of the jungle, until we reached Mengkuang Halt, where we lay up until dark and then crossed the line. We slept in a hut on the outskirts of the village, intending to proceed to the camp, which was four miles to the southeast, on the following day, but at about 2 a.m. all the *kampong* dogs started barking, and we took to the jungle. Next day we heard that some Japs had come down the railway and searched the village, probably as a result of the shooting on the Triang river.

In the darkness we made our way through the rubber and along a jungle track until we emerged into a huge clearing. It was a most wonderful experience for me to see a sky full of stars after living in the jungle for more than four months. As day broke I found we were in a large tapioca plantation where starch and flour were made. We walked through acres of tapioca for over an hour, and jungle-cock, the first I had heard, were crowing from all directions. Their call is exactly like that of a domestic fowl, but ends more abruptly. The guard post of the camp was at the jungle edge over-looking the tapioca and palm-oil plantations. While we were still half a mile away, I picked up the white shirt of the sentry even without my glasses – showing that these guerillas had as little idea of camouflage as the others I had lived with.

In this patrol there was about a hundred men, and another sixty lived in a smaller camp a few miles further north. Here I met many old friends from Menchis. As the camp was supported by the prosperous Chinese of the tapioca plantations, the food was excellent, though they complained very much of the lack of rice. I was most warmly welcomed here, and every morning the Hailam quartermaster used to come round and see that I was supplied with coffee, sugar, cheroots, and even *samsu* (spirit distilled from rice).

I was disabled for six weeks with ulcerated legs resulting from leech-bites, cuts, and scratches I had sustained on the journey from Mentakab. On my shins and ankles I soon had about twenty stinking and suppurating sores about the size of a shilling and a quarter of an inch deep. Pus poured out of them and, as a result of the infection, the lymphatic glands in my groin were so inflamed and painful that I could hardly walk, much less go hunting, as I was longing to do. Only Chinese medicines were available, and none of these seemed to do any good, though one, which they called *kow-yok*, had hitherto proved most effective. This was a substance like Stockholm tar which they smeared on cloth or paper and left as a covering over the wound. Not only did it draw out the poison, but it remained in position even under water and protected the wounds, which were extraordinarily tender, from being touched by twigs or attacked by leeches.

The Japs kept a very strict control of Western medicines such as quinine and antiseptics, but they had overlooked the fact that Epsom-salts compresses are the best possible cure for poisoned wounds, and I could obtain an unlimited supply of these crystals. Cotton wool was unobtainable, but kapok pods made a good substitute, and I used to apply pads of this soaked in a concentrated solution of Epsom salts and kept in place with pieces of palm leaf. In spite of this treatment the wounds kept open week after week, and then at last started to heal up suddenly for no apparent reason. Certain food, such as pumpkin and rotten fish and above all *samsu*, had an immediate bad effect on the wounds and I had to give them up altogether. Many of the Chinese in this camp suffered from the same trouble, but they were so tough they could go on working as usual.

Unlike the other camps I had visited, this one was built on a low hill less than 200 feet above sea level and was surrounded by swampy and miasmal jungle. Consequently most of the men suffered from chronic malaria and other strange fevers. The leader of the patrol died while I was there, and several others were so ill that they had to leave the camp and return to their homes. This particular fever was supposed to be caused by curious white hairs with forked roots which grew on the sufferer's chest, and the cure was to rub this part of the body with fowl's feathers dipped in hot water until the white hairs came away. I have actually seen the offending hairs after treatment but where they came from I cannot say. If these hairs are not eradicated in this way, the patient will die – and he usually did. Another thing that made this camp most unhealthy was that the stream from which we obtained water was black and stinking from the refuse of a tapioca factory which entered it.

One consolation was that even if I had been able to travel, I could not have gone on to Johore until January 1943, for in late November and early December it rained day after day as I never thought it could rain even in Malaya. The Pahang river, fifteen miles to the north, overflowed its banks, and our own streams rose over twenty feet, so that we found ourselves on an island and had to use sampans to reach the *kampongs* to obtain food. However, there was now excellent bathing within a hundred yards of the camp, and the fact that I spent at least an hour a day in the water probably cured my ulcerated legs.

The day after I arrived in this camp I set about running a course of lectures, for the men had absolutely no military knowledge and were very keen to learn. In the British Army manner I wanted to give a concentrated course to the section commanders and other officers who, I presumed, would be more intelligent than the others, and to let them assimilate the knowledge and then pass it on to the men in their section. But when I went into the large *atap* lecture-room, I was astonished to find none of the leaders present. On expostulating at this, I was told that if the officers were to be seen at my lectures by their men it would be a confession of ignorance and they would lose face! The patrol leader was quite adamant on this point, and the only way I could get over it was to talk to the men in the morning and then to give the same lecture to the leaders in the privacy of the headquarters hut in the evening after the men had gone to bed.

When I broached the question of my going down to Johore to visit Cotterill and Tyson, I was surprised and delighted to find that the suggestion was welcomed. It appeared that this camp was on the Palong river in the point of Johore that runs northwards between Negri Sembilan and Pahang. They were with a party of Chinese bandits who were extremely well armed. The Pahang group were very keen to 'convert' these robbers and draw them into the fold – and at the same time secure some of their weapons and ammunition. But there were two difficulties. The only route known to them was hazardous for them and quite impossible for a European. Also, it took between two and three weeks. The question was: Could I, from my knowledge of map-reading, find a safer and more direct way? The other difficulty was that the envoys they had already sent had been so frightened by the bandits that after a few days there they had slipped out of the camp at night and returned without having accomplished anything. Could I use my influence through Cotterill and Tyson – who seemed to be on excellent terms with the bandits – to win them over?

Fortunately they had a map of Malaya, though it was on a small scale. This showed that although the distance was more than thirty miles in a straight line, the boundary between Pahang and Negri Sembilan led across the jungle almost from camp to camp. Provided the path which must originally have been cut by the surveyors had been kept open, we could use it for about five-sixths of the total distance and the journey could probably be accomplished in three days.

To begin with we had to cut a track southwest through the jungle for three miles to meet the state boundary on the summit of Bukit Senorang (1,033 feet) at the northern end of a small range of hills. These, being the only elevation in this part of Pahang, stood out magnificently, when one could catch a glimpse of them, from the low swampy surrounding jungle. As this track would be often used, we took the two best jungle men in the camp, who cut a patch a yard wide while I kept them straight with a compass. Although we worked all day, only returning to the camp when it was too dark to use a *parang*, it took three days to cut these three map-miles of track. We were delighted to find that there was an excellent path following the ridge, and as those who had already been to Palong assured me that there was a similar track running in for several miles where the boundary meets the Sungei Palong, it seemed reasonable to assume that we should find a path open for the whole twenty-five miles of boundary which we had to follow.

On this journey I was accompanied by Ah Ching and three of the Triang guerillas. On the first day we reached the summit of Bukit Senorang and followed its sharp ridge southeast to the Sungei Lui. The Sakai in this area had a craze for attaching to the very tops of some of the tallest trees huge wooden propellers, so cut that as they whirled round in the wind they emitted a weird noise which could be heard at a great distance. The object of these contraptions was probably to scare away devils. Certainly they were very cunningly made, and the Sakai who erected them must have been most expert climbers. Much to my disappointment the track faded out after a couple of miles, and we wasted so much time looking for it that we only just reached the Sungei Lui by nightfall. From the top of the ridge we had seen that all the jungle between us and the railway line a few miles to the east was being opened up by the Chinese, and we had to be very careful to avoid being seen by these people, who were not known to the guerillas and therefore not to be trusted. We made a simple lean-to shelter of unplaited *ataps*, and dined well off a mouse-deer which I had caught with my hands. As I was waiting alone, while the others were making a reconnaissance to find a way round a clearing where some Chinese were working, this little animal about the size and colour of a hare came tripping down the hill and I managed to pounce on it and hold it. Its slender hooves were only the size of a pencil, and it had curiously elongated tusks in its upper jaw. In Malay folklore the mouse-deer occupies the same position as Brer Rabbit in that of the American negroes, and Ah Ching told me many amusing stories about the *kanchil* and *pelandok*, the two species that occur in Malaya.

We spent most of the next morning trying to find the state boundary, which from now on also marked the limit of the Sungei Lui Game Reserve. Though a wide path started off in the right direction, it ran too far east and there was no sign of the *batu* (literally stones) marking the surveyed boundary. After a few miles the path went still further east, but we had the good fortune to fall in with some Sakai, and they not only knew where the *batu* were but led us through their villages and proudly showed us one of them in the jungle. The *batu* consisted of a piece of two-inch iron piping sunk in a block of concrete and projecting only a foot, sometimes even less, above the floor of the jungle. Of a path there was no sign, but a careful examination showed that about ten years before a track had been cut and the saplings that had not died were now about four inches thick with clumps of shoots growing from the point at which the trees had been severed.

If the jungle is once cleared and then allowed to grow again it becomes thicker than ever, and here the going was so dense that we had to cut almost every yard with our *parangs*. The vegetation was also of the worst possible kind. Not only were there thickets of a very close-growing kind of bamboo, but there were miles of swampy jungle covered with *mengkuang*, a kind of gargantuan leathery grass which has pointed blades twenty feet long and four inches wide armed with a row of curved thorns along each edge, and a third row, pointing in the other direction, down the central ridge. The survey marks were a furlong apart, and every eighth one – marking the miles – was much larger. The only way we could find them was to run a very accurate compass course, pace out the requisite distance, and then search right and left.

It took us six days to reach the Palong river, travelling each day from dawn to dusk. I had stupidly left the provisioning of the expedition to the Chinese, and after the second day we ran out of rice. But that night a remarkable coincidence occurred. I shot a pig. This was remarkable not only because it was the first pig I had ever shot – and at that time I had already been out after them twenty or thirty times – but because of the peculiar circumstances in which I shot and recovered it. I went out that evening quite determined to secure meat of some sort, as this seemed to be the only way of making certain that the Chinese would accompany me, and I was afraid that without them we should never find the Palong camp. Almost immediately I came upon the fresh track of a large pig, and I followed it for half an hour until I heard a strange gurgling noise in front of me. The jungle was very thick, but I crawled on hands and knees beneath the *ataps* and rattans. Suddenly, only ten yards in front, I saw a hideous pinkish-coloured animal looking straight at me and, as I lay on the ground, towering above me. For a moment I thought it was a newborn elephant, then I realised it was a huge pig sitting on its haunches in a wallow in the red laterite clay. It was an indescribably hideous spectacle, sitting there with its evil wrinkled snout dripping with mud and its diabolical pointed ears, and I must confess that I was too much astonished to shoot until it had dashed off into the jungle. Only then did I give it a hasty shot with my rifle, and with a loud bark like a dog it crashed out of hearing. When I came to examine its tracks I was amazed to see that I had hit it and there was a thin trail of blood. But it was already getting dark, and after pursuing it for a short time I had to give it up and follow my own tracks back to the camp.

An hour later, just as we were eating the last of our rice, we heard a gasping noise coming from the jungle in the opposite direction from which I had been out hunting, and on going there with a large bamboo torch to give us courage, we found my pig breathing his last. The bullet had passed through his lungs and he had gone in a wide circle which had brought him right back to our camp. This pig, an old boar, was a very large one. He stood about three feet high and must have weighed nearer two hundredweight than one. His tusks were about six inches long and as sharp as a knife. We cut off enough meat to last us a week and grilled it in the ashes of the fire.

Two days after this we reached the wide Sungei Serting. One of the Chinese tried to cross the flooded river in a Sakai canoe we found under the bank. He was swept downstream, however, and we never saw him again. As he was unable to swim, I am afraid he must have been drowned when the canoe overturned. At last we managed to cross the river where a huge fallen tree made a natural bridge, and soon picked up our line of *batu* again. For the next four days we cut steadily towards the Palong river. The meat was soon finished, but I shot another pig as well as a couple of monkeys, so that we had plenty to eat and the Chinese seemed perfectly happy on a meat diet varied by the heart of a species of cabbage palm which we used to cut up and boil. At last, two miles short of the Palong river, there were signs that somebody from the south had reached this point on the state boundary, which soon developed into a wide track. In the jungle nearby we found several tiny lean-to *atap* shelters with sleeping-platforms of sticks, and round about were innumerable monkeys' skulls, the carapaces of forty or fifty mud-turtles, and a carpet of fish-bones and skins of durian (a luscious jungle fruit). We took a hut each, but I passed an uncomfortable night. The whole place swarmed with cockroaches, the mosquitoes were terrible, and as the platform was not nearly strong enough to support my weight, a stick broke whenever I turned over.

Next day we were rather alarmed to see footprints of shod feet on the track and to find a machine-sewn pocket handkerchief, but we met neither Jap nor Malay, and soon crossed the Palong river and cut across five miles of rolling jungle to meet it again further down its course – and we were in Johore. Next day – New Year's Day, 1943 – I was shaking hands with Cotterill and Tyson. They had been left with a transmitter and a Chinese operator supplied by 101 S.T.S. to report on the advance of the Japanese. Later, in January 1942, they had been recalled to Segamat. On the way their wireless operator, who carried all their money, as he did their shopping and paid their coolies, was murdered and robbed by another Chinese. They had then worked their way south, mostly by raft, until they reached the Keratong river, only to hear that the Japs were already in Johore. After this they had lived with an old Chinese couple for a month until they had been invited to join this band of armed Chinese.

Tyson was suffering from what we imagined to be a bad chill, but it was probably pneumonia. He was one of those unfortunate people who become really ill as a result of leech-bites. Cotterill told me he had been severely bitten in the small of his back some months before and had never properly recovered. While I was there he grew steadily worse – though even then we had no idea how ill he really was, and on January 8, much to our surprise and sorrow, he died.

The Chinese in this camp were indeed bandits, but they were cheerful and likeable rogues, and they did not suffer from the political and social inhibitions which made the guerillas in some respects so infuriating to live with. The nucleus of the gang had in pre-war days distilled illicit *samsu* and sold it in Segamat. Under the Jap occupation they found themselves without a job or money, so they had collected some weapons, and forming a band of about forty, operated against Chinese *towkays* who were helping the Japs. Cotterill had been asked to drive a car for them on one of their raids, which took place shortly before my arrival at Palong, but he thought it wiser not to identify himself with such activities. He told me that they had arrived back with suitcases full of loot – tinned food, suits of clothes, bales of silk, jewellery, and seven thousand dollars in cash. They claimed to have made a fair division, as was their habit, leaving the *towkay* with half his possessions to carry on business.

Though the food and general standard of living were much more luxurious than in the ordinary guerilla camps, discipline and organisation were non-existent. The leader, who had no control over his men, had taken the wife of a Chinese he was alleged to have shot, and she ran the camp – in so far as it was run at all. Half the men lived with their women in squalid shacks in the jungle edge, while the rest, including the Europeans, slept in a tin-roofed hut out in the clearing. Cotterill told me these men also used to capture Malay women in the jungle by firing over their heads until they stopped. Nearly half of them were heavy opium-smokers. Unlimited *samsu* was available, and free fights were common. It was almost impossible to sleep at night, as the men took it in turn to puff at the opium pipe, and the drug made them extremely garrulous and talkative. I have always wondered what it is like to smoke opium and longed to try, but I resisted, not because I was afraid of becoming an addict but so as not to lose face with the guerillas, who would be bound to hear of it.

In spite of their lack of organisation, the bandits were first-class guerilla material, and thirsting to have a crack at the Jap. They were, moreover, well able to do so, being better armed than any camp I had hitherto visited, though they had already – before Cotterill and Tyson joined them – thrown away several boxes of grenades, not knowing what they were. They had four machine-guns, ten tommy-guns, thirty rifles, and an almost unlimited supply of ammunition, which they used to blaze off at trees – being extremely gratified if they succeeded in hitting one. But they had no military knowledge – and admitted it – and were consequently the best pupils I ever had. Our lecture-room was a Malay mosque, and as Ah Ching could not understand their dialect and they could not speak Mandarin, I had to address them in Malay, having carefully learned the more difficult words from Cotterill beforehand.

I now heard the true story of the goodwill mission that had been sent over to Palong by the guerillas at Triang. It appeared that two most ill-chosen envoys, the headquarters propaganda man and the music instructor – both bespectacled and rather knock-kneed youths – had immediately set to work to teach the bandits to speak Mandarin and to sing 'The Red Flag' and the 'Internationale.' Somewhat naturally they were met with silent and even ribald hostility, as it was at once apparent that the instructors were far more interested in politics than in fighting the Japs. After a few days the two envoys, fearing for their lives, had slipped out of the camp at night and had made their way home, bearing frightful stories of the orgies and lawlessness of the *orang samun* (robbers) at Palong.

The week I spent at this camp was one of my happiest in the jungle. It was a joy to be with my own countrymen again, and for the first few nights Cotterill and I talked until the small hours. It was especially good to laugh again. After a whole year in the gloom of the jungle it was a wonderful experience to be living in this beautiful fertile valley with smiling paddy fields and gardens, bordered by hibiscus hedges and sweet-scented coffee bushes, where even the tapioca had variegated leaves. The Palong river, too, was quite unlike the mountain torrents of Perak, or the swirling brown waters of the Pahang jungle. It reminded me of a stream in the Yorkshire dales as it flowed merrily over shingle beds and ledges of grey rock. There was also as much fruit as we could eat – bananas, papaya, pomelo, champada, and jack-fruit. Every day while I was there I shot a pig. They could not resist the tapioca and rubber nuts, and used to come out of the jungle at dusk and remain in the clearings until well after dawn.

One day when I was out hunting *rusa* alone rather far from the camp, I met an armed party of the bandits returning from Tasek Bera, where they had been buying rice. On recognising them – they always wore wide-brimmed Australian hats and were festooned with leather bandoliers and holsters – I came out of the elephant grass where I was hiding and advanced to meet them but, thinking I was a Jap, they immediately opened up with tommy-gun and rifle. Fortunately they were full of *samsu* and shot high. I slipped away and returned to the camp by a short cut, and soon afterwards my assailants swaggered in boasting that they had met a large force of Japanese, whom they had completely annihilated!

The bandits asked me to stay with them, train them, and lead them into battle with the Japs. The prospect was terribly attractive, but I had promised Lah Leo to return to Mentakab and instruct the new intake of two hundred recruits, who were to form a reserve against the time when more weapons should be forthcoming. In any case I felt that my work was with Communist guerillas and not with bandits – however charming they might be – so I reluctantly refused, but promised to return to Palong if my other plans went awry.

Cotterill, to my great surprise and disappointment, was not interested in any plans to leave Malaya. He thought his chances of survival were greater if he stayed with the bandits and patiently waited for the British forces to return.

I was also most disappointed to hear that there was no communication between this camp and the rest of Johore, nor was there a word of information of any Englishman living there. But while I was at Palong, the leader of the Bahau (Negri Sembilan) guerillas arrived on a visit. He was of a much rougher type than most of the other guerilla leaders, and he seemed to be on good terms with the bandits, though the latter told me, laughingly, that the Communists were all the same. They only wanted to secure their arms and would then have no further use for them. The Bahau leader was very anxious for me to visit his patrol and give some instruction, but as this would entail my crossing into the state of Negri Sembilan, he said he could not possibly invite me without permission from his group headquarters, so it was arranged that I should visit his camp from Pahang in a few months' time. Meanwhile, he would find out all he could about the presence of Europeans in Johore and would make arrangements for me to go on there after spending a month at Bahau.

On January 9, 1943, Ah Ching and I left Palong on our return journey. Before I went, I left three closely written and illustrated notebooks, being my diary since July 12, 1942, with Cotterill, as I considered they would be very much safer with him than wandering about Malaya with me.[1] Following the route that we had cut with so much difficulty, we returned to the Triang camp in only four days.

[1] Cotterill lost my diaries when the Japs attacked the Palong camp in April 1944. Even if I had looked after them myself they would inevitably have been captured together with my diaries for 1943, which the Japanese took when they attacked the Batu Puteh camp in May 1944.

CHAPTER TEN

Jap Trouble in Negri Sembilan

(Use Map No. 2 and Map No. 5)

I was held up at Triang for a whole month with another attack of ulcerated legs, and when I returned to the Mentakab camp early in March 1943, I found thirty new recruits already in residence. At this time it was the policy of the guerillas in Pahang to train at least as many reserves as there were men already in the camps. These reserves, mostly youths in their late teens or early twenties, were given two months' very strenuous training in weapons, demolitions, minor tactics, drill, P.T., propaganda work, and the inevitable singing. After that a few of the best of both sexes were picked out for permanent duty in the camps or as special propaganda workers outside, while the rest returned to their homes to await the day when there would be enough weapons available for all trained men to take up arms and fight.

During the two months that I now spent in the Mentakab camp training the recruits and those of the old gang who had so far failed to pass their examinations, I had much more news of Europeans in other camps than I had had during the whole of the previous year. Later in March a Pahang headquarters man called Siouw Ling visited the camp. He was an outside worker, which accounted for my not having met him before, and had just returned from Gua Musang in Kelantan, a hundred miles to the north. He brought me a letter from one Creer, dated November 1942 and addressed to 'Colonel Jarmann' – a reflection both on Chinese politeness and pronunciation. This letter asked for any news of the war, as the writer understood that I had a wireless set. He also wrote that Bob Chrystal was with him and that both were well. Chrystal added a postscript to the letter, which had been censored, but I gathered that Robinson and Quayle were still at Perak headquarters, though both were very ill. After they had completed their work of training the Perak guerillas, Chrystal, together with Noone, had undertaken a two months' journey with the Sakai and had reached Gua Musang to find Creer already installed in the guerilla camp there.

In September 1942 my friend Ah Loy and about eight others had left the Menchis camp somewhat mysteriously. I now gathered from Siouw Ling that they had gone about a hundred miles up the east-coast railway line to form a new guerilla patrol on the border of Pahang and Kelantan near the villages of Merapoh, Pulai, and Gua Musang. The Chinese who lived in this isolated valley were very independent and bitterly opposed the Japs, with whom they had had several pitched battles. Indeed, Siouw Ling told me that the Japs dared not enter the valley at all and had even used aircraft in an attempt to drive the guerillas out of Gua Musang. This patrol was in touch with the Perak group, fifty miles over the Main Range to the west, and also carried on a private war with a rival band of Chinese guerillas (whom they referred to as bandits) whose head-quarters were at Kuala Krai, another fifty miles further north up the railway line.

We also received a visit from the Bahau leader whom I had met at Palong, and the leader of the whole Negri Sembilan group, who was known as Martin. This man, who was much paler in complexion than any other of his nationality that I have met, had been the interpreter for the second course of Chinese at 101 S.T.S. and had been put into the jungle at Tampin by Broome and Davis before they had had to leave Malaya for Sumatra. Li Fuk, the original leader of this party, had gone up to take charge of the Perak group.

Martin was extremely intelligent and spoke excellent English. He told me that the Negri Sembilan group had patrols at Bahau, Kongkoi, Titi, and Pertang and were in a very flourishing state. They had gone into action even before the fall of Singapore, and in reprisal for this the Japs, as soon as they had established them-selves in Negri, had carried out a most brutal massacre at Titi, the Chinese mining centre of Jelebu District, in which some thousands of guerilla supporters – men, women, and children – had been put to death. Martin described how a recent raid on a police station had failed, not one of the six grenades which they had lobbed through the window at night exploding. On the other hand, they had carried out a successful ambush against lorries containing Japanese, Indian, and Malay troops, and had captured arms from isolated police posts. As a result of these activities the Japanese were known to be planning a concentrated attack against the guerilla. In order to prepare for this, Martin was very anxious that I should go down to Negri and give them some instruction in defensive tactics.

In nearly every camp that I had visited in Perak, Selangor, and Pahang, I had been told of the large number, from a thousand downward, of white men – usually Australians – who were living with the guerillas in the jungle near Titi. I was, therefore, interested to hear from Martin that whereas during the fighting several hundred soldiers – mostly Australians – who had been cut off had taken to the jungle and were helped by the Chinese, since the fall of Singapore only one European had been living in their camp, and this was an Argyll and Sutherland sergeant called Andy Young.

Martin brought me a letter from Young, saying that he was ill and asking me to go and visit him. I gathered from his letter and from Martin's report that relations were somewhat strained between Young and the guerillas. I was glad to accept when Martin proposed to collect together all the junior leaders from his three camps so that I could teach them for a month, after which I should visit Bahau, do a month's training there, and then go down to Johore.

For me to proceed from Pahang to Negri Sembilan, however, required the sanction of general headquarters, and this took another two months to obtain. Meanwhile, I agreed to join a team, under Whu Bing, which was going to train recruits near Menchis. Martin promised to send a runner to escort me to Negri when permission had been granted.

Before I left Mentakab camp a party of about twenty men, who had left the camp some four months before, returned from an expedition to the Slim camp in south Perak, where they had been sent to collect weapons. After the debacle on the Slim river in January 1942, the Chinese in that area had collected an enormous number of weapons. These were used to augment the armament of practically all the camps from Perak to Pahang. Indeed, when I visited the Slim camp in October 1943, the supply was still not exhausted. As many of the weapons had spent several months at the bottom of the Slim river, they were in a shocking state of repair.

On this occasion our men brought back fifteen rifles, some of them with the last foot of the barrel sawn off – the British service rifle was always too long and heavy for the short-armed Chinese – some without magazines or sights, and all in unbelievably bad condition.

Our journey across the jungle to the new camp north of Menchis was uneventful. It was interesting that as we passed through the outlying *kampongs* in the valley of the Sungei Pertang, the Chinese brought all their legal and domestic problems to Whu Bing to settle – though he was only twenty years of age. The guerillas stood for them as the one representative of law and order in Japanese-occupied Malaya.

At last in the middle of June two runners arrived to take me down to Negri. The journey took four long days, though the distance on the map was only fifteen miles. We travelled southward in the valley to the east of the main road as far as Menchis. There we took to the mountains and went westward almost to the camp where I had first joined the Pahang group, and then south to the Jerang river, where we met the track which follows that river through Sakai country to the Kongkoi. Two of the nights we spent in Sakai villages. They had made very large clearings where they grew hill-paddy, maize, and tapioca, as well as patches of tobacco and various gourds. They lived in villages of about a dozen small bamboo and bark huts, each of which contained one family. There was also a special hut which was set aside for the use of travelling guerillas; here we were given fowls, eggs, rice, and huge sweet Sakai bananas, for all of which the runners insisted on paying.

When we reached the line of Malay *kampongs* along the Kenaboi river, which we had to traverse on the way to the camp, we heard from some Chinese squatters that only a few days before a large force of Japanese cycle troops had come in by the side road from Kongkoi and had beaten up the Malays whom they knew to have been helping the guerillas. All the way from Kampong Telekong, where we joined the Kenaboi river, to Kampong Pelong, the last of this line of villages, about two miles southeast of which lay the guerilla camp for which we were making, the houses and paddy-fields were deserted. The Japs had killed a few of the men as an example and had removed the rest to another place. But they had not burned down the houses or even removed the fowls, goats, and a herd of about forty water-buffalo. Perhaps this was a decoy to lure the guerillas out of the jungle, for almost every day a strong force of Japs, reinforced with Sikhs and Malays, patrolled the track on bicycles.

It was astonishing, as we passed by, to see *kampong* after *kampong* of attractive Malay houses surrounded by their coconut groves, fruit trees, hibiscus bushes, and vegetable gardens, all completely deserted. Even the durians lay ungathered beneath the trees, a sure sign that there were no Malays or Chinese in the vicinity. We gathered a dozen of the huge prickly fruits and took them behind the spreading roots of a large tree to enjoy the greatest of delights – a durian feast. While we were stuffing ourselves, a cycle patrol of about a hundred Japs, Sikhs, and Malays (the Japs being badly disguised as Chinese) passed only thirty yards from us along the track. They were heavily armed with tommy-guns and rifles, and were obviously looking for trouble. We, with only three pistols among the four of us (we had picked up one of the local guerillas *en route*), were intent on avoiding it, so we lay very low behind our tree as they passed.

It appeared that the Sikh Chief of Police in Jelebu had sworn to exterminate the guerillas and had started a serious drive against them about a week before my arrival. On our way down the Kenaboi in search of a patrol, we passed a burned-out camp which had been attacked only a week previously. The guerillas had been sitting around all ready packed up to move to a new camp, when the Japanese had opened fire. One girl was killed and two men wounded, and much gear had had to be abandoned.

The new camp, a few hundred yards up the Sungei Nap, was several hours further on. As we had already been delayed by the Jap patrol, we did not reach it until midnight, finding our way by the light of bamboo torches. The guide we had picked up knew the exact position of the guard post, and as we approached he kept on shouting his name in a loud voice to his comrades, while I, who was at that time wearing a wide-brimmed Gurkha hat, kept close to one of the torches to show that I was not a Jap. However, the guards must have been in a very bad state of nerves, for one of them shot at me at twenty yards' range, thinking – so he admitted later – that I was a Sikh, though I was clean-shaven. Fortunately for me the other sentry, who was a girl, did not agree with him and knocked his rifle up as he shot.

Here I found all three of the north Negri Sembilan patrols, about 150 men and women, living in one camp for safety. They were in a very harassed state. Two of their number had failed to return after a visit outside to obtain food, so they were preparing to abandon this camp, although they had only occupied it for a few days. My friend Martin, the leader, was very sick with a strange fever, as a result of which he could neither eat nor sleep. Whenever there was an alarm he had to be carried into the jungle on a special stretcher bed on which he lay in readiness. This fever, which I later had myself, was probably tick-typhus and caused several fatalities in the camps.

Here I met Andy Young, who was one of the few survivors of that gallant Company of the Argylls which had fought the Japs from the Grik road in the north of Perak southward until they were but a scattered handful. After wandering barefoot and half starving in the jungle edge as far south as Gemas, Young had been looked after by the Chinese and then handed over to the Pertang patrol, whose area was to the south of the Kuala Klawang-Bahau road. He had spent a year with them, almost dying of beri-beri, malaria, and tick-typhus. His patrol had had several fights with the Japanese, and he had distinguished himself by shooting an officer of such high rank that mourning ceremonies were held in every state of Malaya.

At first Young got on very well with the guerillas, though they had no common language – indeed, his Scots brogue was so broad that even I could barely understand him! His greatest asset was that he had a very fine tenor voice, and he soon learned to sing most of their songs far better than they themselves could, though he had absolutely no idea what the words meant. He was a first-class instructor and had taught them bayonet drill, which they did instead of P.T. every morning, and he used to do his share of sentry duty and other jobs. After a time, however, he fell ill and stopped working. Such disaffection is always regarded in the camps as the prelude to desertion, and the men were actually talking of taking preventative shooting measures when I arrived. Young's joints were somewhat swollen with beri-beri and he was sleeping twenty hours a day, only getting up for meals. But his trouble was mainly mental, and after a few days with somebody to talk to, he began to look quite different and was a most valuable assistant when I gave my course of instruction.

Two days after I joined the patrol they moved again, this time going two miles down the Kenaboi river to below its junction with the Sungei Triang, a white and turbid river coming from the tin mines of Titi. As we were expecting an attack at any time, I could only give a concentrated course of a week to the section commanders, but Martin had already taught them all he had learned at 101 S.T.S. and I found them very enthusiastic and efficient. They were particularly keen on using booby traps, and I fixed up a number of charges with trip wires so that if the Japs attacked the camp, they and about twenty-five yards of track would be blown up together.

After I had completed my course of instruction, Martin asked me if I would like to join a hunting camp at Kampong Pelong, where about a dozen of his men were living. Their job was to hunt pig and shoot the water-buffalo that the Malays had left behind and to raft the meat down the Kenaboi river to our camp. It was always a great pleasure to me to get out of the jungle and live in the *kampongs*, and I enjoyed myself very much in the hunting camp, which was only a hundred yards in from the paddy-fields and coconut groves. Our custom was to wait until the Jap patrols had returned home and then come out and shoot a water-buffalo from the herd which we had kept under observation. We would cut up the enormous carcass by the light of bamboo torches and, stark naked to avoid ruining our clothes, carry the gory joints down to the river.

We then made a raft about four feet wide and thirty feet long by lashing together a double layer of four-inch bamboos. The central ten feet or so was raised by lashing on an additional deck of shorter poles, and the load was placed there, amidships, where it kept comparatively dry. As soon as it was light enough to see the feathery bamboo groves overhanging the bank, we would start poling the raft downriver to the camp. This was always most exciting, as the current was very strong and the raft, being very long, was extremely unwieldy. Often there would be submerged tree-trunks jammed right across the river, so we would have to jump overboard and haul the raft bodily over. It was wonderful to be able to see the jungle from outside without being buried in it; to swing round a corner and gaze upward at unbelievably steep walls of variegated greenery stretching a thousand feet above us to the blue sky, and to see masses of nasturtium-coloured creepers overhanging the bank.

There were excitements, too, for as we had to pass the sites of the two camps from which the patrol had already been driven, we never knew when we might meet the Japs. One early morning, as we swept round a corner, from my vantage-point seated on top of the buffalo meat I caught sight of two bearded Sikh police and a Jap sitting in the middle of a fallen tree-trunk which bridged the river. Fortunately they were looking the other way and we were able to jump into the water and pull the raft into the side without being seen.

While I was living in the hunting camp at Kampong Pelong I had a severe relapse of malaria after a year's complete immunity from any sort of sickness except the universal ulcerated legs and scabies. The day I had my first attack I was out with two guerillas collecting durian. As I felt the approach of the nausea which usually preceded the shivering bout, I hurried back to the camp with one of the men, leaving the other to load the fruit on to the raft ready to be ferried down to the main camp at dawn next day.

Not long afterwards I was lying on the sleeping-bench wrapped in blankets; my companion was bathing in the stream and two or three other men were stamping and winnowing rice. Suddenly a shot rang out from the sentry post a hundred yards distant on the edge of the jungle, and this was followed by a burst of tommy-gun fire and a few more rifle shots. Within some ten seconds we had grabbed up our gear and were out of sight in the jungle, where we stopped to pull on our clothes. Later we collected what gear we could carry, hid the rest, and, skirting the paddy-fields, set off for the main camp, where we found our sentry and four others who had been out after pig. But my companion whom we had left with the durian was never seen again, and we presumed he had been surprised and caught by the Japanese.

A few days later the Japs caught two of our men who had gone outside to get food, and as a result it became necessary to move camp once more. The news reached the camp late one night and we were told to pack up and be ready to move at noon next day. At about ten o'clock in the morning, when I was at the other end of the camp trying to persuade the 'nurse' to give me two out of the total supply of twelve quinine tablets, the whole ground was suddenly shaken by the tremendous detonation of my booby traps, followed by the clatter of tommy-gun and rifle fire. Within one minute the camp was clear. The guard was only a hundred yards distant across a small valley and almost in sight of the rest of the camp. The two sentries, having pulled the booby-trap line and emptied their magazines, slipped away into the jungle, so that although I rushed back to the small hut where Young and I slept, I was the last out of the camp. Young, who was hiding in the jungle nearby, shouted that he had got all my gear there, and I hurried to join him. It was only later, when the Japanese were already in the camp, that I realised I had left my webbing belt hanging in the *atap* roof and that in the pouch were my precious Zeiss glasses and a Rolex watch that I had had for thirteen years.

As I was suffering from malaria, I had had to give up my rifle to a more able-bodied Chinese, and I only carried a .38 pistol. My task was to act as rearguard for half a dozen sick men and three Gurkhas, all of whom were unarmed. Almost at once we ran into another party of the enemy, mostly Sikhs, who had entered the camp from behind by another track. I had a lively – if rather one-sided – exchange of fire with the leading Sikh section, who were armed with tommy-guns. I knew that the Sikhs – like the guerillas – were very itchy-fingered in emergency and would be certain to empty the whole magazine the moment they saw a target, so I deliberately drew their fire by putting my head round the left-hand side of the tree behind which I was hiding. Then, as they paused to change their magazines, I took careful aim round the other side of the trunk. In this way I shot two of the leaders – they were only ten or fifteen yards away – and just as I was preparing to make a bolt for it, the Sikhs lost their nerve and the whole party retreated in disorder.

An hour later, as we lay hidden in a bamboo brake above the camp, we heard voices shouting in Mandarin, 'Comrades! Comrades! Come back, come back, the enemy have all gone away.' But this was a favourite Japanese ruse, and it was not until evening, when we recognised the voices of our own men calling, that we returned.

The Japs had pulled down every hut and used the material to make an enormous funeral pyre on which they had burned the bodies of those who had been killed by the booby traps or in the later action. The stink of burning flesh was revolting, but this did not deter my less squeamish friends from raking away the ashes to count up the score of skulls – which was eight. We had suffered no casualties, but the gear of all those who had been out of camp, which we had hurled far into the jungle, had been found and carried away; and all our cooking-gear had gone, as well as our meagre reserve of food, though every man carried a small bag of parched rice as an emergency ration.

We slept in the jungle near the camp, and before dawn the whole party rafted across the Triang river and moved a mile up a side stream to the foot of a steep slope. As we had nothing to eat since the previous morning, we set about preparing breakfast. It had rained all night, and I was suffering from violent fever again and lay miserably on the ground waiting for a drink of hot water. Suddenly the sentry rushed back to say that the Japs were upon us, so we ran up the steep hillside, then stopped to listen. Unfortunately I chose this moment to have a most violent rigor, and had to be gagged to silence the chattering of my teeth.

It transpired that the Japs had sent in three separate parties, each of about two hundred men. For a whole week we were hunted through the jungle and kept on meeting one or another of these parties. Messengers were sent to Pahang headquarters asking that they should make ready to receive our patrol, which was now reduced to about a hundred. The Sikh Chief of Police had clearly made it too hot for us to return to the Kenaboi, though it was surely without precedent that a whole group of guerillas should be driven out of their own state into another.

Three days more took us back to the camp where I had left Whu Bing training the reserves. This was now the headquarters of the Pahang group, since the old camp at Mentakab, after being occupied for nine consecutive months, had again been attacked by the Japs. After an all-night conference the men of the two groups were re-formed into three patrols: one to remain in this camp, five and a half miles due north of Kampong Menchis; another to move to a new site halfway along the Menchis-Mentakab bridle-path, where vegetable gardens had already been prepared to support it; while the third – the new headquarters patrol – was to move to the Bentong area, the cradle of the original Pahang group which had been formed more than a year before.

It was about the first week of September 1943 that Ah Chong gave me a mysterious message that I was to go at once to the headquarters of the Perak guerillas, where somebody wished urgently to see me. This was all the more incomprehensible as for over a year I had been trying to get permission to do just that very thing. Ah Chong also told me that at Perak headquarters they had got a new kind of tommy-gun of smaller bore and with the magazine in a different position – the Sten gun. I came to the conclusion that at last somebody had reached Malaya from India. Before I left, we had a great feast and concert, and Ah Chong and Martin, with much ceremony, presented me with a red enamel five-pointed star which I was to wear as a hat badge. It was with great sadness that I left his patrol, who had looked after me so well for more than a year.[1]

I set off with a party of six Chinese, who were taking this opportunity to bring back more weapons from the apparently inexhaustible supply at Slim. But they were poor guides and often lost the way, so that instead of passing the night in well-supplied Chinese *kongsi*-houses we sometimes travelled for two days with only one meal, consisting of our emergency rice ration cooked in our tin mugs, and frequently slept in the jungle in pouring rain. As a result of incessant fever, and the tapioca diet, I found that all the

---

[1] Two years later when Force 136 officers parachuted into this area, it was found that many of the camps had been disbanded or had removed further west, perhaps to be nearer the main road and railway. I myself was the first European to enter Bentong after the surrender, and I found to my sorrow that many of my friends had died. Andy Young had apparently succumbed to fever early in 1944; my interpreter Ah Ching had been fatally wounded in the neck in a skirmish with some Chinese 'bandits' at Kampong Batu Talam; and Whu Bing had suffered so much in health that he had had to stop living in the jungle.

power seemed to have gone from my leg-muscles. Though I could go well downhill or on the level, when it came to climbing, especially at the end of a long day, my legs simply would not work and I had to be pushed from behind or towed with a rattan line.

(Use Map No. 1)
Our route took us to a new guerilla camp on the Sungei Ribu, about two miles east-northeast of the old Kuala Kubu. Here there were fifty ex-bandits who were being turned into self-respecting Communists. This part of the journey, excluding three days' halt near Bentong when I was too ill with fever to travel, took seven days of extremely hard going. From here a journey of a night and a morning should have taken us to the camp at Kerling, but our two local guides were completely incompetent. It was the old story – the guides travelling entirely by memory, and once they were lost not realising, although the moon and the railway appeared, first on the left and then on the right, that we were going in a circle, and I, fully aware of our erratic course but not being able to do anything about it as I had no idea where we were making for.

Next night we reached the camp which lay about two miles east of Kerling on the slopes of Bukit Bertram. In this camp we had to wait for a whole week, as the guides who were to accompany us were out collecting some gelignite which they were to take to Slim and exchange for rifles. This explosive was in a damp and most dangerous condition and might have detonated itself at any moment. The main Kerling camp contained about ninety men and girls, and there was a smaller camp of about half the size some three hours' walk distant. The larger camp had three machine-guns, six tommy-guns, and twenty-five rifles and shotguns, and was the smartest and best disciplined camp I had visited.

I met here a most intelligent English-speaking Chinese, who had been a despatch rider in the Volunteers and was used to the Western way of looking at things. With him as interpreter I gave a short but intensive course to the fifteen junior leaders of the two Kerling patrols. They were tremendously keen and seemed to get on far better than any course I had yet taken. I realised once again how much I had been hampered by the lack of good interpreters. The actual situation of this camp was known to the Japs, but they were apparently afraid to attack it, having been beaten off once already. This was the only instance I heard of where a patrol did not move camp at once after they had been discovered.

In this camp I met six of the men who had taken part in a dramatic break from Kuala Lumpur jail a few months previously. They told me that about 130 prisoners, most of them guerillas or alleged guerilla supporters, had staged a mock quarrel among themselves. When the Sikh warders ran to quell the disturbance, the prisoners disarmed them, took the keys, opened all the cells, and made a rush through the main gates. A few were shot by the sentries on duty, but the majority got away. I saw the scars where the Japs had pushed needles beneath their fingernails and burned the flesh of their faces and chests with cigarette ends and hot irons. The chief outside worker of this camp had been permanently crippled because the Japs had made him kneel down and had then jumped on the back of his calves. When that failed to make him speak, they had put poles across his shins and, with a man standing on top, had rolled them from knee to ankle.

From Kerling, three days and nights took us to Tanjong Malim. Once again the guides completely lost themselves. This was particularly infuriating for me, as I was now back in the country where we had operated nearly two years ago, and I knew every track and stream. At last we halted at a small *kampong* just north of Tanjong Malim, and the whole party slept for twenty-four hours, only waking up to eat large meals of rice, fried beans, and brinjols.

Four very strenuous days then took us due north along the edge of the mountains. We were travelling against the grain of the land and had to climb one mountain spur after another, toiling across the deep intervening valleys with their swirling rivers. At last we waded across the wide Slim river just south of Kampong Ulu Slim and reached a camp beside the Sungei Rasau, five and a half miles north of Slim river and four miles southwest of the camp where my party had first joined the Chinese guerillas in March 1942.

Ever since leaving Tanjong Malim I had been suffering from a high fever, which was not improved by our having to spend the nights lying soaking wet in the jungle. Our guides, too optimistically hoping to reach a Chinese or Sakai house, were almost invariably caught out by darkness and rain before we had time to build a shelter. I was only just able to keep going by filling myself up with quinine and aspirin, of which, fortunately, we had plenty at this time. My strength and resolution only just lasted out. My leg-muscles were impotent, and I had to be pulled up the last long hill to the camp, completely collapsing when I reached it.

I was now terribly ill with blackwater fever, which was brought on – so the experts tell me – by having chronic malaria and taking a little, but never enough, quinine. As well as the symptom from which the disease derives its name, I suffered frightful vomiting and dysentery, accompanied by such agonising pains in the small of my back and across my pelvis that it seemed as if all my bones must come apart. I had to be held down by two men to counteract the violence of uncontrollable rigors.

For a whole month I was as ill as it is possible to be without actually dying. Then, for some reason, I gradually recovered and by the middle of December was able to travel again. Our destination was the Bidor camp, about eighteen miles as the crow flies to the north-northwest and across the deep valley of the great Sungkai river. This is the heart of the Sakai country, and we depended on them to show us the way; but just at this time Japanese aircraft were bombing the camp at Bidor and all the Sakai had fled into the hills. We crossed the northeast corner of Trolak Forest Reserve, then followed the Sungei Liat down to meet the Sungkai river. The Sungkai was still a mountain torrent about fifty yards wide, and we spent the rest of the day following it upstream looking in vain for a crossing. After spending a miserable night at Kuala Tesong, shivering in torrential rain under a single groundsheet, we returned to where we had slept the night before by the Sungei Liat and at last found a young Sakai headman who agreed to show us the way.

Three delightful days now took us right up the Sungkai river and over a high pass into the Sungei Gepal valley. The Sakai here lived in beautifully built houses, often high above the ground in bamboo groves. Their clearings, sometimes 2,000 feet up on the mountainsides, commanded wonderful views down the deep wide valley of the Sungkai or northward towards the high peaks of Perak. At this time they were living largely on hornbills, which they caught with bird lime, and which tasted delicious provided the meat had

179

not been kept too long. I was enchanted with these shy little brown men who were so friendly once we had won their confidence. Again I wished I had been trained as an ethnologist so that I might learn all about them and be able to study their hunting methods and their customs.

(USE MAP No. 3)

When we came down into the Gedong valley, we were somewhat alarmed to find a wide track that had been recently cut by the Japs. They had gone in on a compass course with apparently no reference to the lie of the land. The route was littered with the paper wrappers off packets of cigarettes and biscuits. In one place they had bivouacked for the night, but though they were miles from the nearest guerilla camp, they had not dared to light fires. The amount of gear they had left behind was quite astonishing. We picked up three excellent pairs of socks, some handkerchiefs, a leather belt, a torch, mosquito coils, half-eaten tins of M. & V. rations (British), and small bags containing sufficient remains of biscuits and sweets to give us all a meal.

Soon afterwards we met some Chinese who were living in a hut in the jungle. They told us that about two hundred Japs, Indians, and Malays had entered the jungle and had synchronised their attempted attack with the bombing of the Bidor camp, which we had actually seen and heard from the hills near Sungkai a few days before. The Japs had bombed a camp and vegetable gardens, which had been abandoned for some time. All the ground party had succeeded in doing was to attack a clearing recently opened by some guerilla supporters, to shoot them up – no casualties – and to loot and burn down their huts. A Chinese who had watched the party on the move said he had not believed it possible for men to move so slowly, clumsily, and noisily. We could still see the marks on steep traverses where the Japs in their nailed boots had scraped the earth away as one after another had slipped down the muddy banks.

The Bidor patrol had moved since my guides had set off to bring me from Slim, and it was another day before we found them in a new camp beside the Seroi river. Here I met many old friends from the original Slim camp, and they had a feast and concert in my honour. At this meal there was a meat dish about which there seemed to be some mystery. I found it very good, being less rank than monkey though not so good as jungle pig. After the meal I was told that I had been eating Jap. Whether this was true or not I do not know, but in several of the camps I had been told that they sometimes ate the heart and liver of Japs who had been killed in skirmishes at the jungle edge. Though I would not knowingly have become a cannibal I was quite interested to have sampled human flesh.

Next day we crossed the Gedong and Seroi rivers and followed an old pipeline down to a large *kongsi*-house. Here I was given coffee and told to wait while they sent for the mysterious person I had come four months' journey to meet. After an hour who should walk in but Chen Ping. He told me that two Englishmen, none other – as I had suspected and hoped – than my old friends Davis and Broome, had come in some time previously by submarine and were eagerly awaiting me at their camp some three hours' march in the hills. As we walked through the jungle in pouring rain Chen Ping gave me the headlines of the world news for the last year. On the evening of Christmas Day, 1943, after I had been almost exactly two years in the jungle, I joined Davis and Broome at Blantan camp.

A Malay kampong.

A Malay fishing village.

Typical Malay house in jungle.

The Sakai, the aborigines of Malaya.

Sakai using blowpipes.

Mangrove swamp.

185

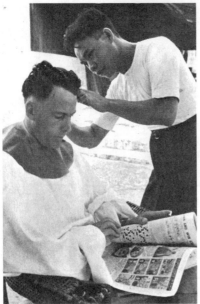

Above: Lieut.-Col. F. Spencer Chapman, D.S.O. and Bar. Left: Richard Broome having his hair cut.

Above: John Davis and Lim Bo Seng.
Right: Itu, the Senior Officer of the Perak guerillas, and Jim Hannah (Force 136).

187

Cooking monkey over a camp fire.

A Liberator plane makes a drop.

Left: The newsletter, Truth, that Chapman published while in Mentakab.
Below: An aerial view over Malaya just before Chapman parachuted back into the Pahang jungle in August 1945.

190

Top: Chapman accepts the Japanese Surrender in Kuantan on September 30, 1945.
Bottom: Chapman (left) with Lieut.-Col. D. Headley of the Malayan Civil Service
(right) and another British officer.

CHAPTER ELEVEN

Force 136

John Davis and Richard Broome had been responsible, among others, for laying the foundations of the escape route from Singapore to Sumatra. During the last days of Singapore this party spent their time working out a route through the chain of Dutch islands, leaving food dumps at intervals along the route and contacting the Dutch and natives to ensure their cooperation. They helped many hundreds over this route, and eventually followed it themselves through Sumatra to Padang, where they were in time to escape to Ceylon in a junk.

The instructional staff of 101 S.T.S. managed to acquire a small steamer and early in February made their way via Batavia to Colombo. In course of time they were absorbed into a much larger organisation, later known as Force 136, which was interested in disrupting the Japanese tenure of all occupied countries in every possible way. By the middle of 1942, when the tornado of the Japanese advance had at last spent itself and been held on the eastern frontiers of India and the fringes of Australasia, there was at last a breathing-space when Force 136 could take stock of its potentialities.

The situation in Malaya was not at all good. In the first place, there was a serious shortage of men who knew the work or the country. Even if suitable British and Asiatic agents could be found and trained, how were they to be introduced? Until the new improved Liberator bomber reached Malaya in April 1945, there were no planes capable of reaching Malaya from available bases in India, except for the old Catalina flying-boat. Submarines could be used, but at that time only two were available in Far Eastern waters – both belonging to the Dutch Navy – and they were fully occupied in operations against enemy shipping and could be used only with extreme danger in the shallow mine-infested Malacca Straits. The few ports there would be strongly held, and the rest of the coast was guarded by impassable mangrove swamp reinforced by sandbanks. There were no assured and reliable contacts in Malaya. And the blind landing of agents was thought to be an uneconomical, if not suicidal, undertaking.

In spite of these difficulties, the Malayan Country Section was formed in July 1942. Basil Goodfellow was in charge and as advisers he had Davis and Broome. Every available scrap of information about Malaya under the Jap occupation was collected and studied. It was little enough. In October 1942, a Chinese managed to get from Singapore to Penang, then overland through Siam to China, and at last to India. Careful interrogation revealed that although tens of thousands of Chinese had been massacred by the Japs, the steady flame of resistance was burning stronger than ever. Even the Malays, who had bowed to the Japanese occupation, now saw the rottenness of their new overlords. Chinese morale was very high and the people still supported the guerillas, in spite of the savage reprisals.

The stage was set for the introduction of agents. The conclusion was that Europeans who knew the languages and the country should be used to direct Chinese, who could more easily collect information and make contact with the guerillas. The Europeans would probably have to join the guerillas in the jungle and with their radio equipment send out information collected by their Chinese agents. Once contact had been established, it should be possible to get in touch with any of the European stay-behind parties which were still functioning and to build up an organisation to smuggle in more agents, arms, medicine, and any other requirements. It might even be possible to get agents out who could be trained in India and smuggled in again.

Davis and Broome were keen to go, but where were the Chinese who could accompany them? About this time an outstanding young Straits-born Chinese who had been educated at Hong Kong University was contacted at Calcutta. His name was Lim Bo Seng. Although he was very keen to take part in an operation, it was first arranged that he should go to Chunking to collect Straits-born Chinese who would be suitable to enter Malaya. As soon as the Chinese agents had been chosen, they had to be trained for their dangerous and specialised work. Those who were to be wireless operators needed at least a two months' course.

The plan of the first operation, known as Gustavus 1, was for one European and several Chinese to embark in a Dutch submarine from Colombo in early April 1943, then to transship by night to a Chinese junk in the north of the Malacca Straits, and to persuade the crew to land the party somewhere on the west coast of Malaya between Penang and Port Swettenham. The Chinese in the party would then contact the Chinese ashore and through them the local guerillas. Some of these would then be persuaded to return to India for interrogation and training. After a month ashore the European would come out in a Chinese fishing craft, contact the submarine at an agreed place off one of the islands in the Straits, and hold a conference. Another British officer, a radio transmitter with a Chinese operator, and several agents would then be landed, while a certain number of Chinese from the mainland would return to India on the submarine. If no suitable fishing craft were seen, the submarine would go in close and carry out a daylight periscope reconnaissance of the coast, and the party would land by collapsible boat with their stores in tow.

(Use Map No. 5 and Map No. 4)
At 8.30 p.m. on May 24, 1943, John Davis and five Chinese agents left the submarine in the middle of the Malacca Straits and started to paddle shoreward in their three folboats. A Chinese junk had been contacted, but the occupants were too old and stupid to understand what was wanted of them, and Davis had to carry out the alternative plan and make a blind landing. The sea was glassy calm. At 11.30 p.m. they heard the welcome sound of surf, and half an hour later made a landing on a beach to the north of Tanjong Hantu, which lies to the north of the channel between the Dindings and the island of Pangkor and near the port of Lumut. Landing was difficult, but all the gear was kept dry and safely put ashore. At dawn next day further reconnaissance proved the beach to be entirely deserted. The boats were dismantled and hidden in the jungle. With each man carrying about 70 lb., they then set off to find a safe place to cook a meal. Almost immediately Davis, who was in the lead, blundered straight into a Malay man and woman, who walked off as fast as they could, refusing to stop and speak. This incident made the party redouble their vigilance.

The next four days were spent working their way most care-fully through three or four miles of semi-jungle to a safe hideout half a mile from a rubber estate near Segari and therefore within reach of suitable contacts. Davis decided to send out the Chinese one at a time to make contacts, as two would inevitably be trapped by cross-questioning. A Hokkien called Ah Ng was chosen to go first, not only because he was the keenest and most resourceful, but because his dialect would be most useful in that district. He was dressed in his oldest clothes, as it was planned he should pretend to be destitute so as to arouse sympathy. His story and the amount he could ask for were left entirely to his discretion. If he did not return within four days, Davis would have to make a new attempt.

Next day he met Ah Ng, as arranged, at the edge of the jungle. All had gone well. He had found a rubber-tapper overseer called Kong Ching and his wife, to whom he spun his hard-luck story, only to be told uncompromisingly that he did not speak or look the part. He changed his ground accordingly and after twenty-four hours of almost non-stop talk these people became his staunchest friends and agreed to go to all lengths to help him once they were assured he was not a guerilla – of whose extortions they appeared to be very much afraid.

Another of Davis's agents, one Ying, a Hylam, had chosen to get work in a coffee-shop, as being the best place to gather infor-mation and meet the other agents. Inquiry led him to a coffee-shop in the centre of Segari marketplace near the bus station – an ideal position. Here the proprietor, who was very understaffed, offered him $10 per month as under-coolie. He accepted straight away and in half an hour he was at work, the proprietor having promised to obtain the necessary documents for him. One of his first customers was Ah Ng, who was quite astonished when he saw who served him, as he had no idea Ying was already established. Ying was very happy there, though the hours were long. He liked his fellow-coolies and the food was excellent, and his master turned out to be a great friend of Kong Ching.

Meanwhile, another of Davis's men, Tsing, crossed by motor-boat to the island of Pangkor to start making arrangements for a boat to take Davis out to the submarine R.V. He crossed over with-out difficulty, but once there his apparent aimlessness was noted by a Malay policeman, who questioned him. Being unable to give any satisfactory answers, Tsing blustered indignantly and insisted on being searched. Fortunately, though dressed in his oldest clothes, he had $60 in his pocket, and this reassured the policeman, as the poorer a Chinese was in Malaya at that time, the more suspect he was. Nevertheless, Tsing was arrested and taken to the police station, where he insisted that he was able to obtain a guarantor. He was allowed to go unescorted to find one, and contacted the unofficial headman of the village, one Choy. Tsing hastily improvised a story that he was a patriot who was embarrassed by having to hide a European and his own mother and sister. He had temporarily settled them and was anxious to come out into the open and go into business with $1,000 capital which he had saved.

Choy, having once been persuaded to help, set about the problem of Tsing's cover with energy and ingenuity. He introduced him to his friends as the son of an old acquaintance, and by the time the day was out had set him up in business as a fishmonger. He gave him smarter clothes and insisted on his behaving as a well-to-do young man in order to efface the impression of the day before, when he had been taken for a vagrant. He also bearded the corporal in his police station and so reassured him that Tsing was even given a passport to allow him to enter other states.

Next day Tsing returned to report to Davis and brought him the welcome present of some fresh fish. Within a week he had consolidated his position so well that his new firm had already dispatched two consignments of fish down the coast. It would obviously be much easier to keep R.V.s if they could be combined with legitimate trading. But to do this it was necessary to borrow a boat from Choy and to get his help in arranging the trading voyage. This proved impossible without telling him the real reason of the voyage. On being told, he readily consented to make himself responsible for all shipping arrangements. He had a most suitable boat available, with a crew of two very reliable Hylams.

Choy also told Tsing that he was in close touch with eight hundred guerillas who lived near Sitiawan, that their second-in-command visited him frequently to buy rice, and that regular collections were made for them on Pangkor. He did not disguise the fact that although relations were very cordial, the town was really being blackmailed for its security. It was arranged that Tsing should sail from Pangkor at dawn on June 22, pick up Davis and any of his Chinese that he wanted to take out with him at the beach where they had first landed, then continue the trading voyage, and eventually make the R.V. as arranged on June 25. On the day of the R.V. a scarlet blanket was hung over the port side and the sail was raised and lowered as recognition signals. At 11.30 a.m. Davis spotted the submarine periscope and the junk dropped anchor.

This sortie and the following ones – Gustavus 2 and 3 – were entirely successful. The upshot was that Davis went out with Broome, who had led Gustavus 2, so that they could together train the required personnel in the light of new information and experience. On August 4 Davis returned and got in touch with the local guerillas at Sitiawan and heard for the first time that I was still alive, with guerilla headquarters in Pahang. He arranged that a message should be sent to me through Perak headquarters asking me to join him. Meanwhile, two guerillas were attached to him as personal assistants. Unfortunately the Japs had got to know that there were Europeans in the neighbourhood and Davis had to move his camp several times.

Gustavus 4 left Trincomalee on September 12, 1943. Broome and Captain Harrison, an ex-Malayan rubber-planter, were on board the submarine and the arrangement was that one or both of them should reinforce or replace Davis – this should be decided by conference at the R.V. On the morning of September 23 they sighted the junk at the R.V. off the Sembilan Islands with Davis making recognition signals. Broome returned with Davis to his camp in the jungle near Segari, dumping a wireless set in the jungle near where they landed.

By this time Ah Ng was already established as a relative of Kong Ching with his miscellaneous trading business in Ipoh, where Ying was living as his assistant, and Lim had been established at Lumut as his representative. Ah Han, another agent, had found it quite impossible to work in Ipoh because with his limp and unusual features he had been too often recognised, and had to return to camp. Tsing's fish business had prospered under the auspices of Choy, and both he and Ah Ng had established many valuable contacts, not only with the Chinese but with the Japs, who were only too anxious to associate themselves with any profit-making concern, however disreputable and shady.

On September 30 a representative from Perak headquarters arrived. He was then using another name, but it was my old friend Chen Ping. As the Japs were extremely active in this area and were already on the lookout for Europeans, every possible precaution had to be taken and it was not possible to make a start for the interior, where they planned to establish their permanent camp, about six miles east of Tapah, until October 8.

The plan was that Broome should go out to keep the submarine R.V. arranged for November 6. In spite of fever Broome left camp at the end of October, but Chen Ping reported that the Japs were very active in all the Bidor and Teluk Anson area and that they were patrolling the road. Broome returned to the camp while Chen Ping kept the R.V. himself. It was impossible for a European to come in at this time, so Lim Bo Seng, who was to have landed with a British officer, came in alone and made his way by car with Chen Ping to the nearest point on the road, then walked up to the camp. His stores, including two of the new and much more portable B.2 radio sets, had to be left at Jenderata to be brought in when possible.

My first fortnight in Davis's and Broome's camp was one of the happiest I have ever spent. In the first place, the situation of the camp was magnificent. Built at more than 2,000 feet above sea level near the summit of an isolated hill called Blantan, it commanded a superb view of both the plains and the Main Range. In the far distance was the zigzag silver line of the Perak river and beyond it again the open sea of the Malacca Straits. On clear days we could make out the tiny Sembilan islets and further north the rugged outline of the larger island of Pangkor and the hills behind Lumut.

Davis and Broome, being the very antithesis of each other, made a perfect team. Since they had first met when they were both learning Chinese at Canton, they had been inseparable, though they rarely seemed to agree and spent most of the day in apparently acrimonious argument. John Davis was short, very strongly built, and full of vigour and determination. He was a good boxer. As he hated conventional Malayan 'Clubland,' he had always spent his leave trekking far into the jungle, often with only his coolies for company. He was a man who went his own way – almost uncompromisingly so. Richard Broome possessed a most balanced and logical, if somewhat cynical, brain for a man of his age – he was thirty-five at this time, and Davis two years his junior. But he was quite the laziest man I have ever come across, being prepared to sit and read a book – apparently without a twinge of conscience – while others worked. Davis would conceive and expound half a dozen different plans. Broome would take no notice, being apparently engrossed in his book. Suddenly he would look up, explain just why such and such a plan would not work, give his opinion of the situation, then return to his book. He was almost always right – and fortunately Davis knew it.

When I joined them, Davis was in excellent health, though somewhat yellow, but I have seldom seen anybody look as ill as Broome. For two months he had been suffering from a strange and virulent fever which would not react to quinine or atabrin. He was emaciated and haggard, and almost green in colour.

The food at Blantan, compared to what I had had in the guerilla camps or even in the outside houses I had visited, was excellent beyond belief. The three Chinese were all good cooks, and one of them was an absolute artist. At that time we were able to get every sort of Chinese delicacy, from sea-slugs to sharks' fins, as well as such mundane things as beef, pork, many kinds of fish, chicken, eggs, and fresh vegetables, through the food lines so efficiently laid on by Chen Ping. Another joy was that there was plenty of reading material. We had a complete Shakespeare, *Fifteen Poets*, *Pickwick Papers*, and *Nicholas Nickleby*, Borrow's *The Bible in Spain*, Marryat's *Midshipman Easy*, a volume of essays, a dictionary, and a book of crossword puzzles. I was able to contribute an edition of William Morris and a Bible that I had brought from Slim.

The guerilla bodyguard, hand-picked by Chen Ping from neighbouring camps, consisted of about twelve assorted Chinese under the leadership of one Ah Yang – a bulky bespectacled student who took life far too seriously and had no sense of humour. He was unbelievably erudite, having read all of Marx, Engels, and Shaw.

But he had been educated far beyond his intelligence and lived in an unreal world of his own so that it was difficult to meet him on common ground and we were never at our ease in his company – especially as he would go to all lengths to avoid telling the truth, even in quite unimportant matters. However, he took his duties most conscientiously, ran an efficient guard and food-carrying system, and was much respected by his men.

During these halcyon days I made the acquaintance of the Chinese agents, a few of whom were permanently in the camp, while others came to report from time to time. Lim Bo Seng, who spoke flawless English and was in every way a most attractive and outstanding character, I got to know best. As he had only just arrived and plans had not been made for his cover in the plains, he was living in the camp and helping to run the outside organisation from there.

Ah Han had at first been installed at Ipoh, but he had had to give up his work outside and was now living in the camp, where his background, sense of humour, and knowledge of Mandarin made him an excellent negotiator between Davis and the guerillas. Unfortunately, though we lived together for a year, we had no common tongue, as he spoke neither English nor Malay. The same applied to the gentle and good-natured Lee Chuen, the wireless operator, who had to wait still another year for his wireless and spent his time sleeping and having malaria. This was his first visit to Malaya, and unlike the others, he was a northern Chinese, coming from Shanghai.

Ah Ng appeared one day with a box of a hundred cheap cigars and two bottles of Japanese 'hooch,' made from rice spirit flavoured and coloured with burnt sugar and called White Stag whisky. He was small and pale, and always looked harassed. But such was his business acumen, courage, and initiative that from the very beginning he was the key man of the outside organisation. In a way this was unfortunate, in that the others relied on him and visited him too much, especially when in difficulties. After launching himself as a relative of Kong Ching at Segari he had quickly gained a great deal of influence both there and in Lumut, and before long had started business in Ipoh. Unfortunately there was never enough capital available to put Ng on a sound and safe footing, and he had therefore to spend most of his time looking after his business instead of being able to concentrate on his real work as an agent. If any difficulty arose, he never fell back on Davis, but settled it himself before coming in to report.

We received several visits from Tsing, a large and rather blustering Chinese, who was inclined to panic. It will be remembered that he had been installed in a small fish business with several partners at Pangkor and was helped by Choy, who was very friendly and fatherly to him. His job was to maintain the sea R.V.s by junk. Ying, who was keen and at times courageous, but rather weak and easily led astray, had started as a coffee-shop boy in Segari. Later he took over from Tsing and, despite failures, kept some of the later R.V.s. I also met Sek Fu, who had acted as Davis's bodyguard in the Segari camp. He was somewhat nervous and excitable for work of this sort, but had just been installed – by Ng, of course – as owner of a coffee and sundry shop in Tapah, which was only six miles from our camp at Blantan.

Two other permanent members of the party were Black Lim and Ah Su. The former had been attached to Davis from the guerilla camp at Sitiawan. He was very strong and brave, but inclined to lose his head in an emergency. He was completely illiterate, but spoke several Chinese dialects and very fluent *kampong* Malay. As he was a good jungle traveller and handy man, he was particularly valuable in a camp of Europeans and Chinese who had never had to live by their hands. Ah Su was an oldish man and an opium-eater. He became a valuable addition to the party, as he caused us a great deal of amusement, was never ill, and did all the unpleasant chores. Both Su and Lim were Fuchows and therefore kept each other company, speaking the weirdest and most cacophonous of all the Chinese dialects.

When Chen Ping had first met Davis at Segari in September, he agreed to convene a conference with a plenipotentiary from guerilla general headquarters. Owing to the tardiness of their communications, it was not until January 1, 1944, that this man reached our camp at Blantan. He became known to us as 'The Plen,' and that is the name which I shall use for him in these pages.

The Plen was a young-middle-aged Chinese of great charm, considerable intelligence, and quiet efficiency. He had a large mouth and perfect even teeth, and when he became animated his eyes grew round and his eyebrows rose about an inch and a half. The conference lasted two days and was most cordial; it was attended by the Plen and Chen Ping on the one side, and by the three of us and Lim Bo Seng – who interpreted from Mandarin to English – on the other. By way of credentials, Davis produced a letter appointing him the Supreme Allied Commander's chief representative in Malaya. The Plen represented the joint committees of the Anti-Japanese Forces and the Anti-Japanese Union – the former being the armed guerillas living in jungle camps, and the latter the numerically greater organisation, including perhaps half the Chinese in Malaya, who provided money and helped in other ways.

In the first place they agreed to cooperate fully with the Allied Commander-in-Chief for purposes of defeating the Japanese *and* during the period when the Allied armies should be responsible for the maintenance of peace and order in the country. We – representing Southeast Asia Command – agreed to supply arms, finance, training and medical facilities. Throughout the conference the Plen was most meticulous in getting a clear-cut decision on every question, discussing each point in detail, and it was equally clear that he meant to stand by everything he said. We had agreed at the beginning that no questions of post-war policy were to be discussed and that our whole mission was military. We were all very pleased with the results of this conference, and it now remained for us to carry out our side of the bargain. This depended on keeping in touch with our headquarters at Colombo by submarine and, as soon as we could, getting our sets up from the coast and establishing communications by wireless.

So far we had at Blantan only enough weapons, ammunition, and medicine to supply ourselves and, for a short time, Ah Yang's guard. Further supplies that had come in on the various sorties had been dumped at Lumut and Jenderata, and Chen Ping had set about getting them up to Blantan. But here we were to find a weakness, not in the will, but in the executive abilities of the guerillas. Outside the jungle, in the towns and large villages, their power was limited owing to their lack of contacts among the richer merchant and shopkeeping classes. And so, though they themselves and our own Chinese agents had comparative freedom of movement in the fifty-mile strip between the jungle and the coast, when it came to the safe conduct of Europeans or the transport of a few hundredweight of stores, their arrangements either broke down or were so slow as to be ineffective.

Owing to Jap activity in the area, it was deemed impossible for a European to keep the January R.V., so this was kept by Ying. He left Blantan for the R.V. a few days after my arrival there, and I was able to write a résumé of my activities for the last two years, some notes on the fate of my companions, and a report on the guerillas on a small square of paper. This, together with the other reports, was carried by Ying wrapped in a rubber sheath inside a tube of toothpaste. The return message was concealed in the brain cavity of a large dried fish – a very usual article of food for Chinese to be carrying. When the time came for Broome to leave the camp for the February R.V., Chen Ping fell ill and at the last minute was unable to make the arrangements, so Ying was again instructed to keep it and carried very full reports from us all. Unfortunately this R.V. was never kept.

The camp site at Blantan, though beautiful, was not at all se-cure, and while we were there we were continually apprehensive. In the first place, it was far too near the outside. Jap activity on the jungle edge was increasing, and we could expect little warning of an attack. It was in the worst possible defensive position, as it could be approached from the valley on either side and along the ridge from each end; Ah Yang's guard was so small that only the usual path of approach from the southwest could be guarded. Worst of all, the air cover was negligible.

In the middle of February I set off with Ah Chu, a droll Chinese who acted as our contact man with the Sakai, to seek a new site for the camp. From Blantan we could look across to several suitable places on the lower slopes of Batu Puteh, and it was there we went. A succession of Sakai guides brought us, after two days' walking, to the house of a headman called Pa Kasut – literally Father Boot – where we hoped to find a suitable site.

Like all Sakai houses, Pa Kasut's hut was built well above the ground on the slope of a hill, so that the front of the house was about ten feet above the ground. It consisted of one large room, thirty feet square, under a single ridge of *atap* thatching, while each gable had been extended by a penthouse roof to cover eight-foot extensions of the main room. Except for the uprights of the house the whole framework was of bamboo. The floor was of inch-wide symmetrical slats of bamboo lashed with fine rattan to the floor-joists with a half-inch space between the slats. The main part of the house was surrounded with a three-foot balustrade of flattened bamboo surmounted by a single large bamboo, which fenced off the penthouse extensions so that they resembled loose boxes. At night the *atap* eaves continued flush over this rail, but in the daytime the lower six feet of the roof could be bent up and supported on props several feet above the balustrade, thus allowing plenty of sun and daylight to enter. As the ridge-pole of the roof was twenty feet above the floor, there was ample room for a loft, whose floor of bamboo made a ceiling to the lower room and increased the feeling of space, while giving the room really beautiful proportions.

Pa Kasut and the men were out hunting and no one knew when he might return, so we settled down to wait in one of the loose boxes that had been allotted to us. Although these Sakai had not been outside since the fighting had started two years before, they were neither frightened nor shy and seemed quite pleased to see us. Some of them knew Ah Chu by sight, as they had carried rice and sweet potatoes to our house at Blantan, and a few had attended the Sakai dance which our Chinese had arranged to entertain the Plen.

The women were naked to the waist, wearing only a *sarong* of cloth or bark. Some had red, white, or ochre paint smeared on their faces, and a few had by way of ornament a match-stalk thrust through the piece of flesh below and between the nostrils. All were smoke-stained and unwashed, but a few were comely if not beautiful, with luxuriant black hair tied in a bun held up with a bamboo comb. The children were quite enchanting – little naked gnomes with round, dark eyes and enormous potbellies.

During the day the hunters returned, singly or in small parties, but not one had secured any game. Some of the youths were not yet in their teens, but like their fathers they carried the eight-foot-long blow-pipe and bamboo quiver for poisoned arrows ornamented with strange conventional designs. They were dressed only in a scanty loincloth, each carrying on his back a small bag closely woven with fine rattan to hold his tobacco, flint, steel, and tinder, and if he were an older man, the apparatus for preparing betel nut for chewing. Many of the men wore twenty or thirty strings of minute bright-coloured beads looped over their shoulders so as to cross in front and behind, and more beads or an amulet of some sort round their necks. Some of them also wore a circle of woven and patterned bark to keep their hair in place, and into this they tucked bright flowers.

It was not until after dark on the following evening that Pa Kasut appeared. He had spent the night at the settlement at Kelundor, a right-bank tributary of the upper Woh, and had returned with a young hunter from there and his ten-year-old son. Their arrival was most dramatic: they appeared from a dark and rainy night, and before they took any notice of anybody, they sprinkled wood ash from the fire out of the doorway – to prevent the entry of any evil spirits that might have been following them.

Pa Kasut was a little old man with no teeth, a bad cough, and a childlike simple expression – far too old, one would have thought, to be allowed out hunting alone. Later acquaintance modified this view, and though he always seemed frail, he was kindly and had a whimsical sense of humour. Like many of the older Sakai he had an inordinate fear of the Japs, and this prevented him helping us as much as he would have liked. Next day he rather reluctantly took us round his clearings, very much afraid – can one blame him? – that we might want to come and live too near him and thus disturb his peace. He told us the water was bad, that it always blew and rained, was bitterly cold, and was very bad for malaria – all of which, except the condemnation of the water, turned out to be true.

Our requisites were: a site open to the west for wireless reception; water; *atap* for thatching; a not too long and difficult path to the *kampongs* from which we got our food; and, while the house itself would have to be built under the trees to hide us from prying aircraft, we wanted an open place beside it where we could get a distant view and enjoy the sun. We found just such a place on the left bank of the Ayer Busok (or stinking water) a few hundred yards above its confluence with the Woh. In the middle of February, our whole party moved over from Blantan.

205

It had been our intention to build one house for our guard and another for ourselves, but while Ah Yang's men were building their house in a strip of bamboo jungle beside the clearing, the whole party took up temporary quarters in a large hut that Pa Kasut's family had inhabited the previous year. *Atap* had to be cut and carried from a considerable distance by the Sakai, and when Ah Yang's men had once built their own house, they seemed so reluctant to start all over again to build ours that we decided to stay where we were and bought the house from Pa Kasut for $10.

The house was completely in the open, though surrounded by secondary bamboo jungle. It had obviously been built by the same excellent craftsman who had made Pa Kasut's, with a similar design, except that one end of the house had been raised a foot or two above the rest of the floor to make a sleeping-bench. We made shutters at this end, so that as we sat on the sleeping-bench leaning over the bamboo balustrade, we had a superb view over the old clearing down to the junction of the Ayer Busok and Woh rivers, and across to the nearer side of Bukit Silun. It was a great joy being able to look down on to the tops of the trees, for a whole new world of beauty was revealed – a world quite unrealised as one walked in the jungle beneath, though even here, suddenly encountering a carpet of fallen blossom made one suspect what lay above. As the Malayan jungle is evergreen, none of the trees shed all their leaves at once, but the foliage of most species undergoes a complete change during the year and many of the trees in the course of their annual cycle are densely covered with a mass of gay blossom, white, yellow, pink, or scarlet, and often so sweetly scented that even the dark jungle beneath is full of the fragrance of the invisible flowers above.

Although the camp was only slightly higher than the Blantan site, being not far above the two-thousand-foot contour, it was the coldest regular camp – as opposed to a bivouac – I have ever known in the jungle. Even if we wore all our clothes and wrapped ourselves in two blankets, we were still frozen at night. This was largely because, being a Sakai house, the sleeping-bench and floor were eight feet above the ground, and being just at the summit of the steep hill rising from the river, it seemed to receive a perpetual bath of cold air. We extended the roof at the back of the hut to

206

cover a basement kitchen with clay fireplaces, shelves, and tables, and a staircase leading to the living-room. Here Lim Bo Seng spent his time, aided by me and most of the other Chinese in turn – since eating was our chief occupation – and assisted by Black Lim and old Ah Su, who carried water and did most of the real work.

We had intended to construct a bamboo conduit from the stream, but so much time was spent in arguing as to how this should be done that it was never even started. We then built bamboo tables and seats, carefully anchoring the former to the uprights of the house so that they did not vibrate whenever anyone scratched himself or combed his hair. Making furniture or anything else with bamboo is a very skilled job, as the wood will turn the edge of most tools, splits on the least provocation, and warps as it dries, and, as nails cannot be used, all joints have to be lashed with rattan. It will also cut careless fingers to the bone with no apparent effort.

One of the arms dumps had arrived from the coast and we were able to distribute a few Sten guns, rifles, and pistols to our guard. I spent a good deal of time training them in jungle-craft and simple tactics, and, as we were so far from the plains, we could give them some target practice on a range in one of Pa Kasut's clearings. Because ammunition had been so scarce in the guerilla camps, very few of Yang's men had fired more than one or two shots – some none at all – and to be able to blaze away a burst of automatic fire with a Sten gun or .45 Colt was a great thrill. We let them fire at point-blank range so that they could occasionally hit the target, and this gave them great confidence.

Once a week one of us would give them a lecture on some non-military subject, such as life in New Zealand or Greenland, how Britain was governed (rather a dangerous subject), or winter sports. And once a week we invited them to a feast – the only time we all ate together – when we squatted in parties of six and ate bowls of excessively fat and greasy pork, delicious curried chicken, and rich soup made of chicken giblets, groundnuts, and cucumber. This was a very happy Robinson-Crusoe-like existence, but all the time we were waiting for something to happen – a submarine R.V. to succeed, or a wireless set to arrive at camp. And week after week went by and still nothing happened.

Soon after we had moved to Pa Kasut's, the food position became more difficult. The Japs, possibly having followed Davis's and Broome's trail to the place where they had entered the jungle, carried out a savage massacre in the *kampongs* near there, burning down the houses and driving away those they did not kill or capture. From Blantan it had been quite easy for Ah Yang's men to go to a certain hut at the jungle edge of the *kampong*, where our outside men had collected the vegetables that had been grown there and the dried fish, coffee, and other food that had been bought in Bidor and Tapah, and to bring them back to camp the same day. But from Pa Kasut's it was a very long day's march to reach the same *kampong*, and the return journey with heavy loads took a day and a half. Even if the men slept at the Blantan house, the whole trip took three days. Though Yang's men had been increased to fifteen, they still had to guard the camp and carry on with their training. They could easily have supported themselves, but our party were mere passengers as far as carrying food was concerned.

Chen Ping and Yang between them at last succeeded in opening up new food lines. Contacts were made near the 9th Mile on the Cameron Highlands road, and it proved possible to buy a certain amount of food there, but gone were the days when we could get Chinese delicacies from the towns. Rice became so short that we had to mix it with sweet potatoes and tapioca that the Sakai used to bring in. We cut ourselves down to one fish dish and one vegetable dish per meal, and coffee and sugar became luxuries. At the same time we tried to become more self-reliant. We bought some goats from the Sakai and kept fowls. We ate bamboo shoots, made curries out of palm cabbage, and started gardening.

Soon after we had settled down at Pa Kasut's it was time for the March R.V., but the Japs were still so active on the jungle edge immediately outside our camp area, as well as at Teluk Anson and Pangkor, that Chen Ping once again said it would be extremely risky for Broome to try to get down to the coast. The fact that the last R.V. had failed made us doubly anxious, and as Ying was absolutely certain he had made no mistake we were afraid that something had gone wrong at the Colombo end. Perhaps they knew that the R.V. had been compromised and were no longer sending the submarines. It would be difficult enough for Broome to reach the R.V., and if anything went wrong it would be practically impossible for him to return again. This was Chen Ping's advice, and we did not feel we could go against it. It must be remembered that the guerillas considered themselves entirely responsible for our safety, and if they said it was impossible for them to take us safely to the coast, we had to accept their verdict. So Ying was again sent to keep the R.V. Once more it was a failure.

While we were awaiting the verdict of Chen Ping, Frank Quayle reached our camp at Pa Kasut's. It will be remembered that in April 1942, before Hayward and I had gone south to look for guerilla headquarters, he, Chrystal, and Robinson had been left at the Slim camp to train the guerillas in Perak. He looked fairly well, but his hair was greyer and he had lost weight since I had last seen him. He had stayed the whole two years with the headquarters camp and had an interesting tale to tell. A few months after I had gone south, the Slim camp, which had long been known to the Malays as Ulu Slim, had been attacked by the Japs, and though there were no casualties among the guerillas, they had to move further north and cross the Sungkai river to the Bidor jungle. After a month there they had followed the Woh down to the Cameron Highlands road and lived up the Sungei Jor, some distance north and on the other side of the road. He had no information about Chrystal and Noone. Apparently they both lived in the camp until the autumn of 1942, when they decided to leave, having become more and more infuriated by the guerillas. They had gone over the Main Range into Pahang, and though reports had occasionally come back, Quayle had not heard of either of them for over a year.

Quayle had been ill most of the time, though at first he had been able to instruct in demolitions and help them with any mechanical repairs to their arms. Often he had had to be carried from camp to camp, and had been nursed through several severe attacks of fever. He was full of praise for the way he had been treated by the guerillas and undoubtedly owed his life to them. They had always given him the best of whatever they had, though, like Chrystal and Noone – and myself too – he hated their politics and some of their methods.

One of our great difficulties at this time was shortage of money, Davis and Broome had only brought in a limited amount and we were running very short. Davis had agreed to bear the total cost of Ah Yang's guard, and with the prices of foodstuffs rising, it cost a great deal to maintain more than twenty people. In addition to this, very considerable sums of money would be needed to carry out the agreement we had made with the Plen to subsidise the guerillas, and more capital was needed to put Ah Ng's business on a sounder footing. It was therefore decided that Lim Bo Seng should go outside to raise money. We felt that with his ability and experience he would be able to put Ng's business in order and thus not only help to raise money but release Ah Ng for his real work. Accordingly about the middle of March he was installed in a house in Ipoh, where he rented the top floor and posed as Ng's uncle. Once again we were reluctantly compelled to centralise far too much on Ah Ng. But he was the only man capable of securing the necessary passes, which had to be done by personal influence and judicious bribery. It was intended that Lim Bo Seng should return to the camp as soon as he had put things straight below.

About March 20 Ying arrived at Pa Kasut's with a letter from Kong Ching saying that Ng had left for Singapore to continue his financial discussions. Ying also said that the night before Choy had had a mysterious visit from two men claiming to be guerillas' representatives, who had demanded money with menaces. Choy was said to have kept his head and had not disclosed his relations with the guerillas, but this visit was most alarming, for Choy not only knew all about our submarine R.V.s but for a long time had been our chief agent in Pangkor for financing the Sitiawan guerillas. In the light of later events it seems clear that the two mysterious visitors were Japanese detectives.

It was now time for the April R.V., but as the two previous ones had failed it seemed unwise for one of us to go. It was most important to keep this R.V. and re-establish contact, which had now been broken for three months. A Chinese unencumbered by a European would have ten times more chance of keeping it and of extricating himself from any trouble that might arise. Accordingly Ying left about April 6 to keep the rendezvous. The same evening he was back in camp with Tsing, whom he had met on the way.

210

A major disaster had occurred. Tsing was almost speechless with nervous excitement. He said that Choy had been arrested on the evening of March 23. Tsing himself was arrested on the following day and confronted with Choy, who now appeared to be a completely broken man and admitted having given everything away. Tsing then had to confirm what Choy had said, but avoided adding anything to what the Japs already knew. Tsing had been taken to Ipoh and lodged in the headquarters of the Jap counter-espionage organisation, where some Japs, some Chinese detectives, and a few girls in their employ lived in a large and comfortable house. He was very well treated. The Japs apparently hoped to reform him by kindness and win him over to work for them – more direct methods of persuasion would no doubt come later. This was their usual method of making captured guerillas or agents speak. He was not locked up, but was kept under constant guard.

On March 28 he was being looked after by two women when one of the Japs wandered into the room stark naked – a Japanese habit. This outraged the natural Chinese modesty of the girls to such an extent that they walked out of the room, thus giving Tsing his chance. He got up, too, as if it had been already agreed, and said he was going to have a bath. He managed to climb out of the bathroom window, which was on the second storey, and clamber down a drainpipe to the ground. He then ran down the street and jumped into a taxi, telling the Chinese driver to drive towards the main road. When he had recovered his breath, he confessed that he was an escaped guerilla and wanted to go to Bidor. The driver responded magnificently and shouting '*Tai ka t'ung pau*' (we are all of one blood), proceeded at full speed down the road. Having reached the coffee-shop at the outskirts of Bidor, where he was known, Tsing borrowed the taxi fare from the local guerilla supporters, paid off his driver, and rushed up to our Blantan camp.

On hearing Tsing's story, we immediately, with Chen Ping's help, sent out runners to warn Lim Bo Seng and Sek Fu. We could do nothing about Ah Ng in Singapore or Lim in Lumut, the only hope being a warning via Lim Bo Seng – if *he* could be reached in time. But we were too late. Though messengers went out repeatedly, they were unable to find Lim Bo Seng or Sek Fu, or to hear any word of them. The only scrap of news we were able to pick up was that one of the Hylam sailors on Choy's junk had said that he had seen Lim Bo Seng and Ng being interrogated. The only good news was that the long reports we had all written to go out by the submarine had not fallen into the enemy's hands. Tsing said that on seeing the Japs come in at the door of Choy's house he had managed to run into the bathroom and stamp the tin of Andrew's Liver Salts, in the bottom of which the reports were concealed, into the muddy floor.

Our party now consisted of the four Europeans; Ah Han, who now took over the leadership of our Chinese; Lee Chuen – still patiently waiting for his wireless set; Tsing and Ying, now unemployable because known; and Black Lim and Ah Su. We felt that the camp was safe for the moment, as the Japs would be kept busy for some time ferreting out details of the organisation in the plains. In any case it would take them a long time to penetrate so far into the mountains, and all the Sakai had been told to give us warning as soon as the Japs set foot in the jungle. All we could do was to put the camp in a state of readiness and wait. As the chances were against the Japs appearing, it did not seem worth while abandoning our gardens and our good Sakai contacts and moving somewhere else, though we immediately started studying the map for the time when such a move should be necessary.

The camp was a difficult site to guard, as it could be approached by the upper track from Pa Kasut's house or by the lower path which came up from the Woh, so we kept an all-day guard on both these tracks and an all-night guard closer in. We also prepared some strong defensive positions overlooking the ways into the camp so that, if we had warning of their approach, we could hold the enemy for a short time while the stores were carried away into the jungle. One other thing we did was to carry all the spare food and gear we were not actually using to a rock chamber half an hour's walk from the camp up the Ayer Busok, which was to be the R.V. if we were attacked.

The sudden and complete destruction of all our hopes and plans left us in the position of mere guests – fortunately still paying guests – of the guerillas, dependent on them for our very existence and impotent to carry out a single item of our side of the agreement we had signed with the Plen. Our only hope for the future lay in Chen Ping being able to bring up one of the two B.2 wireless sets still buried at Jenderata and in the uncertain possibility of another blind landing being made. And that could be successful only if Colombo realised that the original R.V. area had been compromised. Perhaps our greatest worry was that we were completely unable to give the Royal Navy any warning of this grave danger.

Fortunately we still had money enough for our own support for about a year, together with vital medicines. We immediately suggested to Chen Ping that the guerillas should try to borrow money on a large scale on the strength of Davis's written authority from SEAC, and this they undertook to do. We also urged them to try to hurry up the arrival of our wireless equipment from Jenderata. The guerillas' acceptance of our humiliating position was most gratifying. This was largely due to the very friendly relations we had established with that outstanding character, Chen Ping. At no time were we allowed to feel that we were in any way an encumbrance to them, and they gave us every possible assistance. Meanwhile, we could do nothing but wait.

CHAPTER TWELVE

Search Party Through the Mountains

Pat Noone was an ethnologist. His work consisted largely of studying the aborigines in the jungle, and he had published a brilliant monograph on a Sakai tribe called the Ple-Temiar, who inhabit the extreme north of Perak. Both Davis and Broome had known him before the war, and Davis had sometimes accompanied him on his journeys into the jungle.

When Quayle joined us in March 1944, our news of Noone was brought up to date. He had joined the Perak guerilla headquarters camp in May 1942 after an abortive effort to reach Siam with six British officers, who had died one after the other. For some time he worked with the guerillas as their Sakai contact. Like most intelligent people, he was extremely interested in the theory of Communism, and he and Chrystal spent much time reading any available books on the subject and in long discussions with the guerilla leaders. But they soon became dissatisfied with the Chinese interpretation of Communism and decided, much against the guerilla leaders' will, to go off on their own. Noone's complaints were that their Communism had an unreasonably anti-British bias and that the leaders consistently and deliberately deceived him, allowed him no freedom of movement or action, and bungled or interfered with his work to an unjustifiable degree.[1]

He and Chrystal set off together, but as they were both extremely independent-minded, they soon agreed to part company. Noone's idea – according to Quayle – had been to live with the Sakai in the Temengor district, southeast of Grik, in the extreme north of Perak.

[1] In June 1944, when travelling with some guerilla guides from Perak headquarters, I noticed they were using, to roll their cigarettes, some paper with English writing on it. On piecing it together, I found it was a memorandum (though incomplete) written by Noone, giving the above reasons for parting with the guerillas.

(Use Map No. 3)

When our March R.V. failed and there seemed little prospect of getting in touch with Ceylon for some time, I found myself increasingly restless. The search for Noone, therefore, seemed just what I wanted, and would give me an excuse to see new country and new people. I planned to go straight to Kampong Jalong and make further inquiries from the Sakai there, travelling through the high mountainous hinterland well to the east of the ordinary route, in Sakai country, where no Chinese or even Malays normally penetrated. We had good maps of this area, and Davis had actually traversed part of the route in pre-war days and knew that there were Sakai paths all the way. From Jalong, depending on my information, I could either double back and cross the watershed eastward to Kelantan or follow the Korbu river to the Temengor country and on to Grik. It would probably be necessary to replenish my stores at Jalong, but Chen Ping, though he seemed rather vague about this part of the world, said there were guerillas in the south of this area who would of course help me, but towards Grik we must beware of bandits.

I decided to take only Black Lim with me. I liked him because being unable to read or write, he was much less politically minded than most of the guerillas and he could be relied on to do what he was told. Mentally he was almost subnormal, but like many illiterate people, he had an astonishing memory, being able to speak four Chinese dialects and very fluent Malay; and once he had been over a track he could always remember the way. Lim was also extremely good with his hands and had more than his share of the Chinese genius of improvisation. Finally, he was a very strong traveller and would not keep me back.

We took one pistol and a grenade each, and as well as the normal essentials for jungle travel, a fair supply of dried food such as salt fish, prawns, ginger, and curry powder, since we expected to get only tapioca from the Sakai with a little rice and sweet potatoes if we were lucky. We also took several pounds of salt, which for its weight, is the best trade article – except for tobacco, which we ourselves could not get in sufficient quantity. It was arranged that Mahanut, the headman of our local Sakai, should introduce me to Pa Blanken, the intelligent and influential leader of the Bot

Sakai at the foot of the Cameron Highlands road, who would introduce me to the next headman – and so on. Thus, being properly sponsored, I should secure the fullest possible cooperation from the Sakai

We set out on April 13. Mahanut, always surly, was in an exceptionally bad temper that day and, saying he had fever, refused to carry my rucksack, which at the beginning of the journey weighed about 45 lb. I, too, had not recovered from my last attack of malaria, and as it was one of those airless oppressive days that are common when rain is expected, I felt completely exhausted when, after five hours of hard going, we reached the first house of Pa Blanken's country.

Pa Blanken himself was a youngish man with a low forehead, thick lips, and rather ape-like figure. He was extremely shrewd and, in his rather offhand way, was always most cooperative and seemed prepared to take any risk to help us. Unlike any other Sakai that I had met, he wore a wristwatch and owned a few acres of rubber beside the Sungei Tedong. He was also a wily hunter and had been lent a shotgun by the Cameron Highland guerillas, for whom he shot pig and rusa on a fifty-fifty basis. He at once agreed to provide two guides to take us up parallel to the Cameron Highlands road to Pa Senapat's, the next stop. The following day was a very heavy one, and we were travelling for ten hours. Unfortunately one of our guides was again too ill or too proud to take a load, and I had to carry my pack half the day. This was especially annoying as we had to cross a number of Sakai bridges, often over deep ravines, formed by a single tree-trunk. These were, in any case, most troublesome and a heavy rucksack still further upset my balance. Our route led us first up the Bot river through an extremely long and steep series of clearings and then along a high ridge parallel to the road, of which we had occasional glimpses. At midday we rested in an empty Sakai house surrounded by yellow flowers.

The track now followed the left bank of the Batang Padang river, which was here twice as wide as the Woh. Sometimes we could hear Jap motor transport on the road on the other side, and once, when a gong was beaten loudly quite near us, we took fright and ran into the jungle. But it was only a return-to-work signal of a riverside power-station. A steep climb, most exhausting at the end of a long day, led us first through jungle and then up a newly planted clearing to a small deserted Sakai hut. The next day was wasted, as our guides did not succeed in finding Pa Senapat's Sakai until the evening, since they had moved far into the hills. But we had a very pleasant time watching the Jap cars crawling up the road, and making a curry of the succulent stems of yam leaves.

On April 16 we set off with three very jungly porters, descended to cross the Sungei Sekam, and followed the Batang Padang and then the Jor river upstream, wading in the water well over our knees, and feeling ourselves a very easy target for any Japs who might have come down from the road a few hundred yards on our left to watch the river. A short distance below Jor Corner we dashed across the road and for half an hour threaded our way parallel to the road through a most unpleasant bamboo thicket to the back of a coffee-shop beside the road, where our Sakai collected a young Chinese who was alleged to be in touch with the guerillas. We bought a little rice and some cooking-oil here and after an hour's wait, during which we watched some noisy Japs enter and leave the coffee-house and were greatly afraid of treachery, he produced two Sakai who led us at terrific speed across the Jor river and up the Sungei Chevei to a tiny hut hidden in a thicket.

Next day two new guides arrived: a smug little man wearing a *songkar* (a small round velvet cap) and a young man whose wife accompanied him all the way, carrying their small child tied in a cloth on her back. We returned to the Jor river and spent most of the day following it up almost to its source. As there was no path, we waded up the river itself with the dense jungle rising steeply on either side, getting occasional glimpses of recent or abandoned clearings on the hillsides far above us. At a height of 4,000 feet, on the col between Gunong Duri (5,020 feet) and Gunong Bergantong (4,724 feet), we found several very small Sakai huts.

We stayed the night in a minute house only ten feet square with such a low roof that I had to crawl in on all fours. At one time during the course of the evening there were over twenty-two peo-ple in this hut, and I was very much afraid that the whole bottom of the structure would collapse and drop us ten feet on to the ground.

Some time after dark there was a commotion outside and we grabbed our things and dispersed into the jungle, thinking that the Japs had somehow managed to follow us here. However, it was only a Sakai headman named Panjang and two of his womenfolk on their way home from Kampar with rice. I was interested to meet this man, of whom I had had such good reports from Quayle and the Chinese. He was certainly most impressive, being very tall – for a Sakai – with a heavy moustache and a mat of short black hair coming low down on his forehead. He had a very deep voice and slow, dignified speech, which he accompanied with stately gestures of his enormous hands. While we were talking, Panjang's womenfolk cooked rice for us all, and with our dried fish and curried prawns, and some freshly trapped rats and a pangolin (scaly ant-eater) provided by our host, we feasted till 3 a.m., while I gave a discourse on the war situation.

On April 18 we followed a long-disused path called the French Trace. Well before midday we reached an empty Sakai house by the Sungei Kampar, and our guides went out in search of the owners while we dug up tapioca roots and cooked a meal, hoping to continue our journey in the afternoon. But there had been a scare in this area and all the Sakai had moved into the hills, and our guides said they could not find them until next day.

On April 20 we set off again with two bullet-headed Sakai who shouted all day to each other or to anybody we met. This shouting habit was most embarrassing, as I had carefully trained myself to make no unnecessary noise in the jungle, and my ears had become so sensitive that I would stop and listen at the very snapping of a twig. This day's march took us first up the Kampar river, usually in the stream itself, but sometimes following a path on one side or the other. Soon we struck very steeply up the Sungei Tudong, a tributary to the northwest, and had an increasingly magnificent view across to the high peaks of Jasar (5,565 feet) and Ruil (5,680 feet) in the Cameron Highlands.

We followed a very steep but well-defined track for some distance until we heard the sound of chopping ahead. Our guides stopped and said in enormous whispers that we must approach very carefully as these Sakai were of another family and noted for their timidity. They went ahead, and soon we heard the usual shout-

218

ing in progress, so advanced to find a very bent and aged Sakai sitting on the ground eating the heart of a cabbage palm, which he had just cut down.

The old man led us to a curious long, low house built, quite fortuitously I think, in a curve. Here we were regaled with rather high rat and tapioca baked inside bamboo. It was good, but rather too gamy. We had to change guides here, for it seemed that in this district each family of Sakai kept very much to itself and a guide knew his way to the next house but no further. Another two hours along a most complicated maze of tracks, following ridges up and down over steep passes and past clearings, some of which were well above the three-thousand-foot contour, brought us to another hut where a man had just prepared a stew of a blue pheasant he had caught in a noose.

From this hut four or five Sakai accompanied us, and the noise of their shouting must have been audible for miles. Towards evening we reached a large house at over 3,000 feet on the eastern shoulder of Gunong Chabang (5,610 feet), though the peak itself was not in sight. Across the deep valleys of the headwaters of the Raia, Gruntum, and Kampar rivers was the finest mountain view I had seen in Malaya. The whole magnificent range of the Cameron Highlands with Gunong Suku (5,894 feet) in the foreground, and several six-thousanders behind it, lay right across the eastern horizon. In contrast to the great mass of Batu Putah, which is impressive but always rather shapeless and grim, here were graceful peaks – almost aiguilles in spite of being covered by jungle – of real beauty, each with its own distinctive outline and character. I spent half an hour sketching this remarkable skyline. The sketch, alas! was later taken by the Japs.

Next morning we set off by a long detour to visit a durian tree under which some ripe fruit had been collected only the day before, although it was not the durian season. We were unlucky, as a bear had been there before us and there was nothing but empty shells. At midday, after six hours of really hard going, we reached the tiny house of the Sakai headman of Raia.

Our host, like many of the Sakai headmen we met, was young and intelligent. In previous days he had been outside and had visited Ipoh, ridden in a train, and been to the cinema. He even possessed an alarm clock (which did not go) and other bric-a-brac which looked most out of place in a Sakai hut. Since the occupation, however, he had not ventured out of the jungle, having heard frightful tales of Jap atrocities. He had heard of the Chinese guerillas down at the bottom of the Raia valley, but had never met any. Certainly they never used this route. Although the headman had managed to keep out of the way of the Japs, he had suffered in that he had had practically no salt or tobacco since the occupation, and as he could obtain no cloth, his wife and two rather shy and attractive daughters were clad only in skirts of soft bark.

Next morning, April 22, the headman and one of his sons accompanied us, though they only knew the way as far as the Sungei Penoh. It was a continual surprise to us to find how insular were the Sakai. They knew every tree and pool in their own familiar hunting ground, but many had never been to the neighbouring valley or settlement. Our route took us for three hours up and down a very steep ridge almost due north, which we followed to its summit (about 4,000 feet) and then descended a very steep northwesterly ridge for a thousand feet to the Sungei Penoh. This track was almost overgrown with thickets of wiry bracken, which seems to get in and flourish wherever the country has been opened up at all, and we scratched our knees and arms very painful in forcing a way through.

At the bottom of the hill was a poor hovel where a wild, dirty, and gypsy-like woman was looking after three sickly children. She and her husband – who was away on a hunting trip – did no cultivation, but lived entirely on what his blow-pipe and the jungle provided. When we arrived, she was roasting some small hard green jungle bananas, and that seemed to be the only food in the house. She said she did not know the way but she would go and find a guide for us. Leaving the three children to look after each other she took us at tremendous speed down to the river and then left us for two hours while she went to collect guides.

From now on the day was a nightmare for me. I had not been going well the day before and had had no appetite in the morning. From long experience I ought to have known what was the matter with me – malaria – and filled myself up with quinine. That morning the long ascent had been very burdensome, and when we lay waiting for our wild woman to return I suddenly felt very ill indeed. On taking my temperature, I found it was 104 degrees. This was more than awkward, as to return to the headman's house would mean climbing the frightful hill that we had just come down, and we had no idea how far ahead the next house lay. The map showed that it was at least four miles further to the Kinta river and there might not be any habitation on the way. The unknown evil seemed preferable. The way, at least, lay downhill and in the right direction, so I took fifteen grains of quinine and slept until our new guides appeared, and the headman and his son, after receiving a dollar each, returned home.

Our route followed the Penoh river downstream, sometimes in the bed of the stream, more often along muddy tracks on one side or the other. After several hours of this, in which I found it extremely difficult to keep going, we left the Penoh, which by now had become a fair-sized river, and followed a tiny tributary very steeply up to the right. Had I known what lay ahead of me, I should have insisted on making a shelter and sleeping beside the river, but our guides said the hut where we were to spend the night was only just up the hill, so I took another fifteen grains of quinine and went on. The path soon left the stream and followed a ridge through *atap* palms for about a thousand feet of steep ascent. This took me some hours, as I had to stop and rest every few yards and pull myself up by holding on to the trees. My leg-muscles seemed to have lost all their power and would not work. For the last part of the ascent I had to be towed by the Sakai with a rattan line.

When at last we reached the Sakai house, in spite of my fever, I was most excited to see one of the most remarkable huts I had ever visited. It was at least twenty-five feet off the ground and was entered by a tree-trunk staircase resting in the centre on a fifteen-foot stump. I was so giddy that I had to crawl up on my hands and knees! Next morning my temperature was below normal, and as the Sakai here had no food I decided to travel.

The day's journey took us back down the hill to the Penoh, which we followed two miles to its junction with the richest and most famous of all tin-mining streams – the Kinta river. The Penoh was now too wide and swift for us to walk in the river, and to my relief we followed a good path, sometimes along rocks above the rapids and sometimes cutting across loops of the river through pleasant level groves of bamboo, carpeted with brown and yellow leaves. In the early afternoon we passed through a succession of very fine clearings with maize nearly ready for picking. Among it were little patches of spinach, sweet potato, pumpkin, and cucumber, also some fine plants of tobacco. Finally we stopped at a well-built hut just where the Sungei Termin joins the Kinta.

The Sakai here seemed much more civilised. and we could expect them to become increasingly so – and therefore less reliable – as we followed down the Kinta river. At this point we were only four miles from the roadhead from Tanjong Rambutan. The Sakai told us that a few miles down the river at the head of a pipeline lived a Chinese with a Sakai wife. I decided to send Lim down to contact this Chinese, buy what he could, and find out the local news. While he was away, I followed my usual custom, and collecting the Sakai together, gave them a talk on the war situation, telling them why we must win in the end and that they must keep out of the way of the Japs with the certain assurance that they would soon be driven out of Malaya. But as usual the Sakai had all the right ideas, partly from what they themselves had seen of Jap methods and partly from the excellent and far-reaching guerilla propaganda. I inquired after Noone here. Though they had all heard of him and one man had actually met him before the war, they assured me that he had not passed this way for many years. Lim returned after a few hours, but had only been able to buy some tobacco leaves and half a bottle of cooking-oil, as the Chinese himself lived almost entirely on tapioca. He told Lim that the guerillas occasionally visited him and that they were all very frightened of the Malays, who were most untrustworthy.

By the following morning I had completely recovered from my bout of fever. We left Kuala Termin at first light, as we had to go through country which was often visited by Malays. We soon crossed the Kinta river, which was here forty yards wide but not nearly so deep and swift as it had been higher up, and an alarmingly large track soon brought us to the very fine house of Panda, the headman at Kuala Yang-oi, to whom Panjang had recommended me.

He was a most dignified old man, and everything in his house was clean – comparatively speaking – and beautifully made. He was very helpful and sent two of his sons and another man with us as guides. There was considerable uncertainty about the track, and our guides admitted that they had not dared to pass along this way since the occupation, as the Sakai over the watershed to the north were said to be untrustworthy. Working largely from our map, we crossed a high deserted clearing and came down in the Seno-oi valley.

Here we came upon an old and bearded Sakai cutting a shaft for a pig-spear. This man turned out to be the father of our third guide, but he had not met his son for some years, although they only lived a few miles apart. The old man led us to the most magnificent house I have ever seen in the jungle. In the centre was the ceremonial dance floor, as big as a tennis court, beautifully made with two-inch-wide slats of bamboo, and with the *atap* roof far above it. This was surrounded by a square of living rooms, each with its own roof and with half-cylinders of bark taking off the water where the drainage from the two roofs met. Each family lived in a 'loose box' with a low, flattened bamboo balcony and steps leading to the great central room. At one end of the dance floor was a small musicians' gallery built out, and here were two Sakai drums. Out in the centre of the room was a huge log with four holes in it for stamping rice. The whole house, as is usual, was built out over sloping ground, so that the upper side, which was entered by four well-made staircases, was ten feet above the ground, while the lower side was nearly twenty feet up. The walls, instead of being open, were of plaited sections of *atap* which could be raised to admit light and fresh air. At one time there were sixty-four people, all residents, in this remarkable house.

Everybody was very friendly, and the headman, who had a pointed grey beard, made us welcome with grave courtesy. He had a pure Malay wife, who was dressed in a gay bodice and *sarong* and wore a great deal of jewellery. We bought a chicken and were given some sweet potatoes and seedling leeks. We had just started our meal in a corner of the main floor which had been set apart for us and covered with clean grass mats, when suddenly a man who had just returned from hunting started praying in a loud sing-song voice as I had heard the Malays pray. This, in itself, was sufficiently remarkable, but as he spoke or rather sang his words very fast I could not gather what he was saying. Lim, who seemed very concerned, told me that he was telling the others that we were bad people, fugitives from the Japs, and that if they helped us it would bring only misfortune to them, and that they ought to have nothing to do with us.

The situation was critical. The bearded elders sat immobile and seemed to reserving a judgment. Some of the younger men joined the speaker in excited discussion and obviously agreed with his point of view. At this stage Lim, who fortunately spoke extremely fluent Malay, got up and started to argue with him, and soon, speaking with great vehemence, secured everybody's attention. He spoke at the top of his voice for nearly an hour and by that time had succeeded in silencing our adversary and winning everybody over. That night we slept with our pistols beside us, as all the Sakai here were armed with pig-spears – stout poles six feet long and surmounted with heavy flat metal spearheads.

There was no further incident, and on April 25 we left our hosts with every expression of goodwill. With new guides we descended steeply to cross the Sungei Seno-oi a short distance above its confluence with the Sungei Gajah, and then climbed right up an *atap* ridge to a huge rambling dark hut reminiscent of an old English country house with its floor at a number of different levels and with odd rooms built on at various times, each in its own style. Behind this Sakai hut to the west rose the massive face of Gunong Korbu, the second highest mountain in Malaya, towering 5,000 feet above us, with serried outcrops of bare grey rock alternating with the blue-green jungle.

Here we changed guides and skirted a long solidly constructed bamboo fence, the only one of its kind I have seen built by the Sakai. Our guides took us steeply down to cross the Sungei Gajah and then right up to the head of this river with Gunong Chondong (4,803 feet) on our left, and over the watershed at 3,843 feet to the Sungei Korbu valley. All this day we kept Korbu on our right, but so thick was the bamboo jungle that we only rarely got glimpses of its rocky crags and terraces. For a few miles on the north side of the watershed we threaded a maze of tiny tracks, usually following streams and skirting patches of thick secondary undergrowth where there had once been clearings. A long descent brought us to a large Sakai house overlooking the Kuala Termin. Here the people were the most hospitable we had yet visited.

Next morning we crossed the Korbu by a tree-trunk bridge with a bamboo handrail on either side. It is the only bridge of its kind I have seen in Sakai country, and it reminded me of one across a Himalayan torrent. The Korbu river, draining one of the highest massifs in Malaya, has carved out for itself an exceedingly deep valley, parts of which are almost a gorge, and there are long stretches of small waterfalls and rapids where a slip would mean death, as the volume of water, particularly after recent rain, is tremendous. As the water was reasonably low at this time, we were sometimes able to walk over the massive bare grey slabs of rock in the bed of the river, but often we were forced to crawl along tiny slippery traverses among the wet rocks overhanging the gorge, holding on to roots with our hands. Sometimes we negotiated an exposed corner by walking along bamboos supported by pegs stuck into crevices in the rock. The Sakai only renew these when they actually break, and as I am about half as heavy again as the normal Sakai, they went over first, then watched my crossing with great interest. Sometimes we had to renew the pegs before attempting to cross. Whenever tributary streams came in, their lower waters fanned out over slabs of bare rock, so steep and slippery that we had to take off our rubber shoes and cross in bare feet. As usual when travelling with Sakai, we had to cross the river several times – which was only just possible at certain places known to our guide – follow up side valleys, and ascend and descend long ridges to avoid completely impassable stretches of the gorge.

We travelled down the river for three hours before coming to another hut, which lay at the top of a steep clearing where there was a fine crop of maize. Our guide went home from here, and we collected rather a garrulous old man who carried an *atap* fishing-rod and talked all the time. To reach the next house we had to descend for a thousand feet down an unbelievably steep and slippery track through bamboos to the river, cross it, and then climb a similar track on the other side. We stopped at a clearing overlooking the mouth of a tributary of the Korbu called the Sungei Kuah (gravy river), where there were several small huts. The people here seemed to be very prosperous. In the hut where we stayed, for instance, they had a dozen goats, twenty or thirty fowls, some bags of rice and – most welcome of all – plenty of large Sakai bananas. They were very generous and friendly people.

In the evening a very smart young moustached Sakai headman came in with an extremely beautiful wife, who looked almost Javanese. For a moment I thought they were Malays, especially as he used the formal greeting, '*Selamat tuan*,' which I had never heard before from a Sakai. He gave us a handful of home-grown tobacco and some bananas, and promised to guide us towards Jalong on the following day. He told us that the Chinese – whom he did not seem to like very much – had never come up as far as this, but he had met them further down the valley. He had heard of Noone and said that he had been at Jalong some years before, but he had not heard anything of him since the occupation. This dapper young headman, accompanied by his wife, guided us on the following day down the river to the next house. Its owner, Mudah, took us along to the next headman, Bras (or rice), who was the most prosperous Sakai I had met.

He was a young, clean-looking man, wearing a pair of grey shorts and a much-worn drill jacket. His wife, dressed in Malay style, was equally clean and not nearly so shy as most Sakai women. The house was very large and well built and there was much more privacy than in most Sakai houses, the headman's room even having a door. On arrival we were given coffee with sugar in it, and before the meal a china bowl of water was provided for washing and a comb and mirror to make ourselves tidy. I felt quite ashamed here, as I covered about two square feet of the clean bamboo floor with blood from leech-bites on my legs and feet. All the way down the Korbu valley they were as bad as I have known them anywhere.

After lunch we had a long talk with the headman. He knew nothing of Noone's whereabouts – though of course he knew his name – but said that the old headman at Jalong might be able to help us. The man's daughter, Ajang, once the most beautiful of all the Sakai, had some years before the war taken part in an exhibition of Sakai culture which Noone had organised at Singapore, and though Ajang was now away from her home, the father might know Noone's whereabouts. Bras also told us that there was no jungle route from the Korbu valley to the Temengor district and Grik. The only way was through the Chinese village of Jalong, and neither he nor any of the Sakai there would take us past Jalong without the acquiescence of the Chinese who lived there.

Chen Ping had not told us of a guerilla patrol at Jalong, but as we were still south of what he called the bandit country, we thought any Chinese there would be reliable and would help us. Bras himself came with us to introduce us to the old headman down at Kampong Jalong, though he said he could not take us on to meet the Chinese, as they lived in the other headman's district. He seemed very much in awe of these Chinese and said it would be unsafe to go there and advised us to return. But we only laughed and said we were all allies against the hated Japanese. Soon we were to regret that we had not taken his advice.

Soon after leaving Bras' fine house the track became much wider and we came on the fresh tracks of elephant. These were tame ones that had been used before the war to carry supplies to the huge Chinese tin mine far into the jungle some miles up the Larek river, which we soon crossed just where it runs into the Korbu. These elephant were now used by the Sakai to carry their rice down to Kampong Jalong. The Korbu river was here much wider but less torrential. We followed it down, walking on the wide flat slabs between the water and the jungle, until we were able to wade across it in a place where it was very broad and only thigh deep. On the other side we joined a fine wide track.

Late in the evening we reached the old headman's house. He was very friendly and regaled us with hot sweet coffee, but said that his daughter Ajang had been away for years and that he had not seen or heard of Noone since the war. The Sakai are not very accurate in computing time, but it certainly appeared that Noone had not come this side of the mountains on his way from the Perak headquarters camp, or he would certainly have called in here. The old man told us that no Sakai had gone to Temengor since the Jap occupation and there was no one who could take us, but that the Chinese were in the habit of using that route on their way to Grik.

227

There seemed nothing for it but to go and visit the Chinese at Jalong. I was reluctant to do this as we knew nothing about them, but Lim was much in favour of the idea, and perhaps I was too easily persuaded. Even if the Chinese refused to help us, I felt that we ought to have a few days' rest and buy some food before making any further plans. The journey had taken us fifteen days, on two of which we had not been able to travel. Following the excellent Sakai custom of starting at dawn and getting in at midday, except when we had dawdled or made double journeys, we had never been caught by the rain and only once had to stop for it.

The old headman was very reluctant to send a guide with us to the Chinese house, though it was only half an hour's walk downriver. But after repeated assurances that they were friends of ours and would be glad to see us, he at last sent a couple of men with us. We recrossed the river to its left bank and after following the elephant path for a short distance soon emerged at the head of a large area of cultivation nestling between the jungle and the river. Among the patches of vegetables of all kinds were two Chinese huts of brown *atap*. It was indeed a pleasant change from the jungle, and as we walked through the gardens towards the first house I felt the same pleasant anticipation of comfort and good food as the mountaineer experiences as he returns to a luxurious Swiss hotel after a long sojourn in the high Alpine huts.

CHAPTER THIRTEEN

Capture

The house to which our Sakai guides led us was occupied by four Chinese who were absolutely astounded to see us, especially when they learned that we had emerged from the jungle. They had always considered the Jalong valley as a safe *cul-de-sac* immune from surprise approach – except by the Sakai – from the hinterland. After shaking hands I explained in my best Malay who we were and the object of our journey and asked them if, after resting a day or two with them, they would help us on our way. The Chinese, after much whispered confabulation, said they could not discuss the matter until their leader came, that he lived two days' journey down the valley, and that they would immediately send one of their number to bring him. Meanwhile we must have a bath, change our travel-stained clothes, and make ourselves as comfortable as possible.

In the normal Chinese way we undressed in the house and, wearing only our underpants, went down to bathe in the small stream which ran through the vegetable plots ten yards in front of the hut. On our return we found the leader – an unctuous, rat-faced little Hokkien with protruding ears and a mouth full of gold teeth – armed with my .38 revolver, which he carried most dangerously cocked, looking very consequential and aggressive. He explained that as they did not know who we were, or why or how we had come there, they must insist on searching all our gear. We found they had already taken possession of Lim's .45 automatic, our extra rounds, and our two grenades. They then went through all our things, and, apparently finding nothing suspicious, explained that they had had orders to confiscate all our weapons, but that these would not be taken out of the house and would be returned to us the moment permission came for us to proceed.

This seemed not unreasonable, though we rather wondered how they had got these orders since the messenger had not yet returned. The Chinese, who are so accustomed to finding traitors among their own numbers, are inordinately suspicious of strangers, and while they might have accepted me without credentials, Lim was regarded with the utmost suspicion. As soon as we had finished supper, I wrote a polite letter to their leader explaining who we were and where we wanted to go, and asked him if he would come himself or send an officer to confer with me as soon as possible.

Next day the rat-faced man asked if he might borrow my .38 to go and shoot a traitor further down the valley as this man, if he heard that I was in the neighbourhood, would immediately go and inform the Japs. I could hardly refuse this, but made him promise to bring back the pistol that night. Next day, when I asked him for my pistol, he said that all our weapons had been sent down for use against the traitor, but he would guarantee that they would be brought back on the day after. We did not see any of those weapons again, though we were pretty certain that they were kept concealed in the house and were carried by the two men who were on guard each night. When I demanded an explanation, the leader said that he had written to his headquarters about us but that nothing could be done until a reply came and that might take several days. Each day I wrote a strong letter to 'headquarters,' but a whole week dragged by without anybody coming to see me or even condescending to write. Meanwhile Lim and I were beginning to wonder who these Chinese were. On the surface relations seemed cordial enough, yet we were never allowed to go anywhere alone and there were always two sentries on duty at night. It gradually became obvious that we were prisoners.

The house was about twenty feet square with walls of plaited *atap*. A platform had been built over one end of the hut to form a loft, and it was here that Lim and I slept. If we wanted to go out in the night, we had to descend a creaky ladder and climb under or over the table which had been pulled across the doorway, thus disturbing the guards, who would come outside and watch us till we returned.

In the same house were two very old tobacco-growers who in fact owned the house and gardens. The 'guerillas' were apparently billeted on them. There were also four other young Chinese who were away all day building a house and making a clearing to grow vegetables in the jungle. Although these three groups ate different food and cooked their meals separately, they all seemed to be under the orders of the rat-faced man. None of them seemed to like him and, though they seemed too much afraid of him to speak freely, we were conscious of a most unpleasantly strained and suspicious atmosphere in the house.

One day one of the old men was left alone with me and after taking every precaution to see that he was not observed, he confided to me that these 'guerillas' were *orang jahat* (bad men) who had been forcibly billeted on them and that they were forced to give money to fight the Japs, but it was never used for that purpose. He told me that Rat-face had said that Lim and I were friends of the Japanese, and if either of the old men was found talking to us alone he would be reported to headquarters and punished. Lim was of the opinion that these men had nothing to do with the Communist guerillas. Certainly they knew none of the songs and slogans of the camps and did not seem to recognise the names of any of the leaders – though they may well have pretended ignorance for security reasons.

We could probably have escaped in the night, with or without our gear, as it was obviously impossible to maintain an effective all-night guard with eight men, four of whom had been doing hard manual work all day, and we knew that our guards were usually fast asleep by the early hours of the morning. But we did not want to lose our weapons or admit defeat by giving up our search for Pat Noone. I therefore decided to send Lim back with a letter to Davis explaining what had happened, and saying that I would hang on for another fortnight, if necessary, as I was very reluctant to abandon my plan of going on to Grik.

One night, I stealthily put aside a share of the food, medicine, tobacco, and money for Lim, and at dawn he shouldered his pack and quietly slipped out of the house while I engaged the two guards in conversation. Unfortunately one of the others saw him from a peephole in the loft and raised the alarm. All six Chinese then rushed after Lim, who continued nonchalantly making for the jungle. I set off in the rear to keep the peace, as I was afraid that in spite of my orders Lim would start putting into practice some of the 'unarmed combat' tricks I had taught him and which he had been longing to try out for the last week. We stood in the track arguing for an hour in furious Malay and at last arrived at a compromise which 'saved face' for them and for me. I would agree to postpone Lim's departure for four hours if they would guarantee to bring a headquarters official to confer with me within the same time. This they agreed to in spite of the fact that they had repeatedly assured me that the local headquarters was two days', and main headquarters two weeks', journey away.

After a hasty conference Rat-face's stooge set off on his bicycle and returned in an hour's time to say that Lim could go at once. This was most satisfactory, though no headquarters official appeared as had been agreed. From now on I became more and more disturbed and felt sure that Rat-face was playing some deep game to my detriment, but I was still determined to go on to Grik.

One day one of the vegetable-growers, who had once worked on a European rubber estate and always addressed me in very polite Malay – if none of the others were near – told me that Rat-face had quarrelled with the Communist Chinese and was playing a lone hand, and that he had written to the nearest guerilla headquarters saying that he would hand me over to them if they sent him a thousand dollars. This was disquieting enough. Worse was to follow, for a few days later one of the old tobacco-growers told me that in the Kampong Jalong shop he had seen Rat-face talking confidentially to a Chinese who was a notorious Jap agent. Another most disturbing circumstance was that for the last two mornings Jap two-engined planes circled low over the valley for nearly an hour.

I came to the conclusion that these men were probably deserters or plain bandits posing as guerillas, and that they were trying to sell me to the Communists or to the Japs – whichever would pay the higher price. Very reluctantly I gave up my plan of going on to Grik, and decided to give them the slip as soon as possible and return to Davis and Broome. I had been away for a month. Even if my suspicions were unfounded and I was later allowed to continue my search for Noone, it would be at least another month before I should return home, and by then almost anything might have happened – I might even have missed a submarine R.V.

It was now May 10, my fourteenth day in the camp and my

thirty-sixth birthday. It seemed an auspicious day to escape. A month's rest and adequate, if simple, food had made me extremely fit, and I thought I could get home in a week even without any help from the Sakai. That evening I surreptitiously packed up all my gear in my big rucksack. Though it was not their turn, Rat-face and the stooge were on duty. Something had made them suspicious. The guards would drink coffee until far into the night. Then they would take it in turn to keep awake, but usually morning found them both sprawling fast asleep across the table.

In those days we always carried with us an 'L-tablet' – L for lethal, in case we should be captured by the Japs and have to face torture. I had long since lost my tablet, but Davis and Broome had given me some morphia pills which could be used for the same purpose. I had no intention of killing my sentries. I just wanted to make quite sure they would sleep soundly. Unfortunately I had no idea of how much to use. My lethal dose consisted of eight tablets.

I decided to give them four each. That evening I joined them at coffee, and having previously crushed up the little white tablets, it was quite easy to slip them into their mugs before they stirred the sugar. I waited till they had drained their mugs and then, feeling singularly elated, I left them and climbed the ladder to my loft. They talked noisily for some time. Quite suddenly, there was silence. Whether they ever woke up or not I do not know – or care.

To make doubly sure, I had already removed part of the *atap* wall in one corner of the hut so that I could slip straight out into the night without walking past the sentries. Shortly before midnight I tiptoed down the ladder from the left, pushed my bulky pack through this gap and crawled out after it. It was a pale starlit night with a clear white moon riding high above the silver tree-tops. There was a low pall of ground-mist over the river. Never have I been so conscious of the brilliance of tropical moonlight, made more intense by contrast with the inky shadows of the jungle. As I picked my way between the dewy sweet-potato plants, I felt like an aircraft illuminated by the beams of innumerable searchlights. When I reached the jungle I took out my torch, which was fitted with a green filter. It gave enough light for me to follow the track and place my bare feet carefully, for I dare not wear shoes lest I should be tracked.

I had some difficulty crossing the Korbu river, as it had been raining and the water was waist deep and very swift. Without the steadying weight of my pack I should probably have been swept away. As it was, I had to inch my way across, leaning into the strong current for balance. I had no difficulty in retracing the track past the old headman's house and upriver whence we had come. Here, padding along the footpath in absolute silence, I almost walked into a herd of pig which crashed away in the jungle with loud sharp barks, sending my heart into my mouth. I then had to recross the Korbu and follow the slippery rock slabs on the further bank.

Above Bras' house I had to leave the track I knew, and it took me some time to find the pre-war elephant track up the hill to Larek mine. At last I came out on to the old mining-ground. This was most remarkable country. The various branches of the Larek river flowed out of a wide basin surrounded by a circle of high mountains. Although this valley was in the very heart of the jungle and had not been visited by anyone except the Sakai for several years, it showed everywhere signs of man's hand, especially in the bed of the river, which in many places the miners had tried to control with neat containing walls of stone or wooden breakwaters, now derelict. For a long distance on either side of the river, the jungle had been cleared many years ago and there were large areas of open level sand and bare red laterite hillocks, where bracken, ferns, and magenta and white ground orchids flourished. I felt like an explorer suddenly discovering the remains of a former civilisation.

All at once I heard a dog bark and realised there were Sakai about. I tried to find them, but they were not used to the presence of other human beings in this remote place and fled, probably thinking the hated Japs were after them. This was very disappointing, as a Sakai could so easily have led me back on to my old trail and in any case they are always good company. I wasted most of the afternoon tracking Sakai, but though I once thought I could smell a trace of smoke, I could not find their houses or camp-fires. That night I slept in an old Sakai lean-to hut in the middle of a mile-wide stretch of bare sand where there was less danger of surprise than in the closed jungle.

Next day I cooked my breakfast of rice and curried prawns long before dawn and was away as soon as it was light enough to travel – about half-past five o'clock. I followed the Larek river until it divided, and then took the right-hand branch, because there was at first a faint trail beside it. Here the river had been painstakingly built up with stones to ensure a good flow of water for the tin mine, and higher up there were several conduits bringing in additional water from side streams. Soon the gradient steepened, as is usual when approaching a watershed, and the vegetation became increasingly thick and thorny.

When I at last reached the summit of the ridge I suffered a bitter disappointment. Although the map showed that the boundary of a Forest Reserve ran along the watershed, there was no vestige of a path. Instead, the going was of the most impenetrable kind. For some hours I fought my way along this ridge, making pitiful little headway with my bulky pack. Ahead I could see the high peak of Chondong (4,803 feet) still separating me from the Korbu-Gajah watershed, where I had hoped to pick up my outward track. So killing was the going that I thought it would take me at least another day and a half of heartbreaking toil to reach it. I therefore decided to go down the other side of the watershed into the Ulu Chemor, where the map showed evidence of plenty of Sakai settlements, to find a guide to take me over to the valley of the Kinta river and back to the country I knew.

At midday I stopped on the Larek-Chemor watershed and ate the cold remains of the rice and curried prawns that I had saved from breakfast. The descent to Ulu Chemor was as difficult as jungle going can possibly be without being actually impassable. A few saplings had been neatly sliced off by *parangs*, just where the isolated runnels of water joined to form the first rill of the Sungei Chemor, so I imagined that it was a regular Sakai highway. Thus I was misled into following the stream downhill, instead of doing what experience had taught me, namely to forsake the stream for at least the first thousand feet of its mad tumble to the plains, and to follow down the crest of the spur between two watercourses.

As the volume of water increased, so did the angle of descent. At first it was easier to follow the granite bed of the stream, lowering myself from rock to rock, and sometimes relying on the roots or branches of trees, than to traverse the steep muddy banks above.

But soon a roar that I had hoped was the wind in the tree-tops turned out to be a series of waterfalls, and here, wherever I tried to climb out on to the bank, I was always forced sooner or later back into the spray-filled gorge of the river. Once I half fell, half lowered myself down the almost vertical gully of a side stream only to find myself cut off by a wall of steep rock and roaring water. Fortunately I had wound a length of rattan round my waist for just such a contingency, and was able to climb back up the side stream and pull my rucksack after me. I then determined to have no more of the watercourse and climbed laboriously uphill for half an hour until I came out on to a steep *atap*-covered ridge. As I had hoped, there was a Sakai track running up and down the ridge. Footmarks led upward, and I followed them for an hour until the path finished at an empty hut where somebody had recently cut some pineapples, and where a black cat was still in possession.

I had now been travelling for ten hours and was extremely tired. As I had had to discard my rubber shoes so as not to slip while clambering down the stream, my feet as well as my shins were cut and bruised, and the weight of my rucksack had rubbed a great deal of skin off my shoulders and waist. After a good rest I followed the track downward for a long time until it returned to the Chemor river. Here to my horror it crossed over and went straight up a steep ridge on the further bank. Luckily the Sungei Chemor had now lost much of its former impetuosity and it was possible to wade down it.

It had started to rain, and the evening was closing in. My back and shoulders were so sore that each step was most painful. I was very tired indeed. However, it seemed easier, if not wiser, to go on in probability of reaching the warmth and hospitality of a Sakai house than to stay in the rain, build myself a shelter of banana leaves, light a fire, and cook my solitary meal. I cursed myself for not having left well alone and stayed at the empty Sakai hut on the ridge. Suddenly I saw the track of a heeled boot in the sand beside the river. My first thought was that it was a Jap, but I knew I was many miles from the outside and I was certain Japs would not come so far into the jungle except perhaps to attack the guerillas. Though I knew there was a camp at Chemor, I thought it was many miles from here and I had not heard that they had had any trouble with the Japs. I came to the conclusion that either a Sakai had got hold of a pair of boots left behind by British soldiers, or that a patrol of Chinese guerillas, wearing boots taken from the Japs, had passed this way. I decided I must not camp and light a fire until I had solved this mystery.

Very soon afterwards, at about 5.30 p.m., I came round a corner of the river and saw two Sakai, bathing naked in the water. This was luck indeed. I approached very cautiously, keeping well in to the bank, as Sakai are very timid and I was afraid they would run away if I gave them half a chance. When I was about twenty yards away, I stepped out from the bank and said quietly in Malay, 'Don't be afraid. Don't be afraid, I'm not a Jap: I'm an Englishman and I want you to help me.' At the sound of my voice the Sakai stood still. I saw somebody move on the further bank. He was wearing a high-crowned jockey cap with a yellow star on the front – a Jap cap. He looked like a Chinese, and my first thought was that I had stumbled into a guerilla camp – they often wear captured Jap hats and use Sakai guides.

Suddenly the truth dawned on me, and I began to edge towards the bank. The man I had seen – a Jap sentry – started jumping from foot to foot, shouting at the top of his voice and waving the muzzle of a tommy-gun at me. When I continued to move towards the bank, he raised the gun to his shoulder and shouted, 'Hands up! Hands up!' I obeyed. What else could I do? I had no weapons. I was completely exhausted after twelve hours' hard going. With my rucksack I could not have run a yard, and I should have been shot if I had tried to slip it off and dive into the jungle – anyway I was surrounded by now by a crowd of gesticulating Japs and bearded Indians. All at once I started to laugh, because, in all our plays in the camps, the Jap comes on to the stage grimacing, waving his arms, and shouting, '*Killy-kollack; killy-kollack!*' And here were Japs, dozens of them, all grimacing, waving their arms, and shouting, '*Killy-kollack; killy-kollack!*'

The Japs closed around me and jostled me up the river bank into their camp. Several prodded me with rifles and tommy-guns, and one, braver than the others, rushed out of his tent and hit me over the head with his rifle. Fortunately the stock snapped with a loud crack and the butt broke off, so the blow did not hurt at all, though I fell to the ground as a precaution. I struggled to get up again, but finding it impossible with my rucksack still on, I started to slip the straps off my shoulders. At this the Japs thought I was fumbling for a weapon or preparing to escape and several of them threw themselves on to my feet and held my wrists to the ground. In doing this, one of my captors discovered my wristwatch and was just about to take it off when an officer came up and, parting the crowd, started to question me excitedly in English: Who was I? Where had I come from? Was I alone? Where was my gun? Where was I going to? Meanwhile others were patting my pockets in search of weapons and starting to undo my rucksack, and another effort was made to remove my wristwatch. Seeing this, the officer pushed the man back and, waving the crowd aside, took me over to his tent.

I estimated that there were about a hundred Japs and two hundred Sikhs and Punjabis in this party, though I had no opportunity of making an exact count. About fifty Japs, including the officers and N.C.O.s, slept under a single long lean-to of canvas, while the other Japs and all the Indians had similar shelters, though made of leaves. In front of each tent a large fire was burning, and they had just finished their evening meal. The Indians stood around in attitudes of sullen hostility, almost indifference. The Japs seemed to ignore them, as if they were mere coolies.

The officer in charge, after assuring himself that I was alone and unarmed, put a guard over my rucksack and started to question me. He was young, clean-shaven, pleasant-looking, and very polite. He spoke fairly good English. His first words were, 'You are English gentleman: you must not speak lie.' That was all very well, but I had rather a lot to explain away and I asked for a drink of water to make time.

I did some quick thinking. I had two empty holsters but no weapons of any sort. I had maps of the whole area marked: Reprinted in India, 1942 – therefore obviously smuggled in somehow since the occupation – and, idiot that I was, with my route marked in pencil. I had a letter, from Davis, dated April 12, 1944, introducing me to Noone, and my Singapore identity card as 'Major Chapman' with a photograph which was an obvious likeness. I also had a very detailed diary of events since leaving our camp at Pa Kasut's.

Most of it consisted of pages and pages of ethnological details of the Sakai, bird and hunting notes, and tirades against the bandits. Fortunately all security details were written in Eskimo, and any place names were in a code of my own which worked on the association of ideas – my associations – and therefore virtually uncrackable. But the Sakai names were written in clear. Though I had no desire to protect the bandits, I would have risked my life to protect the Sakai who had helped us. Clearly I must get rid of this diary.

I had finished three cups of water and my captor and a Malay-speaking N.C.O. interpreter were getting impatient. They were filling in time by going through the contents of my rucksack. The food – alas! for my precious curry powder and fresh chillies – was given to the Indians. The diary was examined and put back together with the maps, and the identity card carefully scrutinised. Now, for the first time, the officer seemed to realise I was a soldier and examined my 'uniform.' I was wearing an old pair of *kampong*-made sheet-rubber shoes, and khaki trousers and shirt. On the shoulder-flaps of the latter were leather crowns which I had cut myself and sewn on. As soon as the officer read that I was a major and recognised my crowns, he jumped to his feet and saluted – surely the height of Japanese politeness!

I started speaking in Malay, thinking that if I lied myself into too much of a muddle I could always blame my lack of command of the language. I got on very well with the N.C.O., and he paid me the compliment of saying that, as I spoke such good Malay, he imagined I must have lived in the country many years – anybody who knows just how good my Malay was in those days will realise what a very polite people the Japanese are! However, just as we were really beginning to get on well, the officer, who knew no Malay, insisted on carrying on the interrogation in English.

I told him a long story. I *had* lived with the Chinese guerillas in Pahang some years before, but they were Communists and were even more of a danger to the British than the Japanese. I had quarrelled with them and had had to run away from their camp with a man called Davis – an officer who had been cut off and left behind by our retreating forces. Davis and I had gone to live with the Sakai near Bidor, but we had quarrelled and, as Davis knew

Noone, he had given me a letter of introduction to him and I had to set off to Grik to look for him. At Jalong the Sakai had told me that Noone was not in north Perak so I had turned back. At Larek I had met some Chinese robbers and they had taken my weapons, then let me go. I was now trying to find my way back to Davis, though I was afraid he had probably gone back to Pahang.

The officer listened very carefully to me. He made a few notes, looked some facts up in a file, and conferred at length with another officer. Then he started firing questions:

'Do you know Mr. Robinson?'

'Yes, but he has died of fever.'

'That is so. And Mr. Quayle, why has he left that camp and gone away?'

'I do not know. I have heard of him and want to meet him. He has probably quarrelled with the communists.'

'Where is Mr. Noone?'

'I do not know. Do you?' (No answer).

'Do you know of a party of Englishmen living near the Cameron Highlands?'

'No. I have heard of them and have been looking for them, but I hear they have all gone over into Pahang.'

'Who told you?'

'Oh, some Chinese.'

'But I thought you said you had parted company with the Chinese?'

'Yes, but these were the Chinese robbers at Larek.'

'Do you know an Englishman called Colonel Chapman, who is leader of all the Communists?'

This was indeed a two-edged compliment! When I went into the jungle I was a major, but the Corps Commander had said that in order to have more prestige with the Chinese guerillas, I should have the honorary (unpaid) rank of Lieutenant-Colonel. I had, when dealing with the guerilla leaders, called myself Colonel Chapman until I joined Davis and discovered I was still only a major. I knew that in 1942 the Japs had put a price on my head – though, I thought then, and still think, an inordinately small one! Apparently he had not connected my name with that on my identity card. But he had it in front of him and was bound to find out sooner or later.

'Yes. He is my elder brother. Have you any news of him? I heard he had been killed in an ambush in Pahang.'

And so it went on. I explained that I was sick of living with Sakai and eating rats and tapioca, and how I hoped they would let me come down to Ipoh with them where I could see some pretty girls again and drink Japanese beer. And how nice it was to be among civilised people once more. I hated the Communist guerillas. After all, they had turned me out of their camp and insulted me, and I would give my hosts any information they liked on the following day, but now I was terribly tired. All I wanted was a good meal and a night's rest. When we got to Ipoh, I would tell them anything they wanted to know. This all went down very well, but they were still rather worried about my family relationships and were busy scrutinising my identity card and comparing the photograph with the original.

I had discovered that we were going down to Ipoh on the following day, and after some thought I decided I would escape that night rather than try to slip away *en route*. This would mean that I should get only one meal and a short night's rest, but 2 a.m. is the best time to escape unless one has a very long way to go before dawn. Oddly enough, I never had any doubt whatsoever that I should be able to escape. It was just a matter of choosing the most auspicious moment. Consequently I had no sense of fear, only a feeling of excitement that a new adventure had fallen so fortuitously in my path, and extreme annoyance with myself for being such an idiot as to walk right into a Jap camp. On the other hand – how was I to have known it was a Jap camp? They had had no sentries out, and it was unprecedented for the Japs to be camping away into the jungle like this, at least two days' journey from the nearest road. My extreme and utter weariness must explain both my carelessness and my subsequent light-headed fearlessness.

The officer, while questioning me about the Larek 'robbers,' had produced his own map and on this was a pencilled, arrowed route – I was not the only fool that marked my maps – running from Chemor over the Chemor-Larek watershed a few miles south of where I had crossed it, and down the elephant track to Jalong, and another arrowed route ran in from Sungei Siput to converge on Jalong. Now I understood the aeroplanes that had circled so assiduously over Jalong. Probably the usual exaggerated rumours had got out that there were 'hundreds of Englishmen' in Jalong, and the Japs were taking action. I assumed that a small party would escort me to Ipoh while the rest carried on with their original plan.

I knew that I could travel twice as fast as the Japs in the jungle, especially as I should have to leave my rucksack behind, and I planned to double back along my tracks to Jalong and warn the Sakai of the impending attack. I should be able to make it in a single day. The bandits could look after themselves. It was the Sakai I was worrying about.

The first thing to do was to get hold of my diary, which was reposing in the bottom of my rucksack, and to put on the strongest clothes I had for the morrow's journey. I knew I should not be able to wear my rubber shoes because the Malay-speaking Jap had shown great interest in them, asking where I had got them from and how much they had cost. They had rubber bars on the sole and made a very conspicuous pattern. I should have to go barefooted. They had no objection to my having a bath, though six armed guards stood around me while I waded naked into the stream and poured the ice-cold water over me. I noticed that my shoulders and hips were bruised and bleeding from the rucksack, and my legs were scarred with scratches and leech-bites. After the bath I put on clean underclothes, my stoutest shirt with long sleeves, and a pair of khaki drill trousers. Then I sat in the officer's tent by the fire and was given as much rice – lovely white rice from Siam – and salt fish as I could eat. My host apologised for the lack of variety and for the absence of whisky, but said he would make up for that when we got down to the plains.

I then asked if I could get my pipe out of my rucksack and was allowed to fumble inside it while several guards watched me closely. Fortunately the top of a rucksack is narrow, so, although they were observing me carefully, I was able to find the small soft-backed notebook in which I kept my diary in tiny writing, to roll it up, and put it inside a handkerchief. I then produced the handkerchief, wiped my nose with it to show what it was for, and asked if I could put it in my pocket. This was allowed. The other two things I needed for my journey were my compass and medical set – especially quinine to ward off my fortnightly attacks of malaria, and sulphathiazole powder to treat the scratches and leech-bites on my legs and prevent them developing into ulcers. The map I could do without, as I had memorised the lie of the hills and watercourse. Unfortunately I could not palm the compass and medical set, so took them over and showed them to my host and asked if I could take some quinine. This was a tactical error, as he got very excited, thinking, I presume, that I wanted to poison myself, and he put the medical set and compass in his own pocket. He was very interested in the latter, apparently not having seen a prismatic oil compass before – he himself wore an ordinary dry compass strapped to his wrist.

It only remained to burn the diary which I had extracted from the handkerchief and rolled tightly up. In order to get a little shadow from the brilliant light of the bamboo fire, I asked if I could hang up my blanket to dry. Then, having found my old bamboo-root pipe – which was not difficult as I had hidden it under the groundsheet – I filled it and went to the fire to light it. I carefully chose a fair-sized bamboo brand, then, standing in the shadow of my blanket, lit the pipe and at the same time pushed the rolled-up diary inside the hollow stem of the bamboo. Having lit my pipe, I threw the brand back into the fire, where it was soon consumed.

I made one more effort to regain my compass by asking the Jap if I could show him how well its luminous patches showed at night. This delighted him, but he was careful to put it back in his pocket. I then spent a pleasant half-hour smoking my pipe and looking through Japanese illustrated periodicals – full of pictures of the stupid British. By way of conversation I asked him if he knew the whereabouts of two Japanese I had known at Cambridge: Prince Hashisuka the ornithologist, and Kagami the skier. Though he seemed flattered by the nice things I said – quite sincerely – about his countrymen, he could give me no news of them.

Once he asked me what future I imagined there was in staying with the Sakai in the jungle, as the British had already lost the war. I replied, without thinking, that I was waiting for the British to return to Malaya, when I would come out of the jungle and join them. At this he gave a scornful snort, and thought the story so good that he passed it on to the others, who shouted with laughter.

At about ten o'clock we turned in for the night. I was very relieved to see that my host showed no inclination to do anything so unmannerly as to tie my hands. We wished each other a very cordial good-night and soon there was no sound but the cracking of the fire and the heavy breathing of my bedfellows.

CHAPTER FOURTEEN

Escape

Although my hosts did not attempt to tie me up, they took no other chances. There were three sentries who seemed to be particularly interested in my welfare. An N.C.O. carried a pistol – I saw him take it out of its holster, cock it, and push it into the belt of his raincoat. A sentry with fixed bayonet strolled up and down beyond the fire in front of the tent. Another with a tommy-gun hovered on the edge of the firelight and seemed to be watching the jungle as if they expected my friends might attempt a rescue. Alas! how little fear there was of that!

The N.C.O. stood on the far side of the fire and seemed to be in charge of all the guard, as other sentries appeared from beyond the range of our fire, took orders, and disappeared again. All were practically, if not smartly, dressed in leather – usually nailed – boots, puttees cross-gartered with their tapes, loose-fitting breeches, shirt and tunic, high cloth caps of varied design, and a useful-looking belted raincoat with a hood that pulled up over the cap.

My tent-fellows slept in all their clothes, including boots, and were thus able to dispense with blankets. I lay between my English-speaking friend and another officer in the centre of the tent and therefore directly in front of the fire which was only a few yards from my feet. It was quite light enough to read, and the encircling jungle night looked inky black by contrast, though I knew there would soon be a moon. My neighbours seemed to fall asleep instantly, but were restless and noisy sleepers. We were so crowded that one or other often rolled against me or put a knee affectionately over mine and I had to push them back, observing with satisfaction that no amount of manhandling seemed to disturb them – though my guard showed signs of disapproval.

In the days when I was a fieldcraft instructor I had read every book on escaping and used to lecture on the subject. But none of the methods I had advocated seemed to be of much practical use now. My first plan was to pull up the canvas at the back of the tent and to slip out that way. But it had been tightly pegged down and my bedfellows were too close to allow me to work at it. My next plan – the obvious one – was to go to the edge of the jungle to relieve nature and then to make a dash for it. I rehearsed this, but the N.C.O. on guard called up two sentries with fixed bayonets, and they stood so embarrassingly near me that nature refused to function and my guards were obviously suspicious.

My next idea – one of desperation – was to set the officer's clothing alight and then to slip away in the ensuing hubbub. I was allowed to smoke my pipe and managed to put some bamboo embers among my neighbours' spare clothes, but there was insufficient draught and nothing came of it. After this I went to sleep, thinking that after all I would have to escape on the way down to Ipoh.

At about one o'clock I woke up. The N.C.O. on duty had been changed and the new one did not seem so vigilant. I watched him closely, and while pretending restlessly to stretch my arms, I was able little by little to ease up the canvas behind my head. Before I could continue operations I had to do something about the fire which, in the chill early morning, had been made larger and more brilliant than ever. I now had an inspiration, which traded, most ungenerously, on the natural good manners of my hosts. After a few preliminary hiccoughs, I got up, retching horribly, and pretended to be violently sick. I had saved up spittle for some time and the results, especially the noise, were the most realistic. The N.C.O. was quite sympathetic and I explained that the heat of the fire was so great that I was unable to sleep and was indeed – as he had seen – very ill. He immediately called up the sentries and together they damped down the fire and raked it further from the tent.

From there the firelight still shone on to my blanket sleeping-bag, but I was able to put on my rubber shoes (which I should have to wear until daylight) and then to collect some of the miscellaneous gear belonging to my bedfellows – a haversack, a tin hat, some spare boots, and a dispatch case (which, unfortunately, I could not open and which was too heavy to take away), and pushed them down into my sleeping-bag, tastefully arranging the boots to resemble my own feet thrust into the corners of the bag. Meanwhile, with legs doubled up, and watching the guard through half-closed eyes, I worked myself further and further back into the angle of the tent. A Japanese rifle caused much discomfort to my backbone. I thought how careless it was of them to have left it there, and wished I could have taken it with me, but it would have been too much of an encumbrance.

I waited till one sentry was out of sight, the other at the far end of his beat, and the N.C.O. not actually looking at me. Then, in one movement I thrust myself violently through the opening at the bottom of the canvas. I heard a 'ping,' as a peg gave or a rope broke, and a sudden guttural gasp from the N.C.O. – and I was out in the jungle.

I crashed through a bamboo thicket, raced in brilliant moonlight along the trunk and branches of a huge fallen tree – a balancing feat I could never have accomplished in cold blood – dived through some undergrowth, then half fell into the river. I slithered down between the rocks for a short distance, then stopped to listen. There was not a sound, not a sound of any sort: no shooting into the jungle, no voices, not even the snapping of a twig. I could only imagine that my captors were listening too, and I slid a long way further down the stream – once going right up to my armpits in a deep pool. It was then that I discovered that my watch was missing – a disaster for my subsequent navigation: the leather strap must have caught on something in my dash for freedom.

I was now below the camp. My plan was to make a fairly wide detour, to strike the river above the camp, and then to follow it up until dawn, by which time I hoped to get on to the Sakai path I had found the day before and to follow it over the watershed to Larek.

I clambered out of the stream and felt my way up through the steep undergrowth on the far side, for only an occasional gleam of moonlight filtered through to the floor of the jungle. When I was some distance above the noise of the river, I paused to listen. There was still no sound of pursuit. After half an hour I struck a good track and came out into a moonlit clearing where stood, among the tall wet grass, a long-deserted Sakai house built some eight feet above the ground. The thatched roof gleamed in the brilliant moonlight, accentuated by the deep shadows beneath the eaves and under the house. It was so still that even the huge black and white banana leaves stood motionless and there was a sweet fragrance of some forgotten flower growing in the clearing. I could see the moon now and the constellation of Aquila with its bright star Altair, so could get my bearings accurately, as I still had a fair idea of the time and knew from experience in what quarter of the sky Aquila would lie at that hour of the night.

I decided to follow up the stream, keeping well up on its right bank, and was delighted to find a Sakai path starting off in the right direction. However, it soon ended in two very small graves with little *atap* roofs over them and I had to take to the thick jungle with the stars lost to sight and only an occasional glimpse of the moon to check direction. At last I came upon a wide but overgrown path along an *atap* ridge, but as I kept on losing it in the darkness, I lay down to await the dawn, for travel, even if it is not exactly in the right direction, is ten times as fast along a path as in the thick jungle.

As soon as it was light enough I took off my shoes and followed the track eastward. After an hour's excellent going, I came to a track heading steeply downhill to the south. Perhaps this would join the one I had discovered yesterday and I ventured a long way down it, but dared not follow it as far as the river because I was still too near the Jap camp and I was certain that at earliest dawn they would send patrols up and down the Sungei Chemor. I therefore returned to the ridge track and followed it in a northeasterly direction until it fell steeply for a thousand feet and I came to a large river. To my horror this river, instead of flowing from left to right, was flowing in the other direction! There was a fine cave here beside the river with many signs that it had been used by Sakai. I spent some time drawing a map in the dust and ashes, trying to work out where I had gone wrong.

I retraced my steps up the long steep hill and followed a path eastward down to another rather smaller river, but still the water was flowing in the wrong direction, and realising that I had now left it too late to follow the Sungei Chemor with impunity, even if I were to find it, I determined to follow this river up to its source and then to cross the Chemor-Larek divide further north.

Dusk found me on top of the watershed. It would be very cold up there at night, especially as my clothes were soaked through with sweat, so I retraced my steps to a sheltered dell I had noticed, to bivouac for the night. Since I had no knife, I could not make much of a shelter but managed to hack off some wild banana leaves with a stone, and putting some below me and others above, I was soon asleep, and though it rained hard in the night I was no wetter than when I had turned in.

As soon as it was light I went up to the top of the ridge and started to run down the other side, hoping soon to see the great scar of the Larek mine or perhaps the high cone of Gunong Korbu. The jungle was very thick here and, though I was going steeply downhill, the tree-tops obscured what lay below. It was not until I found a clearing where several trees had fallen that I had any view and then, to my consternation, instead of Larek and the inner jungle, I saw the west-coast plains and the Malacca Straits beyond. I could have wept with disappointment. Once again I sat down and tried to work out where I was and how I had got there.[1] The problem was completely inexplicable and I knew that the only certain solution was to retrace my footprints over the watershed, then follow the river back to the neighbourhood of the Jap camp, there to work out my plans afresh – possibly to slip southward on the edge of the jungle.

This plan entailed grave risk, but I felt certain that the Japs, having given up their search for me in the vicinity of the camp, would follow their original plan and go over to Larek, cutting a wide track which I might later be able to utilise. Though I was not yet beginning to lose strength, I did not expect to be able to travel at this rate with only water as a diet for much more than a week, and once really lost one can wander indefinitely in the great jungle, each day becoming more exhausted and correspondingly less vigilant. The Sakai all seemed to have fled, and there was little hope of finding them, so I spent the rest of the day in vain search for a path crossing the watershed and returned that night to my shelter of banana leaves.

---

[1] Careful examination of the map later gave me the solution: I had kept too far to the left (my invariable habit in fog or jungle) and descended to a northern tributary of the Chemor – hence my bewilderment at the reversal of the current. I had followed this stream due north to cross the watershed where it runs east and west and to descend a tributary of the Sungei Kuang in a north*westerly* direction – hence the view of the plains (actually near Jalong and Sungei Siput).

Next day, with some difficulty, I retraced my steps to the cave beside the river and prepared to sleep in it. But I found that the Japs had already visited it in their search for me. It was covered with boot-marks and littered with paper. As they probably knew I had been there, although I was going barefooted at that time, I did not dare to sleep in the cave, though it was raining again, and made myself another shelter of banana leaves. Nearby I found some plants of tapioca, and though there were no roots on them I ate the leaves. I had often eaten them cooked and imagined they were edible raw. But I was mistaken, as I had terrible pains in the night, accompanied by a morbid thirst.

By the middle of the next day, May 16, I had made my way back to the deserted Sakai house a quarter of a mile above the Jap camp and was sheltering inside during a torrential downpour. Judging by the litter, the Japs had been here too since my last visit, but there was no sound or sign of smoke from their old camp in the valley below. As I was still feeling very ill as a result of eating the tapioca leaves, I found a hiding-place beneath the derelict sleeping-bench and was soon asleep.

After some time, I was woken up by voices underneath the house and looking through the cracks in the floor I saw some Japs and Sikhs – I could not count how many. This must have been a patrol which had stayed behind to look for me. Possibly they had seen my naked footmarks underneath the hut, though the rain would have obliterated them outside, for two of the Sikhs climbed laboriously up, with loud-voiced encouragement from the others, and entered the house. But the floor was so rotten that they satisfied themselves with a perfunctory glance round. After sheltering for some time and talking loudly, they at last set off in the direction of the plains. Judging by the size of their packs, they were going for good.

An hour later, just as evening closed in, three naked Sakai came running along the track which passed beneath the house. I dared not call to them, and in any case they would have fled; but the mere fact that there were still Sakai around gave me fresh hope. I tried to track them, but it was too dark, and by next morning, after I had passed a very comfortable night in the hut, the rain had obliterated all but the heel-marks of the Japs' boots.

Next morning was the fifth day since I had escaped from the

Japs. Since then I had eaten only a few rattan berries and the tapioca leaves which had made me so ill, but I was drinking enormous quantities of water. Unless I was going to leave my bones in the jungle – with or without the help of a Japanese bullet – I had to do some serious thinking, and it was symptomatic of my physical state that I was very reluctant to do this, being much more inclined to rush on, anywhere, instead of pausing to work out a coherent plan. Surprisingly enough I was not at all exhausted, but I felt curiously light-headed – as if the top of my skull were a foot higher than normal. On three of the four days since my escape I had travelled furiously, with hardly any rest, from dawn till dusk – more than twelve hours – but in spite of always going to bed soaking wet, I had slept right through each night and oddly enough was really enjoying myself. I had no doubt whatsoever that I could carry on for many days yet, even without food. I knew enough about the Japs – their paper-chase trail and enormous heel-marks, their loud voices and their bad eyesight, and, if it should go as far as that, their bad marksmanship – to feel quite confident that I could get the better of them. I was certain that the main body of the Japanese had gone over the watershed to Larek and Jalong. Though I was still anxious to warn my Sakai friends, I knew I should catch up the Japs or run into their rearguard if I went that way just yet.

When day dawned, I heard a cock crowing far below on the other side of the ridge from the Jap camp by the Sungei Chemor. I was pretty certain that it was a jungle-fowl, and that indicated the presence of an old clearing, and as Sakai are in the habit of visiting their old houses and gardens, I hoped a track would lead me to the present settlement. As soon as I left the track I was involved in a series of extremely steep rocky gullies, choked with thorns and rotten vegetation. After an hour of very precarious scrambling and the usual drill of lowering myself down on a rattan line, I came to a wide path pockmarked with heel-prints and littered with cigarette wrappers and empty food-bags. This was clearly the path that the main Jap patrol had followed on their way to the camp where I had been their ungrateful guest.

This wide path soon brought me to a very large Sakai village with six or seven beautifully built houses capable of holding about a hundred and fifty people. Goats and fowls walked about in the sunshine. There were clumps of pineapples and banana trees hung with bunches of fruit, and on the opposite side of the valley were several clearings carpeted with the soft even green of tapioca bushes. Looking down the wide Chemor valley, I could see the blue foot-hills of the plains framed between its variegated jungle-covered sides.

The village was of course deserted and the presence of the very dead bodies of a young girl and an old woman showed that the Japs had come this way. I was certain that as their goats and fowls were still here, the Sakai would return, so I lay up in the jungle edge to watch, being rather disturbed by the noise of a Jap plane which spent the whole morning circling low over this part of the jungle, perhaps – I flattered myself – searching for me. Sure enough, I soon saw two tousle-headed dark faces peering out of the jungle on the other side of the clearing and I went across to talk to them. The Sakai were very friendly but literally shaking with terror. They told me that some days before, the Japs had suddenly appeared and attempted to surround the houses. The Sakai had started to flee into the jungle, but the Japs opened fire, and as well as the dead I had seen, many were wounded.

They gave me some ripe bananas and a *parang*, but they could not spare me a flint and steel. I tried repeatedly to persuade them to take me over the watershed to the Kinta valley, but this they absolutely refused to do, saying that they must try to collect their womenfolk, who were scattered all over the jungle, and that there were still parties of Japs and Indians about.

I tried to follow the route they described and spent several hours following up a tributary of the Sungei Chemor, but night found me high up in a trackless area of waterfalls, steep rocky outcrops, thorn-scrub, and a tangle of heartbreaking undergrowth. Fortunately I now had a *parang* and was able to make a comfort-able shelter of *atap* in which to spend the night. Next morning, May 18, I again tried to get over the watershed into the Kinta valley, but though I fought my way to the summit ridge, there was no sign of a track. Since the descent seemed even steeper and the vegetation more thick and thorny, I retraced my steps to the Sakai village.

As soon as I got near, I could hear that something unusual was going on. Peeping through the edge of the clearing, I saw several Sikhs running about trying to round up the remaining goats. Apparently the Japs had established a regular patrol between Chemor and the camp from which I had escaped, and probably over the top to Larek and Jalong also. If this was so, not only was it unhealthy for me to stay in this area, but I could expect no help from these Sakai.

When I had been trying to follow the Sakai's directions over to the Kinta, I had noticed a wide path leaving the left bank of the stream and going uphill to the southwest. I now followed this over a high ridge and down to another stream, where the track disappeared. Sakai tracks have a way of following streams, where the going is often easiest, but if one is unaccompanied by a Sakai it is very difficult to find where the track leaves the stream and takes to the hills again. So it was on this day. Presently I picked up an overgrown track, and soon came to a steep valley where the jungle was being cleared. Soon the track was wide enough for a car, though grass-grown, and I turned aside to walk in a rubber estate, which gave more possibility of a safe retreat. Presently I found myself overlooking the head of a motor road, where were several large vegetable gardens with Chinese women hoeing, wearing black blouses and trousers and huge conical hats. I saw one larger house, apart from the rest, and creeping round through a forest of tapioca bushes I went in at the open doorway.

Here I found six Chinese men, who seemed delighted though somewhat astonished to see me. After a bath in the stream (while one of them kept watch on the road) and a large meal of rice cooked with sweet potato, a stalky green vegetable and dried fish, one of them gave me a small home-made pipe and we settled down to talk. It appeared that I had come out near Kinding Tea Estate, about three miles above Tanjong Rambutan. The men said they could put me in touch with the guerillas, but in the present disturbed state of things it might take a week or more. They told me it was quite impossible for me to stay there and took me back to a tiny hut on the very edge of the jungle. There were half a dozen other fugitives in this small house, underfed and dressed in rags, several of them in a high fever from malaria.

I gathered from them, and from stories I subsequently heard, that at this time the Japanese had just started a drive against the *kampong* Chinese on the jungle edge the whole way from Grik to Kuala Kubu – about 150 miles. This was probably the most savage of any of their organised massacres. Each morning two or three two-engined planes would circle low round and round the area between the main road and the edge of the jungle. At the same time a cordon of trucks full of Indians and Malays would be placed every fifty yards along a section of road to shoot anybody attempting to break out. The cordon would close in. Young able-bodied men were taken away and seen no more – probably they were ordered to go and fight elsewhere for the Japs or to work in the labour camps, and murdered if they refused. Girls, even children of twelve or thirteen years, were often raped at once or taken away to fill the military brothels. An enormous number of Chinese were tommy-gunned or bayoneted. Others were driven into the *atap* houses and burned alive. Everything in the houses that was of any possible value was taken away – every cent of money, watches, trinkets, clothes, cooking utensils, even the vegetables from the gardens.

Next morning, May 19, I watched these Jap planes circling round and round so low that I could see the pilot's helmeted face looking down, and I wondered how they could manoeuvre their large two-engined machines so low among the steep valleys and wooded foothills. I even went out to the edge of the rubber and, though I could not get a view over the *kampongs*, I could easily hear the noise of firing and the heartrending screams of the victims. While I was there several half-demented fugitives came running up the lane into the jungle.

At midday one of the six men at the tapioca *kongsi*-house came up and told me that a thousand Sikh police had been posted along the jungle edge to intercept and kill anybody who tried to escape that way, and that though they wanted to help me, it was impossible just then and I must go back into the jungle. Of course I did not believe this story, but I determined to go right back past the Sakai village and the Japanese camp to Larek, and to strike my old trail somewhere at the head of the Korbu valley.

The same afternoon, May 19, I left this stormy refuge. They could give me only a few pounds of rice, half a cigarette tin of salt,

254

a handful of groundnuts, an old sack to use as a blanket, and eight home-made matches. At the same time the dozen or so Chinese fugitives who were there, believing the ridiculous scare about the thousand Sikhs, set off, carrying their miserable possessions, to return to the hell that was still going on in their *kampongs*. I wondered which of us was being the more stupid.

I spent the night in a small Sakai shelter I found beside the Chemor river. I suffered a bitter disappointment here, as the home-made matches that the Chinese had given me would not light. After wasting four of them I decided to keep the other four and dry them out in the sun before trying them. I ate my groundnuts, together with a pocketful of sweet-potato leaves which I had picked in the Chinese garden.

Early next morning I visited the Jap camp to look for my wrist-watch and pipe – without success – and followed an excellent track which the Japs had cut over the top, about a mile north of my route to Larek. In the middle of the sandy waste, where I had camped on my way over from Jalong, I counted the cold ashes of fourteen large fires, but the Japs had built no sort of shelter. There had been no sunshine by which to dry my remaining four matches. Indeed, it had rained solidly all day, and though I managed to make one splutter by the old trick of first rubbing it up and down the short hair of the nape of my neck, I was unable to make it burn.

Next day, May 21, I followed the wide Japanese track past another of their camps, as usual littered with paper, and right down to the Sungei Korbu where they had turned downstream towards Jalong. I went upstream and at last came to a Sakai hut right up in the hills on the right bank of the Korbu river. I walked into this house before the occupants had time to flee, and found there several of the headmen I had stayed with five weeks before. Instead of giving me the usual cordial '*Tabe tuan*' (Greetings, sir), they bowed to the ground and gave me the formal '*Selamat datang*' (Peace attend your coming). At first I could not account for this change in their attitude, but it gradually appeared that my bandit friends, after my escape, had thought that it was I who had brought all these disasters to their peaceful valley. But I was soon able to make matters clear and to hear their story.

It appeared that a few days previously the Japs had suddenly appeared in the jungle – the Sakai had no idea whence they had come. They had captured several Sakai alive, shot others, burned down the houses, and either removed or destroyed the huge stores of rice which had been collected for the bandits. Bras, the young and intelligent headman, had disappeared: perhaps he had been killed. The Sakai were very disgusted with the Chinese, who had fled at the first sign of danger and not stayed to protect their jungle allies. All the Sakai were in a bad state of nerves, and for my own safety as much as theirs, wanted me to go to a still higher and more remote hideout for the night. But I was very reluctant to do this, as I was very tired and my feet had been rather badly cut about after travelling so far barefooted without having had time to harden them properly beforehand, and usually at such speed that I could not pause to avoid rough and thorny places. In any case, there was little possibility of the Japs coming up as far as here.

I was given as many plates of delicious dry fragrant Sakai rice as I could eat, together with a huge bowl of pumpkin cooked with salt, pepper, curry, chillies, and shoots of wild ginger – certainly the best dish of pumpkin I have ever tasted. We smoked until dark, and I was just beginning to think I had never enjoyed food so much or eaten such a quantity in a few hours, when I saw that my hosts were about to kill no less than six old roosters. They were afraid that their crowing would betray the presence of the house to the Japs. Among us we finished off all six fowls, though they were terribly tough, and enormous quantities of rice.

The next morning, May 22, I set off early with a guide. Before I went I managed to persuade the Sakai to give me a flint and steel and some tinder. We reached the house which Lim and I had called the *jagong* (maize) house, because it stood in a clearing planted with this grain. Here my guide failed me – the only time a Sakai let me down. After waiting some time for him to return I realised that he had abandoned me. The next morning I set off on my own to find the elusive watershed, but after twelve hours of exhausting travel through the worst sort of jungle, I found that I had moved in a large circle, finishing up within a few hundred yards of my starting-point. Next day I had no better luck, and in addition felt the first warnings of a bout of malaria. I realised that I had to find my way back to the *jagong* house and lie up there. Soon, as the fever got hold of me, my strength ebbed, and for the last part of the journey I had to crawl on my hands and knees, eventually arriving long after dark.

I reached the *jagong* house on the night of May 25 and was very ill there with malaria for more than a fortnight. I was able to keep account of time by cutting a notch each day on the pole beside my bed and, though I had the usual alternations of uncontrollable shivering and high fever with a racing pulse, I was never, as far as I know, actually delirious. My chief trouble, other than the fever, was twenty or thirty running ulcers on my feet and legs and one over my hipbone, which resulted from many deep cuts and leech-bites. Since I knew I should be completely immobilised till these were better, I forced myself to bathe them four times a day with a solution of boiling water and the last few grains of my salt. I would then cover them with maize leaves to keep out the dirt.

The Sakai did not discover my presence for the first few days, but subsequently they used to visit me from time to time at odd hours of the night, usually to split and dry bamboo torches for fishing. They were far too frightened to come so far down into the valley during the hours of daylight, as they were still dominated by terror of the Japanese, who, they said, had made their headquarters at Kampong Jalong and were gradually working up the Korbu valley searching for guerillas and Sakai and burning down any houses they found.

I had been very uneasy on this score myself, and had taken elaborate precautions. My bed was on the floor in the far corner of the hut. I had made a small doorway in the *atap* wall so that I could slip through and crawl down the trunk of a felled tree which was there and into the edge of the jungle. I had also made a screen of maize stalks so that the tree-trunk would be invisible to anybody approaching the house along the main track. There was a small dun-coloured terrier bitch which seemed to belong to the house, though like most Sakai dogs it completely ignored my presence and refused to make friends. But the owner told me it hated Japs and would bark as soon as they came near.

On June 2, the dog started growling, and going to the door of the house, I could hear voices and the chop-chop of *parangs* coming from down the track. As no one but a Jap would want to make the perfectly adequate path wider, I smothered my fire with a pile of ashes I had kept for the purpose and slipped out through my getaway into the jungle. Peeping through the leaves, I saw two Japs and about a dozen Sikhs enter the hut. The small dog barked furiously and one of the Japs had two shots at it, but missed. The party spent some time inside the house, then set it alight and left it. Fortunately it had been raining all night, and the *atap*, being soaked, was reluctant to burn; I was able to beat it out with a stick, so that the only damage was a large gap in one wall.

On June 8 my fever reached its climax, and for some reason I was quite certain I was going to die. It was an unpleasant sensation to lie there alone in the depths of the jungle, convinced that I had only a few hours to live. My chief feeling was one of annoyance and frustration that the great efforts I had made since escaping from the bandits had been entirely wasted and that no one would even know how hard I had tried.

Next day I woke up long after sunrise. I found that the fever had completely left me and I was ravenously hungry. Though I was still very weak, I could now walk across the house without holding on to the roof-beams. My ulcerated legs had practically healed during my enforced lying up, and I felt I might be able to set off after a day's rest. I went out into the clearing, collected some maize, scraped the grain off the cobs with a rattan-thorn grater, as I had seen the Sakai do, and roasted it inside a bamboo. The result was delicious, and I ate till my stomach was distended.

That evening one of the older Sakai came in to cook some tapioca, and after considerable argument I persuaded him to take me upriver to the house at Kuala Termin. He warned me that this house had been burned down by the Japs, but I could not believe they had penetrated so far into the jungle; in any case I hoped he might be able to contact the Sakai there and persuade them to take me over the watershed to the Kinta valley. On June 11 – exactly a calendar month since I had escaped from the bandits – we set off. I should really have rested for a few more days, but I felt so much better that I was impatient to be off. I went terribly slowly, especially uphill, but rallied when the old man said it was no good going on and we should return. Towards evening we reached the clearing near the Kuala Termin house, but instead of crossing the Korbu by the 'Himalayan' bridge, we struck straight uphill, following a typical *atap* ridge. This was too much for me, and I lay down and slept while my guide went in search of Sakai. Just as it got dark he returned with two men whom I remembered, and between them they pulled me up the hill with a rattan line. I could still walk along the level, but uphill my leg-muscles simply refused to work. After climbing for at least a thousand feet we reached a small empty but newly built *atap* hut, hidden away off the ridge in the middle of a thicket. The Sakai, apparently, had fled still further into the hills.

While I was examining the house and the food that they had left for me, the three men disappeared. I never saw them again, though I waited till well after daylight on the following morning. It poured with rain at night and I felt rather miserable, as I was not at all certain that I could find the bridge across the river, much less the house at Kuala Termin, which would set me off on the right track. And even if I found the track it was one of those that meandered up a succession of small streams and would be very hard to follow.

I therefore set off with some foreboding. I was surprised to find how well my legs went after a long sleep, and I could even keep a good pace uphill. I found the house without difficulty. It *had* been burned right to the ground, but I satisfied myself from the lack of litter and the absence of boot-marks and fresh cutting along the tracks that no Jap had ever been near here and that the fire must have been entirely fortuitous. The Sakai are very careless with their fires, and it was pure chance that the conflagration had coincided with the Jap drive against Kampong Jalong further down the valley.

I chewed sugar-cane in the clearing near the house until my gums were sore and then set off to retrace the way by which Lim and I had arrived two months before. Luckily a Sakai had gone the same way earlier in the morning (though the two men from here had assured me that none of them knew this route) and I was able to follow his naked footmarks and to cast back when I lost them. Evening found me near the house which commanded such a magnificent view over Tanjong Rambutan, and I hoped that I should be able to find the pig-paling which ran along the ridge and that this would lead me to the house. However, I was unlucky here. As it

259

grew dark, I lost my Sakai's footmarks, could find neither fence nor house, and had to sleep out in the jungle.

The following day, June 13, I ate some sugar-cane that I had brought with me and spent another hour or two searching for the house. As I could not find it, I determined to drop downhill to the Sungei Gajah, follow it down to where it joined the Seno-oi river, then follow up the latter until I reached the huge house where Lim and I had had trouble with the oratorical Sakai. I found the Gajah without difficulty. It ran at the bottom of a valley whose steep sides were scarred with old clearings that came right down to the bank. The river was very swift and deep and in some places flowed through gorges, and I had to find my way overland. Once I was swept away by the current and was carried down some distance and badly bruised before I could regain the bank.

I joined the Seno-oi about midday and tried to follow it up, but the volume of water was enormous and I could find no sign of a track on either side. I therefore returned to the main river, feeling that I had done all I possibly could to find the Sakai, and with a clear conscience started to look forward to the good food, security, and companionship of a Chinese *kongsi*-house. I had been following down the joint streams for some time when the character of the river changed. The rapids ceased and I was now able to let myself be carried down at the edge of the current, occasionally checking my speed by clinging hold of boulders. This was a somewhat precarious but extremely rapid method of descent.

When I pulled myself ashore once to rest, I saw some fresh footprints in the sand. A large party of Sakai had been there only a short time before. I determined not to lose these tracks and followed the sandy marks where the little men had jumped from boulder to boulder and again when they took to the shore. In the late afternoon I came upon them and approached cautiously so as not to give them a chance to run away. When I spoke to them I recognised some of the men from the large house up the Sungei Seno-oi, and on inquiry discovered that it was now deserted, though the Japs had not been near it. They resolutely refused to let me go back with them to their new house in the hills, but said that if I followed down the river I should soon come to a Chinese *kongsi*-house at the head of a pipeline. I was still trying to persuade one of them to show me the way when I realised they were already disappearing into the jungle, and soon I was alone again, with two small cooked fish and some tapioca that they had left for me.

After eating this I continued to follow the river down. There was, as the Sakai had said, a good track. At first, to avoid another rapid, it led parallel to the river in and out of side valleys and round rocky spurs. Then it crossed the river, led through a large and very pleasant bamboo grove, across a swamp, over several deserted clearings, and at last to a couple of timber-built Chinese houses at the head of a bicycle track and pipeline.

In this house were five Chinese. They promised to put me in touch with the guerillas, but as Malays in the employ of the Japs were liable to visit the house at any hour of the morning, they refused to let me sleep there. After giving me some food they took me to an overgrown clearing half a mile downriver, where there was a hideout which had been built for two Chinese fugitives. It was raining heavily, and although they lent me a four-foot-wide conical umbrella-hat, I was soaked to the skin by the time we reached the refuge, and during the night I had a relapse of malaria. I stayed in this hut for three days and was very glad of the rest and security, for I was so weak that if I got up too suddenly I had a complete blackout and fell down again, and only came to from the pain of hitting the ground. Each evening the Chinese would bring me a meal of rice and sweet potatoes with fresh fish, sweet-potato leaves, and other vegetables, and I used to keep enough to eat in the morning, though at this time my appetite was poor and I could not sleep well as I was suffering from violent toothache. There was a hot spring near the hut, just the right temperature for a bath, and this was a great luxury as well as being very good for my cuts and bruises.

On the third night in this refuge, being unable to sleep, I was sitting on a log outside listening to the hunting cry of a tiger, when my attention became fixed on what I thought was a singularly bright and constant firefly. Suddenly I realised it was a light which was gradually approaching. In case it was an enemy, though this was unlikely in the middle of the night, I hid in the jungle, but soon recognised the voice of the leader of the pipeline Chinese and came out to meet him.

With him were another oldish man and a young and very charming Chinese who was introduced to me as Ah Sang. I was in touch with the guerillas once again.

CHAPTER FIFTEEN

Traitor-killing Camp

(Use Map No. 3)

Ah Sang was well informed of the progress of the war in Europe and gave me the first news I had had for some months. The Russians were driving the Germans out of the Crimea. A 'second front' had been opened in Italy, where there was heavy fighting; and – which I hardly dared to believe – British and Americans had landed in force in France and the invasion of Europe was at last in full progress. At this news, I was more than ever anxious to get back as quickly as possible. I felt certain that by now we had probably re-established wireless communication with India, that a submarine R.V. would have already been arranged, if not already carried out, and that the war would be over before I even got out to India. I was burning with impatience, and when Ah Sang suggested that we should start off as soon as it was light, I willingly agreed, though I was really in no fit state to travel, especially after a sleepless night.

We left the pipeline early next day, June 16. I was delighted with my new companion. He was a typical Straits-born Chinese, well mannered and quietly efficient, brave without being foolhardy, and very easy to get on with. Unfortunately I only spent three days in his company. He took me to an *atap* hut near Tanjong Rambutan (we passed, in fact, the hut where I had stayed a month before, on first emerging from the jungle) and handed me over to a tough, burly-looking Chinese in khaki called Lau Ping, who was to keep me in his camp until permission had been obtained from headquarters to guide me back to Davis and Broome. That night several Chinese tried to extract my aching tooth with a pair of pliers, but the operation was unsuccessful and it was some months before the tooth had ached itself into insensibility.

Lau Ping's camp was only a day's march away, but I was so enfeebled that I could barely keep up with the guides, who travelled at an appalling pace. After fourteen hours flat out we reached a large *kongsi*-house, where I had a bath and a good meal, though

I was too tired to sleep. Next day Lau Ping and I left the house before dawn, he wheeling his bicycle. I upbraided him for making me do the terrific journey the day before, saying that as I was ill it might easily have strained my heart. He merely said that he had been told that I could travel as well as any Chinese and that if they could do it, I could.

After an hour's walk along cart-tracks, over rivers, and through countless tapioca plantations, we followed a small stream up a steep little valley with tapioca growing on either side. At the very top of the stream in a little dell backed by secondary jungle was an *atap* hut, so snugly placed that it looked as if it had grown there. As we approached, Lau Ping gave a shout, and immediately eight men rushed out and pointed four tommy-guns and as many rifles at us, a most formidable armament. This was one of the traitor-killing camps I had heard so much of, and it was to be my sanctuary until permission came for me to proceed on my way. This turned out to be yet another month.

The hut itself was marvellously hidden and in a perfect defensive position. Behind the hut the small stream, after being dammed up to provide a pool for drinking-water and bathing, lost itself in a trackless waste of secondary undergrowth and tin-tailings. Apparently they had only finished building it a few days before, having been driven out of their last hideout by a Japanese attack.

The hideout was only about five miles east-southeast of Ipoh, and three miles northeast of Simpang Pulai, quite near the junction of the Raia and Senju rivers. Here lived about twenty men, though there were never more than a dozen at home at one time, and sometimes only one or two, as they were continually coming and going on jobs which might last half a day or a couple of weeks. Their task was the systematic and ruthless elimination of informers – a job which they carried out with remarkable energy, enthusiasm, and success. A camp of this nature had been operating from the jungle edge in the fifteen miles between Tanjong Rambutan and Gopeng since soon after the surrender, though by now there were only two foundation members left. They told me, and I believe it from what I saw myself and heard from other sources, that they had lost count of the number of traitors, informers, spies, and police they had killed, but that it was well over the thousand mark

– Chinese, Sikhs, Malays, Japs, and Tamils (in that numerical order), both men and women, and with every imaginable weapon, from grenade and tommy-gun to *changkol* (a heavy hoe used in place of a spade) and their bare hands.

As a rule they hunted in small parties, usually only two or three. If they went into Ipoh itself to remove some sleek and urbane Chinese who had let his avarice overcome his patriotism, they would carry pistols thrust well out of sight beneath their shirts and meet their victim in a coffee-shop that he was known to frequent, perhaps in the very centre of the city. The moment a shot was fired, every man and woman within hearing would rush madly from the place to avoid implication, and it would not be difficult to escape in the ensuing tumult. In the rural districts, if perhaps they had to deal with a spy sent to report on guerilla activities, they would enter the *kampong* openly carrying tommy-guns or rifles.

Sometimes, just to keep up the morale of the country districts, they would attack local police stations – hence their astounding armament. In this way several guerilla prisoners had been liberated, and once they had managed to destroy all the records in Gopeng Police Station. Another of their ploys was to put an embargo on any work that was being done for the benefit of the Japs. If coolies started working tin, a few shots would be fired above their heads to make them run into the jungle; pipelines would be damaged, petrol-stores set alight and carts of produce overturned in the road.

One day two of them returned to camp with a sack full of women's clothes and jewellery. They belonged to a girl whose brains they had beaten in with a *changkol* that morning. It appeared that a month or two before, half a dozen Chinese prostitutes had come to live in a large *kampong* where there were many tapioca *kongsis* – also many guerilla supporters. Each week one of the girls would make a journey to Ipoh, ostensibly to visit her aged parents. A guerilla, becoming suspicious, followed her into the town and was not surprised to find that her 'aged parents' lived at the Jap military police headquarters.

It is noteworthy that of the twenty men whom I met in this camp, in an area which I had not previously visited, at least five had already met me, and usually in one of the other states. For in

265

these outside camps, as soon as a man becomes known to the local police and informers, he is shifted to another area where he starts again with new cover. One man, who had over 150 killings to his credit, had already operated in Pahang, Selangor, and north and south Perak. This man had been wounded three times, captured five times, and twice tortured; on one occasion, after being tortured, he had been left for dead; twice he had bribed his Malay guards and twice escaped. He spoke very clear Malay, and I spent a long time talking to him on the rare occasions when he was not out on a job. His parents, wife, and two children had all been killed by the Japs; of his six brothers and sisters, two had simply disappeared and the rest were in guerilla camps in Pahang, though he had not seen them for two years. He told me quite candidly that he was not the least interested in the Communists' scheme for a Malayan Republic, as he thought the Chinese and Malays would never get on together without the help of the British. All he seemed interested in was killing Japs and anybody who helped them. He had no plans for after the war.

This camp was far more businesslike and less self-conscious and schoolboyish than the main camps, and I was far happier here. They got on with the job instead of spending half the day singing songs and making speeches. They usually told the truth and had something else to talk about besides the Malayan Republic and the advantages of life in Soviet Russia. On the other hand, it must be admitted that the discipline was very lax here – quarrels, almost unknown in the jungle camps, were frequent, and while some men seemed to be working all day, others did not get up till late and took no part in the daily chores.

The guard system was curious. An alarm clock went off at 4 a.m. and two men would mount guard at the top of the hill, fifty yards in front of the hideout, until dawn, an hour and a half later. During the day no guard was kept. All the Chinese in the area seemed to know the camp, and it was assumed that ample warning would be brought of any daylight attack.

The food was far better than I had enjoyed in any of the jungle camps. All they had to do was to bicycle into Simpang Pulai and back, then carry the loads for less than a mile up to the hideout. Each day we would have the usual two meals: any amount of rice cooked with sweet potatoes and two 'vegetables' – one fish, usually a kind of large skate or ray with cartilage instead of bones, and the other a leaf or root vegetable. Once a week we had coffee and sugar, otherwise we had Chinese tea made by boiling the whole leaf in water. Our diet was augmented from time to time with the meat of pig and jungle-fowl which could be shot within a hundred yards of the hideout – my companions never worried about the sound of firearms. There were reported to be both bear and wild goat (*kambing gurun*) within a mile of us at the source of the little stream that ran through the hut, but at this time I was too ill to go hunting. For the whole month that I was in this traitor-killing camp I was in very poor health, and was afraid that I had radically strained myself by travelling too hard before I had recovered from my attack of malaria.

I was able to get a good deal of reading matter, the lack of which was perhaps the greatest continuous ordeal of my sojourn in the jungle. I was given some copies of the English edition of the Jap newspapers, and read with great interest that the Japs had captured the leader of a British parachute troop in the Perak jungle and shortly expected to round up the rest of the gang! I hoped that my friend the Japanese officer had not had his head cut off for allowing me to escape. From one of the M.C.P. presses I also received several cyclostyled news-sheets under the title of *The Voice of Malaya*. These were excellently produced, though the contribution of Russia was greatly exaggerated.

The books that were brought to me were borrowed from a Chinese – probably he had collected them from a planter's bungalow during the fighting. They were: *Buried Alive*, Arnold Bennett; *The Last Command* (film story), Claude Houghton; *The Murdered Mahout*, Sexton Blake; *The Bronze Eagle*, Baroness Orczy; *The Man of the Forest*, Zane Grey; *Ivanhoe*, Scott; *The Patent-Leather Kid*, Rupert Hughes. I read all these twice or three times, but was unable to obtain any more, as the Japs had banned all English books in this area and anybody found in possession of them was liable to have his head cut off.

On July 4, after I had been in this camp just a fortnight, Lau Ping appeared with a boy of fourteen or so who always accompanied him and was treated as a mascot by everybody. Lau Ping had had

267

a letter from Perak headquarters and brought me $200, a bottle of quinine tablets, and also a pistol to replace the one I had lost to the bandits. Lau Ping said it would be another fortnight before the two runners came – which was just as well, for I was not yet in a fit state to travel. Although I had not had an attack of malaria since leaving the pipeline *kongsi*-house three weeks before, I was yellow as a grapefruit and took thirty grains a day for three days as a preventative.

On July 12, soon after dark, there was a sudden shout down the track and we all turned out. It was Lau Ping and his mascot, accompanied by two runners from headquarters.

The guides said the journey had taken them five days, but I knew it would take me very much more. Fortunately, however, they did not want to start for a few days, and I was certainly much better than I had been a week before: my ulcers had all healed save two or three; I was sleeping properly, and my appetite had returned. If only I could persuade them to take the journey easily, I was sure I could get home all right. I spent an hour each morning walking up and down the track in front of the hideout to get my muscles back into working order. I copy the account of this journey from my diary.

July 16. – Got to sleep late last night as we had a farewell party and they made me yodel and sing every Chinese song I know – about twenty now. Up at five. Sweet-potato-rice and the green stalky vegetable. Only the two runners and myself; they carry all my gear except .38 – in a holster I made out of canvas – and *parang.* I have been given a light blanket for the journey and a spare shirt and shorts. I shook hands with them all and felt quite sad to leave, though I am longing to get home and hear the latest news.

We started off up the Senju river – miles of level red sandy tintailing country where it would be possible to land parachutists and possibly even a plane. Lots of pipelines here, most of them derelict. As usual a line of Chinese paddy clearings follows the river far into the jungle. I went surprisingly well but was painfully slow uphill. We soon took to the real jungle and followed a Sakai track right up a long ridge and traversed along the western side of the

Main Range with occasional glimpses back to Simpang Pulai, and once, only a few miles to the west, we had a good view of the red-tiled buildings of the small town of Gopeng far below us.

In the afternoon we descended steeply for some miles – here I go as fast as they can – until we reached the house of a Chinese living with some Sakai. Very happy. Grand feeling to be on the move again – and going home. I washed my clothes and lay in the sun.

July 17. – Headache. Very heavy dew. In the morning there was a scare that a party of Malays were coming up to assess the rice crop for the Japs and we had to retire to a Sakai house in the jungle which was built about thirty feet up a tree and had to be reached by a most unsafe bamboo ladder. They were cooking bamboo shoots, which the Sakai do not generally deign to eat. A Sakai went out to the shop four hours away and owing to the presence of Malays he did not return till late, so we lost another day. Three of us ate five cigarette-tin measures of rice – in the camps the ration is half a tin per man per meal, measured before cooking, of course. They say a working coolie eats two tins per meal. Twelve tins to a *gantang*, which is 8 lb. Also had dried fish, bananas, and coffee with sugar. Could not sleep. Acute toothache. My ulcers are breaking out again and very painful.

July 18. – Left just before 4 p.m. Passed many old Sakai houses and soon reached the rubber. All downhill going following huge pipe-lines to the Kampar river. Here there were several Malays about and we had to wait till dusk, then walk along a bicycle track beside the biggest pipe in Malaya. It is five feet high and belongs to the firm known as French Tekka. Crossed a river and reached huge corrugated iron coolie-lines for the men looking after the pipeline. Stopped and talked to the Chinese coolies, who seemed very glad to see me. Now we follow up a river with a succession of rubber smallholdings and clearings. Millet is the main crop, also ground-nuts, ginger, and acres of sweet potato, and every kind of vegetable. These people on the edge of the jungle may not have security, but they seem to have everything else they want.

We stopped at the last house before the thick jungle and were well looked after by two married couples. The Japs were here last year and two of the children were shot.

July 19. – Up at 5.45 a.m. Sweet-potato-rice and groundnuts cooked with seedling leeks in soup. Heavy rain, so did not get away till ten o'clock. Terrible going over a newly cut clearing of bamboo for two hours. Nothing is more exhausting and exasperating, as each pole goes right down under you and is as slippery as hell. Then up a long steep ridge for two hours and an hour's descent to a river – Sungei Rias. We are fairly near the town of Sungei Siput, and there is a main road only half a mile away. They say the Japs come here almost daily, as they know that the guerillas use this route and have a camp up the Dipang river.

Two of us hid while one of the runners went out and found a small house where we could lie up.

July 21. – Terrible day. Attack of fever coming on, so took 40 grains of quinine during day. Got up at 4.30 and cooked tapioca-rice and fish mixture. Away at 6. Went down to the river and followed it right up into the hills for a couple of hours, usually walking in the water. When we reached the steep upper section near the water-shed, we left it and soon crossed a high pass. Very hot and close today and am going very badly uphill.

On the far side we descended very steeply indeed through old clearings. Very slippery and fell a good deal. We now had to descend and cross the Cameron Highlands road, but the guide was not certain of the way and we wasted at least two hours, crawling up and down through thorny thickets and waterfalls looking for a Sakai who is supposed to live here. This was a failure, and I was very tired and bad-tempered. We followed a stream down for an hour or so, and then the guide said we were near a big *kongsi-*house where the Japs were making paper from bamboo, and as some of the Chinese coolies there were unreliable we should have to make a detour. This took us two hours of purgatorial work. Quinine was fighting my fever all day and I felt ghastly. We struck up into the hills, lost the path, and had to traverse across a hillside covered with the worst kind of thorn jungle – probably very old secondary jungle, as Sakai have had clearings all over this area for hundreds of years.

At last we got down to the Cameron Highlands road, somewhere by the 18th Mile – just south of Jor Corner. We crossed the road and fought our way down to the Jor river and then to its junction with the Batang Padang river, which we followed down for another two hours. It was very slippery, and as I was now almost exhausted, I kept on falling. We could hear Jap lorries on the road above. Crossed Kuala Sekam and started to climb the 1,000-foot hill to Pa Senapat's. When we reached the small house where Lim and I stayed more than three months ago I could go no further and had to lie down. The house had been burned down, but the bamboo framework and the floor still stand. I am completely done in and can only just move. My guide went up the hill and sent a Sakai youth back, and I was able to go on up with him – an hour's climb up a steep face to the house. It is a fine new hut with split bamboo walls and four large partitions inside with one end left open for light.

There are three Chinese here, one of whom I had known at the Slim Camp. They spend their time with the Sakai and go out to remove informers and guard food lines, etc. We cooked two fowls and a huge dish of wood mushrooms and sweet-potato-rice. Felt much better, though dazed with quinine. I wanted to take the short cut over the Sekam-Woh watershed and down the Kelundor river to our camp, but Pa Senapat says he doesn't know it.

July 22. – Feel fairly good, bar quinine hangover. Two of the Chinese out gunning for an informer. Bought five eggs from the Sakai ($1) and made a mushroom omelette. The men all went off hunting with their blow-pipes at 6.30 a.m. and the women soon afterwards to collect tapioca and water – which is very scarce up here. Pa Senapat and his wife have the same father, but different mothers. The small girls all smear their faces with red stripes, the stain being made from a small berry. Eight hunters, as a result of the day's hunting, brought back four small squirrels, three rats, and a bird the size of a thrush – and most of the former had been caught in traps. I don't know how the Sakai existed before they started cultivating crops.

In the evening all the Sakai sang songs in the most beautiful harmony, the men keeping the deep, organ-like notes going, while the women sang shrilly, and beat time with empty bamboo water-pots. It was most moving, but quite impossible to learn. Later on several youths danced a whole series of incredibly energetic steps. The dance went on without a moment's pause for three hours until the naked dancers' bodies glistened with sweat in the firelight and they practically dropped with exhaustion. It reminded me of an Eskimo witch doctor's seance, but was far more light-hearted.

July 23. – Dry rice and salt fish. Away at seven. Descended to the lower clearing, then turned southeast and coasted round the hills, followed a stream, then crossed a deep valley, and after three hours reached the deep gorge of the Sungei Lengkok. All the way along were the remains of old Sakai clearings, houses, and a network of paths. Once we heard someone singing, then met four women carrying huge loads of tapioca and sugar-cane. Each had her hair wreathed with yellow flowers.

All the afternoon we went up and down hills, over and along streams, through bracken and bamboo thickets, across old clearings, and at last came right down the hill to Pa Blanken's settlement by the Sungei Tedong. For the last four hours we were on the same route that Lim and I had followed on our way out, but now practically all the Sakai houses we had then passed have been burned down and there are no people about. Pa Blanken's family live in four small and very well-built houses, as opposed to the communal large house system usually followed by the Perak Sakai. The end walls and floor are made of strips of bamboo, and the *atap* roof is extended over the sides to make shelters. Pa Blanken tells me that the Japs beat up our camp a month ago and we have lost all our heavy gear and moved up into the hills – he does not know where. Hell! No casualties, however.

July 24. – The new camp is a few hours up the Telom valley and we should get there tomorrow morning.

July 25. – Up at dawn. Washed and packed up. Away at 6 a.m. with one youth as guide. I met Ah Chu (our Sakai liaison man). He said I looked so thin and ill that he wouldn't have recognised me, and certainly I felt at the very end of my strength as we climbed for two hours, traversing in and out of valleys and crossing streams and deserted clearings. When we got near the camp, I yodelled and they were so unaccustomed to the sound that they all turned out and I was met at the guard post by a row of Sten-gunners! I have been away 103 days – and I am glad to get back!

CHAPTER SIXTEEN

A Year of Frustration

(Use Map No. 4)

Black Lim, I discovered, had safely arrived with my message from Kampong Jalong only three days before the attack. He himself had had a narrow escape from a Jap patrol on the way, and a Sakai with him had been killed.

I was very anxious to discover what damage had been suffered in the Jap attack on our old camp at Pa Kasut's, and how the enemy had discovered our hideout. The others told me that soon after I had left on my abortive trip in search of Noone,[1] they had been greatly cheered by the arrival of two agents by submarine from Ceylon, Chang and Chen, who had made a successful blind landing on Pangkor Island at the end of April. Also a message from Chen Ping said that most of the heavy stores from Jenderata were at last on their way up to Blantan. After the depression caused by the collapse of our outside organisation, this was good news indeed. Davis and Broome left Quayle to look after the camp and hurried down to Blantan with a carrying party. On the way back with the stores – which included the heavy batteries and hand generator, but not the B.2 wireless sets – they suddenly came across a whole string of still-warm camp fires on the track near the junction of the Woh and Telom rivers.

They realised that the Japs had come in from the 7th Mile on the Cameron Highlands road, and were probably at that moment attacking the camp. It was too late to warn Quayle. All they could do was to hide the stores in the jungle and wait in an empty Sakai hut till the Japs had gone. The Sakai told them that there had been no casualties and, after the Japs had gone, guided them to the house where Quayle and Yang were sheltering. Quayle reported that he had had practically no warning of the attack, and that the Japs had followed up the fugitives so fast that the reserve stocks of

[1] To this day, I am sorry to have to record, there has been no authentic news of Pat Noone, and one must assume that he died of fever while living with the Sakai.

food and medicine, dumped in the cave, had all been lost, as well as all the heavy gear which had been hidden in the jungle as they fled.

Our material losses were very serious. The Japs had found a rucksack containing all our money, our medicines, including all our vital quinine, a copy of our signals plan, and a number of maps. It also contained my diaries and collections for the last year and a long report on my two years' work which I had written to be sent out by submarine. Fortunately Davis had taken our most secret documents with him to Blantan. It was nevertheless a serious blow. The batteries and hand generator had easily been found in the undergrowth by the Japs, who had also taken all our cooking and household gear, spare clothes, and blankets. It seems probable that the Japs spotted our camp from the air. They certainly knew its exact position and came straight to it.

After regaining contact, the whole party had moved down the Woh and spent a miserable month at Juit. The three Europeans, deprived of quinine, had been prostrated with malaria, and food had been very scarce indeed. At last they had found this camp site near the upper sources of the Telom river, and had only been established there for a fortnight when I rejoined them on July 25, 1944. Gurun camp (we borrowed the Sakai name: *kambing gurun* being the *serow* or mountain sheep) was ideally situated except that, like Pa Kasut's, being on the shoulder of Batu Puteh it received its full share of the rain and mountain mist collected by that great massif. Also, as we were almost 2,500 feet above sea level, it was very cold at night and in the early morning, though never quite so cold as at Pa Kasut's. We were to use this camp for a whole year without interruption by the Japs.

The site chosen was on a narrow and gently sloping step on one of the steep sharp ridges that run down from Batu Puteh to the Telom river. The camp could be easily defended, provided that the enemy approached up the main track – which, fortunately, the Japs almost invariably did – but as in all Sakai country, the jungle was a maze of tracks and many of them came in from behind. The normal approach ran straight up the steep side of the ridge, and this had been cleared a little to give a good field of fire from the guard post a hundred yards below the camp. On the other side of

275

the ridge a steep track ran down two hundred feet to a tiny stream which supplied us with water, and on to a number of deserted clearings by the upper reaches of the Telom.

Yang's party, which was gradually increased from fifteen to thirty during our year's sojourn here, lived in a single hut about fifty feet by twenty-five. Fortunately there was plenty of bamboo and *atap* nearby for building. A flattened bamboo sleeping bench ran down each side, leaving a wide space in the middle where they kept a fire of huge logs burning night and day. One end of the hut was quite open, while the other was closed in with *atap*, but at the top shutters could be propped out to admit light. The whole of this end of the hut, to a depth of fifteen feet, was made into a stage about a foot higher than the sleeping benches. Down either side, just under the *atap* eaves, was a long bamboo desk so that the men could sit on the outside of the sleeping benches and write. Later on a headquarters hut was built nearby, where Yang and his quarter-master spent most of the day writing at a high bamboo table piled with books, grenades, boxes of ammunition, quack Chinese medicines, and innumerable notebooks laboriously filled with potted knowledge.

As was customary in guerilla camps, the kitchen was down by the stream to save carrying water, and as the steep muddy track became more and more slippery, a series of steps were cut and reinforced with logs. Here under an *atap* roof was a bench for bags of rice, fish, and vegetables, and on the ground were two huge clay fireplaces built round the hemispherical cooking-pots. We walked through the cookhouse to reach the washing-place, which, as the flow of water was so small, had had to be dug out and timbered. A hundred yards above the camp this stream disappeared altogether under a pile of boulders, but it never ran dry.

A small parade-ground had been made in front of the men's hut on the only available patch of level ground. It was not as big as a tennis court, and Davis waged a perpetual war with Yang to prevent him enlarging it by removing several clumps of *atap* and cutting down the trailing bamboos which grew to a height of fifty feet and then spread to thin clusters of greenery, thus providing just enough cover from the air. From this camp we had a clear though limited view over the plains in a southwesterly direction and could just descry a zigzag silvery line which was the mouth of the Perak river.

For the first six weeks after I rejoined the party we were living in exceedingly cramped temporary quarters just beside the men's hut, though we still cooked and ate our meals separately. Our party was now twelve: the four of us, Han, Lee Chuen, Tsing, Ying, Chen and Chang (the two new arrivals, whom I now met for the first time), Black Lim, and old Ah Su. Of the other four – Lim Bo Seng, Ah Ng, Lim, and Sek Fu – there was still no word.[1]

John Davis had more or less recovered from his bad attack of fever, but had lost a great deal of weight. Richard Broome was better than he had been at Blantan, but was still very frail and yellow. His condition was anything but robust, and he never became acclimatised to existence in the jungle. Frank Quayle was in a bad way again, as he had painfully swollen legs and was unable to walk. He had his fortieth birthday in this camp and was never really well. Our Chinese agents were all suffering from intermittent fever and at this stage were quite unable to help to carry food or undertake any other heavy work. Lee Chuen, particularly, was very prone to sudden and violent attacks of malaria and could not get rid of chronic scabies, that most irritating of skin diseases, from which I had always suffered in the Pahang camps but from which I was now entirely free. Ah Su and Black Lim were our two strong men, and they carried water up from the stream and did most of the heavy chores of the camp.

Han took over the cooking and with his ready tact and command of Mandarin he used to help Yang in the rather invidious task of dividing up the food between the two camps. There was inevitably a certain amount of mild friction between Yang's men and ours. At Blantan and Pa Kasut's, where our men were busy coming and going on their own work and where food was plentiful and we had any amount of money with which to buy it, things were easier and though we lived on a considerably higher scale than did Yang's men, yet they were still much better armed, clothed, and fed than in any other guerilla camp I had visited. But now

---

[1] Ah Ng, Lim, and Sek Fu were found still to be alive when the Japs surrendered, but the gallant Lim Bo Seng, alas! had died under torture.

things were different. Although we Europeans found it extremely difficult to exist in the jungle on the food of Chinese coolies, Davis rightly insisted that the twelve of us should live alike and share any medicine or luxuries we had. Now that we were more than ever dependent on Yang's men, with food and money so scarce, we shared all the food that came up equally in proportion to numbers between the guard and ourselves. This meant that Yang's men, while continuing to live very well by their standards, accumulated considerable stores of luxuries such as coffee, sugar, ginger, etc., as well as essentials like salt fish, prawns, and vegetables, while our party, who – especially the Europeans – depended more on the 'vegetables' than on rice and potatoes, always seemed to be short.

Our food lines were limited by an unfortunate circumstance. At the time Pa Kasut's had been attacked, the camp at Bidor had had an alarm and had moved in from their site on the Gedong river to a position on the Telom less than a mile from our camp – though when we had moved to Gurun we had been quite unaware of this, as camps were never allowed to know each other's positions. Chen Ping ought to have prevented this, but things were happening so fast at that time and he had so many responsibilities that he failed to do so. This meant that we had to leave all the Bidor jungle edge to them, and food lines had to be so arranged that carriers from one camp never met those of the other. Another disadvantage of the proximity of the Bidor camp was that every time they fired a shot at a pig or had a little target practice, we thought it was the Japs. Yang blew the alarm whistle – a dread sound that never lost its capability of making one's heart miss a beat or two, and we were given the inconvenience of grabbing all our gear and falling in outside the hut in readiness for instant departure. And had the Japs ever found their way to the Bidor camp, they must inevitably have followed up the wide, well-trodden path that led within a few hundred yards of it and up the hill to Gurun.

In August we moved across to the new house that Yang's men had at last made for us. At Blantan and at Pa Kasut's we had not been able to design our own dwelling, but here we could do this and had plenty of time to carry out our ideas. The site chosen was a hundred yards above Yang's big *kongsi*-house and on the other side of the parade-ground. The ridge was very narrow here and immediately above our hut the level part ended and the ground rose very steeply towards Batu Puteh. We soon cut another row of steps down to the bathing-pool, and on the far side of the ridge so as to drain into the other valley, we built our latrine – not an architectural triumph with steps, platform and handrail such as I had made at Pa Kasut's, but simply two poles running out from the hill and supported on a crosspiece. As the tapioca diet gave us all violent attacks of diarrhoea, we dared not have the latrine too far from the house.

A raised sleeping-bench of flattened bamboo ran across one end and along one side of the house, and a large bamboo was placed along the front of this bench, so that we could sit there in comfort with our feet on the floor, which had been carefully lev-elled and was soon stamped hard and firm. At the back of the bench a bamboo wall ran up for a couple of feet and was finished off with a rail against which we could lean. Shutters filled the gap between the rail and the overhanging *atap* eaves.

So far it was like any Chinese hut, but its really magnificent features were its tables and chairs. The tables, each of which was made to seat six, were constructed of poles driven into the ground and topped with smooth planks off the wireless cases. Against the tables and right along the open side of the house was a continuous bench of smooth bamboos with the frames so constructed that the seat and back were tilted like an armchair. On the other three sides of the tables we made bamboo stools on legs driven into the ground. As we had no rails, everything was made firm with rattan lashing. The bamboo, which was bright green at first, soon toned to a very attractive pale ochre.

At the end of the hut opposite the shorter sleeping-bench was a row of shelves from floor to roof and an opening leading down three or four steps to the kitchen, which we preferred to have under the same roof instead of down by the stream as in other camps. This meant that water had to be carried up each day, but we used to go down to the bathing-place to wash. In the middle of the floor between the tables and sleeping-benches a fender of four logs enclosed a fire. At this height its warmth was most acceptable as soon as the sun had set, and on cold misty days we were glad of it at any time. It also served to keep the mosquitoes and flies at bay.

279

Gradually we worked out a routine which changed very little as we waited month after month for Chen Ping to find new wireless batteries. Each morning Yang would blow his whistle – how we grew to hate the sound! – at 5.30 a.m., and his men would all shout a loud good-morning to each other and tumble out and parade in full marching order with all their possessions in rattan bags on their backs. It was not light for another half-hour, but experience showed that dawn was the favourite moment for the Japs to attack.

We would also get up, roll up our blankets, and pack up our gear in case of an alarm. It very rarely rained at this time of the morning, though there was often a cold and clammy mountain mist. Each of us would fill the time in in his own way until Ah Su had lit the fire and prepared the coffee. We were all very bad-tempered at this bleak hour of the morning and used to keep out of each other's way as far as possible. Davis would just sit huddled up in a blanket, looking very cold and miserable, and refuse to speak to anybody until after coffee, when he would take his stick and walk down the hill past the guard post and sit alone in an old Sakai clearing from which there was a superb view right down to the Telom and across to Blantan and the plains beyond. Davis felt the constricting gloom of the jungle and was always looking for open spaces with a view of the plains. As leader of the party he fretted most at the frustration and protraction of all our plans.

Broome, who always looked ghastly in the early morning, used to do a little P.T. – his only exercise of the day – and then go off a suitable distance into the jungle and either play his home-made flute or sing Gilbert and Sullivan and other songs to himself. Quayle always pretended not to hear the whistle, or that he was ill, but once up he became most energetic. He very rarely left the camp, but was always busy making something – a new kind of lamp, a pipe, or a piece of furniture – and until it was light enough to do this he was to be seen walking up and down the open space between our house and Yang's waving his arms and doing sterto-rous breathing exercises – a process which, for some reason, infu-riated the rest of us! I felt terrible in the mornings, but rather than sit in liverish taciturnity I used to make myself go through a regular table of exercises. I hated being so unfit and longed to be able to travel as I used to. This was very good self-discipline and kept me warm and occupied during the miserable half-hour when it was still too dark to read.

Coffee used to appear between six o'clock and half-past, sometimes sweetened, but for weeks we were without sugar. Later even coffee was unobtainable and we drank local Chinese green tea – made with complete leaves and stalks. Ah Han would have breakfast ready by about 8.30 a.m. There would be rice and tapioca with two 'vegetables,' and soup. There would be a dish of fish, working out at, perhaps, two sardine-sized fish each, and another of some vegetable – pumpkin, bamboo shoots, *petai* (the large, bright green, rank-tasting fruit of a jungle tree), or even yam or sweet potato, cooked with *belachan* ('a stinking paste of prawns and fish-fry' – Winstedt's dictionary), curry, ginger, chillies, or anything else that would give it a strong enough flavour. Each man would fill his cup with rice mixture and then, if there were no casualties – which was unusual – we would sit in two parties of six round our tables. As soon as the last man sat down, we would dive at the 'vegetables' with our chopsticks or spoons. Unfortunately, when we were all very hungry and there was little food, the meal used to develop into a race, and there were frequently acrimonious accusations that one or the other of us was getting more than his share. After this we would agree to eat more slowly, but meal by meal the speed would increase until after about a week we flared up into another argument.

Davis always refused to ration the food for the same reason that he refused to allocate and divide up the essential chores among us – namely, that he hated any sort of organisation and what he called 'militarism' and never gave an order if he could possibly help it. His theory was that there were more than enough men to do the little work necessary, and therefore if one man wanted to sleep all day, there was no reason why he should not. If another man liked chopping wood and helping in the kitchen, he was at liberty to do so. Davis was probably right, and in fact each man did what he liked to do, but it seemed to me too idealistic in theory to live up to under those conditions.

Sometimes I used to go out hunting immediately after early-morning coffee, though on dull days it was not possible to see the rifle-sights in the jungle until seven or eight o'clock. This was by

281

far the best part of the day, when the jungle smelled sweet and exciting, and the undergrowth, especially in the clearings, was heavy with dew. My hunting was not justified by results, as in the whole year at this camp I only shot one pig – and that was near our old camp at Pa Kasut's, where I often used to go and spend a day or two when I felt I needed a change. The fact was that the Woh and Telom valleys had been inhabited by Sakai for so long that all the game had been killed off. In all the eighteen months that I lived in this district I only saw monkeys once – a herd of pig-tailed monkeys below our camp at Gurun. We used to hear the deep booming of the *siamang* ape up in the mountains, but we never actually saw them.

Davis was of an energetic disposition, but was not at all interested in hunting and was completely impractical when it came to making anything with his hands. He would sometimes spend hour after hour just sitting by himself in a hollow under a tree and – presumably – thinking. I always envied him this power of mental hibernation.

Broome, whose health gradually improved during these months but who was never robust, usually found some occupation for himself that did not involve too much physical exertion. He would spend hours carving a nude figure or a set of chessmen, making a patent bamboo pot-lifter, or a clay model of the area round the camp. He rarely chopped wood or helped to prepare a meal, and it was quite an occasion when he went down to the stream to wash himself or his clothes. Indeed he seldom went more than a hundred yards from the house, and when we had anything to read he would not even go as far as that. On the other hand, he was capable of great mental effort and would spend hours writing a Gilbertian opera at the expense of the guerillas, or making up crossword puzzles, and at one time he spent an hour or two each morning teaching the more intelligent of our Chinese to speak English.

Quayle was spasmodically active and, being an engineer by profession, he was very useful with his hands. When he was interested in a job, he would attack it with great energy. He also had a passion for acquiring abstruse knowledge, and though he was the world's worst linguist, would spend hours and hours laboriously learning Chinese characters or the Arabic script of the Malayan language.

I have always been horribly energetic and must have driven the others to distraction by my restlessness, especially when they were feeling ill. When I was fit, I was quite happy going out hunting all day or exploring deserted Sakai clearings for the occasional cucumber, tobacco plant, or chilli tree that they had planted and subsequently forgotten. When I was too ill to leave the camp, I spent my time making things or cooking.

I have always been extremely fond of cooking and often used to spend three or four hours a day in the kitchen. When our house was fully furnished I made an oven just outside the cookhouse. The walls were built of rocks covered with clay, and the roof consisted of a semicircle of bark also covered with clay and with a handsome bamboo chimney. Unfortunately the clay consisted mostly of earth and I had to repair it almost daily, as it cracked with the heat and washed away with each rainstorm. The oven itself was made out of a four-gallon kerosene tin with a door and three shelves, and as it stood on a tip platform above the fire and there was an outer metal door, it was completely surrounded by hot air and was most efficient. After we had been at Gurun for a few months we managed to get plenty of tapioca flour, which made excellent pastry when mixed with coconut oil. Whenever we secured any joints of wild boar or goat, I used to roast them with sweet potatoes – which when cooked like this were almost indistinguishable from English roast potatoes. Even pumpkins, when stuffed with chopped pork, prawns, and seasoning, and baked in the oven, became quite an appetising dish.

At one o'clock we had coffee again, and as tapioca seemed to go straight through one's stomach, we were always ravenously hungry by then. In the afternoon there was a strong temptation to go to sleep, but because we usually felt so heavy and liverish on waking up again, we tried not to sleep in the daytime. The evening meal was at 4.30 or 5 p.m., and was exactly the same as the morning one. This was followed by coffee or soup at eight o'clock, and we usually went to bed before nine.

Books were the great problem. In normal life one longs for time to read. Here we had absolutely nothing to do – but practically no books. After the attack on Pa Kasut's camp we only had *Pickwick*, an excellent but small volume of essays, and the Pocket Oxford Dictionary – which I read right through from cover to cover, a thousand pages of it. I also had a Bible that had somehow survived the attack on Pa Kasut's, but it is a strange thing that, for some curious reason, not one of us was able to read it. Here were four men – a civil servant, a policeman, an engineer, and a schoolmaster. None of us was what is called religious, yet we all agreed that at one time or another we had said to ourselves that if ever we had time we should like to make a real study of the Bible, especially the New Testament. Yet, now, in just such circumstances, we simply could not read it.

It was not until we had been at Gurun for three months that Ah Yang at last produced some books. There was a treatise on shoeing horses written in 1873, six manuals on the cultivation of rubber and one on palm oil, two ancient copies of a magazine called *Lucky Star*, some books from the Watchtower Press about a remarkable new religion invented by a Judge Rutherford, a thousand-page grammar in Chinese and English, a delightful selection of English diarists, an Agatha Christie, and *Drago* by 'the author of *Rio Rita*.' This was clearly part of a planter's library and was at least a varied if not a very readable selection. At the beginning of December another load of books came in, but these were a great disappointment to me, as they were the ones I had collected at the Ulu Slim camp and I had read them all several times. However, we now had a good selection and only wished we had had it earlier.

Davis was a non-smoker, but Broome and Quayle were fairly heavy cigarette-smokers and I liked my pipe, especially when time hung so heavy on my hands. In the old days at Blantan and Pa Kasut's we could get plenty of cheroots of varying quality, made from locally grown tobacco, and these satisfied all three of us. At this camp tobacco was usually scarce, and sometimes we were reduced to collecting leaves from the plants in abandoned Sakai clearings and preparing a coarse and potent mixture ourselves. Sometimes Yang procured the fine-cut *hong yen* (red tobacco), but cigarette papers were unobtainable, and these had to be rolled in cones of newspaper. In a pipe it smoked too hot. The best mixture was known as 'tobacco Siam' and was too strong to smoke in cigarettes – except for Quayle, who could smoke and inhale anything, even at 5.30 a.m.! – so both Broome and Quayle had to become pipe-smokers. Since pipes were unobtainable, we used to spend many-hours making them.

A great fair-weather sport was darts, and much ingenuity was required to improvise a board. Quayle made a composition of clay and crushed *atap* stalk, but it weighed half a hundredweight and was always cracking. Broome favoured a sheet of bark and spent many an hour cutting samples off various kinds of tree, but it proved impossible to straighten these without splitting them. I tried to level a surface of a growing trunk, but there was no suitable tree just where we wanted it, and all the wood was so hard that the darts bounced out again. At last Yang managed to obtain a double-handed saw, and we cut a wedge out of one of the thin flat buttresses that certain kinds of tree throw out near the ground to support their weight. This had a quarter of an inch of firm bark on it and held the darts perfectly.

When it came to marking the board, none of us could remember the places of the figures, and we had to make them up. Quayle, who was a good draughtsman, painted the figures and blacked in the alternate spaces with Chinese ink. The body of the darts was made of shaped wood, the point by filing down a nail, and the wings of paper. We passed many happy hours playing this excellent game. I was the champion, but was sometimes beaten by the Chinese, who became very keen, dancing and shouting with excitement in a close game.

Another game that did much to preserve our sanity was Mah-Jongg. Most of our Chinese were already expert players. They made a very beautiful set of bamboo tiles and painted them with a box of watercolours that Lee Chuen had brought in with him. A game that was very popular for a short time with us and never lost its appeal for the Chinese was Monopoly. Broome, who had an astounding memory, made all the cards, etc., and it was very satisfactory to be sitting in the middle of the Malayan jungle buying property in Soho and putting up luxury hotels in Park Lane and Piccadilly. When our Chinese played this game, they used to get wild with excitement and shout and scream so loudly that it was quite impossible for us to play any other game or even to read!

What really prevented us from going completely off our heads or quarrelling violently with each other was the writing and round games we played in the evenings, as long as there was enough oil for our lamps. The most popular was certainly the good old-fashioned Quiz. Each of us would prepare twenty questions and then ask them round the other three. We soon outgrew general Quizzes and confined them to a special subject – South America, the Great War, food and wine, the Stage, or even the *Pickwick Papers*. Davis and Broome had known each other intimately for so long that they could always answer each other's questions. Quayle would stump us with some abstruse problem, when it would be discovered that he did not know the answer himself or had looked it up wrong in the dictionary.

We had some playing-cards, but only Broome and Quayle knew how to play Bridge. They tried to initiate Davis and me, but as they could never agree on the finer points of the game or how to teach it, we soon gave it up. The others used to play Patience and Chess. In normal life I had always considered cards and indeed any organised game as a waste of time, and would much rather watch birds or fish, or go for a walk, and in the evening talk or read a book. But now I wished very much that I could use up the hours in this way.

Another entertainment that was rather an ordeal at the time, but which at least served to break the monotony of our evenings, was the concerts that Yang used to organise every month or so, usually to mark some Russian anniversary. We were always expected to take part in these, and however much we ourselves disliked standing up and singing songs or making fools of ourselves, our contributions were always greeted with great applause and were presumably enjoyed, if only as a change from the normal programme. When the guerilla performers sang their own folk songs or indulged in buffooning, they were a joy to watch and listen to, but tradition demanded that they should sing dreary propaganda or political dirges, and that their plays should follow the traditional pattern that I had learned to know so well in other camps – and under Yang's uninspired leadership the Gurun plays were duller than ever. Fortunately our Chinese introduced some variety, as Tsing and Ying were born buffoons, and Han, who in these days affected long hair and a sparse moustache and beard, could bring the house down by simply standing on the stage. Lee Chuen, who had the expression of an angel, would fix his eyes in the rafters of the roof and sing sad songs of Shanghai.

Richard Broome, however, was the star performer. He had an excellent baritone voice and seemed to be able to remember both the words and tune of any song he had ever heard. His most popular number was 'The Music Goes Round and Round,' which he sang with lively pantomime.

Davis only knew two songs: 'Nine Green Bottles' and 'The Drunken Sailor,' but he was made to sing them both at every concert and if he forgot the words there were plenty of prompters, as all the Chinese soon learned to sing them, though they had not the faintest idea of the meaning. Quayle and I had both learned some of their own songs in the various camps, and it always gave them great delight to hear our versions of these. My yodelling and Eskimo songs were as popular as ever. Our most ambitious effort was a production of *The Monkey's Paw* in Malay, in which Davis and Broome were the old married couple, Quayle the son, and I the friend from overseas. This was a tremendous success – at least, we thought so – but here again the audience entirely missed the point. It was very difficult to put on any turn involving the four of us, because it was rare for all of us to be fit at the same time, and a play might have to be postponed five or six times – which was most discouraging for the cast. A great attraction of these concerts was that halfway through, sweet coffee and rather indigestible tapioca cakes were handed round, and these were most acceptable, especially when our own supply of sugar had run out.

Looking back on these wearisome months, it surprises me how little we quarrelled – except occasionally over the matter of food already referred to. Yet we were living under the most difficult conditions it is possible to imagine: one or more of us was nearly always ill, often very ill; food was so short that we were usually hungry and what there was upset our stomachs; the unnatural existence in the gloom of the jungle was extremely trying both to health and nerves, and we had no work to occupy our minds or muscles. We seemed to be making absolutely no advance in our efforts to regain contact with India as month after month passed without any sign of a battery. Until that time we were mere guests of the guerillas without being able to do anything to help them or the war in general. And we were not only living on top of each other, but cheek by jowl with a party of Chinese who were equally frustrated and whose whole outlook on life was so entirely different from ours.

Quayle and I had been thrust by the chances of war into somebody else's 'show,' and it was inevitable that – if only subconsciously – we should feel in the position of guests, if not intruders. Although I liked both Davis and Broome, and now number them among my closest friends, circumstances and the vagaries of our characters used to cause innumerable minor irritations which might easily have developed into bitter feuds and quarrels – yet they never did. I greatly admired Davis's forthright and absolutely straightforward character, yet I found him infuriatingly uncompromising in argument. I was delighted with Broome's wit and scholarship, but his indolence drove me to distraction. I hated the daily race for food which – to me – seemed so unnecessary, and, even though I enjoyed doing it, I resented working while others slept or did nothing – and my enthusiasm and restless energy must have been equally infuriating to them. Fortunately we all had the good sense to realise that however much we got on each other's nerves, we just had to live together, and therefore made the best of it. But such is the depressing effect of insufficient food and bad health that of my three and a half years in the jungle these months were by far the worst.

CHAPTER SEVENTEEN

We Get on the Air

When the Japs had attacked our camp at Pa Kasut's, we had lost all our batteries and the hand generator. However, the B.2 sets, still on their way from Jenderata, had been saved, together with two large cases of wireless material. The latter were found to contain a pedal generator and dynamo and a small receiving set. Unfortunately they were all completely ruined, owing to bad packing. The receiving set was useless and the wiring of the dynamo rusted through. The pedal generator, a machine with the framework and saddle of a bicycle, but which could be jacked up so that the chain charged a dynamo instead of turning the back wheel, was very rusty but could be repaired.

Our efforts were now concentrated on getting motor-car batteries and either rewiring the ruined dynamo or procuring another. But such was the inefficiency of the Chinese when it came to carrying out a job like this that it was four months before we even got a battery that would work and another three months before we had the apparatus necessary to charge the batteries sufficiently to be able to transmit.

The chief trouble was that our contact with Chen Ping was limited to a visit about every six weeks or two months. We could never be certain of getting in touch with him when we wanted to, however urgent the matter might be. Chen Ping was a very much overworked man. His chief job was as liaison officer between Perak headquarters, somewhere on the other side of the Cameron Highlands road, and the outside. He also seemed to be responsible for liaison between Perak headquarters and the various other camps in the state, and with general headquarters somewhere in Selangor. Also he was a sick man and his activities were continually interrupted by attacks of fever. Yang himself – presumably on security grounds – seemed to have no traffic at all with the men who were supposed to be charging our batteries and rewiring the dynamo, and our contact with them was therefore limited to the rare visits of Chen Ping or his runner.

At the end of July, when we discovered that the dynamo was useless and set about trying to have it repaired, Chen Ping's runner appeared with the news that several columns of Japs had been sighted in the jungle making for the Bidor camp – which was less than a mile from us. Whether this was true or not we never discovered. At the same time, there was a report that the Japs had sent ten Sakai who were working for them to the 7th Mile as informers, their task being to try to get in touch with any Sakai who might know anything about us and whence we had moved from Pa Kasut's. A few weeks later the Japs carried out a massacre near Blantan and our food lines in that area had to be entirely closed down. Certainly for the first few months after the attack on Pa Kasut's camp, the Japs were very active on the jungle edge and whereas a Chinese carrying food might be able to establish his innocence, one found with a battery or a dynamo would inevitably be tortured and probably put to death.

It was abundantly clear that for us to 'get on the air' was going to be a long and difficult task, but there was still a chance of re-establishing contact with India by means of submarine rendezvous. In April 1944 Chen and Chang, after a blind landing at Pangkor, had made their way to our camp at Pa Kasut's. Before they left the submarine a new series of R.V.s had been arranged for the subsequent months. But owing to the attack on the camp and the move which followed it, it had not been possible to consider getting to the coast until the August R.V. It was quite out of the question for a European to hope to get through while the Japs were so busy on the edge of the jungle, and anyway at that time none of us was fit enough. It was therefore arranged that Chen should go. He had not been compromised by the collapse of our outside organisation. As he had originally come from the camp at Sitiawan he knew that part of the country, was familiar with the ways of submarines, and would be recognised by whoever came out from our headquarters at Colombo. He and Chang were the only two of our Chinese who could safely go out into the plains, and it was arranged that Chen should stay with his family near Sitiawan and start building up another outside organisation.

When the time came for Chen to go out to keep the August R.V. a great difficulty arose. Owing to the recent massacre near Blantan, it was impossible for him to go out that way – whence he had come in. He would have to go out further south through the country controlled by the Bidor camp. We were out of touch with Chen Ping at that time and Yang said he had no authority to get in touch with Lau Leo, the head of the Bidor camp, and resolutely refused to do so. When, at last, we persuaded him at least to write to Lau Leo on our behalf, the latter replied that he could not possibly help us without higher authority, and there the matter had to end. At last we regained contact with Chen Ping and on September 7 Chen went down to Lau Leo's camp to be escorted to the jungle edge. He was unable to keep that or subsequent rendezvous, but he remained in the plains and from time to time sent in letters which contained valuable information.

In October Chen Ping was away attending a conference at general headquarters near Kuala Lumpur. Before he went he had brought us the dynamo, which had been rewound, but it was still quite useless and would not charge, so we had to send it down again. Meanwhile we had secured a complete bicycle from·outside, and with a certain amount of 'improvisation' Quayle had produced a fairly efficient pedal generator which we kept hidden in the jungle in case the camp was attacked. On October 22, Yang, after four months' efforts, produced a motor-car battery – but alas! his men had carried it upside down and all the acid had run out! He also said that a second battery was on the way up, and that they might be able to secure another dynamo off an old motor-car, but it had to be repaired and would not be up for another month – and we knew what that meant!

We now had to decide a matter that had been under discussion for some time. Where were we going to establish our wireless station? The two B.2 sets were still in their cases in a hideout near our camp. If we unpacked only one of them, it and the pedal generator and the batteries would be more than we could guarantee to carry away in the event of the camp being attacked. We had once thought of setting up the wireless at a high clearing, about an hour's walk along the escape route, but this would have meant Lee Chuen and one of us living there. Eventually we decided to open up the station at Gurun itself, especially as things were now quieter outside. The Japs were either too busy in Burma and elsewhere to worry about us, or they had assumed that we had left the district entirely. A plan for evacuating all the wireless gear in the event of an attack was worked out and rehearsed, while a large hole was dug underneath the fireplace in our hut – as traces of disturbance would not be visible among the ashes – and all the heavy spares were secreted there.

On November 5 John Davis and I walked down to one of the lower clearings to collect sweet-potato leaves. It was an oppressive thundery day and out in the open the heat was so unbearable that we were glad to return to the jungle. On our way home at about 10.30 a.m. we suddenly heard bursts of machine-gun fire and the uneven roar of manoeuvring planes straight overhead. We were in a particularly thick part of the jungle, and though we ran frantically up and down the track, we could find no place where we could see through the tree-tops to what was going on above. When we returned to the camp, the others were agog with excitement. There had been three huge four-engined bombers very high overhead – they thought they were Superfortresses – and they had heard the deep drone of others in the clouds and had seen the Jap two-engined fighter bombers in pursuit.

That same afternoon two batteries came up from below. They had been carried right side up and were giving charge. We collected the set from its hiding-place in the jungle and hung the aerial from the top of Yang's flagstaff to our hut. This set was in perfect condition, as it had been properly packed. The ants had eaten away the outer wooden case, but within was a sealed tin box coated with half an inch of pitch, and inside that again the set in its ash case. Lee Chuen found that he had not forgotten how to connect it up and tune it in. To our joy the set was alive. Within a few minutes we had picked up All India Radio from New Delhi and were listening to the news. We heard – my diary records – that General Sir John Dill had died in the United States, that the Prime Minister of Japan had made the gloomiest speech ever uttered by a Prime Minister at war without actual surrender; that in the Philippines the Japs had lost 2,400 planes compared to the Americans' 400, and that twice the weight of bombs had been dropped on Cologne as the Germans had loosed on Coventry in November 1940. Antwerp and Budapest had been taken and all Greece was liberated. Then we heard that at 10 a.m. that morning thirty Superfortresses had dropped bombs on Singapore and that all had returned safely to their base which, 'according to Japanese reports,' was in India.

We still had no dynamo and had to rely on batteries being sent out for recharging. But nothing succeeds like success, and after we had circulated our first news-sheet we soon received more batteries as well as supplies of distilled water and acid. But most of them were old car batteries and if they worked at all their life was very short. Sometimes we only had enough juice to get the headlines of the news and sometimes we could not receive at all. We only had a pair of headphones, and while one man dictated what he heard another feverishly wrote it down. Each week we produced a long news summary and Han transcribed it into Mandarin for Chen Ping to circulate.

These events had an extraordinarily salutary effect on our health and spirits: though we were still far from being able to get on the air, we at least knew what was happening in the world outside, and we were helping to spread the good news. On December 3 we had a letter from Chen Ping to say that Chen had gone out to try to make the November R.V., but that bad weather had prevented it. He also said that more batteries were on the way up, which was very good news because we had not been able to receive for some time. On December 20 another rather cryptic letter came from Chen Ping saying that a British party had got in to Johore by sea, presumably by submarine, and that he could take them a message from us. A signal was therefore enclosed for them to relay to Colombo saying that we were hoping soon to get on the air and would they be prepared to pick up our signals. We were afraid that after more than a year's silence they would by now have stopped listening for us to come upon the air.

On January 11 some more Superfortresses passed above our camp in ones and twos, heading north-west. They were so high that in spite of their vast size and a clear sky they looked extraordinarily misty and attenuated. These were the first Superforts I had ever seen, and I was tremendously excited. We all cheered and cheered as each was sighted. Superforts seemed to bring us luck, for on the same day a new dynamo arrived together with the old one which had again been rewound, but was still quite useless.

The new dynamo was off a motor-car and was in a very bad state of repair, and the sprocket would not fit our pedal generator. All our efforts were now concentrated on being able to charge our batteries. Up till now we had rarely had enough power to receive more than the headlines, and to transmit had been quite out of the question.

Fortunately we had a good team. Quayle, a trained engineer, was an inventive and skilful craftsman. He knew the theory of electricity and how a dynamo should work, though he knew little about wireless and had never seen a B.2 set. Lee Chuen was a professional operator from China who had also been trained in our system in India. He had not operated a set of any sort for over a year, though he had read and re-read his rules of procedure and had kept his hand in by daily tapping practice with his key. But Lee Chuen was very intelligent, had infinite patience, and unlike so many Chinese would always listen to what anybody else had to say. He and Quayle used to work day after day trying to make one good dynamo from two dud ones and to turn it with the pedal generator. At last they succeeded. It was very hard work, but if one man turned each pedal vigorously by hand, we could just get the battery plates to bubble – which indicated a charge going in. The chain was very poor and kept breaking, and it was very difficult to anchor the machine down so that the alignment was not continually being shaken out of the true by the violent pedalling required.

On January 14 we received the news again after a three weeks' silence and were relieved to hear that the German salient had been held and that United States forces had landed on Luzon after closing the Leyte campaign. But it was always very difficult after a prolonged gap to pick up the threads of the news, as names of new generals and places would be introduced which would mean nothing to us. We had only some indifferent maps in the back of our out-of-date *Pears Cyclopaedia*, and it was very difficult to follow the various campaigns. Now that the batteries were really being charged, we built a special shelter for the generator and shored it up with wooden supports so that we could pedal it by foot, but even now it was very hard work, and the dynamo was in such poor condition that it needed two or three hours' hard pedalling for us to be able to receive for a quarter of an hour.

On January 21 I felt very ill and found that my temperature was 105 degrees, and for the next three weeks I was laid low by a very virulent fever which we thought was tick-typhus. This was a most unpleasant disease, and I gather that the others rather wondered at times if I would pull through or not. Personally I ceased to care very much either way. Day after day my temperature would be 102 in the morning and 103 or 104 in the evening. I could eat nothing and had terrible pains across the small of my back and behind my eyes. The worst symptom was that I could not sleep properly. Each evening I would fall asleep at about midnight and then wake up again at two or three o'clock in the morning and be quite unable to sleep any more. Fortunately there was still a tin of Klim which had been kept in reserve, and for two weeks I could take nothing but milk, sometimes with an egg beaten up in it. At this time two of our hens were laying well, and later I was able each day to have two eggs cooked with a little rice, and by the middle of February my temperature was down to normal again and I could get up. But I had lost a great deal of weight and what little colour I had had before, and could not walk without a stick.

It was unfortunate that I chose this time to be so ill, as it was a most exciting month. Towards the end of January the pedal generator was putting enough power into the batteries for Lee Chuen to be able to transmit, and by this time he had set up his complete station. Unfortunately we only had the Mark III signals plan and this had already been compromised when the Japs had attacked our camp and captured a copy. We were therefore not at all optimistic of being heard, but after five days we were picked up, and on February 1, 1945, we successfully transmitted our first message.

There were now three things to be done: to convene a meeting with a representative of guerilla headquarters, since at last we were in a position to help them on the lines of the agreement we had made just over a year previously; to get Broome out to Colombo, not only to make a full report but for his health's sake – and it was now taken for granted that after my recent illness I should accompany him; and to receive a parachute drop. The last of these was the most urgent, as our charging machine required daily attention and it needed all Quayle's ingenuity and everybody's energy in relays to be able to come upon the air twice a day. Yet from the time we started to transmit on February 1 until the parachute drop on February 27 we came up regularly on every schedule.

The code we were using was a very laborious one, and if a single mistake were made the message would not make sense and all had to be done again, so we often had to work far into the night coding and decoding messages. Our headquarters at the other end seemed to us not only unnecessarily verbose but extraordinarily stupid. Either they would explain obvious things at great length – thus wasting hours of our time deciphering – or they would refer casually to things we could know nothing whatever about. When we had to ask for enlightenment they would reply as if we were all congenital idiots. Also, our headquarters, for obvious reasons, did not give us any more information than necessary about other parties that were operating in Malaya, and when we heard of these activities through Chen Ping, we felt that we were being treated like children and kept in the dark. This misunderstanding between headquarters and the field is inevitable unless there is personal contact from time to time, and we realised how necessary it was for one of us to get out as soon as possible to Colombo and made a detailed report.

One of the first signals that we received told us that Davis and I had been awarded the D.S.O. Colombo wanted us to take a daylight drop of four 'bodies' and a vast quantity of stores within a week. For this they required a dropping zone (D.Z.) at least 300 yards long and 100 yards wide. The only place where we could hope to find such a space was among the tin-tailings between the jungle edge and the road. As it would take us several hours to carry the stores away into the jungle, we did not think it safe to take a drop there by daylight and had to postpone it to the 'moon period' a fortnight later. In these days we had few weapons and most of our ammunition was faulty. We certainly could not afford to provoke the Japs to an engagement either on the D.Z. or if they were to follow us back to our camp.

Unless it is safe to send planes over in broad daylight, there are three times for taking a drop in enemy-held country – first light, last light, and during the moon period. With a country that is so far away from its base as Malaya is from Colombo it is very difficult, after a flight of eight hours, to strike the dawn or dusk period exactly. First light is the more dangerous time. If the plane is late in arriving over the D.Z. and has to spend some time in searching for it, enemy fighters may come to the attack and will be able to pursue it all the way home in broad daylight, and if enemy troops arrive on the D.Z. they will have all day to search for and engage the carrying party. Last light is a safe time, but the plane has to cross the dangerous coastal belt in full light and, if it arrives late, may not be able to locate the D.Z. in the gathering darkness. A slight advantage is that the carriers will be able to do their work under cover of night. A drop during the moon period is safest, and in Malaya there is the additional advantage that in general the nights are less stormy and overcast than the days, and there is therefore less danger of the plane running into a mountainside. A Liberator bomber – the type of plane used for all the drops into Malaya – needs several miles to make its turn and therefore must have plenty of room and good visibility to manoeuvre.

The moon period lasts for four days on either side of the full moon, and it was eventually agreed that we should take the drop on February 25. Davis went out and reconnoitred a suitable D.Z. in some old tin-tailing country a few miles east of the Tapah-Bidor road. It was a perfect place, level and sandy, and well clear of the mountains. The only disadvantages were that it was rather dangerously near the road, and a stream ran across one end of it.

Meanwhile, signals went backward and forward arranging the details of the drop: the exact date and time over target (T.O.T.) would, for security reasons, be given later. We asked for one European, to bring us up to date with developments at our headquarters, and one Chinese operator to assist Lee Chuen, and we asked modestly for a few clothes, combs, tooth-brushes, and books for ourselves. But Colombo came back saying that they were going to send two Liberators and drop three Europeans, one Chinese, and two tons of stores. It was all terrifically exciting, especially when we heard who the newcomers were to be. They were sending Majors Hannah and Harrison, both ex-Malayans known to Davis and Broome, and two radio operators – Cpl. Humpleman and Chuen. (Why is there so little variety among Chinese names?)

Chen Ping had come in to see us before going south to attend a meeting at his headquarters, and he was in excellent form. We were all in much better heart now that there was something definite to look forward to and it seemed that all our work would not be wasted after all. We heard from Chen Ping that two Europeans and four Chinese had done a blind drop in the Sungei Siput area. The Japs had arrived on the spot soon afterwards, but the six 'bodies,' who had been dispersed in landing, had been collected by the guerillas.

We heard in our news bulletins that the Russians had occupied Budapest and were only fifteen miles from Berlin, and that the Americans had recaptured the Philippines and landed in Iwo Jima. Little was said about the progress of the war in Burma after the Akyab landing, but we felt that war in Europe was about to end and that the campaign in Malaya would open in a few months' time. My great fear was that if I went out by submarine in March I should miss the fighting in Malaya and three years of my life would have been wasted. I was making a quick recovery from my last unpleasant illness, but I feared that once in India I should be made to take at least four months' sick leave and probably sent home, and thus I should miss the Malayan campaign completely.

I had no love for the guerillas' politics, but I had considerable affection for the rank and file. I felt that knowing them so well and being trusted by them, my job was to stay and fight with them against the Jap and to act as liaison between them and the Allied invading army, while Davis stayed at guerilla headquarters and did the job for which he was so admirably fitted, and Broome was attached to our headquarters at Colombo. My military knowledge was completely out of date, but the new instructors who were to be dropped in would soon put that right. They would also bring in medicines and good food, and a doctor had been promised on the following drop. I therefore made up my mind to stay and wired Colombo to that effect.

Meanwhile arrangements went forward for taking the drop. Our reception was to be a simple 'T' of five fires, 100 yards apart on the upright of the T, which was to lie along the axis of the D.Z., and 50 yards apart on the cross-stroke. The fires were to be lighted the moment the plane was heard – it always circled once over the D.Z. before coming in to drop – and a man was to stand beside the central fire and flash a letter which would be given to us at the last moment, together with the Time Over Target.

The charging motor was now so overworked that it needed very skilled nursing to keep it going at all, and we feared that it would break down before we had been given the recognition letter and the T.O.T., especially as Colombo had to postpone the drop to the night of February 26–27. At least a hundred carriers would be needed, as the containers, each of which was six feet long and weighed 2 cwt., would have to be carried bodily off the D.Z. and well into the jungle before dawn. They would then have to be broken down and each man's load made up. The carriers were armed with bamboo poles and rattan slings, and it was hoped that four men would be able to carry one container, at least for a short distance. Chen Ping had arranged that the camp below us would provide fifty carriers, we could raise thirty, and the rest would be Sakai whom Chu was assembling. Somebody had to stay behind to look after the camp and get the wireless gear away in case of an attack, and as I was still convalescent I had to undertake this unpleasant task. As soon as the carrying party had gone off at dawn on February 26, I set to work to enlarge our table and benches to accommodate the expected guests and to build a shelter for all the stores that were coming up, and the day passed all too quickly.

The long-awaited night was still and cloudy, but the moon shone through from time to time and it was never really dark. From a viewpoint near the camp it was possible to get an unobstructed view of the plains, and as it was only eight miles in a straight line to the D.Z., I hoped to see the Libs come over if they circled inland. The T.O.T. was to be at midnight, our time, and as this hour approached, those of us who were left in camp became more and more excited. As a result of having done too much work, my temperature had gone right up again, so I lay down in the hut, having arranged that the others would call me as soon as they heard the planes in the distance. Twelve o'clock came and nothing happened. Then one o'clock, then two; still no sound of the Libs. At last, at 2.20 a.m., when we had almost given up hope, we heard a faint hum of a plane approaching from the coast. For half an hour the noise of engines increased, grew faint, and then approached again. The planes did not come anything like within sight and we had no idea how many there were. Even now I had an awful fear that something had gone wrong and they had failed to find the D.Z.

Perhaps the reception party had given up waiting and gone home, or finished up their fuel and not been able to keep the recognition fires going. However, all was well. I will take up the story in my diary:

Thursday, March 1, 1945 – One of the happiest days of my life! Feel better today, but temperature up again last night. Day of feverish activity. Re-clayed oven and cleaned out drains and finished off the shelter for the stores. Loads coming up all day. I told Yang's quartermaster to send them over, but he said he had had orders that they were all to go in the headquarters hut and refused to comply. After a violent argument I won my point, but only by giving him a signed statement that I had overridden Yang's orders. How difficult Chinese are! As the loads came up I unpacked them and stacked them on the bamboo shelves I had put up. Lovely to see all the medical stores; also tins of bacon, cheese, fruit, chocolate, and all sorts of concentrated rations; cases of cigarettes and tobacco; new clothes and shoes; weapons and ammunition; and above all – books. The new Winchester 30 Carbine is a joy, short and light and very handy – ideal for the Chinese. It is semi-automatic, holds sixteen rounds in the mag., has aperture sights and a cunning safety catch you press with the trigger finger – a perfect weapon for the jungle.

The books are a wonderful selection: a few war books – John Brophy's *Target Island*; Gibbs's *The Battle Within*; Henriques' *The Journey Home*; Feuchtwanger's *Simone*, and James Hilton's *The Story of Doctor Wassell*; Sackville-West's *The Eagle and the Dove, The Song of Bernadette*, also two Dickenses, Clemence Dane's *He Brings Great News*, and Harvey Allen's *The Forest and the Fort* – altogether a superb selection.

All Yang's men were in by midday and our party straggled in later completely done in. Chuen came in first. He was wearing a dark green commando's beret, long green canvas boots with rubber soles – American jungle boots – and green battle-dress with lovely blue parachute wings over his left pocket. He is a little cheerful man and speaks fair English. Then came Humpleman, very young, blue-eyed, with a bland and serious manner; then Jim Hannah, lean, dark, hook-nosed, moustached, and over forty. At one time he was a journalist and in the rubber slump in Malaya he worked in Australia. Then came Harrison, short, with red face and sandy hair – a very silent Scot, also a planter. John and Richard brought up the rear, absolutely exhausted but very contented.

After a meal they had got out on to the field and had everything ready an hour before midnight. Then they waited and waited and, as nothing happened, they got more and more worried and despondent. One hour late, then two hours. It was bitterly cold, and at last they were just talking of returning home when a faint drone was heard from the west. They were so excited that their hearts almost choked them! At last the Lib came over. Apparently she followed up the Perak river, then came across on a bearing. The moon was shining brilliantly and the sky was covered with high, white, fleecy clouds. The fires, freshly stoked with dry *atap*, burned up brightly, and Quayle with his torch flashed the recognition letter faster and faster with growing excitement as the great Lib, after flying round in a wide circle, swooped overhead, vast and glistening in the moonlight. Suddenly four little white balls seemed to appear in the plane's wake, and four tiny black forms were seen swinging from side to side below them. John, Richard, and Frank all agreed it was the most exciting moment of their lives. While they were still lost in wonder, things started happening. Hannah and Harrison landed beautifully and were immediately fielded, but Humpleman fell in the stream and was retrieved soaking wet. The containers and packages, which had been released immediately after the bodies, now came down and all landed safely.

Very soon another plane was heard approaching. They thought at first it was the same one back again, but it turned out to be another Lib. A new shower of parachutes burst open, and more containers and packages started to float downwards. This time some of them drifted off the tin-tailings and landed in broken ground and undergrowth nearby. As the chutes collapsed and became less conspicuous after landing, it was necessary to note where each one fell and immediately send a party to recover it. A count revealed that they were still four short, and these could nowhere be found. It was very much feared that the first Jap plane over in the morning would see the parachutes and a search party would arrive. While some continued the search for these, others carried what had been retrieved into the jungle. The containers were vast and heavy. Each was slung from a pole, but six Sakai could only just stagger a few yards with them, and they had to be broken up on the spot and hidden in the jungle. The loads were all dumped at a safe place and some of the party returned to search for the missing chutes by daylight. (It was later discovered that these four packages, which contained grenades and pistols, had, owing to some error, never been dispatched.) Still no sign of the Japs.

There were several Chinese squatters there, and they helped to search, knowing exactly what was happening. Chen Ping did not put in an appearance, so Yang organised the carriers and did a first-class job. Lau Leo's fifty men were there – a very fine lot of men, sturdy and smartly dressed, and thirty-five Sakai, who did marvellously. I wonder what they thought of the drop! After a meal the party moved off. The Sakai came on at speed, making Blantan before dawn and going straight on to Gurun. Hannah says the pilot knew he was a little late, but not two and a half hours: we think the R.A.F. or Colombo probably slipped up between Indian and Malayan time and Greenwich Mean Time.

John and I are lieutenant-colonels! Richard a major, and Frank a captain. Lovely green battle-dress and jungle boots for all of us. When the party reached camp, Yang arranged a guard of honour for them with flags and messages of welcome hung on the trees – I was stripped to the waist, sorting stores. I am so yellow that Hannah thought I was Chinese! We had a bottle of Australian whisky, then all went over to Yang's for a concert. No letters for me – apparently I am still officially 'missing, believed killed.' Marvellous to see new faces and hear fresh voices. So many new inventions one feels – and probably looks – like Rip Van Winkle. Mind in an absolute whirl! How did I ever think of going out by submarine?

The most notable result of the drop was an immediate and revolutionary change in our health. For the last year, even when we had had quinine, the four of us had been incapacitated by malaria for between a third and a half of the time. Hannah and Harrison brought in a new drug called mepacrine. We took a single small yellow tablet each day, and though it gradually stained our skin the same colour, it was absolutely effective, and from the very day we started taking it none of us had another attack – and, as far as I am concerned, have never (touch wood!) had a recurrence to this day.

One curious and disconcerting result of our improved food was that we seemed much more liable to blood poisoning. Before, if our legs were scratched in the jungle or bitten by leeches, we had been able to prevent the wounds becoming infected by the application of sulphathiazole powder, but now this no longer seemed efficacious. Davis started a crop of jungle ulcers – from which he had been comparatively free for a year – and I was very much frightened by a number of diffuse and inflamed swellings on my legs which were as painful as boils but never actually broke the skin. I had to take an internal course of sulphathiazole before the trouble was cured.

The new party had brought in a fair supply of food, and we did not stint ourselves, as a large stores drop was expected as soon as we could make arrangements to receive it. We kept to the same Chinese ways of eating our food, but bacon, fried cheese and onions, and curried bully were substituted for bamboo shoots and salt fish, and three or four times a day we had tea, coffee, or cocoa with plenty of milk and sugar. Now that we had baking powder I could bake millet-flour bread in my oven, as well as jam tarts and sausage rolls.

Within a week our energy had increased in the most extraordinary way, and after a fortnight even I, who had only just recovered from tick-typhus, found that in an hour I could climb a hill that had taken me three hours a year before. And the newcomers, who on first seeing us had been horrified at our cadaverous appearance and unhealthy colour, could almost see us putting on weight and returning to normal. We had new clothes and soap to wash with. Nylon tooth-brushes took the place of ones we had made ourselves out of pig's bristles, and we no longer had to make one Gillette blade last three or four months by stropping it on the palms of our hands. We had books to read, maps on which to follow the daily news, plenty of good tobacco and cigarettes, the occasional tot of whisky, and, above all, something new to do and talk about.

It was fascinating and bewildering to hear of all the latest developments: first-hand accounts of the flying bombs and rockets at home; the story of Cassino; Wingate's Chindits (Mike Calvert, I heard, was one of his Brigadiers); and the bridging of the Chindwin. Through the irony of fate – or the Deity's misplaced sense of humour – while I had been wasting my war years learning how to keep alive in the jungle, Hannah, who had spent much of his life in Malaya, had been attached to a Ski and Mountain Warfare School in Iceland. Harrison had already been dropped into Burma and had come as far as the coast of Malaya by submarine. We were astonished most of all to hear of the activities of Force 136. Apart from operations in Burma, Siam, French Indo-China, and the Andamans, several parties had been dropped blind into other parts of Malaya to contact Chinese and Malay resistance movements, and one party of five officers and twelve other ranks had made a blind landing in south-east Johore from a submarine based in Australia, and had been in regular wireless communication with Colombo in spite of being chased around by the Japs.

Humpleman soon got his new radio station working, and we could give up our daily war with the pedal machine. We had a small steam generator which worked off a wood-burning boiler, and the station was kept so busy that we had to run the generator all day and far into the night. Now that we had reliable communication with our headquarters, two- or three-page signals were coming in and going out on every schedule, and while the three operators were kept busy, the six of us often worked till midnight coding and decoding. Before the station closed down it had been transmitting or receiving for an average of three or four hours a day for eight months and was only switched off if a Jap plane flew overhead. Although we were only ten miles from both Tapah and Bidor, the Japanese radio direction-finding was so poor that they had no idea of the existence of our station.

We learned that submarines operating in the Straits of Malacca had been sinking all Japanese shipping from the size of junks upward, and the Chinese survivors who had been taken back to Ceylon for questioning had given a good deal of general information of conditions inside Malaya, though reports of the activities and organisation of the Chinese guerillas were vague and contradictory. Our headquarters were therefore enormously relieved to hear that our relations with the guerillas were still so good, but it was now more than ever important for us to regain contact with guerilla headquarters and carry on from where we had left off fourteen months before, after our preliminary conference with the Plen. Our only intermediary was Chen Ping, and now, just when his presence was most needed, we lost touch with him completely for several weeks.

Although we had lost touch with guerilla headquarters, Colombo were prepared, on the strength of the agreement signed in January 1944, to start arming the Chinese at once, and most of the signals traffic was concerned with ways and means of doing this. On our side, with our intimate knowledge of the terrain and of the Chinese guerillas, we gave our views of their fighting potentialities and the role in which they could be used to the greatest advantage, and to what extent liaison could or should become advice or even leadership. We also gave our opinion of equipment and rations.

It was very difficult, especially in the continued absence of Chen Ping, to work out exactly what form our liaison with the guerillas should take. They were already organised into seven independent 'Anti-Japanese Regiments,' and each of these regiments – we called them groups – had a headquarters and, as a rule, five patrols. Colombo's basic plan was to drop in a Group Liaison Team (G.L.T.) to each headquarters, and a Patrol Liaison Team (P.L.T.) to each patrol. The G.L.T. was to consist of an officer (the G.L.O.), three radio operators, and an interpreter; the P.L.T. was to include an officer in charge (the P.L.O.), and his second-in-command, two radio operators, and an interpreter-instructor who would be Chinese. Each patrol was to be made up to a hundred men and in certain strategic areas to a hundred and fifty, and was to be armed.

Hannah was to be G.L.O. Perak, and Harrison to be one of his P.L.O.'s. The first patrol in Perak to be armed was the neighbouring one at Bidor. We planned to take the stores drop for them and some food supplies for ourselves on a jungle D.Z. during the March moon period. Hannah and I, who were to organise the reception of this drop, found a perfect D.Z. only a mile below the Bidor camp on the Sungei Sui about a mile above its junction with the Gedong. Here were a whole line of overgrown Sakai clearings, now occupied by Chinese squatters who were growing vegetables for the Bidor camp; and one of these clearings was a good 400 yards long and comparatively level. The 'bodies,' including a doctor for us and the P.L.T. for the Bidor patrol, would be dropped at the same time on the D.Z. we had used before.

The Bidor drop was arranged for March 25, and we were much looking forward to it, as by the middle of March we had run out of the luxury stores brought in by Hannah and were back to bamboo shoots and sweet-potato leaves, and were right out of tobacco. It was planned that soon after this drop there should be another to the Perak Headquarters patrol, which we understood to be somewhere near the 9th Mile on the Cameron Highlands road. Harrison and Broome had found an excellent D.Z. on one of Pa Blanken's clearings by the Sungei Bot. Harrison was to take this drop, introduce the new arrivals to their patrol, then move north to Sungei Siput and prepare to receive another P.L.T. there.

In the absence of Chen Ping, we tried to make arrangements with Lau Leo, the Bidor leader, to take his own drop, but although he was tremendously keen to arm his patrol he refused to accept any responsibility without orders from above. When we tried to get him up for a conference he pleaded sickness. We also tried to get in touch with Itu at Perak headquarters, but a message came back to say that he was away. None of the guerilla leaders would act on their own initiative, and it seemed clear that they were waiting for definite direction from their headquarters on the whole question of co-operation. Chen Ping still did not appear, and at last we had to postpone both the Bidor and Perak headquarters 'drop,' as no arrangements for reception could be made in Chen Ping's absence. This was a bitter disappointment.

Meanwhile, in spite of these setbacks, there was plenty to do. We had to collect bamboo shoots and sweet-potato leaves as in the old days. The wireless traffic was still considerable, and the overworked steam generator was starting to give trouble. I was extremely busy writing training pamphlets for the guerillas. From time to time in my years in the jungle I had composed illustrated manuals on weapons, demolitions, tactics, fieldcraft and direction-finding, leadership, and training. Some of these had been duplicated by the guerilla press and distributed among the camps, where they were the only manuals available. These pamphlets were now three years out of date and in the light of new information had to be entirely rewritten, and this was at least a month's work.

At last, on April 1, Chen Ping arrived. He had had typhoid fever, and this had delayed him for a fortnight on his way back from a conference at his headquarters in Selangor. The next three days were spent in conferences in a special wireless hut that we had built some distance up the hill at the back of the camp. These conferences were conducted in Cantonese, with Broome interpreting for the benefit of Hannah and myself. Chen Ping informed us that a representative from general headquarters would arrive about April 16 to discuss matters with us; and we were glad to hear that this was to be our old friend the Plen. Chen Ping said that he (the Plen) was not fit and he would have to take the risk of coming up outside the jungle. He asked us not to take a drop on the jungle edge for a full fortnight before his arrival, as otherwise the Japs would be on the lookout and his life would be endangered. This was a reasonable request and as it was obviously most important to come to a proper agreement with guerilla headquarters before any more arms were dropped in, we had to agree once more to postpone all drops until the moon period at the end of April.

About this time I decided to go out with Broome when at last we could arrange a submarine R.V. Though Colombo could obviously give us no definite information on the date of 'D Day' Malaya, it was apparent from the length of time they allowed for the build-up period that the campaign would not open for some months, and until that time Davis alone could more than cope with any liaison work there might be. The men who had come in said that on joining us, the actuality was so very different from what they had been led to expect that they thought I should be most usefully employed briefing the G.L.O.s and P.L.O.s who were to come in. Davis was very anxious that I should do this, as it would greatly lighten his task if the incoming men knew exactly what to expect and how to act towards the guerillas. At that time I had great schemes for training and bringing in a special British force, to be attached to certain patrols to undertake special military tasks which were beyond the guerillas' capabilities. The acceptance of this plan would also satisfy the growing ambition that I had to do both a submarine journey and a parachute drop before the war was over. I put up to Colombo the suggestion that I should return and they agreed at once. Quayle, apart from being hardly fit enough to walk to the coast, had determined to stay on and become one of Hannah's P.L.O.s.

On April 15 we heard that the Plen had reached the jungle edge outside Blantan, and next day Davis, Broome, Hannah, and I set off to meet him. Humpleman and his wireless station also accompanied us, as we wanted to keep in touch with Colombo during the conferences. Our arrival at this conference was dramatic. The journey took seven hours of hard walking, as we had to cross the Telom, climb up to our old camp on the top of Blantan, follow down a tributary of the Gedong, then cross several miles of steep foothills. Broome, who was never a strong traveller, completely collapsed a mile short of our destination and had to be revived on rum. He only had about an egg-cup full, but in his exhausted state it went to his head and we had to support him into the camp. Here, to our horror, we found a guard of honour drawn up awaiting our arrival. However, we put his head in the stream, and a few minutes later he was able to stand fairly steadily and take the salute.

In the meeting we had had with the Plen and Chen Ping at Blantan in January 1944 there had been a certain air of cautiousness and even cynicism. But at this conference the atmosphere from the beginning was one of complete understanding and cordiality. There was no bargaining whatsoever. It seemed clear that the Plen had come from his headquarters with instructions to 'get on with the war,' and there was not a point of disagreement throughout. He was perfectly frank about the powers and limitations of the guerillas, and whenever we hesitated to ask him to do things, he not only consented but usually broke in to go further than we asked. No written agreements were made or were necessary, as the conference was largely devoted to methods of carrying out the agreement previously made. The principle arrived at was the tactical decentralisation of the guerillas, increase of powers for all their officers, and encouragement of individual initiative.

After spending most of the night encoding and sending reports of the conference to Colombo, we returned to Gurun with the feeling that all the guerillas would now be told that it was their duty to co-operate to the full with British officers. The days of shilly-shallying and secretiveness were over.

CHAPTER EIGHTEEN

The Submarine Pick-up

(USE MAP NO. 4)

Now that we had taken a parachute drop and our liaison with the Chinese was on a sound basis as a result of our successful conference with the Plen, our single remaining task was to get somebody out by submarine to Ceylon. The first problem was the choice of a rendezvous. A study of the chart showed that there was a small bay called Tanjong Blangah (also known as Emerald Bay) facing straight out to sea on a small island, Pulau Pangkor Laut, lying just to the seaward side of the larger fishing island of Pangkor. That this bay was only two miles from the Japanese coast-watching station on the hilltop above Pangkor harbour made it all the more immune from suspicion, and its proximity to the fishing centre implied the presence of innumerable small craft among which the sampan carrying us over from the mainland would be more likely to pass unnoticed.

The Navy agreed at once to this R.V., and after considering the moon and tides, they proposed May 13 as the date for the pick-up. Recognition was to be by means of a device known as Eureka and infra-red torch. We were not in possession of these aids, but they were to be sent in by the next drop. The pass and counter-pass words were also arranged to eliminate the possibility of Jap ambush, and the submarine would send an armed 'ferry party' ashore for us under cover of darkness. During the preceding day, if all was well, we would display a white sheet at the point where we wanted to be picked up.

Unfortunately the fact that we had promised not to take a drop before the Plen's arrival meant that the first suitable day for a drop was April 26. With the drop coming on that day it would just be possible for us to collect our Eureka and infra-red torch and then, setting off a week later, to reach the coast in time to make the R.V. But when Colombo changed the date of the drop to April 28 we realised that it would be cutting things too fine and that we must do without the additional recognition apparatus, relying simply on a torch with an ordinary red glass filter – which we had.

Chen Ping seemed to have a pretty fair idea of the sixty miles of country between our camp and Pulau Pangkor, and as his advice was always worth taking we had several conferences with him to arrange details of the route. We were to set off on April 27, to give us two days' travelling before the drop so that we could be well clear of the dangerous area. Ah Yang was to accompany us until we were on board the sampan, and to arrange for local guides at each stage. As, owing to the drop, we had to start seventeen days before the R.V., we arranged to lie up for a week in a safe place on the far side of the dangerous area. It all seemed unbelievably easy, so much so that we felt it was essential to take every precaution to avoid anything going wrong at this final state. We left Gurun camp soon after daylight on April 27, travelling as light as possible. Davis and Chen Ping, with a small escort of guerillas, came with us to the edge of the jungle so as to be near the D.Z. where the drop was due on the night of the 28th.

After heavy rain all night the Telom river was so swollen that we were only just able to cross it. Only five hours' fairly fast travel brought us to an old sawmill, now ruinous and almost covered over with a pale green climbing plant. From here we waded up a slippery ditch for half a mile or so and found ourselves at the very camp where we had had conferences with the Plen, having approached it from exactly the opposite direction. We spent the afternoon there, drying our clothes, lying in the sun, drinking coffee, and eating as much as we could of rather a dull meal consisting of rice and small squares of a large and over-salt fish. Davis accompanied us as far as the sawmill, then, wishing us good luck and goodbye, returned to the conference camp to be ready to organise the reception party – consisting of over 150 people – for the following night's drop.

We all felt very depressed at the coming parting. When people have lived and worked together for as long as we had, a bond holds them together, a bond which is certainly never expressed – probably not even realised till the time comes to break it. And although there had been times when John and I had argued ourselves speechless, I felt quite a lump in my throat when Richard and I went on through the Straits rhododendron and bracken and left him standing forlornly alone.

From now on it was entirely new country. The track, after crossing a few streams, left the great jungle, and for half an hour we traversed a number of rolling ridges where the trees had recently been felled, and there were Chinese huts and vegetable gardens among the debris of fallen timber. Although all the Chinese here were known to be friendly, we were careful not to be recognised as white men. We had previously put on our Chinese clothes, pulled our old felt hats well down, and covered our faces and hands with a strong solution of potassium permanganate. Chinese trousers have no pockets, but the coat has four small pockets without flaps. In the lower two I carried my grenade and .32 automatic, and in the upper two my compass and spare ammunition. I carried my own rucksack, as was my habit, while Broome carried the Sten gun. The steep wet laterite track was incredibly slippery in our gym shoes, and we kept on falling. Several times Broome, carrying the Sten in the ready position, filled the barrel with mud as he fell, and we had to stop to poke the barrel clear with a stick.

Soon we came out into the rubber, which did not seem to have been cleared since the Jap occupation, as it was covered with undergrowth and elephant grass to a height of six or seven feet. There is always an extraordinary feeling of exhilaration as one leaves the oppressive jungle behind and emerges into the freedom and open skies of the plains. It was good to sniff the fecund scents of hot earth and pigs and *kampongs*, and to hear the happy cries of children and the barking of dogs. As I trudged silently in my rubber shoes along the hard-beaten track, I felt an almost breathless excitement at the prospect of what lay ahead – a prospect I had hardly dared to contemplate in the last three years. As my thought went forward to the submarine, to Ceylon, to India, and perhaps to England, I realised I had sometimes been very, very homesick.

Just as we were about to cross the main road at about 9.30 p.m., we heard a car coming and a Jap lorry chugged slowly past, making a noise like a traction engine and obviously burning the Japanese synthetic petrol made from rubber. Further away we could hear the snorting of a train and the unaccustomed sound of its whistle. As a matter of form we sent a scout ahead and then dashed across the tarmac road. The whole countryside seemed to be deserted. Beyond the road the ground levelled out, and we followed a succession of tiny zigzag paths through a maze of old tin-mining ground, secondary jungle, and elephant grass cut by streams. Then we passed between the gigantic pylons bringing electricity from Chenderoh dam to work the open-lode tin mines upon whose brilliant lights we used to look down from Blantan and Gurun camps. I felt a pang of shame to see such easy targets still unscathed after we had lived for over a year so near them.

At midnight we climbed an isolated range of hills a few hundred feet high, and crept into a tiny hut thatched with grass, where we were to lie up the following day. We did no cooking in this hut, but our guides prepared the meals in a nearby house and brought us any amount of coffee, rice, and vegetables. They also brought some grass mats and old sacks to sleep on, but with the coffee and the mosquitoes, and the pleasure and excitement of what seemed like another life, it was impossible to sleep, so we sat outside and smoked our pipes and enjoyed the fragrant night. It was now overcast, but the moon was visible and it was very light. We could easily see the dark shapeless mass of Batu Puteh, where we had lived for the last year or more, and the plain spread out at our feet. The night was still, but the trains seemed to be very busy in the neighbourhood of Tapah Road.

Next morning we were up at 5.30 a.m. from force of habit, and our Chinese brought a meal of rice and a dish of salt fish cooked with prawns and small pieces of pork. The far side of the hill was covered with rubber trees, but near our hut was typical tin-tailing ground with little laterite cliffs, cracks, and gullies, densely overgrown with Straits rhododendron, bracken, and seedling trees, with several kinds of mauve and cream ground-orchids flowering. I spent most of the day creeping about watching birds – three brilliant varieties of kingfisher, several kinds of doves, bee-eaters, woodpeckers, jungle-fowl, minas, bulbuls, and that sweet-songed black and white mimic – the Straits robin. It was a very pleasant day, filled with the possibility of being a free agent once more, of dreams of meeting one's friends again, and of being able to sleep at night with no haunting fear at the back of one's mind.

Chen Ping, who had been away all day making arrangements

for the next stage of our journey, together with our small escort of old friends from Gurun, bade farewell to us and set off back to the sawmill to be in time for the drop, the excitement of which they were loath to miss. I was indeed sorry to say goodbye to Chen Ping. He had been my first English-speaking contact among the guerillas at Tanjong Malim in March 1942, and when I joined Davis and Broome at Blantan in December 1943, he, as their most trusted adviser, was the first man I met. And to Broome, who could converse with him in his own language, he was, more than any of the other Chinese, a real friend.

As our next guide we collected a great character – one Ah Tong. He was an incorrigible joker, and he looked, and probably was, half Malay, having too dark a skin for a Chinese and a mop of curly black hair. He told me, and others corroborated the fact, that he had accounted for eighty-seven traitors, spies, and informers. We now had three Chinese with us: Yang, who was in charge but had never been over this ground before; Ah Tong, who had a general working knowledge of the area; and a local man found by Ah Tong, who might be changed several times during the night's journey and who would be told only enough to enable him to hand us over to the next guide.

We left our camp an hour after sunset and soon realised the value of minute local knowledge, as our way for the first few hours led along tiny zigzag paths, through Chinese gardens, beside tall plantations of tapioca, between neat lines of sweet potato and other vegetables, across single-plank bridges, and sometimes actually through disused houses, in at one door and out at the other. We tried to look as much like Chinese as possible, being plentifully stained with permanganate, and I sank my chin and crouched as low as possible to disguise my height and distinctive walk.

After four hours' travelling we entered a large rubber estate, and very soon it became apparent that our guides were completely lost. We were then making for the railway which runs north-west and south-east, and we planned to cross it just south of Tapah Road junction, where a branch lines goes off south-west to Teluk Anson and Bagan Datoh. Our guides were travelling by memory alone and, once they could no longer recognise any landmark, had absolutely no idea in what direction to go. After they had wandered in a complete circle for some time and all the dogs in Asia seemed to be barking at us, I took out my compass and showed them that they were actually going away from the railway. This they refused to believe for some time, and it was only after we had reached a certain house with particularly clamorous dogs for the third time that they realised that they were indeed lost. However, about this time a train chugged past some distance behind us and at last they were convinced. We soon reached the railway line, which lay in a wide clearing with rubber on one side and jungle on the other. They were looking for a tiny path which led through a clearing on the far side, and we now had no idea whether we were above or below it. They set off to reconnoitre, while Broome and I lay beside the line. Three trains passed, heavily laden and unlighted, burning wood – judging by the showers of sparks that shot into the air.

For some time now we had been keeping an eye on the time and an ear to the sky, as this was the night that four Liberators should be passing almost exactly overhead on their way to our D.Z.s. As we lay waiting, we heard the first one approaching from the sea just before midnight, and for the next two hours the night was punctuated with the heavy drone of their engines. It was now overcast, but still very light. The planes came singly. Those that flew directly overhead, at a height of about a thousand feet, we could see quite easily, but on their return, half an hour later, they were already high enough to be invisible. It was a most exciting sight to see them passing so easily and unopposed over enemy country, and we experienced a vicarious thrill as we crossed our fingers for those on board who at that moment were preparing to jump and probably wishing they were anywhere else in the world.

At last our guides returned, saying that they had no idea where we were, so we all started walking southward along the line. This seemed the safer direction, as we knew that Tapah Road Station must lie to the north. Presently we found the 147th milestone (from Kuala Lumpur) and some coolie-lines, both of which we were able to identify on the map, but as we did not know where our guides' track lay, this was not much help to us. As we cast first south, then north, then south again, I took some measurements of the railway line which I hoped would be useful to me in a few months' time. Unfortunately, as we repassed the coolie-lines a Tamil came out, and as it was a very clear night he must have seen our party and could probably make out Ah Tong's tommy-gun. We were a little worried that he might telephone the Japs further along the line, but at last our guides found the track for which they had been searching, and we turned off the line into quite the most unpleasant going of our journey.

This was part of the abandoned Sungei Manik rice scheme, where all the trees had been cut down many years ago and nothing further had been done. It would have been difficult enough even if we could have seen where we were putting our feet, but when a tangle of leaves or a foot of slimy water prevented this, we were continually sliding and falling about and became increasingly worn out and exasperated. At last cultivation started again and we passed both Malay and Chinese huts, being careful as far as possible to avoid being seen, though we had the usual trouble with dogs.

At 2.30 a.m. we crossed the railway line that runs from Tapah Road to Teluk Anson. As with most branch-lines and even parts of the main east-coast railway, the Japs had taken up the rails to send overseas for making armaments, but the track showed evidence of being still used as a bicycle- and foot-path. On the far side of the line we entered a very large low-lying rubber estate, where we continually crossed wide drains on bridges made of iron rails. Soon after this we crossed the Batang Padang river by a suspension bridge, and it was difficult to recognise in this turbid thirty-yards-wide torrent the Sungei Woh, Busoh, and Telom, whose limpid headwaters we knew so well.

Another hour of swampy rubber brought us suddenly to the Degong road a few miles south of Ayer Kuning. It was now 4.30 a.m., and Tamils and Malays were already cycling or walking to work. Dawn found us in an area where the undergrowth was fairly thick, so we lay down and rested while our local guide went off to try to find his bearings. It had now clouded over again and was starting to rain, but we were so tired that we just covered up any exposed flesh against the mosquitoes and fell asleep, taking it in turn to keep guard. Finally our guide returned, saying that he had found the track but that we had to be particularly careful as this was a dangerous place, since the police from Teluk Anson were in the habit of coming here to hunt pig.

The whole area was intersected by paths where many people, fortunately mostly Chinese, were walking or cycling to work, while others were wandering here and there in search of firewood. At last, after running the gauntlet of these people, dashing across tracks and hiding in the undergrowth whenever our guides signalled that anybody was coming, we reached an area where, between the adult trees, the whole ground was densely covered with rubber seedlings ten to fifteen feet high, limiting the visibility to a few yards. Here we lay up about thirty yards from the nearest path, while Yang and our guides went to look for food. After an hour they returned with a pot of rice and a dish of long beans, pineapple, paw-paw, and sweet coffee. In spite of the voices of stick-gatherers all round us, we passed the whole day here undisturbed except by the rain and mosquitoes. In the middle of the afternoon Yang sent a note to say that he had found a place where we could safely lie up for a week and that he had made arrangements for the sampan for the next part of the journey, but that we must not smoke or talk, as there was an alarm of some sort – probably occasioned by our having been seen on the railway line – and a party of police had arrived from Teluk Anson on bicycles and were carrying out a house-to-house search.

Ah Tong had had a bad attack of malaria all day and had been lying groaning with a high temperature; but as soon as we started to move soon after dark, he set off and carried his load and tommy-gun as if nothing were the matter. A path of grey and slippery clay led us across a swamp which we had to cross by a bridge of half-submerged trees to a small uneven path of jungle about a hundred yards across. We reached this oasis, which was to be our home for the next week, just before midnight on April 29.

In the centre of our 'estate' was a tiny *atap* hut about twelve feet by six and only high enough for us to stand upright in the centre. One half of it contained a sleeping-bench covered with a soft but uneven pile of *atap*, while in the other was a small log table and benches. The roof leaked and the mosquitoes were terrible. A tiny track led down through the undergrowth over fallen trees to a muddy stream, fortunately just inside the patch of jungle, so that we could get drinking-water and bathe ourselves by day. The average visibility in our sanctuary was rather less than five yards, and even if it had been combed by a large force of Japs, it might have been possible to elude capture. From the edge of the undergrowth, without risk of being seen ourselves, we could look out on each side and watch the Chinese working in their gardens and the boys and girls playing outside the houses, while the noise of children's voices, dogs barking, and the chopping of firewood sounded so close that we often thought people had actually invaded our retreat. Some distance to the south lay a much larger patch of uncleared jungle, and there we decided to go in case of trouble.

While there, however, we had no alarm of any sort. In fact we were never seen, and even the Chinese who provided our food merely knew that they were helping two people – presumably Chinese – who were wanted by the Japs. The two trusted men who brought our meals merely knew that we were passing through – they had more sense than to ask where or why. The food that we were brought during this week was the best we had had for a very long time. Each morning and evening we would be brought an earthenware pot of beautifully cooked white rice and a bowl of chicken, salt fish, or pork, and sometimes fried eggs, as well as a dish of cucumber, long beans, cabbage, or other vegetable. The chicken was quite the fattest I have ever seen, with great lumps of creamy fat.

Unfortunately, to lighten our loads and so as not to deprive those who were staying behind of reading material, we had brought practically no books with us. Broome had a copy of Ivor Brown's *Just Another Word* and I had only my Malay vocabulary. However, I spent several hours a day working on the reports that I knew I should have to write as soon as I reached Ceylon and rewriting the various manuals on fighting in the Malayan jungle which I was hoping to get printed in India for the use of the guerillas.

My spare time in daylight I spent sunbathing – with an eye on the Jap aircraft which used to fly overhead every day – and watching birds, of which I noted sixty-seven species during our week's sojourn, including several I had never seen before. We also saw or heard from our sanctuary six kinds of monkeys, and heard the calls of tiger, *rusa*, and *kijang*. At night I used to watch the stars, and it was wonderful to get an unobstructed view in every direction after the constricted glimpses of the sky we had had in the jungle. In Malaya the Great Bear and the Southern Cross can be seen at the same time, but from the camps it was never possible to see this wonderful sight.

At night we could hear the Chinese shouting, banging empty kerosene tins, and making weird noises by blowing into bottles to frighten away the pigs. One night there was a violent thunderstorm and gale of wind, and we must have heard nearly a hundred trees or branches come crashing down with a terrifying rending noise, and we were greatly afraid that one of the several enormous dead trees above our hut would come through the roof. I had another near escape that night. I heard a dry scratching noise on the *atap* beside my head and, not daring to move, I asked Broome to switch on his torch; this revealed an enormous black scorpion crawling towards my face.

On May 4 Yang returned and brought two bottles of *samsu*, a tin of cream biscuits made with tapioca flour, some bananas, and two hundred locally made cheroots. Yang said that all plans were made for us to travel on May 8. Practically all the rest of the journey was to be done by sampan, and since the Japs were in the habit of patrolling even the smaller streams and searching boats for smuggled goods, we could travel only at night. May 8 was the last and tenth day in our sanctuary, and although we had enjoyed our enforced rest, especially the good food and the sunshine, we were impatient to be off and the day dragged unconscionably. We had a final meal of pork, chicken, and giblet and cucumber soup, then, carefully removing every sign of our having used the hut, we made up our faces and arms with permanganate and were ready for the road, feeling fitter than either of us had felt for a very long time.

We had one guide besides Ah Yang who stayed with us until we reached the sea, as he knew this area inside out. Before the war this guide had been a boatman on the Perak river, and for the last few years he had worked for the guerillas, carrying messages from Teluk Anson to Perak headquarters on the one side, and to Pangkor on the other. He told me that he had been up before Malay or Sikh policemen about ten times, but on each occasion the matter had been settled privately – that is, by bribery – without it ever coming to the notice of the Japs.

The going was dead level all night. First, we followed a tiny track past scattered huts with walls only of thin sticks through which the lights gleamed. The path as usual led over and along fallen timber covered with creepers, so that we slipped and fell frequently, for there was now no moon and the guides had considerable difficulty in finding the way. Sometimes we passed through little island patches of jungle with gaunt dead trees still standing and shrouded in creepers. We met no other travellers in this strange, flat, eerie land, and the very dogs were silent. About midnight we crossed a long, straight, artificial dyke about twelve feet wide with steep sides, which we followed south-west at full speed for about two miles. This seemed to be an area of paddy and must have been cleared for a very long time, as there were only a few dead trees still standing and practically no jungle. Beside the track were several small platforms with *atap* roofs, and on these, beneath brilliant flares, small parties of Chinese or Malays were sitting gossiping and gambling. Some of the men shouted to us as we hurried past and we became a little anxious.

Soon our guide, who had slipped away some time back, rejoined us with a tough little Hokkien in a straw hat and a very patched blue coat, who now led us for another two miles, still at furious speed, along the summit of a high artificial bank beside a branch dyke. Although it was now long after midnight, from far away to the south came a weird noise as of a great many women and children singing a tuneless song, or rather a number of different songs at the same time, the sort of song that accompanies manual work, but we were not able to discover who was responsible for this strange chorus. At last we turned off and cut across to a much wider dyke, where we embarked in a boat about twenty feet long and pointed at each end. It was rowed in the usual Chinese way with the oars on rowlocks three feet above the gunwale, so that the rower stands and leans on the oars which cross in front of him. Thus the rower can get his full weight behind the stroke and can see where he is going. A strong current was with us, and to Broome and me lying peacefully on our backs in the bows, watching the trees and bushes on the banks sweeping past, the boat seemed to be rushing along at a tremendous speed, a most exquisite change from the last few exhausting hours.

The curves of the bank showed that we had joined a river and left the artificial waterway. This was the Sungei Kroh, and we swept down the last few miles of its course and then, at last, found ourselves floating in the vast Perak river, so wide that we could not see across it. It seemed to be the very ocean itself. I could not help recalling how this same river had carried me to freedom three and a half years before when three of us were, as now, slipping through the Jap lines to safety. So wide was the river that, in spite of the powerful current, it was very difficult without the aid of the stars to keep any sense of direction. The length of rattan which tied down the rowlocks kept breaking, and once while mending this, we swung right round and the boatman set off again upstream, but as there was no landmark visible he did not notice this for some minutes. Rubber and jungle – the former distinguished by the level line of its treetops – alternated on the low banks. The only sound which reached us above the lapping of the water and the groaning of the rowlocks was the faint reverberation of drums from the Malay mosque of some riverside village – a weird and exciting noise. Out in the middle of the river we felt curiously helpless and insecure in our little rowing-boat, especially when told that Jap motor-boats regularly patrolled this part of the river, though only by day. The large river port of Teluk Anson was only a few miles further downstream, and we knew that soon we had to go overland to avoid the loop of the river on which the town lay.

Some hours before dawn we turned off suddenly to the right bank of the Perak river and nosed our way up a tiny creek which soon came to an end. We abandoned our boat and walked overland between vegetable gardens for a few hundred yards to the head of another creek, where we found a rather larger boat moored in readiness. This creek was so overgrown that to find our way we had to use a torch consisting of lumps of blazing and spluttering rubber threaded on the end of a length of stiff wire, and even then it was difficult to follow the course of the stream. Entering this hushed and enclosed backwater, after the fresh breezes and swirling stream of the open river, there was a strange sense of cessation, as if the earth had stopped spinning or we had suddenly entered another world – but a world that was strangely familiar, for this lurid nocturnal view of a jungle creek was just exactly as one had always imagined it – with the impeding branches covered with rank parasite growths and festooned with creepers, stretched out from either side and interlocking overhead; with sodden half-submerged logs clogging the waterway and, together with the curtain of hanging greenery, grasping at our boat as she passed. Once our torch revealed the coils of a water-snake wriggling across the still surface to disappear beneath the overhanging branches. The only sound was the croaking of every variety of frog and startling 'plops' as they dived into the water. Once a tremendous splash in front of us indicated the movement of a crocodile, of which our boatmen told us there were many in these sequestered backwaters.

At last, after half a mile of this winding creek, we brushed beneath a tree and once again found ourselves in the flood of the Perak river, and so great was our speed that in the half-light submerged trees and other stationary snags seemed to rush towards us and roar menacingly past. After a mile or two of the main river, which took us round the promontory running westward from Teluk Anson, we once again turned up a creek on the right bank, and leaving our boat set off to find a safe place where we could lie up for the day. We walked for nearly two miles between a rubber estate and vegetable gardens along a slippery track made of bricks of clay dug up from the dykes alongside. The gardening here was on a much larger scale than we had met elsewhere – whole fields of ground nuts, leeks, yams, and sweet potatoes, and acres and acres of sugar-cane. Our Hokkien guide told us we should have to wait an hour for the tide to come up, and took us into a large hut with earth floor, walls of solid planks, and roof of *nipah* palm. There seemed to be nobody sleeping in the house, but on the wall was a choice picture of a Swatow family all in their best clothes, the old man looking very important and uncomfortable in a collar and tie, probably lent to him for the occasion by the photographer. While we were here, we frequently heard the heavy splashes of crocodiles. The Sungei Buaya, or crocodile river, was quite near.

Soon our guide returned and we continued past a maze of dykes and small bridges with hundreds of native craft hauled out on the banks. Just before dawn we lay down under a boat and were devoured by mosquitoes until our guide brought a Chinese who spoke Mandarin with a very deep voice. He told us that the hut for

321

which we were making could not be used, as two strangers had appeared there earlier in the evening and they might be Jap spies, but that he would take us to a reliable family nearby. Since the other house was still an hour's distance away and as it would soon be light, we were only too happy to agree, and as dawn broke we reached a hut in a small clearing which had been made in the middle of a rubber estate. There was a platform four feet above the level of the earthen floor, and on this were two grass mats with blankets, pillows, and mosquito nets. The only other furniture was a rough table and home-made chairs, a cupboard – rendered ant-proof by standing the legs in latex-cups full of water – and the clay kitchen stove. One curious thing about this hut was that when the tide came up the whole garden was flooded, and only a mud step prevented the water from actually flowing into the house.

After a few hours' sleep we woke up to find ourselves in charge of a small boy of about twelve years who was cooking rice and fish for our breakfast. Suddenly two shots rang out from the rubber behind the hut. Broome and I mobilised at once, thinking that we were surrounded by Japs. But the boy merely said in Malay, 'Perhaps somebody is shooting an informer: it doesn't matter.' After glancing outside the hut with complete nonchalance, he went on with his work! We never discovered who had fired these shots.

That evening we had a special feast of rice, sea-slugs cooked with garlic, salt pork, squares of soya-bean paste which tasted like Camembert cheese, fresh mud-fish flavoured with ginger, and chicken soup. Just before dark, a huge Liberator, gleaming silver in the evening sunlight, flew directly above us quite low and was soon followed by another. This was a most thrilling spectacle and made us feel somehow less dependent on our Chinese guides.

An hour after dark we set off again with the owner of the house as guide, leaving his twelve-year-old son quite happily in charge. As usual, we made ourselves up with permanganate, and it was just as well, as we had to pass through an inhabited area and we felt very conspicuous walking along the banks above the surrounding vegetable gardens. Banana trees lined the paths, and there were many huts, from which came the sound of laughter and children's voices and once the strains of an accordion.

An hour's walk brought us to a tiny creek where we found a

sampan ready stocked with provisions, including two live fowls, vegetables, and fresh water. The boat was about eighteen feet long, of five feet beam, and pointed at either end with the bows decked in to form a small locker. At first the creek was so narrow that we had to pull ourselves along the banks with our hands, but it soon widened out until we emerged into a most fantastic scene, quite unlike anything else I had hitherto encountered in Malaya. This was a vast area of swamp overgrown with clumps of enormous *nipah* palm growing out of the water like some fantastic Brobdingnagian fernery with fronds a foot thick and thirty or forty feet high. Between the roots of these we nosed along, following a channel of open water which wound its way between the over-hanging palm leaves. From time to time we passed other craft, usually Chinese fishing-boats with fires burning on the fore-deck either to attract the fish or to keep away the mosquitoes. Every now and then an ordinary tree seemed to find enough firm ground to flourish, and on the foliage of each of these was a swarm of countless fireflies illuminating the tracery of its branches, all twinkling together like a gigantic Christmas tree. So bright were these myriad points of light that they were hardly distinguishable except by their lack of motion, from the brilliant tropical stars which swung behind them.

After an hour or two of this fascinating, strange scenery we once more emerged into the Perak river, now well below Teluk Anson. Here there was no other craft in sight. After hugging first one bank and then the other we ceased to make any progress and lay up for two hours to await the turn of the tide, while the thin crescent of the old moon rose with a brilliant planet beside it. At dawn we saw to the north-west the shapely silhouette of Bukit Sigari in the Dindings and to the south of it the highlands of Pangkor – which marked our destination. Inland, about forty miles to the east, we could distinguish Batu Puteh and other mountains of the Main Range, which we seemed to have left so many months ago, though in fact it was less than a fortnight. Along the banks of the river we could now see groves of coconut palms planted in neat lines, and prosperous-looking Malay *kampongs* in the clearings. Already there were quite a number of Malay, Chinese, and Indian craft poling downriver with the tide, and some passed quite close to us, but by this time we had put up the *kajang* (a peaked canopy of thatched palm) and Broome and I lay below this out of sight

Once we passed quite close to a three-masted hull stranded in the river, on which some Chinese were working. They hailed our boat as we passed, and Broome and I got the Sten-gun ready, expecting to be fired on. But they were only exchanging the time of the day. I felt singularly helpless on the river, especially in the daytime. In the jungle one could at least show oneself and walk openly and if necessary beat a retreat, but here, swirling along with a six-knot tide, one was absolutely at the mercy of any motor craft that might appear.

As we swept silently downriver we had a magnificent view of a tiger prowling along the edge of the sand between the river and the jungle, probably waiting for pig or deer as they came down to the riverside to drink. Out in the open his underparts, especially the throat and chin, looked conspicuously white as he picked his way delicately along as if hating – like any cat – to get his feet wet. He deigned to favour us with only a casual glance.

At about 7.30 a.m. the river traffic became so considerable that we deemed it wiser to turn up a small tidal creek and tie up. We were now about half-way between the river ports of Teluk Anson and Bagan Datoh, and within the daily motor-boat range of both. But we had so to time our progress as to pass Bagan Datoh in the late evening but with still enough of the tide left to carry us out of the mouth of the Perak river. Twice during the day we heard motor vessels chugging past.

In this peaceful creek we were surrounded by beautiful Corot-like trees with emerald-green leaves, rusty red bark, and irregular straggling branches. As the tide went down, leaving a wide belt of muddy slime, we amused ourselves by watching the antics of innumerable mud-fish, some of them a foot long with square heads like grasshoppers and eyes raised up on stems, crawling and hopping grotesquely in the ooze. There were also hundreds of little turquoise-coloured crabs monotonously dibbling water into their mouths with alternate claws, and another kind with one over-developed salmon pink claw held at right angles across its body. We stood our bucket stove up on the part of the bows that was decked in, and having collected some sticks from on shore, cooked rice and the two fowls. In the afternoon some crab-eating monkeys, tamer than we ever gave them a chance of being in the jungle, sat in a tree above our boat and screamed harshly at us. We drove them away, as our boat was now aground in the middle of the creek and we did not want to attract the attention of any prowling patrol-boat. Once, as the tide rose, another boat did enter our creek, so Broom and I lay flat beneath the *kajang* with our faces covered. But it was only an inquisitive Tamil who had come, ostensibly, to beg a match.

We had moored our boat by sticking a paddle down on either side of the gunwale into the mud, and when the tide came up we floated gently upstream, but were so busy cooking supper that we entirely failed to notice that the paddles were submerged. It took nearly two hours of diving operations to recover them. In order not to pass too near the busy port of Bagan Datoh, we kept across to the right bank of the river, but with our glasses we could see boats of every description anchored in the harbour, and the larger permanent buildings of the port, as well as the native Malay village built up on stilts. The river became wider and wider, and as darkness fell we found ourselves at last in the open waters of the Malacca Straits. In the glow of a lurid and stormy sunset we saw the high outline of Pulau Pangkor, our destination, and the rocky Sembilan Islands further south, while the mass of the Main Range lay crowned with heavy purple clouds, far away inland.

An hour after sunset, when we were rowing peacefully out to sea to pass Tanjong Bras Basah, out of the darkness there suddenly came a most fearsome roaring sound, getting louder every moment. Looking round I saw that we were being swept towards the long line of stakes that Malays used in their fish-traps. In the rushing ebb tide each pole was oscillating furiously and emitting this terrifying noise. The strength of the current was so great that although our boatman rowed furiously, we only narrowly avoided capsizing by being swept against the end of the line of stakes, through which white water was foaming. The noise and movement of these stakes drive the fish into a funnel-shaped trap, in which they are left stranded by the ebbing tide, or in another form of trap, lifted out of the water on a tray of matting. Usually there is an *atap* hut, in which the fisherman lives, built on stilts at the end of the line. As we swept out to sea, there seemed to be very little shipping, just a few junks showing riding-lights, no other sampans, and no disconcerting chug-chug of motor-boats.

We still had two days in hand before the R.V., and the plan was to go some distance south of the river-mouth on this tide and, under cover of darkness, enter a creek where there was a Chinese village. There a hideout had already been prepared for us. A few miles south of the Perak river we ran aground on a sandbank, and remained there for several hours until refloated by the rising tide. However, we felt fairly secure, as there was only a foot of water for a considerable distance all round us and no other boat could possibly approach near enough to see us without a searchlight. Fortunately there were no mosquitoes here, though palpable waves of hot air, laden with strange and exciting land smells, intermittently drifted across from the just visible shore, like some great dragon's living breath. Another two hours were spent in coasting southward, and all the time our guides seemed to be anxiously searching the shore.

At last we saw a low tree-covered point running out ahead of us, and on swinging still further inshore, we entered a creek to the north of this headland. At the mouth of the creek, close against the bank, a large junk with riding-lights was tied up, and there were men talking quietly on deck. Opposite this, leaving a clear passage of only thirty yards or so, was a large barn-like structure with a platform built up on a scaffolding some thirty feet above it. As this was very obviously a coast-watching post, we were more than a little anxious. Our guides later explained that the Malay coastguard had been warned that we were coming in and had agreed not to take any notice of us. Furthermore, it had been arranged that if the Japs manned the station unexpectedly – which they sometimes did – he would have a small boat outside the river-mouth to warn us!

It was about 4 a.m. when we entered the creek, but the fishing village of Sungei Tiang was already alive with industry. We passed long lines of junks and sampans moored outside houses which were ablaze with glaring naphtha flares and full of people gutting fish, preparing nets and lines, and going to and fro. All the way up the creek there was a very powerful smell of pigs and bad fish. At last, after passing what seemed to us with our jungly ideas a very large town, we tied up against a wooden jetty and Yang and our guides went ashore. It was most exciting as we lay waiting in the bottom of the boat beneath the canopy to hear the Chinese talking and shouting all round us, while boats jostled and scraped against ours, and once some fishermen actually walked over our boat on their way ashore.

Our guides at length returned, and we had to follow them along rotten slime-covered piers and crazy plank bridges over swamp-holes to a pig-sty, where we waited for another half-hour. Then we left the village and took an elusive path through a mangrove swamp, and for a most unpleasant hour, we were sliding and falling about in the darkness through knee-deep slime and clay, slippery as only a mangrove swamp can be. At last, just before dawn, we reached a tiny hut in the middle of the swamp, entirely surrounded by man-groves, which actually met over the roof. The hut was roofed and walled with leathery *pandanus* palm and had a plank floor raised a few feet above the swamp. Not far away we could hear the waves beating against the shore, and it appeared that we had dou-bled back parallel to the river and were now only a hundred yards from the open sea and the river-mouth – and the coastguard sta-tion. We could hear the fishermen talking to each other as they put to sea.

Just before we reached this hideout, which, as far as we could judge, had been especially built for us, the local man whom we had collected at the village made us stop while he went ahead to disconnect a most lethal booby trap, consisting of a trip-wire cun-ningly fixed to a sixteen-pounder shell. This shell, together with several others, had been fired at Japanese junks by a British sub-marine and had embedded itself, without exploding, in the soft mud of the foreshore, whence it had been extracted by the Chi-nese. It was strange to be living in the middle of a mangrove swamp, yet so near to the village. All day we could hear the crowing of cocks, the grunting of pigs, and the continuous hammering of boat-builders. Sometimes half-wild dogs came prowling round, and oc-casionally we were disturbed by a weird and horrible bellowing sound which worked up to a climax and then stopped. This was a new sound to me, and our local guide said it was made by a very large type of black-faced monkey. In the afternoon the tide completely flooded the mangrove swamp and came up to within a few inches of the floor, and we saw a number of water-snakes, some of which are very poisonous, swimming past our front door. During our stay here we were fed most lavishly on chicken, pork, fresh fish, and huge succulent prawns, and as much coffee, sugar, and sweet biscuits as we wanted.

Yang was away all day making plans and as usual was much weighed down beneath his responsibilities. I added to these by giving him a letter to post to the Japanese Governor of Perak. In this letter I asked his Excellency if he would be so very kind as to post me, after the war, c/o the Royal Geographical Society, London, the various diaries of mine that he and his friends had taken, as I imagined that they would then be of no further use to him. So far, I regret to say, these diaries have not arrived.

Just before dark Yang returned with two young Hailams who were to take us on the final stage of our journey. He said they could understand Cantonese and knew exactly what was expected of them. We bade farewell to Yang and gave him a letter to Davis saying that we had so far been successful. I also gave him my wrist-watch as a parting present. He had well deserved it for arranging this difficult journey so efficiently. We then waded back through the mangrove swamp to the village – not quite such an ordeal this time, as there was still a vestige of daylight – and, embarking in the same small sampan, we soon passed the coastwatching station on the rapidly ebbing tide.

Once we were clear of the river, one of the Hailams rested on his oars and said, ingenuously, '*Mana mau pigi, Tuan?*' (Where do you want to go, sir?) and we now discovered that our Hailams, though very cheerful and helpful, had absolutely no idea where we wanted to go or why. In spite of Yang's assurance to the contrary, they could not understand a word of Broome's Cantonese or even speak much Malay. They were quite unable to understand why we wanted to be left at Pangkor, and explained that nowadays things were not what they were in the good old days, and even the rest-house was full of Japs. The situation was so funny that we had to be very careful not to roar with laughter. But whatever else Yang had or had not told them, he had certainly instilled into them that they must obey orders, and at last in slow and one-syllable Malay we managed to explain just what we expected of them. They certainly understood when we told them that we were not coming back and that we would leave our Sten-gun, pistols, and grenades at our point of embarkation for them to pick up at a later date.

We decided to keep well out to sea and make straight for our R.V., anchoring during the hours of contrary tide. This would mean passing the most dangerous area in broad daylight, but there was nothing suspicious about a small fishing-boat being in those seas, and it would be just bad luck if we were stopped and searched. Even then we had our Sten-gun and grenades, and if only one boat came after us we might be able to deal with it without anybody else hearing. We were glad to see a fair number of other boats astir, mainly small junks and sampans. There was no sign of the fleet of larger motor fishing-boats that used to operate from Pangkor in pre-war days. This was because any larger craft were liable to be shot up by British submarines and therefore dared not stir out of harbour.

Out to sea we could just distinguish the outline of some of the Sembilan Islands and we passed several lines of fishing-stakes, but as the tide was turning there was no roar, and we could hear the voices of the fishermen who lived in the huts above them. From midnight until 5 a.m. we lay at anchor until at last May 12 dawned, cloudy and overcast. The most northern of the Sembilan Islands, rocky Pulau Agas, lay just abeam. Soon we could see the Lumut hills and later the lower summits of Pangkor Island. There were now only a few small sampans in sight. Some terns with long tail-streamers flew past and a small flight of sandpipers just above the surface of the water. Everything seemed very still and peaceful. By now we could see a white tower on the rocky island off Tanjong Katak – the frog cape. Just after sunrise several Japanese seaplanes appeared from the direction of Pangkor, flying very low, probably scouring the sea for submarines. Soon we left the Sembilan Islands behind us, and after passing the Fairway Rock our hearts rose as we drew nearer to our destination, accompanied by a sense of apprehension lest our luck should turn at the last minute and a motor patrol-boat should suddenly appear out of the Dindings

Channel: it all seemed too easy. The coast-watching station, up a tall tree on the highest point of Pangkor, was now plainly visible, and though we knew it was manned by people in the employ of the guerillas, we lay well under the *kajang* until it gradually went out of sight as we slipped past Pulau Dua and up to the Pulau Pangkor Laut – our destination.

We knew that once there had been a leper colony on this island, but that immediately before the Jap occupation it was uninhabited. As we nosed round, we were glad to see that there were no boats in the lee of the island. The only sign of life was a crab-eating monkey, which, frightened at seeing us so close in to shore, rushed across the belt of exposed rock between the breaking sea and the dense jungle which covered the island. At last we rounded the southern point of Tanjong Blangah, our R.V. itself, and discovered a beautiful deserted bay with a half-mile beach of silver sand, and behind it, on the far side of a low bar, a stretch of level but densely wooded ground surrounded by a horseshoe of steep jungle. We arranged that our Hailams should call here on May 16 – three days after the R.V. – when any possible excitement occasioned by the submarine being seen would have had time to die down. They could then pick up the weapons which we had promised to leave for them.

Yang had provided enough food for several days – an earthenware pot of boiled rice and a dish of cooked salt fish, a four-gallon kerosene tin of coffee, another of water, and a third of packets of biscuits, and at least 200 bananas. We soon unloaded this and hid everything in the hollow roots of a tree, arranging to leave our weapons there, so that our boatmen would be able to find them. By now they had a pretty shrewd idea of what we were up to and were very reluctant to leave us, suggesting that they could easily hide the boat and remain with us till our friends came. In the end we had almost to drive them away.

There was plenty of fresh water on the island. The first stream, which drained the swamp at the back of the bay and then debouched on to the sand, tasted of Epsom salts. Then we found several streams of perfect drinking-water draining the high hill which surrounded the bay. At some time this bay had been inhabited, for we found the remains of the timbers of a hut, and there was some scraggy tapioca still growing at the edge of the swamp. We had kept the *kajang* from the boat, and pitched it just out of sight over the bar as a refuge in case of rain.

As it was still not yet midday when we were left alone on the island, we had the rest of the day and the whole of the next before the pick-up – which was to be at 8.30 p.m. We had imagined that the best place would be one of the rocky headlands which enclosed the bay, and we had arranged to display there a white cloth, eight feet by four, during the morning and afternoon before the pick-up, so that the submarine, with only its periscope showing, could have a look by daylight and make sure that all was well. However, it took us an hour of extremely hard work to force our way along the steep jungle-covered hillside to the headland, and when we got there the waves were breaking so roughly on the rocks that we decided it would be too dangerous for a small boat to come in close and take us off. We therefore came to the conclusion that the centre of our sandy bay was a far better place for the pick-up. It was, moreover, a much safer place to display our white sheet, as we could keep a careful watch and the moment a fishing-boat came into sight off the entrance to the bay, we could take it down. When we returned from our reconnaissance – incidentally nearly getting lost by following the ridge too far and descending into the wrong valley – we made our flag, fixing the piece of parachute silk that we had brought for the purpose to a wooden framework, so that it could be hoisted ten feet above the ground, but lowered at the first sight of danger.

In the evening, about five o'clock, we suddenly heard a loud roar and three Japanese seaplanes came in very low and fast over our island from the north-west, as if making for their base at Pangkor. Not long afterwards the seaplanes flew just over the wooded crest surrounding our bay and straight out to sea, where they disappeared. We were still trying to account for their strange behaviour when the reason was made clear. A vast silver Liberator came in from the north-west, again exactly over our bay and flying so low that it looked simply enormous with its huge, protruding nose, four engines, and double tail. As it approached, I was in the sea bathing and I ran in under the trees. As soon as I saw it was a Lib I rushed out and waved, thinking it possible that it might be coming over to have a look at the R.V. to see that all was well. An hour later it returned flying slightly higher: it must have been doing a last-light drop to one of our parties a little further south.

Next day, May 13, was the great day. Broome and I had a bet of a dinner at the Galle Face Hotel, Colombo, as to which of us would see the submarine first. We had a pretty shrewd idea that it would come in fairly early in the morning to have a look at us, so from 6.30 a.m. onward one of us held up the white flag in the middle of the bay, while the other watched the Straits with field-glasses from the vantage-point of a rocky outcrop. At 7.10 Broome saw two bright flashes, as of reflected sunlight, far out to sea and at the same time we heard the noise of distant aircraft. After that the morning dragged interminably and we began to imagine all sorts of terrible things.

As our white flag must have been visible for at least ten miles out to sea, we decided only to show it for a minute every quarter of an hour. Suddenly, at two o'clock in the afternoon, I saw the periscope quite clearly out beyond the middle of the bay. We rushed to the sheet and raised it, at the same time standing conspicuously naked by it, looking as white as possible. The periscope then came up again about six to eight feet out of the water and very close in, and for the next hour we kept on seeing it going up or down, or rushing past, looking horribly conspicuous – but there was only one small native craft visible far out to sea.

That evening we were all ready by six o'clock, though we had seen no sign of the submarine since three and assumed that, having had a good look at us, she was lying up further out to sea. At seven o'clock we started flashing our red torch as arranged, at first each quarter of an hour and then, when the time of the R.V. (8.30 p.m.) passed, every five minutes. A new moon was shining over the Straits as it grew dark, but it soon set, and as the stars were hazy the visibility was poor and now we could only just make out the arms of the bay. Suddenly, at 9.15 p.m., I saw an indefinite dark shape in the very centre of the bay, and a moment later we heard a hail, 'Ahoy!' Straining our eyes, we could just make out what appeared to be a boat with two men in it. This would be the expected ferry party and probably there was another folboat behind it.

We collected our gear and ran to the edge of the water. Over the still surface of the sea came the password, 'How are your feet?' We replied with the counter-pass, 'We are thirsty.' Then they came back, 'You will have to swim: we have got no boat.' At first I thought it was a leg-pull on their part, as it seemed to us we could see the boat, but when we had made them repeat it twice, I realised that what we saw was the submarine itself and that we should indeed have to swim. Broome, I knew, was a very weak swimmer, but under these circumstances I think anybody could have swum – and Broome swam. We had only light packs. The sea was beautifully warm, and the distance turned out to be no more than fifty yards. Broome had to abandon his field-glasses as he took to the water and I was very concerned for my diaries and reports. We also had to leave behind the remainder of our biscuits and bananas, which we thought might have been acceptable on board. As we clambered over the slippery, barnacle-covered side of the submarine, up the stays, and over the rail, I realised that what I had thought was a small boat with two men on board was actually the hull itself with the three-inch gun and conning-tower silhouetted.

We soon found ourselves in the tiny six-foot-cube wardroom, surrounded by enormous bearded and incredibly young officers dressed only in *sarongs*. Our wet Chinese garments were taken away to be dried. A bottle of whisky was opened in our honour, and we introduced ourselves, trying to appear as if we were quite in the habit of being picked up in the dark watches of the night by a submarine. We soon discovered why there was no ferry party. Apparently the 'sub' that had been detailed for the job – one of the largest, latest, and most luxurious of submarines – had broken down on her way out and this one – *Statesman* – while returning from patrol in the Malacca Straits, had received a signal that she had to go to a certain map reference at a certain time, pick up two 'bodies,' and take them home to Trincomalee.

The journey home took six days, and Broom and I, at least, enjoyed it. The food we thought was excellent, though they were full of apologies for it. *Statesman* was an extremely diminutive craft. Broome slept in the only spare bunk aft, while I slept in a camp bed beneath the wardroom table. The very first morning I was woken at dawn by two excruciating blasts of the klaxon horn and by everybody tripping over my feet as they rushed to 'Diving Stations!' I thought we were being depth-charged at least; but it was merely a Jap plane several miles away and still out of sight that had been picked up by the radar. This happened many times in the next few days, because it was at this time that a Jap cruiser was sunk off Penang by British destroyers, and aircraft were out looking for them. More than once we were sighted by enemy planes, but the radar always picked them up in the distance and we were able to dive before they came near; though they dropped several bombs, they exploded so far away that it merely sounded like the hull being hit with a metal spanner.

On May 19 we entered Trinco harbour and tied up beside the submarine mother-ship, where Innes Tremlett and Claude Fenner, both of whom I had last seen in Singapore, were waiting to welcome us. We then went to one of the Force 136 camps, where we had a bath, shaved off our beards and moustaches, sent our Chinese clothes to the incinerator, and drank large quantities of pink gin.

The same afternoon we flew back to Colombo, but I did not see much of the view. I was too busy reading the first mail I had had for three years and five months.

CHAPTER NINETEEN

Return to Malaya

The evening I reached Colombo from Trinco I stayed with Tremlett, who was head of the Malayan Country Section. Before dinner I happened to see on his shelves a book called *Memoirs of a Mountaineer*. I picked it up to see who was the author, and was astonished to see that I had written it myself. 'Well,' I thought, 'I've been in the jungle a fairly long time, but I've certainly no recollection of having written such a book.' On examination I discovered that my publishers, seeing that I had been officially reported 'missing, believed killed' for three years, had brought out my *Lhasa, The Holy City* and *Helvellyn to Himalaya* under this title. I was only disappointed to find there was no obituary notice inside.

It was probably very good for my mental equilibrium that I was kept extremely busy as soon as I returned to Colombo. As Broome and I brought the first authentic and detailed news out of the country since the fall of Singapore, we had to sit down and compile long reports. He wrote the story of the Gustavus operations and the history of our liaison with the M.P.A.J.A. (Malayan People's Anti-Japanese Army), while I wrote down the history of the British stay-behind parties and the full story of my own adventures in Malaya. Broome flew home fairly soon to his wife and family in England, while I went up to Kandy to see the Supreme Allied Commander and his Chief of Staff, who were then planning the invasion of Malaya. I also flew up to Delhi to see General Roberts, who was to command Operation Zipper – the Malayan landing.

When we were in the field, we had been unable to fathom the attitude of Colombo, but now, seeing the whole picture, we could understand the extraordinary difficulties under which the Malayan operations were being planned.

It will be remembered that after I joined Davis and Broome at the end of 1943, no further submarine R.V. was kept. Early in 1944, the Navy made four monthly sorties, but we failed to keep these rendezvous. On the third sortie, two Chinese (Ching and Chen) were landed blind and found their way to our camp. On the fourth sortie the submarine was heavily attacked for about fourteen hours, and that, together with information that had been received from other sources that the area was compromised, compelled Force 136 and the Navy to abandon further attempts. The radio having failed, contact with us was entirely lost.

Then, on February 1, 1945, the unbelievable had happened. We had come upon the air using our original set and plans. At first, Colombo suspected we were working under duress, but once the security checks had been correctly answered Hannah's party was able to drop to a reception committee, and enough information was sent out by radio for the full plan of the Malayan operations to be drawn up. The basis of this plan was that 3,500 Chinese guerillas would be armed and trained by our liaison teams ready to play their part when the invasion of Malaya took place. A resistance movement was also to be organised among the Malays, but with their freedom of movement in the country they would be more valuable for collecting information than actually fighting, especially as their security was not very good.

On August 6, 1945, the first atomic bomb was dropped on Hiroshima, and three days later a second bomb devastated Nagasaki. On August 17 the Cease Fire order was sent to all Force 136 personnel in the field. Although the Japanese had officially accepted the surrender, it was not known what the reactions of their troops in Malaya would be, particularly since the Japanese Commander at Singapore had announced over the wireless that he would fight.

John Davis, who was the Supreme Allied Commander's representative in Malaya, came out of the jungle to the nearest telephone and rang up the Japanese Governor of Selangor, who suggested that Davis should proceed to Kuala Lumpur for discussion. Davis naturally refused to do this and wirelessed Colombo for instructions. He was told to continue to keep in contact by telephone, and the Supreme Commander, who had been unable to get in touch with Count Terauchi, sent a message to Davis with instructions that it should be passed as quickly as possible through Japanese channels to Count Terauchi. This message set out the surrender terms. The Japanese were instructed to remain in the main centres and maintain order, and the Chinese guerillas were allowed to move into areas vacated by the Japanese.

There was some fear at SEAC Headquarters that the guerillas would usurp the functions of the government and take the law into their own hands, but the fact remains that the M.P.A.J.A. with its Force 136 liaison officers, apart from the Japanese, was the only organised body in the country at that time. During the period between the publication of the Japanese surrender and the arrival of British troops – in remote areas a period of several months – only two serious clashes occurred with the Japanese. This is the more remarkable considering what the M.P.A.J.A. had suffered at the hands of the Japs, and says a great deal for the discipline and order which existed.

Shortly after the surrender there were indications that the guerillas in Pahang might get out of hand. Unfortunately our liaison with this group had not been effective. Chen Ping had been able to give Davis so little information about the location of these camps on the other side of the Main Range that the liaison officer, Major J. R. Leonard, a Malayan Game Warden, had dropped blind some distance from the guerillas' headquarters and had had the greatest difficulty in contacting them. He now reported that they were unhelpful and even hostile. As a result of these reports, Colombo was contemplating dropping one or more Support Groups to give Leonard any assistance that might be necessary in controlling these refractory guerillas. These were the Chinese from Menchis and Mentakab with whom I had spent almost a year, and although I knew that their politically minded leaders could be difficult, I still had implicit belief in the good sense and friendliness of the rank and file. It therefore seemed to me that instead of using force it would be much better if I could be dropped in to settle these misunderstandings by conference. At the same time I should realise a personal ambition by doing a parachute drop.

I returned to Colombo just in time to volunteer to return to Malaya by parachute at the end of August 1945. I had never done my parachute course, but it seemed to me that it was obviously so unpleasant to drop through a hole in the bottom of a moving aircraft that I could see no point in going and doing it several times beforehand just for practice. I thought that as long as I learned exactly what to do, and did it, I could come to no harm on landing.

As news from Leonard's party was still very confused, it was arranged that I should drop to a D.Z. on the Sungei Lipis about ten miles west-northwest of Batu Talam. I was so keen to get back to Malaya that I would gladly have gone in without question by the first aeroplane to hand, but the W.A.A.F. Flight Officer who was responsible for liaison between Force 136 and the R.A.F. discovered that the only crew available was a new one that had not even dropped supplies, let alone bodies. She therefore told me (may she be forgiven) that no plane was available that day. Meanwhile, she rang up the Squadron Leader, who, on being given the facts, immediately agreed to take me in himself – and the next day I was informed that there was a plane available!

We took off at dawn for China Bay and, as I had a Lib all to myself, I got more and more frightened during the ten hours' flight to Malaya. How easy is it to coerce one's timid self into doing such things by simply saying 'Yes' or adding one's name to a list. I felt just as I had some fifteen years before when climbing the snowy slopes at St. Anton to compete in that formidable ski race, the Arlberg Kandahar. We met the west coast of Malaya just south of the Perak river and flew exactly over the Sungei Tiang, where Broome and I had lain up for a day on our way to keep the submarine R.V. We then crossed the west coast and railway and through holes in the cloud could make out the S-bends of the Gap road. How wonderful it was to be flying with such ease over jungle which I had penetrated so slowly and painfully in the years that already seemed like a dream.

By now we were rapidly approaching the D.Z. Muffled up in clothes, wearing rubber boots, spine-pad, and helmet, and squeezed into my parachute harness, I was told to sit on the wooden slipway above the gaping hold through which I could see rags of cloud and the tops of trees tearing past. My dispatcher showed me that the hook which would automatically pull open my chute was firmly attached to the static line running along the roof of the Lib. 'There's your D.Z.,' he said, and as we banked sharply over to circle once before coming in to drop, I could see a minute green clearing dotted with a few isolated trees and a 'T' of signal fires smoking. 'A red light will come on as we approach the D.Z.,' he shouted. 'When the red light turns green, out you go. Keep your arms crossed in front of your face so that you don't hit your head on the far side of the hole, then grip your shoulders or your arms will be blown off! All set?'

I nodded, gripped the raised arm-rail as one does a dentist's chair, and tried to look as if I wasn't scared stiff. The red light came on. I felt like a trussed fowl with the harness cutting into my crutch. My pistol dug into my ribs on one side and my camera on the other. Suddenly through one of the portholes level with my eyes I caught a glimpse of the jungle – a river threading through the trees, and a rag or two of cloud. I was just wondering what the hell the jungle was doing up there when the light went green. A last glance at the startled face of my dispatcher – he was almost as frightened as I was! Damn that icy feeling in the pit of my stomach …

A rush of air; a loud roaring noise; a violent pull – and, yes, my chute had opened all right, and I was swinging free far above the earth. It wasn't half as bad as I had expected, nothing like so terrifying as ski jumping – with which it has a certain similarity – and I was just beginning to enjoy the delectable sensation when my body started to spin sideways. Remembering what I had been told, I reached up and with both hands grasped the harness and pulled myself up. The spinning stopped at once. I was congratulating myself on having the situation under control when I suddenly caught sight of a tree-top approaching at a rate of knots from the starboard side, and I realised the wind must be carrying me sideways. I reached up again and spilled the air out of one side of the chute and the sideways motion stopped. But, though my body missed the tree, a branch snagged the edge of my chute so that I started swinging violently.

All at once I saw the ground coming up at an alarming speed towards me. I remembered I had been told to land in a forward roll – ankle, knee, hip, then shoulder – and I had just tucked in my chin and elbows ready to carry out this manoeuvre when – bang! – the ground hit me violently on the back of the head. Luckily the ground was grassy and soft and, though my neck-muscles were sore and my head ached for a week, I was none the worse. Apparently as my feet touched the ground I was just starting to swing backwards and no amount of forward rolling could prevent the laws of gravity.

As I sat up and prepared to free the harness to stop myself being dragged along the ground, I saw several little dark men running towards me. For a horrid moment I thought they were Japs and fumbled for my pistol; then I realised they were Malays. The Lib flew around again, dropped the rest of my stores to me, and returned to Ceylon. I took a photograph of it, and then stood up and waved to show that I was all right. Next day the W.A.A.F. read in the pilot's report: 'Body appeared to land on head, but got up and waved.' We collected the containers and packages – which included a small collapsible motorcycle called a Welbike – and spent the rest of the afternoon and the next morning floating down the Sungei Lipis on bamboo rafts. Then things happened at extraordinary speed. We had a conference with six Chinese 'bandits' who had been fighting with the Communists, and disarmed them.

Then some Jap envoys came from their headquarters at Raub, twelve miles to the south, and we made some temporary arrangements for keeping the peace. Next day we met M.P.A.J.A. representatives and I accompanied the leader of No. 6 Regt. to join Leonard at Jerantut on the Pahang river. This Chinese was not one of those I had known in 1943, and I found him most deceitful and uncooperative. On September 3 we were the first British to enter Raub and on September 5 passed an astonished Jap sentry and were the first into Kuala Lipis, the capital of Pahang. The people, especially the Chinese, literally wept with joy to see Englishmen again, and we had an unforgettable welcome.

The attitude of the Japanese soldiers was difficult to fathom. They had been told to stop fighting, apparently, but they were certainly not prepared to surrender to a handful of scruffy British officers emerging from the jungle – nor had we been empowered to discuss terms of surrender with them. They continued to carry arms and use the roads, and many of them were distinctly truculent. I remember driving over the Gap road in a small car I had commandeered from the Japs. On the way up the hill I caught up with a Jap armoured car, and, as I followed behind, the gunner in the turret trained his weapon on me and kept me covered all the time I was behind him.

On November 5 I left Malaya and flew back to Colombo, and I

spent Christmas skiing at Gulmarg in Kashmir. A month later I was married at Delhi and returned to England in March 1946. People often ask me: 'What did it feel like getting back to civilisation after spending almost three and a half years as a fugitive in the Malayan jungle?' My friends tell me I was very restless and had a hunted look for some time. Certainly for many months I woke up every morning shortly before dawn and used to get up and go for walk or run, as I could not bear to lie in bed. And if there were any loud noise in the night, such as a car backfiring, before I was even awake I would be out of bed and fumbling for my bundle of possessions, ready to rush away into the jungle. Also, as my emotions had atrophied for so long, I found I was embarrassingly moved if I went to the cinema. A few of my friends found it necessary to form a special protection society to keep me safe from designing females. But they defeated their own objective by including in the protection society the very attractive W.A.A.F. Flight Officer – who is now my wife!

In December 1946 I lectured at the Royal Geographical Society on my travels in Japanese-occupied Malaya. Lord Mountbatten, my late commander, honoured me by his presence, and after the lecture he said that when Operation Zipper landed on the beaches at Morib and Port Dickson there was only one battalion – 1,000 men – of Japs in that area to oppose them. All the rest – thanks to the Japanese habit of believing what they are told, even by the enemy – were hundreds of miles further north in Kedah, where they thought the landing would take place. And to get from Kedah to Port Dickson the Japs would have had to follow the only road and the only railway, which for hundreds of miles ran along the foot of the western side of the Main Range. Here the M.P.A.J.A. and our liaison officers and support groups were waiting for them with Sten-guns, carbines, Brens, Piats, and mortars.

I do not think many of them would have got through.

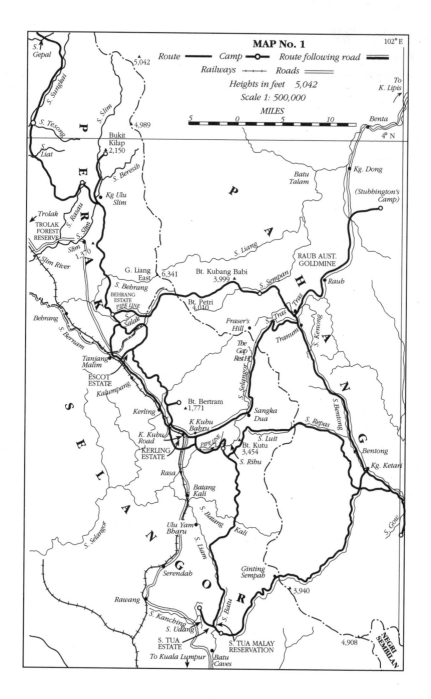

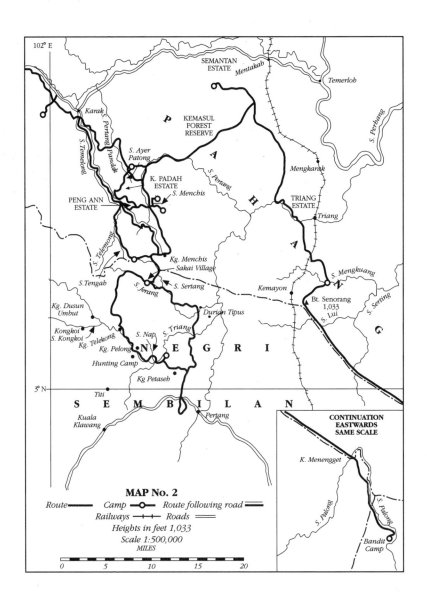

102° E

SEMANTAN
ESTATE
Mentakab

Temerloh

Karak

S. Temelong

S. Pertang Pandak

P

KEMASUL
FOREST
RESERVE

A

S. Ayer
Patong

K. PADAH
ESTATE

S. Pertang

S. Menchis

Mengkarak

PENG ANN
ESTATE

H

TRIANG
ESTATE

Triang

S. Telemong

Kg. Menchis
Sakai Village

S. Tengah

S. Jerang

S. Sertang

Kemayon

S. Mengkuang

A

Kg. Dusun
Umbut

Durian Tipus

Bt. Senorang
1,033

S. Serting

Kongkoi
S. Kongkoi

Kg. Telekong

S. Nap

S. Triang

S. Lui

G

Kg. Pelong

N

E

G

R

I

Hunting Camp

Kg Petaseh

3° N

S E M B I L A N

Titi

Kuala
Klawang

Pertang

MAP No. 2

Route   Camp   Route following road

Railways   Roads

Heights in feet 1,033

Scale 1:500,000

MILES

0   5   10   15   20

**CONTINUATION
EASTWARDS
SAME SCALE**

K. Menengget

S. Palong

S. Palong

Bandit
Camp

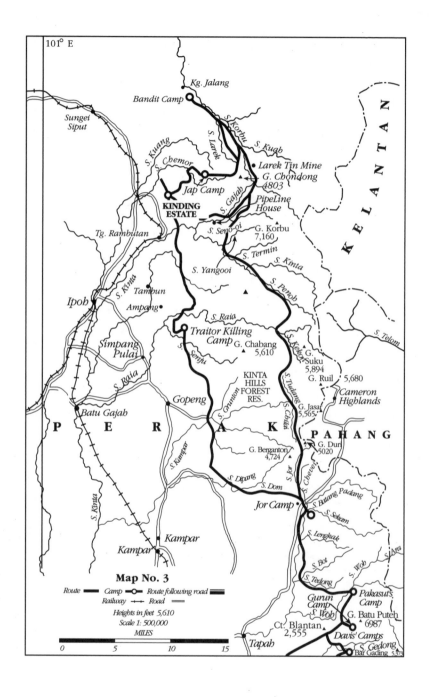

Map No. 3

Route ▬ Camp ●━○ Route following road ▬▬
Railway ━┼━ Road ═══
Heights in feet 5,610
Scale 1: 500,000
MILES

0   5   10   15

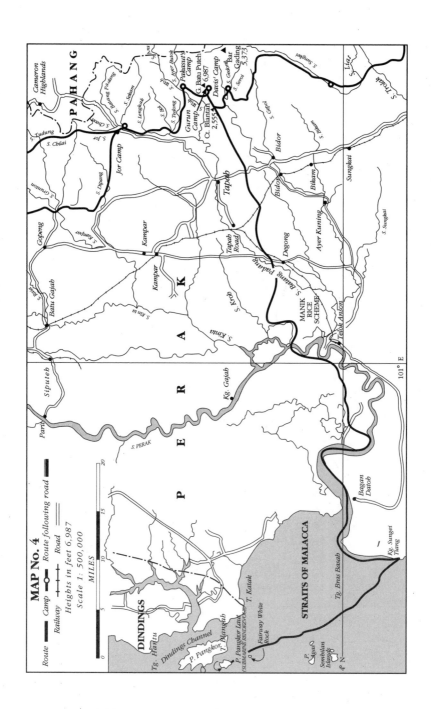

MAP No. 4

Route ━━ Camp ○ Route following road ▬
Railway ━━┼━━ Road ──
Heights in feet 6,987
Scale 1: 500,000

345

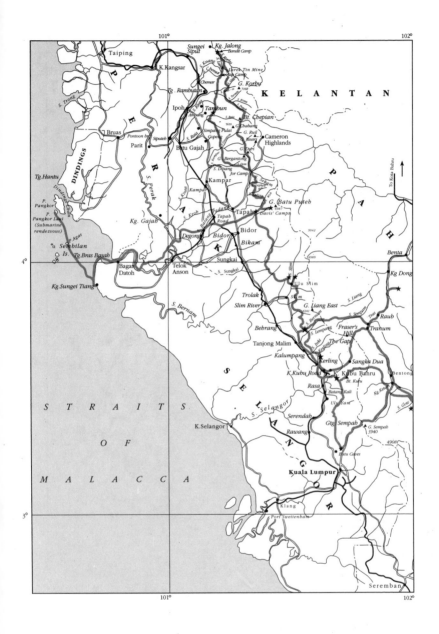

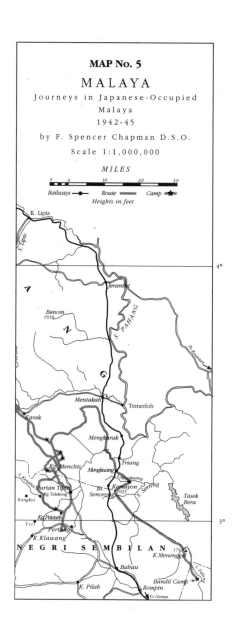

MAP No. 5

MALAYA

Journeys in Japanese-Occupied
Malaya
1942-45

by F. Spencer Chapman D.S.O.

Scale 1:1,000,000

MILES

Railways ● Route ━━ Camp ★
Heights in feet

K. Lipis

S. Lipis

4°

Jerantut

Benom
6916

S. PAHANG

To Kuantan

Mentakab

Temerloh

Karak

Mengkarak

Kg. Menchis

Mengkuang

Triang

Kerdau

Durian Tipus

Kg. Telelong

Bt. Kemayon
1033

S. Seming

Senorang

Tasek Bera

Kongkoi

Kg. Petaseh

Titi

Pertang

3°

K. Klawang

N E G R I   S E M B I L A N 174

K. Menenggal

S. Pahang

Babau

Bandit Camp ★

K. Pilah

Rompin

To Gemas

347

The Author

Frederick Spencer Chapman was born in 1907. He read English and History at Cambridge. Taking part in expeditions to Greenland and to Himalaya, Chapman made the first ascent of Chomolhari, in 1937. He was a housemaster at Gordonstoun when war broke out in 1939. After Dunkirk, he was assigned to a Special Training Centre as a commando instructor.

In September 1941 he was posted to Malaya to help organise local resistance against the impending Japanese invasion. It was the beginning of his career as a truly outstanding strategist of guerilla warfare. His four thrilling, danger-filled years spent in the jungle with the Malayan People's Anti-Japanese Army are the theme of *The Jungle is Neutral*.

At the end of the war, he was a Civil Affairs Officer in Malaya until he was demobbed in 1946. He then returned to educational work – he was the Organising Secretary of the Outward Bound Trust for a year before taking up teaching again as a headmaster. He died in 1971.